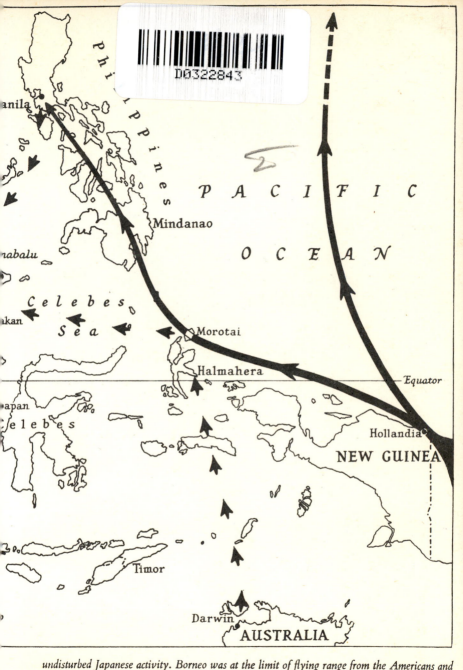

undisturbed Japanese activity. Borneo was at the limit of flying range from the Americans and beyond the limit from Burma.

Continuous arrows show the main allied advances; isolated arrows the flight lines used by Flight 200 attached to 'Z' Special unit for dropping purposes.

(*Map drawn especially, by Royal Geographical Society.*)

WORLD WITHIN

A Borneo Story

Negri Besar ('Great Country'), an upper-class Kelabit, and the author (5′11½″), 1945

TOM HARRISSON

WORLD WITHIN

A BORNEO STORY

SINGAPORE
OXFORD UNIVERSITY PRESS
OXFORD NEW YORK

Oxford University Press

Oxford   New York   Toronto
Delhi   Bombay   Calcutta   Madras   Karachi
Petaling Jaya   Singapore   Hong Kong   Tokyo
Nairobi   Dar es Salaam   Cape Town
Melbourne   Auckland
and associated companies in
Berlin   Ibadan

Oxford is a trade mark of Oxford University Press

© The Estate of Tom Harrisson 1959
Originally published by The Cresset Press 1959

First issued in Oxford in Asia Paperbacks 1984
Reissued as an Oxford University Press paperback 1986
Second impression 1990

Reprinted by kind permission of Hutchinson Books Ltd.

ISBN 0 19 582606 X

Printed in Malaysia by Peter Chong Printers Sdn. Bhd.
Published by Oxford University Press Pte. Ltd.
Unit 221, Ubi Avenue 4, Singapore 1440

To

LOUIS C. G. CLARKE
Trinity Hall, Cambridge

Oldest of friends

Note

Though this story is true, I have modified or altered a few incidents, and some personal or place names, to avoid giving hurt (or conceit). It is also likely I have made some mistakes of dates and name spellings and similar detail in Part III, which reports a period when exact records were seldom possible—and I often did not meet, for months, people I was dealing with (and perhaps believing) a few map-miles over the mountains away.

CONTENTS

Page

I **WITHIN AND WITHOUT**

From the Beginning
1944 . . . *The Plain of Bah*   3

II **STARTING EX 'Z'**

Starting ex 'Z' Special
1932-44 . . . *Melbourne to Manila (via Mass-Observation)*   137

III **THE MOUNTAINED HEART**

Impact of Ants
1945 . . . *Bario, from 5,000 ft.*   191

IV **OUTCOME**

Outcome
1945-6 . . . *High and Low*   305

V **NOW**

Primrose Hill
1958 . . . *NW1*   337

End Note   342

Index   344

ILLUSTRATIONS

Negri Besar ('Great Country'), an upper-class Kelabit, and
the author (5' 11½"), 1945   *Frontispiece*

 I (a) Within Borneo, above the cloud and jungle, seen from
       Mt Dulit, 1932   *Between pages* 100–101
   (b) Borneo, forest and mountain; rice clearing in centre
       foreground

 II The long-house at Bario under the Tamabo Mountains

 III (a) Bario to the mountain top out of sight
    (b) Family fire inside the long-house

 IV Tayun, a young Kelabit

 V Anyi, one of the best Kelabit craftsmen

 VI (a) Man carved in stone relief from a boulder high in the
        mountains on the Sarawak border
    (b) Kelabit girl of marriageable age

 VII (a) Women working in irrigated rice fields at Bario, November
     (b) Women fishing with hand nets in the Bario stream

 VIII (a) Woman making Kelabit pottery at Pa Trap
      (b) Man in Swatow ware bath weighing about 100 lbs.

 IX Penghulu Lawai, BEM, at Bario, 1958   *Between pages* 196–197

 X Dropping Zone under Mount Murud

 XI (a) Penghulu Miri (with belt of silver dollars) and other
        southern Kelabits in 1945
    (b) 'Sarongs from Heaven': Kelabit women in new clothes
        celebrating a war-time occasion

 XII (a) and (b) Views of the final ceremonies and communal
         drinking outdoors in an *irau* feast at Bario

 XIII Bario man with blowpipe and some less formidable quarry
      of those days

 XIV Senghir, the top aristocrat of Balawit

XV   The path westward to the lowlands crosses the Kubaan river

XVI   (a) Kelabit making canoe paddle for use once arrived in the lowlands
      (b) The type of long-house commonly made by Kenyahs and Kayans in the lowlands in the Baram river

XVII   (a) The Ong family with 'Doctor' Ong, key-man of interior medicine in 1945   *Between pages 260–261*
       (b) Nomadic Punans who served as erratic blowpipe units in 1945

XVIII   (a) G. S. Carter, DSO, in our house at Kuching, 1958
        (b) Christian Murut soldiers from the middle Trusan river

XIX   (a) Nick Combe, OBE, MC, with his eldest daughter Sheila at Kuching recently
      (b) Eric Edmeades, MC, second-in-command of *Semut I*
      (c) Bill Sochon and family, after receiving the DSO at Buckingham Palace

XX   Peace in a corner of the long-house

XXI   (a) Kelabit mother and child (1945)
      (b) 'Tom', a Kelabit godson, born 1945, sulking in the special Kelabit way, *kedior*, used by small boys (1947)

XXII   A Kelabit father and son in party dress at Long Lelang, in the head waters of the Akar River

XXIII   Boys learning to blowpipe

XXIV   (a) (b) and (c) Three styles of inland carving

Plate I by Oxford University Expedition to Sarawak, 1932 (see p. 152) courtesy P. M. Synge; IX by John Seal, 1958; XVIIa courtesy K. F. Wong, FRPS; XVIIIa and XIXa from Horace Abrahams for the author; XXIII Junaidi bin Bolhassan and Hugh Gibb for Sarawak Museum; remainder from author, now in photographic archives, Sarawak Museum.

MAPS

A. Borneo in South-East Asia, 1944–5   *Endpapers*

B. Borneo at war; February–November, 1945   *page* 189

C. Borneo from within, 1945   *Between pages* 302 and 303

(*These maps have been made, with the help of the Royal Geographical Society, to help tell a sometimes slightly complicated story. Some attention to them is recommended.*)

FIGURES

The designs on half-titles and end pages are from everyday Kelabit patterns of tattoo, woodcarving, wall drawing, sword handle, hornbill ivory and so on.

ACKNOWLEDGMENTS

The main experience on which the present volume is based was acquired during war service, including service with 'secret' units of the British, Australian and incidentally Dutch armies. But the events are now so long past and of so little importance that, on advice, I have made reasonable use of such experience in general, refraining however—not without a good deal of self-control—from referring to actual documents addressed to me from Higher Authority in a variety of roles over a wide range of distances.

After the Japanese war, I became (and remain) a civil servant in Her Majesty's Colonial Service. I have reason to be grateful to this Service, and in particular to His Excellency the Governor of Sarawak (Sir Anthony Abell, KCMG) and my colleagues in the Sarawak Government generally, for enabling me to carry on work in Borneo, some of which has been of little direct interest and sometimes of direct irritation to them.

Within this framework I have not consulted anybody in what I have written. The thing has taken a long time simmering, with several boss-shots. What now stands was put to paper on a short leave in the United Kingdom, long after the main event—and to some extent in a deliberate mood of removal therefrom. It would be ungenerous, though, if I did not from the start specifically record obligation to three people who will be mentioned later, but who—unlike many of those mentioned—will be able to read what I may write. These are my colleagues in arms, Lieutenant-Colonel G. S. Carter, DSO, now a Shell senior employee in Brunei; Major W. L. Sochon, DSO, until lately Superintendent of Prisons in Singapore; and my second-in-command during parachute operations to be described, Major Eric Edmeades, MC, who is still my neighbour in Sarawak. If I have anywhere in the later part of this story unwittingly seemed to exaggerate my own part in events, I hope these friends will understand that this is an unfortunate habit of writers—including others far less egocentric than I. No such intention is in my heart, from the start.

The lack of references to other books in this one is simply because, while many have been written on Borneo—particularly in the past decade—none have dealt with the period of the present experience; nor with its setting of the far uplands and their remarkable peoples. I have gone out of my way to mention any kind of other publication with validity which even touches on these themes. It would have helped had there been more.

I must thank those, especially Colonel Jack Finlay, OBE (now HM Commissioner of Board of Customs), who have read parts of the manuscript and sometimes corrected it with comment—which, where printable, is printed herewith. I must add those who at one time or another gave me ideas or a quiet place to think, namely: Mr and Mrs Denys King-Farlow, Mr Dennis Cohen, Mrs J. L. Lacon. To Miss Grace Carter I am grateful for her secretarial skill and intelligence. To Mr Fred Warburg I owe an apology.

Finally and above all, I owe all such debts as a man may there bear (unashamed) to the Kelabit peoples of Borneo's far interior, led by their old lion, Penghulu Lawai Bisarai, BEM, of Bario, ably supported by Sigang and many others. They have looked after me, in war and peace, for years. It is among these distant mountain people—who incidentally elevate indebtedness almost above all else—that this Borneo story therefore (and properly) begins.

WITHIN AND WITHOUT

'That is the true beginning of our end.
Consider then we come but in despite
We do not come as minding to content you,
Our true intent is. All for your delight,
We are not here.'

Shakespeare (*A Midsummer Night's Dream*).

Poirot smiled.
'I make a little table—so.' He took a paper from his pocket. 'My idea is
this: A murder is an action performed to bring about a certain result.'
'Say that again slowly.'
'It is not difficult.'
'Probably not—but you make it sound so.'
'No, no, it is very simple. Say you want money—you get it when an
aunt dies. *Bien*—you perform an action—this is to kill the aunt—and
get the result—inherit the money.'
'I wish I had some aunts like that,' sighed Japp.

Agatha Christie (*Death in the Clouds*).

' . . . being able to give a stupendous house-party,
that would go on for days and days
with everything that anyone could want
to drink, and a medical staff in attendance,
and the biggest jazz orchestras in the city
alternating night and day . . .'

Scott Fitzgerald (his *dream*).

FROM THE BEGINNING

1944 . . . *The Plain of Bah*

BY the latter half of 1944 the Japanese had been in occupation of all Borneo—and South-East Asia—three years. By 1944 the first glow of a new order had faded; the signs that this new mastery was only temporary began to multiply rapidly. By the end of 1944 the 'Greater Co-Prosperity' regime was visibly foundering. Before the end of the following year it had been overthrown by force of arms and atoms. It was the singular fortune of the present writer to be the first visible sign, and in some ways symbol, of this transition, reversion or progression, in one of the remotest and until then least known parts of tropical Asia, a part of the world so far within it as to live—up until then—in a sense nearly outside it. Because of the Japs, in this latter part of 1944 the sweet soaring cry of the gibbons, black, white, swift and smart swinging against the canopy green; the faint singing of old ladies making mats by flickering gum-candlelight; and the echoing murmur of wind sniffling out of the cold, mist-laden mountain cliffs down onto the plain below; these and many, many, other noises (tree crash, cicada buzz, mongoose chuckle, the whistle of the blood-red and black hill partridge, grasshoppers, a million moving termites, piglets, bat swing, goat laugh, eagle owl and the legendary noises of the enspirited night—to name a few others) were, for the first time in far upland history, swamped for a few moments by the sound of a great mechanical device.

Lying in the bomb-aimer's blister of an American four-engined Liberator little was to be seen on this first flight. In fact the navigational plot between below and the existing map made, showed us nearly fifty miles out at nowhere. Meanwhile, scarcely dreaming and certainly feeling nothing of the land under our belly, from the clouds something very special was being cooked up for the Kelabits, their dolmens and their dragon jars down below. I was the (unwitting) chef.

3

If what I am going to try and describe is worth describing in any sort of detail, it is first needful to have a clear idea of what those people down there, set in that monster mountain tangle, were caring about, trying for, fearing, loving, ignoring or avoiding *then*. Without some appreciation of goings-on inside their long-houses or within the vigorous bodies of these tall, strong men and thickset jolly women, anything that follows might be too misleading. But in giving such a picture I am forced to fall back largely upon what I learnt later. For I arrived among these people literally on the bones of my arse; and knowing nil. Indeed, at first they knew more about me, even if only mistakenly. In what follows, therefore, I have first tried to give an accurate picture of the Kelabit way of life at one crucial point in its evolution, developing in a particular kind of isolation, and about to be subject to something of a revolution (which is the subject matter of the rest of the book).

Thus, much of what happened in the inside of Borneo within the year may get a sort of interest and even significance as part of a long and infinitely intricate story—rather than simply a hotch-potch splash of this and that. Anyway, I cannot tell all this story in one book or life, only begin to. If there is a failure here to balance two rather different approaches to living, mine and 'theirs', I hope it may be forgiven me. After all, I already have some seventy thick notebooks full of elaborate field observations. No doubt, if I am spared from cirrhosis and the other occupational diseases of the colonial civil servant in the East, the time will come to produce the necessary volumes of apparent scholarship. Until that grinding day, this is no more than an attempt to reconstruct a post-megalithic chapter or two in the history of a little place and a few people including, for better or for worse, the present writer on this subject, within it.

After a good deal of thought and some slight experiment, I have preferred to rely almost *entirely* on my own memory for everything that follows. Otherwise, there is much difficulty (for my sort of 'scientific' mind) in avoiding getting bogged down in detail or over-cautious with trivia.

*　　*　　*

Psychologically, if not exactly physically, smack in the middle of Borneo lies the Plain of Bah. Encircled in a great bowl of mountains, on the northern edge Murud—at eight thousand feet the highest peak in the British part; running south and west from Murud the fifty-mile Tamabo range, which in its northern stages falls in three thousand feet sheer of summit cliff. To the east, the interminable winding spinal range which runs for over five hundred miles north and south to divide British from Indonesian (in 1944 Dutch) territory.

The plain runs out, slowly, slowly downhill between its westerly and easterly ranges, for some thirty miles, forming the head waters of the great Baram River: if anyone happened to have a bottle to cast into the turbulent highland waters—here too high for once to be equatorially hot—said bottle might reach the very distant sea in a year at least.

In a land where nearly all travel is done by river, this far upland plain can only be reached on foot, with high equatorial labour. There are just one or two places on the map of Borneo—and, more widely, on the map of the world—where you can get farther away from a known place-name or a good take-off. But there are few where, in fact, you can be more away from what most people call 'the world'. There are fewer places still where you (or I) are likely to be able to *feel* more remote, more 'cut off 'from the great outside. Or at least, this was so . . .

Every square yard over almost the whole inside of Borneo is covered with tropical jungle. Most of it is unbroken virgin forest, never felled by man. Over vast sectors, no one cultivates. The only regular inhabitants are small parties of nomadic Punans who live entirely by the blow-pipe (pig, monkey, snake, flying fox, hornbill, parakeet) and jungle plants. But on the Plain of Bah and other plains to the north and east, over aching journeys and down centuries recorded only in song, a widely scattered but effective people have built up an elaborate way of life and a high standard of living, exceptional unto themselves. Some of these people (mistakenly but now officially called from the outside Kelabit), live between three thousand and four thousand feet in the headwaters of the Baram and several other great rivers which rise from Mount Murud and flow out to the west in Sarawak, to the north into Brunei Bay and to the east through Indonesia towards Tarakan.

The highest of the Kelabit villages—and the highest settled community in all this great island—is the long-house at Bario, right under the power and blast of the glistening Tamabo cliffs. The place is named for the tremendous assaults of wind hurled down from the surrounding mountains, so that only the best built kind of long-house can persist.

The long-house, a complete village and (even more) a nearly complete living unit within one roof, stands on a small knoll beside a four foot wide brook which is the very beginning of the Baram River—more than half a mile wide down at its mouth among the oil-fields of industrial sophistication. For rather more than a mile the plain spreads dead-flat below, divided into irrigated rice fields, grass land grazed by herds of hump-backed cattle and goats; or swamp of buffalo-wallow, bulrushes and shining tall spears of white orchids, where the land has been used for rice or is waiting to be used again. Thus Bario, on the plain of Bah, is one of few emerald jewels in this jungle land. For once, there are no tall trees, no thick under-scrub, few thorns. Even in the wide territories cultivated by the riverine and lowland people, there are seldom even the smallest *permanent* clearings; they cultivate by slashing and burning, by annually clearing a new jungle patch and leaving last year's to revert—as all so quickly do—to jungle again. Seen from twenty miles and twenty thousand feet Bario is a tiny hole in a great, hopeless, uninviting and seemingly unchangeable sea of the dullest, most uniform jungle green. Tiny, pale, shiny, it registers indelibly, though.

But that cannot have been the way people other than I came to it in the first place. On the whole such evidence as has so far come to eye does not suggest that the high uplands were inhabited *very* long ago. In this sort of country, where nothing much lasts long before it rots, or is flooded out (or overgrown) evidence is difficult to come by. Still, in the last decade a good deal has been learnt about earlier human activities and later human migrations into, through and to some extent out of Borneo again. We know, now, for instance, that at least as early as the upper Palaeolithic Stone Age—at around 40,000 BC—there were people living in the Niah Caves near the west coast. But this population has not yet been found in a number of other caves to the north and to the south of Niah; nor again further inland. At a later end of the time scale, we are now learning from excavation that there was extensive Chinese trading activity and even big business settlement along the west coast of Borneo as early as the T'ang Dynasty, twelve centuries ago.

These and other important human influences seem, however, to have kept mostly to the coast, the sub-coastal plain and the lowlands behind. The tremendous obstacles of jungle and mountain which twist and contort, buckling the river lines and murdering quiet waters, put no premium on pushing far inland except under pressures enough to push mighty hard. For the adventurous heart and the wandering visionary—characters of romance and reality at least as numerous in Asia and in ancient times as in Europe and in history—it was a contest with tremendous difficulties to get behind the Tamabos or over the precipices of Murud and yet come *back* for the family.

Probably, though, both pressure and adventure eventually led the predecessors of the present-day Kelabits into the remote highlands. Their tremendous songs, some of which last days, are filled with heroic figures of exploration, liberally laced with blood as successful achievement. Thus, Lawai will sing in high chanting:

He went over the great mountain up and up into high jungle, to the highest peak and there the sun came out.

He followed the ranges and went so strongly that the mountains rolled and swayed, because he went so swiftly homeward. He went on and on until he came to the rice-clearing of Burong Siwang—his own land.

He came down the hill to the plain and came near to the edge of the village.

He called out aloud and shouted for his father—'Are you there, father, in the village, for Balang Lipang has arrived, he has fought with Tokud Udan'.

All the villagers, his father, his mother, came running out of the house and down the ladder to greet Balang Lipang.

'You have returned, son! Where did you go? You have been very long, these days I have waited for you, a long time—where have you travelled so far?'

'I have been around and about, father. I have reached the land of Tokud Udan, and fought with him three months. I have got his head and so now I return,' said Balang Lipang.

Now spoke Burong Siwang: 'I said my son was the very best. No one under the clouds, no one in all the villages can compare with him. Before others tried to fight him (Tokud Udan) but were always defeated. You have his head! I am so happy, my child.'

They gave out the head cries, gathering at the fence, declaring Tokud Udan's head the finest, 'His face red like a fireglow, he is the very finest.'

Or more mildly, the song of the mighty hunter:

The dogs bay again and Balang Lipang runs after them and sees a huge beast which he does not recognize, he does not know its

7

name, but he spears it—it is unknown to him.

He goes on again, having got the huge beast. For a long time he goes on under the clouds, going into each river valley until he gets another animal—a Wild Ox.

He goes on, round and across the head-waters of the rivers and among the mountains, finding no villages, always in great jungles. He gets many animals of all sorts, of each kind.

(Then) he thinks: 'I have got many animals now, I think I will go back to my father's land.'

He collects up all the animals. They are so many, very many, that he thinks—'They are so many, it will be best if I try to wrap them in leaf.'

He wraps them in leaf and tries them, finds they are very light, so carries them off.

He travels on, carrying the animals for a long time, and grows tired. He sees a large rock and he thinks: 'I am tired carrying these animals. Best I rest here.' And he sits on top of a rock.

He meditates—'Why do I sit here? Perhaps later on people will say I lied? It would be a good idea if I left a mark here now, so that they will know.'

He kicks and makes marks, to remember him by, on the rocks, then .on he goes.

He goes on for a long time, nearly a month, until he comes to his father's land at Long Marong Akan Dalan.

He arrives near to the village and calls out for his father: 'Are you in the village? I have many animals, I got a great number, and one whose name I do not know.'

Burong Siwang hears him and rushes out and comes to the end of the long-house and onto the platform and sees him carry many animals.

'I took the dogs, father, and I have returned with pig, barking-deer, sambhur, leopard, wild ox, and one—the largest—whose name I do not know. What is it?' asks Balang Lipang.

Then Burong Siwang says to him, 'This animal which is so large—how is it that you do not know it? We old people call it Rhinoceros,' he says.

★   ★   ★

When did Balang Lipang of Long Marong Akan Dalan first range the mountains, harass the shy (or sky) rhinoceros? The earliest date we can give to these pioneer, loud-mouth, combative (in words, anyway) Kelabits may be something well after the beginning of the Christian Era. They brought with them one activity which, in an archaeologically unhelpful land, identifies them unfailingly through the heart of Borneo. For, alone of Bornean peoples, the Kelabits have a large scale 'megalithic' interest. They strew their landscapes with works of stone; dolmens, avenues of monoliths, stone bridges and dykes, seats carved out of the solid rock, spread-eagled figures cut into rock faces, huge stone vats for the bones of the departed, grottoes cut into cliff faces for burials, a monster traced on a great boulder in the river bed, a man-eating bird chipped into a single rock away in the jungle; and much else. But it must have taken many centuries to drag this mental load of cultivating stone into the uplands of interior Borneo, where it eventually emerged eroded of detail but still magnificent.

There is not (for long) anything 'lost world' about Bario. This long-house's particular line of stone monuments has lately subsided into the rice-wet plain. You must go up the mountain behind to find one of the strange stone bridges; or into the next and now uninhabited valley for an immense dolmen, and where the lines of irrigation ditches can still be traced through what is now already high jungle once again. Easier, though, to look high up at the long and intricate line of the western ranges. Every mile or two are big gaps, rides, cut out of the forest right upon the crest. Visible from many miles away, several of them high upon the crown of Mount Murud, these are another part of the same fierce activity concerned with the journey of the dead—in this case passage ways for the spirits of great men to travel outward from their last withins.

There is nothing 'lost world' or remote civilization about it. It is part of the pattern of everyday life and death. It is, though, rather more difficult to resist thinking of Bario as that other sort of lost horizon, a Shangri-la. For though still equatorial it is mostly cool; at night, sleep with a woman at your thighs, fire at your toes and the good Kelabit habit of waking every hour to nick one and kick the other. Anything grows, from tobacco and mango to potato and bean's sprout (but not coconut palm; a slight relief). And though the streams are too small for many fish, there are delicious eels, cat-fish, and feeble golden crabs. In the grass there are quails, pheasant cuckoos, warblers; and in the wet rice fields Arctic Phalaropes to be darted by the children's blow-pipes as they flee too far before the polar winter. All around upon the jungle mountain sides, plentitude of game, slime and biting insects. Overhead far hornbills go bellowing the dawn and fruit bats flutter the dusk. The waking cry of morning is the long, lovely laugh of the yodelling gibbon—wa-wa-wa. If you happen to be a human being, what gives the place its special magic is its other humans and the things they have done to make it neither Shangri-la nor a decrepit relic of some obscured past. And it is in this sense that we approach the seething, never silent, long-house of Bario, where someone will probably be singing to his own finely made mandolin at two (if he knew that) in the morning; and the paramount chief of all the Kelabits, Lawai Bisarai, is liable to be snoring on the verandah all afternoon.

To these far people this is the centre of the universe. To them the coast is nowhere. At the time this far story begins the plain had been visited by a half-dozen Europeans, and no Japs. The orphan Bulan had a splendid blue-and-white Ming plate of the fifteenth century hanging in a vine-stemmed frame beside her fire-place at the other end of the long-house, where it comes down to the big buffalo wallow beloved of migrating snipe, wagtails, pratincoles and sand-pipers. Sharing her rice, you might look up through sticky fingers along the whole range of the house—for there are no rooms and any privacy is as impracticable as excessive fantasy—and in the half-light from the roof thatch, pushed up at one place and another (to let out the smoke), now thus insecurely count enough pieces of Chinese ceramic art to interest any intelligent curator. But no Chinese (and only one curator) had sat here.

* * *

The living descendant of Balang Lipang is Tayun. Before we go any further it will be as well to look a little more closely at a typical Kelabit in so far as a typical one ever has existed. Tayun will well serve this purpose. He is unmistakably 'Kelabit'. Not that it is easy to define what a Kelabit is; no Kelabit ever attempted to define it, himself, in words for the record—since no one can write. But looked at high and far, some differences are distinctive enough for everyone to know even if not to notice.

Tayun, like most Kelabits, looks much like most other Borneo people. They are of course closely related, as part of one broad ethnic group, with the Kenyahs and Kayans, less closely with other Dayaks, who occur to the south or east; more closely with the people whom outsiders call Muruts and others to the north and north-west. There are many differences and distinctions among groupings of uncertain value inland in Borneo: different languages and dialects, class and kin systems, customs and beliefs, long-house arrangements, agricultural methods. Some of the characteristics which particularly single out Kelabits such as he are:

(i) that remote upland position, topographically;
(ii) their advanced techniques of irrigation and rice cultivation, agriculturally;
(iii) their open, superficially communal, long-houses, architecturally;
(iv) their concentration of celebrations connected with parental death, theologically;
(v) their active megalithic efforts in connection with the above, conspicuously;
(vi) their powerful physiques, physically;
(vii) energy and initiative, gaiety and personality.

Largely because they live naturally on foot travelling the upland, Kelabits have developed differently from the Kenyah-Kayan type of general physique, powerfully in the back, thigh and leg muscles. They are big-boned, generally strong people; but in use of wrist and shoulder cannot touch the canoeing Kenyahs and Kayans of the lowland rivers.

Take Tayun, anyway; newly full-grown young man, not yet married though plentifully experienced (thirteen girls); and making his own rice field independently for the first time this year. He is five foot eight inches, looks much more because he is massively built and muscled. His skin is palely dark. He would not like it to be darker, so wears a bark coat when working in the open in the sun; and a sweeping broad conical hat of leaf. He admires paleness of skin and finds whiteness just as attractive as do the sung sagas of Bario prehistory, in which shiningly moon-white men with bodies of steel defeat all comers in war and jumping tests (they can and do easily jump over the Tamabos or Murud, their footmarks of prize leaps still to be seen preserved in stone round and about the highland landscape).

Where the girls, Bulan and Dayang, with the big Kelabit breasts, wear their waist-length hair tucked up and pushed through a hole left in the top of their conical bead-hats, Tayun has a bun through which he sticks a metal skewer. Only the older men now fix their buns with curving pins carved out of buffalo horn or antlers; the head of the pin cut out into a lace-mesh design of spirals and curves. Everybody has their hair long. Kelabit hair never curls. It is ordinarily jet black and stays like that all through life; but sometimes a fashion sets the women dying their tresses rufus—just as they get fits of putting henna on their hands, saffron on wide-boned faces. Women are even keener than men in keeping their skin pale, especially upper-face of breasts and shoulders.

Over Tayun's shoulders goes (when he likes) a bark waistcoat, embroidered with a convolute design, edged with red. Under this Tayun wears a loin cloth of plain bark. This is three arm stretches long, wrapped round the thighs and between the legs, free ends hanging forward. Into it he sticks the hinge of a bamboo container with finely carved lid holding blow-pipe darts if he is going hunting; or replaced by a smaller one with tobacco, tinder, quartz flake and a chip of iron for fire striking otherwise. On a belt of woven rattan vine hangs a long and curving bush knife, which he made himself with the help of his crafty uncle, on the Bario forge of bamboo blowers and the single hard-stone anvil. His sword is sheathed in two flat strips of wood, tightly bound together with thin swamp vine, the handle a carved antler of a Sambhur stag; and from the bottom end of the sheath trails a long hank of human hair, with a little goat's hair tuft just above, dyed crimson.

Tayun has two loin cloths and interchanges them as he feels, washing one when he takes it off to bathe in the stream, as he does at least twice a day, morning and evening (being careful always not to expose his penis to the view of others). The rest of his physical furniture is semi-permanent. Under each knee are about fifty *unus*, bands of a special kind of creeper, specially prepared, twisted, secured. These are supposed to strengthen the calf muscles and more subtly to protect the upper part of the body from ephemeral, external, encroachment through the ground. More important, they feel good, look good and cannot be gone without. On his wrists, a few more of the same; and some little bangles made from strips of aluminium cut out of a cooking pot which was traded up from the coast a few years ago and eventually expired on his family fire (so far as cooking was concerned). Round his neck are four long, hanging necklaces. The longest is of plain, deep blue glass beads, some round and some tubular. If he had any sisters, these would be theirs. But his sister went mad and vanished, long ago. So he wears this parental inheritance. This kind of bead is, in any case, a rather more masculine kind. In general, beads are felt to be feminine.

But big ones and glass ones are weighted to the male, who could not properly wear the finer cane, bone or brilliant red ones. His wearing these beads manifestly expresses that he is a person of some property. It does not necessarily mean that he has not got other property—enough to make him rich and superior perhaps. It certainly implies that he is not poor and propertyless—though it is always possible that he has borrowed the beads for a day or two, for the look of it, of course.

His other necklaces are smaller glass beads of recent origin and no consequence, except that they jingle about, shine in the light of the sun by day and flame by night. One string is made of pretty white seeds, very hard, which the girls gather when ripe; they will only last a little while before crumbling, have been put upon him in fun.

Tayun's ears give another impression. While he was still a baby his father—who not long after was terribly mauled and crippled by a honey-bear—took a big thorn and made quick incisions in the top and bottom lobes of each ear. The top hole was gradually expanded by wooden plugs. The bottom one was slowly extended by hanging weights of increasing strain. Now, through the top lobes he has a pair of leopard's fangs, good ones in his case, worth almost a young buffalo. For leopards (which are shy and cowardly—so regarded as feminine whatever their sex, whereas honey-bears are masculine regardless) are hard to find since they live in the trees and hunt pig at night when no man goes out. Once cornered, the leopard barely protests its life; but only one out of many has good, long, unbroken fangs, although most have handsome marbled skins which make dancing cloaks, one of which Tayun has cut into a little seat-mat hanging from the back of his loin cloth, to squat on at special occasions—thus keeping his bottom out of spilled booze.

The leopard's teeth are joined behind, out of sight under Tayun's pouring black hair, by two lines of insignificant beads. The fangs point forward beside his big brown eyes, eyelashes and eyebrows of which have been pulled out for the sake of high masculine beauty, feminine intercourse.

His lower ear-lobes hang almost to the shoulders with brass weights, value objects traded up from Brunei Bay for centuries. When he is doing some hard work, or out in the jungle where branches might easily catch the long ear-lobes, he slips the weights off and puts them in the bamboo container, wrapping the lobe elegantly over the top of each ear. It is considered very sad to have a torn ear-lobe. Sometimes careless parents judge the weights wrong when you are young and rip the lobe.

For girls, the beautiful lobe stretches far below the shoulders and can even be wrapped (when the weights are taken off) round the top of the head. For them a childhood break is almost tragic; certainly one of the few things never to joke about. The unforgivable fight, short of killing, is for one girl to pull out another's ear-lobe.

Girls do not have anything done to their upper ear-lobes—instead while young they have their two top front teeth knocked out. Men used at one time to have these teeth blackened, but since there was contact with the coast more readily, have them gold-plated—if they can accumulate enough gum or bezoar stone or other jungle produce to pay a Chinese down-river dentist the price. Tayun has not yet succeeded to that level of financial achievement. But he does have a crocodile tattooed on one arm; more strictly, a myth-crocodile monster, interchangeable also into scorpion=dog.

Kelabit men do not go much for tattooing. Tayun's girl cousins are elaborately tattooed instead. It takes several years to complete a good girl's tattoo. The chief feature is a minute trellis-work of interlocking dots and lines, looking at a distance like perfect black stockings stretched from the tips of her toes to the tops of her thighs. This is the largest part of feminine costume, which otherwise consists simply of exposed shoulders and bust above a narrow single strip of bark or woven thread, slung above the thighs and slightly open at one side, to reveal the top of the tattoo as it is expiring. For removable furniture, she will have more necklaces, more arm bangles, more ear-lobe weights and a head-dress. Tayun and other men wear hats against the sun or feather head-dresses when formally dancing. The better-off women wear skull caps made of up to a thousand beads, taking them off merely to sleep. In the front of these caps are the most valued glass beads, thin, yellow and orange; *manik tulong*, 'bone beads', they say. A rainbow of colours is built up around. A cluster of women squatting together is brighter than any flower effect Borneo could envisage. Similarly colourful belts of beads are worn by women indoors, about a hand-span broad at the back, narrowing in front and serving to secure the skirt, especially in the more boisterous goings-on at parties.

Dress and design can vary widely within simple limits. There is nothing against Tayun or his girl cousin Bulan borrowing each other's clothes, sticking eagle's feathers in their hair, meeting someone literate on a coastal journey and getting their names tattooed on to forearms, by mirror reflection, upside down. One person may like red beads, another green. There are a surprising number of fancy variations (and variable personal incentives) in how a man can fix his loin cloth or a girl the slit in her skirt!

* * *

Tayun is young and strong, in these later months of 1944. The rice is sprouting young and vivid green at Bario as at eight other Kelabit long-houses dotted about this particular plain and its environs, from the south side of towering Mount Murud to the lower end of the plain where the Baram river begins to widen and cuts its deep impassable gorge as the land rises once more in great bounds, to seal off the Kelabit uplands again, and complete the fourth side of the barrier. These villages were named, in all cases but one (*Batu*=Rock of, *Patong*) after the small streams adjacent to the long-houses. The word for stream or river is *Pa*. A Kelabit thinks of where he lives not as a piece of named land so much as to do with a stretch of identified water. A long-house will move when the tall poles which lift it off the ground are rotting; maybe transferring to another stream a mile or so away, taking its new name.

The villages are, starting at the north end of the plain:

Pa Trap (Palungan)	Pa Mada
Pa Main	Pa Dali
P'Umur	Ra Mudoh (R=P before M*u*)
Pa Bengar	Batu Patong

Long-houses lie within a day's walk of each other; or, after the heavy rains which occur almost every season in the uplands, a couple of days' wade and swim. Up here there are no boats. Everything is on foot. And the Kelabits have developed tremendous physiques, not so much from travelling the plain as from hunting the mountain-side jungles and crossing the mountains to barter salt for porcelain, earthenware pots for cloth, beads for buffaloes.

There is—or was then—no way of getting to Bario or any other of the long-houses without climbing at least as high as one thousand Kelabits standing upon each other's heads. There are really seven practicable ways of getting in and out with no more expenditure of physique than this. For the most part the encircling mountains are impossibly precipitous, their approaches intolerably tormented with gullies; there are small streams to be repeatedly crossed, with wide beds of boulders deceptively over-masked with plants and bushes. It is largely this that enabled the Kelabits to develop to an unusual degree on their own in recent centuries: just as they developed their thigh muscles and can throw any other kind of Bornean in feats of strength.

To the north Mount Murud completely blocks the way. It is possible to climb it; and some great aristocrats have been memorialized with cut clearings on the top, at an enormous expenditure of effort sustained with hundreds of pints of rice wine and half a dozen buffaloes and bulls sacrificed per occasion. But man cannot carry a dragon jar over Murud or anywhere round its shoulders. And where you cannot wisely carry a dragon jar, you cannot fairly call it a Kelabit way of going. These ways are always devious, narrow, and not to be followed by the inexpert. There is no such thing as an open track; not even a permanent one. Where a tree falls, it is not done to cut through the tree: go round it. When the big tiger-hornets—to be stung by six is too much—nest in a tree stump, markers of bent branches send the track winding for a hundred yards: never to return to the previous. As well as that, inside almost everything that Kelabits do is a kind of intricacy, even amounting to spiralism; which cannot equate function with straight lines as of necessity, or conceive of something approaching efficiency as being direct. A square can be an irritation. A line is not something to be followed; it is to be taken along behind, to be gone for a walk with (at will).

In terms of travel results the outcome may sometimes appear disturbing and even absurd. Nevertheless, these people penetrated into this remotest highland. And on several occasions when others have sought to encroach upon or devastate them in force, the efforts have failed largely through outside misunderstanding of big mountain jungle and little water labyrinth.

The Kelabits thus found themselves—or rather found they had put themselves—in a position of strength. They could go out, east, south or west, along seven main yet almost secret ways. But few could get in; and any could be obstructed and suitably beheaded at keypoints along each way, narrow passes, or river fords.

There are four ways out to the east. The north-easterly of these circles right round Mount Murud's cliffs, crosses the spinal range and emerges on another plain of splendid irrigated rice fields in the head-waters of the Bawang—a stream which flows east to gather mighty strength and come out in the end on the east coast, opposite the oil-fields of Tarakan Island. The Kelabits did not make that journey, but traded extensively with these people, who had contact both easterly thus and also back over a northerly spur of Murud into the head waters of the Trusan river, which rises less than half a day away from the Bawang, north-west into the great bay of Brunei. The other three ways out eastward over the spinal range each come into a smaller valley, further tributaries in two hundred miles of the same head-waters heading east for Tarakan. The people on the other side of the spinal range are closely related (the nearest villages very closely), by inter-marriage, language, and custom. These closer villages share the tre-mendous cult of the dead and its associated stone monument activities. Only two miles further east and this cuts out. The Kelabits feel less affinity with people a couple of days' walk away. It takes a fortnight to carry down to Brunei Bay, longer to Tarakan. These north-easterly and northerly ways have perhaps not spelt out much culturally; yet in the acquiring of material things including the things the people value most, the direction has been paramount for at least seven centuries.

From the south—if not entirely, at least more than from any other direction—came the movements of *people* themselves, prototype Kelabits. There is only one big way. In some ways it is the easiest, in that it links more quickly to navigable waterways and to the whole overland trend of Borneo peoples for centuries: pushing in to the island from the south and south-east, working up generally north-west, though with innumerable divisions. This is the main important spine of inconsistency in Bornean human geography. Its uncertainties are both caused by and reflected in the tremendous tangle which is the inside of Borneo itself. This is not a country with a logical pattern. In North Burma, anywhere in Indo-China, or on Java and Sumatra, there are big overall designs of land form which make it quite easy to learn the feel of the place, quite natural to move in certain directions. In the interior of Borneo this sort of geological commonsense ran out millions of years ago. So, it is not only possible but easy for a Kelabit to get lost in his own particular part of the country. There are famous and recent stories of wise hunters and of foolish boys being so lost—and sometimes never recovered.

The southern way leads from the lower end of the plain, the long-houses of Pa Dali and Batu Patong, slap up into the mountains again along winding summit ridges. Up on the very top, near the first night's camp, there is a characteristic group of stone monuments commemorating early war parties and death rolls. From here, slogging up and down minor and maddening dips and falls, a whole day with myriad leeches and a kind of cursing whistle with which the Kelabit expresses physical dismay, comes the second camping place, lean-to huts a few inches off the ground—each set of travellers cutting some new fan-palm or other leaf to refresh the roof against the inevitable night mountain rain. Another long day, going mostly down, past places where the displaying Argus Pheasants have stamped their dancing grounds. The atmosphere of upland begins to slither away. Then, crashing and sliding, through very big jungle, down to the first canoeable river and the smell of true dense equatorial heat, passing an old rhinoceros mud-bathing pit and the first pool famous for big river carp.

Here there are several long-houses of people who are partly Kelabit and partly related 'Saban'. The Sabans—slender built and noted killers with the blowpipe—are still in process of migration slowly into this beginning of the navigable Baram, as also northward, upward, into the Kelabit highlands proper. Most of the Sabans still live to the east in the Bahau river, the second main tributary of the Batang Kayan, which is much the greatest river of north-eastern Borneo. The Batang Kayan is the later 'homeland' of the Kenyah and Kayan peoples, expansive peoples, great tribes who have pushed northward even into historic times; helping to push the Kelabits in front of them, too. Kenyah and Kayan like rivers. If the Kelabit now wishes to proceed further towards the coast in the southerly direction, he must move among these people. That may be in many ways awkward, but offers the enormous advantage of travel by canoe.

Not that the journey can immediately be made. Having come down into the beginning of the lowlands, life is still about a thousand feet above sea level. But all the birds, the snakes, parasites, stinging bushes, butterflies and tree shrews are lowland. Back up at Bario almost every form of life is different. Above three thousand feet, Borneo has a sharply distinct montane life, with a great many forms not only unknown in the lowlands but often peculiar to particular sections of the interior highlands.

In this unfamiliar lowland world, which can only be approached much more gradually along the eastern tracks, the traveller now has access back over the spinal range eastward into the Bahau; or, more easily, turning westward for another three days' walk to the first big Kenyah long-house below the last of the major gorges and rapids on the main Baram river at Lio Matu. These gorges and miles of rapids de-limit the whole upland area (of which the Kelabit country is part).

Finally, there are two western ways. These are formidable but important too. One takes off from the long-house right down at the lower end of the plain; for the other you start climbing almost as soon as you leave the long-house at Bario. Both go smack over the Tamabo ranges at the only two points where these can suitably be crossed. These are climbs to be planned, not lightly undertaken, the man carrying a hundred and twenty pounds, the woman eighty. If there is nothing to carry, there is not much point in the climb. Both ways lead up into those eerie levels of cloudland where it is too wet for most vegetation. The trees are stunted, everything is overgrown with puffily profuse mossy sponge. Where it looks as if one is walking on ground, suddenly something gives way to drop a body unaware into ten feet of moss-soft, embracingly slushy crevasse. In this Sargasso Sea thrown upon the mountain tops it is only a minor compensation that everywhere are exquisitely lecherous pitcher plants, bright tiny orchids and skinny but gay rhododendrons. Flowers and bright plants are only quite seldom to be seen in Borneo and are not things that matter much to people who find their beauties in the art of China and in their own agricultural and other achievements, including words.

From either of the passes on the Tamabos, there is a shattering view out over the whole interior. It is a favourite pleasure of the successful climbers to sit for half an hour, if cloud and cold permit, sharing the sky world with soaring serpent-eagle and edible-nest swifts; smoking, chewing, spitting and discussing the peaks in view. A people who walk everywhere and run (not much done in Asia) for fun, acquire an almost electronic-brain 'feel' for landscape. Even then this landscape is so tortuous, complicated and 'illogical' that the discussion generally ends in argument and in strong personal expressions of comparative, competitive experience, disparaging for those who disagree. As a great many Kelabit discussions end in this way, the party which walks on until late afternoon to camp beside the Kubaan river (now flowing westward into the South China Sea), proceed as amiably as before, constantly joking, roaring with laughter, or roaring out the songs which tell of the pioneer journeys made over these mountains by ancestors many generations ago.

Sounds so often soothe the nearly aching upland calf and ankle, rhythms stand in for wishes and conduct the mind across the considerable obstacles of upland geography thus:

Hear how he went, the giant jumper,
Clear in the sky over every Tamabo,
Higher than cliff or swiftlet soaring,
Whiter than cloud in the driest daylight,
Flying with speed of the falling eagle,
Falcon of hurling rush, invisible that Tokid Rini!
Man beyond human, spirit of everywhere,
Bending Batu Lawi, ignoring Murud, defying the hornbill,
Red of face, his sound of crying,
Breaking the waters on Telang Usan
Mighty as iron, shining like silver,
Roaring like the most fearful of storms, with hail threatening,
To terrify the otters swimming in unknown waters,
Lest river turn to stone, and great rocks fall;
To petrify the women of peoples as yet unseen
Lest the harvest falter and man disappears—
On journeys none have yet quite taken
To lands where man has not yet been:
Even to hunt the rhinoceros, not yet;
Even to follow my dream, not so . . .
At the place where the wild waters tremble
Up to the edge of the moon.

* * *

The rivers which burst through the western side of the Tamabo range eventually also join the Baram, far down in its lowland reaches. In the extreme head-waters of these tributaries, on the outer side of the Tamabos again, there are small long-houses the largest of which (Long Lelang) is within the limits of navigability—with daring—and correspondingly contains an element also of Kayan (river) people, folk who never walk if they need not.

There is plenty to show that the Kelabits were once more widely distributed, especially to the west and south. It was the late Kayan expansion, more than any other, which drove them furthest inland and concentrated them in the uplands, beyond the gorges and falls. But the process was not all as negative as that. They had already pioneered the uplands and expanded down from them, even as far as the coast of Brunei Bay. Their own legends claim, indirectly and politely, that in fact the first Mohammedan Sultan of Brunei—which became the paramount state in this part of the world by the fifteenth century— was a converted Kelabit. There is even something in Brunei's own royal traditions which makes this possible. In reverse, the upland Kelabits remained absolutely isolated from Mohammedan influence. When the State of Brunei at its peak (about AD 1500) ruled far outside Borneo, the only jurisdiction which it exercised over the island's interior was through its monopoly of direct trade with the Chinese, and presently the Portuguese, Spanish, Dutch and English, in that sequence of appearance.

This inland, upland, isolate point has determined much of the human activity thereon; and especially it has enabled some of this activity to develop along its own lines relatively—by Borneo standards—un-hampered or unhelped by the constant, minute bombardment of external influences which characterizes the human process outside.

The Kelabits have thus been able, to an exceptional degree, to keep their own heads.

'Head hunting' is the phrase most easily associated with Bornean peoples. It has played a big part with the Kelabits as with the rest. But whereas so many other peoples were attacked from far away, unaccountably, and sometimes with dreadful massacre, by and large these uplanders escaped such major ravages. That they did not entirely do so was due to their ordinary human vanity, energy and restlessness— here vividly accentuated by a premium on individual display in a social setting where nearly all the everyday emphasis is in the opposite direction; in a community of roomless long-houses like Bario, where everybody is nearly everybody else and nearly everything can be done by everybody in season. When the Kelabits, individually or in gangs, literally stuck their necks out and went making trouble over the ranges, the effects were sometimes more serious than when they stuck to minor feuds and fights, bloody though these could be between neighbours, friends and kin in the long-houses immediately around.

Before one can fully sense this sort of bloodshed—as it had been in the past and could again become in the future—you must know the simple structures of daily life which lead winding and thin out into the emotionalisms and demonstrated eccentricities of ecstatic Kelabitry.

*   *   *

Bario is a long-house much like any other, looking down at it from the air at this moment, perched on the hillock where it has survived (off and on) for some centuries. Rather under a hundred people ordinarily live in it. The nearby long-house at Pa Main has over two hundred; that is big for a hill house. On the rivers, where transport gives mobility for people and harvests, long-houses may run to over one thousand; one house in the Batang Kayan runs over half a mile long.

Bario runs for two hundred and fifty feet, east and west. A track from the easterly verge of the plain winds through the network of irrigation ditches on to the bright green knoll, up a fourteen foot log, with notches cut into it to take the bare feet; through a three-foot hole, for the body to emerge, uncrouch itself, manoeuvre in the carrying basket and rub eyes smarting from the bright plain light; and already feeling the first touch of smoke which makes the inside's darkness white. If anyone were ever so rude—and the Bario people so impossibly negligent as to permit it—he could then pursue this track over the one hundred and more planks of the long-house verandah, out through the other little door at the upward west end, down the slightly sheltered notched log there (for the knoll slopes upward already) and continue away into the mountains for a three weeks' trek to the nearest Government Station, bottled beer and taxation. The long-house *is* the path. In proper practice the newcomer sits down on a slightly raised platform at one side of the long verandah. Physically he relaxes; psychologically he tenses. Or a she even more so of both.

This verandah (for there is no better word for it) is thirty feet wide, running the whole length of the house. On the inner side is a continuous plank wall, reaching between eight and twelve feet high, where it tails up into a confusion of little platforms, cross beams, rice bins and fruit baskets, slung skins of honey-bear and clouded-leopard, piles of rush leaf for mat making, dried ears of maize for next season's planting, fish traps, spear hafts, and unintelligible agglomerations; all hung, strung, perched and crowded, as a false ceiling overhead. Above rises the true roof of delicately sewn palm thatch, the gable ridge sixty feet above the ground, darkly obscure until the gum-candles are lit at night. The roof thatch slopes evenly outwards and the eaves overlap a low wall which encloses the outer edge of the verandah, against the fierce winds, night cold and driving rain of these equatorial highlands.

The only piece of 'furniture', above floor level, is a little rough stool carved with a hornbill's head, the perch of Chief Lawai Bisarai, who is, however, more usually to be found lying down on one of the many red and white mats which are the true furniture—and which are made and traded from the Bawang two days to the east.

This verandah takes the ordinary traffic flow of Bario, from a people exceedingly restless. Anyone can and must come in and sit down wherever he or she chooses along the verandah. A complete stranger will usually sit at the near end, immediately on the left as he comes up from the plain. (Few *strangers* will come the other way, where in a week's travel the only people are in a few small long-houses.) From this humble position—for the ends of the house are humble—unless something is known against him some one of the several people always about the house at any time will come and greet the new arrival in the neat Kelabit way. The words are chanted by the resident, repeated in a higher key by the visitor:

'You have come?'
'We have come.'
'You have come from?'
'We have come from Pa Trap.'
'You are many?'
'We are three.'
'All is well at home?'
'All is well.'
'Good—and all was well on the journey?'
'All was very well on the journey.'

After this essential exchange—and no more—tobacco will be brought out. Then the visitor is usually either asked through one of the four small doors in that long central wall, or moved up to the enlarged platform half way down the verandah—the upper-class focal part of the long-house where the Chief and his family reside.

Many other things happen on the verandah, and young men who have reached the age of energetic sexual enterprise officially sleep there. But there will be plenty of time to see more of all that. So go in with the invited traveller, crouch again through the low door of the long central wall, to emerge into strictly parallel but vastly more elaborate human arrangements.

For the dominant Kelabit arrangement is living in public, then planning inside. Nearly all other Borneans live either in separate houses or in long-houses with separate rooms all along the back-skin behind the verandah. There is not a lot of difference between living in a Kenyah or a Kayan long-house and living in Davenport Street, Bolton, or any other industrial housing. In Bario this is the big tangible difference. The back part of the house is as open as the front. There are, of course, separate and recognized family units. Each family group has it own fireplace, situated on this inner side of the long centre wall. On either side of this fireplace are plain mats—that is, beds. Around this fireplace the family (or such part of it as is around at the time) will eat in the early morning and again after dark. But even one fire may be and often is shared, for short or sometimes indefinite periods, by more than one 'family unit', each with its little allocated territory—observed by adults, more or less—around the shared hearth. And the stretch of ten feet or so away from the fireplace up to the back eaves is always open territory, the highway of all communal comers by night and day, adults and children, invited visitors, dogs, fowls, cats and house-cleansing cockroaches galore.

Each family is responsible for initially building and regularly up-keeping its section. But the house as a whole is a joint enterprise. Although all parts of it are individually owned, as a whole it is everybody's. There can be no thought of prohibiting anyone entering any part of it. And to a considerable extent personal property is mobile within it, also. Many things must not be taken and used without asking the person who originally acquired them. But some things, like axes (two) and other scarce iron tools, move about the house from end to end and fire to fire with almost anthropoid vitality. Others—like the single block of hard stone which acts as anvil and was brought as a joint effort from over the mountains into this plain of friable sandstone —stay wherever convenient. The visitor not very familiar with recent Bario deliveries would probably be unable to detect which children belonged to what families. Sometimes a child will not eat or sleep at his parents' fire for nights at a time. The kids roam the whole house; and —when they are old enough—on the plain around, with an independent but responsible mobility confounding close definition.

In this diffuse mood, a single sort of furniture dominates the interior landscape of Bario. All down the back wall of the house, in a continuous line, are the firm shouldered shapes of big, brown-glazed, eared jars. The older ones made in South China maybe over a thousand years ago; the not so old about Sawankalok in central Siam some six centuries back; the latest by Chinese immigrants, working in the old southern tradition on the coasts of Borneo within the past century. Around these jars centres a great deal of expressed Kelabit feeling. Out of their capacious depths flows a gratifying, sometimes seemingly continuous, stream of intoxicating beverage, the essential fluid of Bario's verbal dynamic.

*   *   *

The other conspicuous items of furniture are brass gongs, often decorated, like the jars, with impulsive dragons in moulded relief. The prize gong is kept in Chief Lawai's part. It weighs about forty pounds. Beaten with the fresh tuber root of cassava shrub, this fabulous gong can sometimes be heard in long-houses a day away. These gongs come from Brunei; like the jars have infiltrated up the rivers and over the mountains in centuries of trade. The oldest gong, jar or bead may be well over a thousand years; but it need not have been in the uplands for any long time. The mobility of objects through central Borneo is not necessarily related to human movement. During the long periods of disturbance and war—including war between immediately adjacent groups—objects of value trotted along from place to place as opportunity permitted. The journey from Brunei Bay to Bario may have taken a piece five hundred years.

Practically everything else to be seen in the crowded setting of the living quarters (or living corridor) is of more or less local origin. There are very few needs the Kelabits cannot meet for themselves. And these few can all be obtained by barter from adjacent peoples. Bario makes its own ordinary mats for personal sleeping; a very good, easily worked sort of rush grows in the swampy parts of the plain. It is a man's job to collect this and trim off the thorns; his wife's to dry the leaf strips and, at leisure, intertwine them, laid flatly on the floor boards to make a plain mat within a few evenings. The sort of mats that should be used in public for the visitor and on social occasions, requires a finer and firmer leaf which only grows on the other side of the spinal range. Bario can make its own cooking pots. But the white clay pocket here is small and inferior. The pots of Pa Trap, where the clay is purer and nearer the long-house, are preferred; pots of Pa Mada to the south are better still. There is a sort of ground-creeping tendril which grows at Bario, most favourable to the making of fish traps—which are much in demand by the easterly people; old Pun Maran makes the very best.

Everyone can make his own cloth of course—out of bark for male loin cloths and embroidered, sleeveless coats worn in the sun by both sexes; out of stripped pine-apple leaf woven on straightforward looms for feminine dresses, blankets, wraps.

Iron is found mostly in an easily workable ore among the lowland Kenyahs. On the upper Batang Kayan are master blacksmiths who make the ground-edged, scroll designed sword-knives (*parang*) without which no proud man steps out of house, and which act equally to cut down a tree or off a head, extract the thorn from the foot or strip the skin of the red-leaf monkey much favoured for masculine skull-caps; trim your own or scalp a neighbour.

There is no money anywhere. Anything can be changed for something else—including human life (or portions in it). The three basic units against which barter standards are generally measured:

1. *Buffaloes*—for major exchanges.
2. *Salt*—the basic unit for measure in small labour values.
3. *Borak*—rice wine, the ordinary way of 'paying' for casual labour (this sort of payment will also almost always involve reciprocating the same value of labour at a later date).

These three things—buffaloes, borak, salt—are always a conspicuous feature of the domestic landscape at Bario and other Kelabit long-houses. So conspicuous that almost every night you drink the borak, someone is almost sure to be paying some other people for something they have done that day; being Kelabits, these occasions cannot be kept private—all who wish may join the fun. The long-house (which anyway collapses occasionally), sways gently in the night, not simply because of the borak absorbed but by virtue, too, of the buffaloes who have come in for overnight shelter under the floor to thump in itchiness their mud-dry night hides rubbed against the posts.

The salt of commerce is to be seen everywhere: hanging in bundles neatly packed and sewn within smoked leaf; stacks of it along with the firewood neatly arranged over each fireplace. Big packages, several pounds weight, hang from the roof rafters—or anywhere near some warmth. This salt comes from natural springs, is one of the great reasons why the Kelabits have been able to remain so independent of external influences. All the other interior peoples of Borneo have to depend on outside salt. Right inside, Kelabits have grown rich by working and trading their salt over the interior. A package of some three ounces represents a day's work at Bario. By the time it gets a fortnight away on the Batang Kayan, a few packages might buy you one sounding gong. Very dark and stinking of iodine, this salt has the enormous added attraction of effectively preventing goitre, curse of so many inland peoples in this part of the world.

The intricacy, elasticity, and apparent illogicality of Kelabit trade beggars brief description. Much of this semi-economic activity is centred in death, connected with the erection of stone monuments, the cutting of those proclaimal mountain clearings high upon the skyline all around the bowl of highland. In that context, it can be more suitably considered emotionally, presently. Immediately, the inborn eye—looking down these two hundred odd feet of long-house—can invisibly calculate enough salt for several thousand days; enough borak for four more jolly evenings (and it only takes four to foment); enough buffaloes moving around to buy at least one of the highest dragon jars and a spare human life:

One salt=one day's ordinary work (say).
Two salt=one Bario-type mat.
Four salt=one Bawang-type mat.
One salt=one Pa Trap pot.
Two salt=one Pa Mada pot.
Thirty salt=one small Chinese pot (two pint size).
Fifty salt=one small simple gong.
Two gongs of this kind=one half-size dragon jar (5 drunks).
Two jars of this kind and ten salt=one ordinary large dragon jar.
Four ordinary dragon jars=one male buffalo calf.
One well-grown male buffalo=thirty yellow glass(='bone') beads (worn in the front of women's caps).
Five buffaloes, five fat pigs, three hump-back bulls, two goats, two ordinary jars, two small jars, two gongs, two fine parang knives, ten mats, ten fish nets, ten fowls, ten Pa Mada pots, ten rolls of best leaf tobacco, one hundred yellow cane beads and two hundred salt=one old dragon jar of red-bodied stoneware (if you can get it).
One old dragon jar=one human life.

The best jars have each their separate mythology. There are about a dozen of them in the uplands. And although the Kelabits themselves cannot date them back to China and the T'ang dynasty, or Siam and Sung, they truly recognize the oldest group as regards manufacture. In fact, the value just given for such a jar is in a way—like all other Kelabit values—irrelevant, absolutely. It all depends on the buyer, the seller and the go-between: for no transaction is ever undertaken direct: let alone multiple variations, to the Kelabit eye, in each jar, buffalo, bead, or (for the flicker of that) any single package of salt, bellyful of borak. When a price has been agreed, naturally that does not mean that it is settled. Payment cannot be made on the spot. To owe is propriety. A thing has not true intrinsic value at any one moment.

Value properties are multiple. They have their major dimensions in some time and any place, *once* (that is) initial existence of the object as it is is accepted. It is not actually as simple as that. For the object you may agree to obtain today, may, after all the preliminaries have been undertaken, appear to you on a later day another object. It is not even necessary that it should appear to you as a different object; all may agree that it is the same. But now, a year or two later, when the buffaloes are ready and your son has spent ten days at the springs making the necessary salt, the object has become different to your eyes.

Meanwhile, the buffaloes you arranged to exchange have in the nature of things become slightly different buffaloes. One of them has gone wild on the mountainside, as they love to do: it is going to require a major effort by all the long-house to erect a stockade, drive it, trap it, tie it and lug it in. Incidentally, the female buffalo agreed has since had a calf; thus increasing its value. In any case no one would ever sell an old jar unless he—jars are inherited in the male line (beads as the main value object in the female), gongs and buffaloes in both—or she has to. It is only when it comes to a she (or worse still childless) generation that a great jar goes back into exchange circulation. Then it becomes a prize of the utmost order. For the possession of that holy jar gives a status almost matching that of a recognized, generation after generation genealogical tree of leadership, head-hunting ancestry, industry, and bravery: the attributes which, along with high value property, make Kelabit aristocracy tick, *altesse*.

The aristocracy in Bario lives in the centre of the house with the big verandah platform where most visitors are—if the house is in full order and mood—entertained on arrival. On each side of Lawai's fireplace, to east and west, are his immediate relatives, also upper class. On each side of them, graded up-hill and down, the class gets less.

Each end of the house lies the least class—though only as a maximum insult among an outspoken people would anyone dare to say so; to *show* your class status verbally and particularly to show someone else's class inferiority specifically, ranks with incest, negligence to orphans, ridiculing animals and neglecting hospitality in the Five Commandments of Kelabitry. No other sin can breed such catastrophe.

* * *

There are two very old jars of ultimate sanction at Bario. The best (that is the most perfectly unscathed, richly brown-glazed, powerfully shaped and strongest decorated with dragons—three) is of course in the possession of Lawai himself.

Lately, this, the king of Kelabit jars, caused some disturbance about the house. It took upon its imperial self, at sudden moments of the night, to issue a powerful booming note, interspersed with melancholy yet carnivorous roars. Nothing of the kind had been heard before. It augured some major disturbance, for sure. Much fear was caused among the women and children—who do not scare easy. So Lawai removed the jar about half a mile and tied it to a special carved, buffalo-horned post on the edge of one of his rice fields out across the plain. Here he must visit it daily.

Later, he will learn the meaning of this strange omen, in yet louder sound. So far, soliciting the spider-hunters, crested jays and white-breasted kites suitably appealed to with offerings of eggs and chicks, has failed to elicit any explanation of the ominous uproar. Bario has seldom been very closely in touch (through Pun Maran) with an outside world of the intangible, a very vague Almighty and an obscurely unpleasant devilry, requiring only great attentions at bad times, epidemics or droughts. An unspecified pantheon of spirits derived directly from Kelabits of the past are propitiated by formulae and at a small expense. What really matters is that the aristocracy, when it dies, should continue to be treated as such by those left to use the inherited property. So long as the death feasts are generous, the monuments conspicuous, these powerful spirits should not disturb the peace. *Should* not . . .

It is not necessarily easy to arrange that the appropriate safeguards for spiritual peace be preserved. The trouble comes when an agreed aristocrat either faces death without direct heirs or disapproves of the doings of these heirs. Practically the only way a son or daughter may earn parental disapproval is by marrying someone of substantially inferior status. Every parent *wants* to back up his children in everything. Only thus can the parent be sure that the children will do the right thing after death, not leave him in the lurch: for ever suspended without getting out. Whatever the far origins of such feeling, their theoretical formulation has become as nebulous as nearly all the philosophical or immaterial judgments which not so much complicate everyday occasion as give depth and excitement otherwise readily lacking in a largely self-sufficient, frequently over-exuberant, way of life.

A parent will back up his children on almost anything. Matters like murder, adultery or even idleness can be seen through rose-grey retina of uncertain or undesired eternity. To marry someone without property is another matter altogether. For this means that the total contribution of the two partners to the consummation of life by death will be watered down, dangerously. For a principal heir should devote *at least* one fifth (better more), of the inherited property to celebrating the departure of mother, father, mother-in-law, father-in-law. Each of these will require celebration with local orgies, sacrifices of animals, removal from the coffin to a special burial urn or jar, and much else beside; to secure the departed's spirit. The complex strain on the family property must be considerable. It can only be offset by the wise use of the varied objects in barter and loan, dead and long-term thinking; and, even more important, by applying body and mind to hard work. The theory of the Kelabit upper class is that it is the industrious and intelligent; the higher you are, the harder you *should* work.

The better-off people are, on the whole, the harder they work, at Bario. To some of them, like Agan and Kampong Rajah, it may become something of an obsession. The good way of life is to work hard. It is not difficult, at three thousand five hundred feet near the equator, in a not over-populated land, to produce all minimum requirements of food, shelter, clothing, tools and comforts. It does require constant devotion and frequent thought to harvest overabundant rice: thus to build up a surplus every two or three years, to entertain five hundred people at one feast. To look after your buffaloes and bring in new stock, trading over the border and leading a beast in slow, cautious stages over the mountains, through the jungle, where buffaloes (which cannot sweat) peel and die over you when you are not thinking. To work day and night every week in the roaring heat needed to boil salt out of the springs. To travel a fortnight away through the mountains and win bezoar stones from the guts of monkeys and the white gum from two hundred foot *damar* trees—items of the highest value for trade outward and eventually for the Chinese cosmetic and aphrodisiac trades.

It is possible for anyone to grow gradually rich; it is not easy. The aristocracy has acquired its riches over generations. The true son or daughter, in this line of thought, must preserve the position and not let go. For it is as easy to squander away your heritage at Bario as anywhere else. To be effectively industrious and intelligent, it takes two. The roles of man and woman are pretty well defined, according more or less to the heaviness of the work and the distance it takes the person away from the main community on their own. Fetching firewood from the jungle and all other jungle work goes to the man. Fetching water from the stream, and most indoor activities unconnected with hunting, fall on the woman. Women do most of the gardening, tobacco planting and preparation; men the salt making (though women often can help), or clearing the space before gardening can begin. Either sex carries as much as they can of whatever they must. And there is no significant privilege a man enjoys (other than from physical necessity) which is not also available to woman, if she so feels.

It would be fantastic for man to fetch water, woman to hunt pig. There is no actual objection to it at all. There are few superstitions about what must not be. It does not arise. A division of labour has been worked out by experience. It suits the setting. There are so very many things to do in upland life and so few things that a family need not do for itself. Simple specializations suit everybody. A man should not know how to fish the tiny brooks which women cunningly drain off to hand-net minnows and shrimps in dry periods (popping minute catch from net with strong fingers into pear-shaped gourd hung with twine over the left ear). Women would not know the way to set big conical fish traps, bigger than a man, which the men make with bamboo and bind with vine to set in weirs at special bends on the larger streams in flood periods. But almost all know almost all. The only other criterion thus: what they have and how they care for it.

Nothing more dreadful can happen to proud parents of privilege than that one of their offspring shall marry far below them. The partnership pattern of their own posterity is threatened. Sometimes it works out all right, afterwards. In any case, the socially lesser partner has to make substantial payment—raised by that side of the family—as guarantee deposit before being admitted to the slippery upward slope. At Bario, though, girls are very much girls. In the face of forced censure, there are always those who will defy. In simple, will marry for love. The word is not there. The feeling is: though inextricably mixed with personal vanity and the obstinate protection of oneself which grows so vigorously in such a close and crowded community. 'I wish— I will—I shall.'

*　　*　　*

The second old and very valuable jar at Bario reflects directly—and, as some think, dreadfully—upon this very situation. Old Balan's jar has also its own separate locality and history. Though at this moment it is where it is, seemingly static, and he is where he is because others fear for its future, all are anticipating real uproar which lies ten years ahead (when Balan is dead, the jar still ageing).

Balan is not strictly a native of Bario. Kelabits are constantly mobile. There are many reasons for moving from one village to another. Fury, spite, anxiety, sexual uncertainty, kin-troubles, come in. Because one long-house may contain too few people of the same status and because people nearer than third cousins are not supposed to marry (they often do), marriages are usually (or at least 'ideally') between different long-houses. The commonest ground for divorce is that neither family can agree to their child living with the other. Serious battles sometimes develop over this, especially if the young people are themselves determined to stay together somehow. On the Plain of Bah nothing is deliberately designed in a middle way. Compromise can occur only by exhaustive attrition; the outsider inexperienced in this process becomes utterly exhausted—at a stage when Kelabit discussion is only *beginning* to move into the phase of using a go-between, has not yet *looked* like becoming local argument; let alone entered the parabola of shadowed violence, or abandoned offence.

Balan's only child, a girl, lives, as he long did, at Kubaan, the larger of the two long-houses two days' walk westward over the Tamabo range. These are Kelabits outside the main stream of present-day, away from the richest upland and the intense contact within. They feel it so. She fell for a local boy: he rating in her parent's eyes as thoroughly bad. This did not mean that he was bad morally. Morally a Kelabit can be as bad as she or he can get away with. The original sins are so extreme that punishment will fall upon the whole community anyway, probably by universal, semi-instantaneous petrifaction. Bad, in the Kubaan or Bario sense, means inferior in status, judged on the scale of ancestry, property, position in the long-house structure and desired industry. A bad man is a low-class man. It is fighting talk to call anyone so. Conversely, it is blush-making to call anyone otherwise. Only aristocrats are good. Either they take that for granted or the speaker is using the term in a flattery which implies uncertainty; and may be insulting by inversion.

Should the speaker be a shrewd aristocrat, however, he may (in his goodness of heart and hearth) thus flatter some lesser person carefully without offence. Benevolent with borak—before the stage when it begins to sting the tongue or inflame shallow-buried self-expression— Lawai Bisarai may often be heard to describe the whole of Bario as good. A couple of gourds later on he may extend his observations to the adjacent village of Pa Trap, and point out that apart from a few of present company's relatives excepted, the whole of that (Pa Trap) lot are bad. For in a set-up where the families within a long-house are much more than neighbours, when you want to knock some about you must go a few miles away—unless, that is, you want serious trouble, which Lawai (like many other Kelabits) sometimes courts joyfully.

A journey can be good. One's health can be good. News nearly always is good. Fruit trees, a joint of venison, a stone earmarked for later carving, the finish of a windmill for scaring away birds from the harvest, a new bone fish-hook—all may very well be good. By the same word and token ('dhor') Lawai is good. And a man who lives at the end of the house, although he may have abundant harvests, many children, much commonsense, high skill in the jungle and a lovely singing voice can hardly ever be better than bad—whatever a momentarily melting Chief Lawai or his hasty, ambitious, generous eldest son good Agan may say to the contrary.

For good and bad alike there is equal opportunity; more than enough land and sufficient of everything else—provided you are reasonably industrious. The odd, 'impossible' misfit character is allowed for. Otherwise, who may exist, securely? All must 'co-operate' (or cohabit) if they are to continue in comfort. The ultra-neurotic woman, who squandered her girlhood in frustrating affairs, has grown embittered and lonely; but she still receives all the help she needs in the fields and in the house—where she shares another fire with a family. For each of those who help her, she reciprocates as she can. Otherwise she could not

continue to exist as a Kelabit. Her anti-social strivings are expressed
with her mouth and in tiny meannesses which nearly all deprive no one
beyond herself (to her intermittent fury).

The ear in a long-house must acquire its own immunities. It becomes,
behind a blunting over-all jamboree of sound, highly selective to what
that particular mind behind will accept (or ignore). Frightful words
spoken in anger need never go further than the lips which formed
them. While all words spoken in heat, drink or hinting no longer exist
next day; unless someone *wants* to make something of it.

'Bad man', for Balan, thus meant no more than that the fellow had
not a buffalo to his name, only one very ordinary big jar—the kind
which the descendants of Chinese who made them hundreds of years
ago (in Swatow) now make at several places on the Borneo coast. Not
as imitations, but in direct tradition with minute differences, which
could not deceive a Kelabit.

Balan did all that he could to obstruct the marriage. Where there is
no ceremony it is not particularly easy to tell when people are
'married', anyway. Frequently the first and the final confirmation of
such an arrangement is conspicuous pregnancy. Even then, there may
be violent dispute. Kelabits cannot conceive that sleeping with a girl
once or intermittently can cause children. And as many girls (before
they settle down) are highly promiscuous (as we shall soon see),
awful arguments may occur—if, as is usual, the girl claims one man
as the father and he does not wish to admit it and marry her. It is unlikely she has lain only with him over the months.

That was not all the problem in the present instance. Balan's daughter
adored the man, wished for no other. If father had been younger and
quicker, he might have nipped things in the bud much earlier. Elderly
and a widower, the fresh man was well bedded down on the family
mat before Pa woke up.

If necessary, such a situation can be dealt with even at this stage.
At almost the same time Chief Lawai's own young close nephew had
gallantly gone to the aid of a niece put in the same class-unconscious
position. Although first cousins, they had married and then kept the
family—otherwise stained by her becoming pregnant from a bad man,
of low class—within its best social level, despite heavy public comment which might have been too powerful with lesser people. (For
although the ear soon learns to select and reject individual voices, when
these become multiple, loud, sustained and also supporting tradition,

the house is soon filled with the sound; then he who ignores can either run away or run amok—as Belalang's father soon will).

Faced with a finality, Balan now said that he would disinherit his daughter. This involved major effort of will. It is a stronger act than killing someone—alas, for men, suicide is one of the activities exclusively allocated as feminine. Even his threat had no effect. And Balan, passing the age where men, after four or five decades of effort, are expected to do much out of doors, needed the comforts which offspring should provide at this stage on the way out. He stayed on for one rice harvest at Kubaan. Then, as his son-in-law's lack (to Balan) of industry grew greatly intolerable, the sore festered. One day, he sent word to his second cousin, Lawai at Bario, to come and fetch him.

This kind of external invitation is the subject of intense jubilation. There is nothing a long-house would rather do than add to its number. Especially if the addition is aristocratic, good stuff. All the blood body of Bario took off over the mountains. Arrived at Kubaan, there was inevitably a tremendous fuss. The head man there, Ngelawan Rajah (himself a relative), properly found in this a grave loss of face for his long-house. Many other material and emotional interests were bound to be upset by the disappearance of one of their oldest and most respected inhabitants. It nearly came to a free fight. Fortunately, there was borak to soothe things over; and statesmanship, to leave some property behind and to spin the whole issue into words which, if remembered, need not be re-registered for some time to come.

So, the second great jar made a further fragile journey, carried in relays, in big baskets on brown backs (sweating on slippery mountainsides with nervousness as much as with heat).

Back in Bario, old Balan could not at once feel at home. After all, he had lived sixty years elsewhere. Every tiny knot in the thousands tied to secure the planks and poles and thatch of the Kubaan long-house was known to him personally. He had taken some part in everything to do with its growth and survival, in every life and mood there. In Bario he knew almost nothing. So Lawai and the whole village turned out to make him a little separate house, ten feet by eight feet, a hut, with a separate log entrance from the outside and single plank causeway leading from his fireplace direct on to Lawai's centre part of the long-house verandah. Here, with simple furniture of mind, but with the wonder jar very securely tied to the wall, Balan re-anchors his future. Now the whole question of his inheritance could become subject for marvellous speculation. As Kelabits trace relationship through the most tenuous links—and sometimes non-existent ones, if convenient—Balan had plenty of 'nieces' and 'nephews' in Bario. It was now a niece's job to cook for him, feed him and generally supply him with the good things of a fading life, all the way from pulped and salivaed sugar cane, through mouse-deer brains sweetly cooked in bamboo, to the freshest dried tobacco neatly rolled and tied in plantain leaf (preferably already lit for smoking). But would Balan live long enough for them to fill sufficient obligations, for him to make them indirect heirs? Could he feel the same obligation? Would his daughter now come to her senses and do something different? The answer could not be yet. And when it came, might contain the sort of sensational unexpectedness which somehow or other injects itself into so many upland solutions: solutions not knowingly designed to solve . . .

*   *   *

Balan, an uncounted sixty and old for a Kelabit, spends most of his time indoors. This is not to suggest that he is not active enough, often sprightly. Rather short, five feet five inches, light (a hundred or so pounds), his skin wrinkled parchment, his long black hair lank with a few tiny traces of grey; two of his teeth have gone, his frequent smile is stumpy, chipper. He amuses the young by wearing, through the holes bored in the upper part of his ears, a pair of long, pointed, tapered, delicately pink prongs, which he carved himself—with much difficulty and an especially strong steel—out of a solid casque on the bill of a Helmeted Hornbill. The shape is an imitation of the usual (for young men) upper ear ornaments, made of the long, white fangs of the Clouded Leopard.

People do not take much more notice of what he says, even though he is an aristocrat and theoretically entitled to serious attention in any serious discussion—for instance on the allocation of land for next year's rice planting or programme for replacing planks and repairing thatch in the long-house. He is said, with chuckle, to be 'a bit like a boy again'. Some men do rather deliberately develop a juvenile touch in old age again; Balan, the name, itself implies that. It is properly a name for a young, unmarried man. There is no rule. Kelabits do not think of names as binding, lasting things. The name of the long-house itself can change. The name of a person can change as the person chooses;

or as circumstances require. By wishing at this stage to be called Balan, the old boy is also in a way expressing his protest against his son-in-law in very public and easily recognized terms. For every day precedent requires, or any way indicates, that since his daughter has a child he should now take a name showing grandparenthood. A grandfatherly name should be a humble one, lest undesirable other-world attention be focused on the little child to its physical disadvantage. Balan is a boasting name: Tigerish.

But Balan feels like boasting. For over his daughter he has put up an exceptional display of personality. He has expressed a sentiment in the public mood, with about the amount of demonstration which the context requires. Rather on the conservative side, no doubt. Still, well in line with propriety and touching up a bit of drama, as everyone desires. To boast with your name is strictly in order. After all, a baby starts out in life with some name which suggests excessive insignificance. If the parents have previously lost children in childbirth, as many do, the baby will usually be addressed as:

'little filth'
'flea'
'rubbish'
'cowpat'

—and these names may be continued well on into life. With adolescence and rapidly growing self-expression, youth may choose whatever name comes to heart. Rajah, Prince, Rhinoceros, Tremendously Powerful, for boys; Bright Moon, Princess, Jewel, for girls. The next stage, traditionally involved with the taking of heads, allows for more ambitious personal claims.

The name of the great man of Bario, Lawai Bisarai, implies 'he who ignores and overrules everyone else'. This signalizes an achievement of early manhood. He speared a man in a drunken party over on the Bawang side. Subsequently taken down to the coast by his elders, mainly because the event was having international repercussions (Bawang being then in Dutch Borneo), he was sentenced, by the only European then living in the whole Baram watershed, to two years' detention. He was given the job of gardener to the officer's bungalow. After a few months, he simply could not stand the lowlands. By a tremendous feat of endurance he got back to Bario, travelling entirely on his own and undetected for two months. His reappearance distressed everybody. They feared to irritate the remote white Rajah's

Government, to whom each family paid one dollar a year and by whom they were otherwise undisturbed. So they took him back again. After a few months he was released and returned, to become in time the most government-minded Kelabit of all. His name exactly expresses how much that mindedness is, and what outside rule feels like, on the far side of the Tamabo mountains.

A great name need not mean a great family. Thus 'One Thousand White Men' is one of the humbler adults of Bario, though a man of great energy and strength, whose views on things involving these qualities receive special hearing through the evening's talk. 'I Am Better Than The Rajah' is quite a boy; no one takes any notice of *him* (yet).

A personal name can also express aspiration rather than achievement. In doing so, it can incidentally satisfy some of the aspiration, is one outlet for self-expression. Old Balan, when on top of his new Bario form, actually does sword dances—mostly left to the younger generation. He also likes to go fishing on his own. He insists on bringing in most of his own firewood despite protests from nephews very willing to serve in this way. He must not, he feels, become too dependent on others. Always there must be a distant implication that perhaps he will presently go back over the mountains to Kubaan. No arrangement must be guaranteed permanent. For that matter, maybe his fury with Kubaan will mellow presently; he can express that at once, by taking another name.

Balan is only one of several people who will nearly always be around in the house. There is the blind widow at the fire one bay from the west end. Her two daughters, buxom, marriageable, are among those who make the most laughter and gaiety about the long-house—as marriageable girls often do, emphasizing their energy, jollity, amiability, which can be taken for granted when they are settled down, after all. The two girls treat their mother a little cursorily, but sufficiently. When old people become incapable, they are a trial; there are so many things to be done, especially at the key-points of agricultural activity, making it difficult to keep regular hours or look after people constantly. For the most part the pale blind woman stays, scantily clad, crouched beside the fireplace, feebly weaving rush mats or cooking interminable tit-bits of old pig-fat, fern top, some grubs the gang of kids have given her, laughing.

Some of the kids will always be around in the house. One or two older ones look after the tiny ones, who cannot yet safely be let to roam the plain outside. The babies, once old enough to be left for spells by mother, are put in basket-work slings. When that is depends entirely on mother. Some start separating from their babies quite soon. This is mostly compelled by the season. At the time of the rice harvest, a woman has so much to do that if she possibly can she will dump the baby. Women have been known to kill their babies or force abortions when the event corresponded with this crucial two months in the year. It matters tremendously that the rice crop should be good and much more than that: that every ear of it should be properly gathered in, trampled, sifted, winnowed, and stored in the big bark bins, in the special rice huts dotted about the plain.

When little children can begin to walk and run, there is constant care lest they manage to fall through a loose floor board, into a fire, or through the end doors clean out of the long-house. Right now, there are two particularly bossy young girls who have happily taken over the whole business of child supervision for the community. Though both under ten, they are also well capable of welcoming through travellers or visitors with barter, answering a shout from Lawai for some bananas, or from Balan—who has run out of betel nut, his particular hobby (which is awkward, as it will not grow up here properly).

It is essential that people should be about all the time. Fire is fear in the long-house. Or rather, the fear that can best be offset by care. The other and deeper danger is that the whole house will be turned to stone. But that unpredictable disaster can arise from a remote act by a remiss individual who unthinkingly makes a fool of a toad or ridicules a minnow stranded in a rock pool half-way up Mount Murud.

It is a long time now, since Bario was burned down. But only last year the Saban Kelabit house away out on the southern track down the Bahau was totally destroyed through a crippled old woman accidentally upsetting some red hot embers. However carefully the fireplaces are made of baked clay, separately set in selected places along one line, accidents will happen. Once, a rat set fire to a house by dragging the end of a burning branch, for no known reason. Another time, a newly acquired mirror, lovingly brought up from the lowlands, was let lie to catch the sun's rays and set fire to the leaf roof. Old people and children get killed in these fires. The loss of jars, gongs and beads is irreparable.

There are times, too, when everybody is about the long-house most of the day. These times are much less frequent among the Kelabits than most other Borneo people. Bad omens provide the reason. If a snake with red head and tail crosses someone's path on the way to work it means bad. If a barking-deer barks on one side of the track it means bad; the other, good. If a tree falls on the mountainside, with a mighty crash, just when a man is felling another tree, it threatens awful. If there is hail—it happens about once in a generation—it spells appalling.

There is quite an elaborate code of these omens. On the whole, though, Kelabits treat them with liberal margins of observation and oversight. It is not necessary to *hear* a barking-deer in the wrong place if something important is afoot. On the other side, it may be extremely convenient to hear one another morning. Only if the omen is conspicuous, the observer important and the occasion significant, need it be taken quite seriously. All work is suspended, for the individual, family or the whole community, according to all the conditions involved. Those affected must do no more out-door work for one or sometimes more days. Offerings are made to the invisible forces of disorder in general. These offerings are put in inverted cones of bamboo strips on posts, placed along the outside of the house or— for bigger occasions—outside on the ground. It had better be an old person who seeks to redress the balance in words addressed outward. Older than Balan of Kubaan is Pun Maran. His whole skin is darkly veined with a decade of ring-worm; the hut he spends most of his days in, on the edge of his rice field, is famous as the only Bario one which has fleas. Pun Maran is Bario's main link with the invisible, which he addresses, scratching:

The barking-deer called across the track, suddenly, my fiery eagle
The barking-deer calling for some thing and we must give—
Help us, powerful eagle, come down, my closest hawk,
Be here over us answering who have nothing to hide or hidden
And we will give you and the everything
Until there is nothing left for you the powerful ones who may eat
    our very lives if you wish and say
But whom we implore this day to relieve our terror, overlooking us,
    overlooking single stupidities and all the ways we have forgotten
    to consider.
Always we are merely the poor plain creatures below who know
    nothing

40

Who plant to starve and laugh only in fear of mighty you
The power by whose endurance we have grown and may we pray
    continue—
Or even perhaps prosper a little
If we unceasingly think of and respect the spirits outside, offering
    all to you,
Here through this fine little pitiful rich hen's egg
Our bodies to you that our fields may not be scourged and our
    plain swept entirely away
In the sweep of great wings and angry neglected feelings.
Pun Maran proceeds, intermittently scratching; and in good time the
bird of his wish is seen in his eyes, swooping in on closed wings, the
poised reassurance.

*　*　*

Ordinarily, nearly everybody in Bario is outdoors none of the night
and most of the day. Most of the year many if not most of the people,
except Lawai, Balan, the blind widow and slung babies, are out
virtually all day. At very busy times the house is nearly empty by
daylight, starts to fill up again as the sun falls way over Kubaan and the
dusk gives just enough light for people to hurry in from the plain, or
the jungle behind.

Dusk is the turn from busy day into busy night. For although the
difference between the two is sharp out of doors and no one does
anything in the dark, inside the long-house is lighter by night than by
day—and far more lively. If such is the mood it may remain so until
the new dawn. The bright young men, like Tayun and Agan, can
comfortably do a whole day and night without sleep, when there is
something not to sleep about. As they wish (or must), they can turn
over on the floor and be asleep in a whisper, for as long as they do not
feel cold—or too warm, from feminine propinquity.

The phase of dream is not, perhaps, so powerful in determining
Bario's waking action as among some other Borneans. In this, dream
and omen, superstitions, animistic idea and the auto-suggestions of
nightmares, are interrelated. They are not very easily held to, strongly,
by mountain people, who have learned by experience—which they
assess and esteem—that in this upland set-up most depends on what
they themselves do. The actual *imponderabilia* of these surroundings

41

are, on the whole, a lot less than those of the average lowland long-house. For instance, it is very seldom indeed that weather or other factors seriously hinder movement and travel in the uplands; whereas, among the great majority of Borneans, who depend on rivers and their wrist for a large sector of living, much erraticism is evident—and frequently not to be explained by any immediately local or predictable event. Of course, it is more complicated than this. All the same, Tayun and Lawai take little stock of dreams except as indications. If they dream of any event actually intended to be undertaken, and the dream is unfriendly to the project, they will likely postpone and conceivably (if not very keen) abandon it. But the dream has not here become a guide, even a dictator, of day-to-day conduct. Days pass, and no one mentions one. It helps, no doubt, that over half of most nights most wise men sleep deeply, wine-abetted. Basically, though, few Kelabits wish (or can afford) to be dreamers of anything less than the achievable years ahead; that struggle is more than sufficient, since satisfaction can never be reached.

Thro' this daylight all the able-bodied men have been working on rice huts. Balan and Pun Maran are exempted by age; as also the indoor regulars, of course. The job for this day was decided the previous evening. It is up to each fireplace to provide one person to help build the rice huts for all of them. These huts have common uprights and roofing: within this each is separately walled, binned and laddered. Actually the 'fireplaces', family groups, with more adults have provided extra; there is not much else doing this day—except that Tayun has taken some of the curl-tailed curs and gone hunting for his own and the general pot. These extra helpers involve the three people helped in reciprocating that amount of extra back on some other job later on. Right now it makes the job easier, quicker, more complete. It is quite a big job. Big logs have to be felled, trimmed and carried in from the forest. Thatch already prepared by the women indoors, carried two cigarette's walk from the house; vine and bamboo collected to bind and fix it as thatch. Circles of wood cut and fixed on the uprights: to keep out rats, of which there are vigorous sorts in the highlands. The surrounding grass and scrub cleared, bark stripped off the few kinds of tree which provide the right kinds (of bark). In amongst the hard work the women of the three families supply a small jar of borak; and about noon a big meal of rice wrapped in leaf, with smoked pork and just a little cucumber leaf as salad.

The men stop as the sun begins to fall into the mountain tops. They must do their own family odd jobs before dark. Several hurry off into the jungle and come home in the full dusk, labouring up the single log ladder with the heaviest branch or trunk they can carry. This is dumped on a rough platform beside the top of the ladder, one side of the low entrance to the house itself. Here in the gathering dark men sit, chat about the day and chop the firewood for night; below buffalo, cattle and goats wander in from the grassland and swamp. Those with animals lean over the edge with open packages of the iodine salt. Every beast likes to lick this stuff. And anyone who neglects to feed his in this way may find they wander far afield after salt licks; thereby difficult to recover when wanted for exchange or for slaughter in sacrifice. Necessarily it is not easy to see whose is which in this light. But each man knows his own intimately. Ten ordinary buffalo cows look and practically feel as different to their owners as ten jars from the same Chinese manufactory, back indoors bubbling (some hope) with borak.

The women have mostly managed to get in earlier. They have to revive the fires and start the rice cooking. The fowls, running free inside and out during the day, become their sudden concern before night. A brood of chicks must be gathered up with hen into a basket slung from the ceiling; otherwise as likely as not a civet, weasel, mongoose, lizard or python may wreck the lot before dawn. In each family section one floor board lifts up. Through this, out of a child-high bamboo, the housewife spills a thick, soupy concoction from all the food refuse, odds and ends augmented by boiled cassava tubers, lily roots and other plant matter which—among these earth-rich people of Bario—is considered unfit for human consumption; and which has been simmering away in a big pot for the pigs.

After the animals, the humans feed. It is inconceivable, at Bario, that the evening meal should be other than rice substantially. Every meal will be rice substantially—unless it is a big feast for the dead with great blobs of buffalo flesh being pushed into anyone's mouth, in all directions. At Kubaan, in a year like the last, when there was too much rain before planting—so that everything was delayed, the harvest late and the finches arrived in darkening uncontrollable hordes—Balan had to fall back a good deal on corn and three or four times even wild sago. Here, in the true Kelabit highlands, he need have no fear of that indignity. Every meal the rice, the white rice, boiled nearly to pulpiness, rolled and swished and packed in leaf, will be more than he or anyone can eat. That much the better for the fattening pigs.

To have the rice truly white is also important. Women pound it from the husked grain, two working together, slamming down in alternate rhythm, breasts swinging, with poles tall as themselves, smashed into the small cups carved out from a solid chunk of hardwood—on which it is comfortable to sleep at any other time. The grain has been dried on the sunny days. Twice a week will do for pounding, coming home specially early those afternoons. But some prefer to do a lot in one day. And if visitors are expected or journeys to be undertaken, all the women may be pounding, pouring with sweat, two or three days in a run.

*   *   *

Every proper housewife serves pure white rice. It is a serious reflection on the manners of a lady if there is any trace of husk or other matter to discolour. So long as everyone keeps on drinking borak, the loss of the husk and germ elements do not matter a jot. For borak is made with plenty of whole grain. Baby starts in on it soon after the breast; takes a gourd of it long before the breast is abandoned.

Tayun and the dogs get quite a big Sambhur doe. Not that the dogs did much. They are brilliant with pig. But only the odd one will scent a deer and the very special one tree a leopard. Tayun and his cousin Anyi, who is married to Lawai's fat, irritable daughter, are Bario's dog lovers. That is: they each have one lead dog which is lovingly fed. Anyi likes to sit, in the evening, with his dog between his knees, dribbling saliva into the dog's mouth—to the apparent satisfaction of both. It is the best dog in the place, just as Anyi is the cleverest hunter; he knows the different calls of at least a hundred different birds, and by pressing a leaf against his mouth and squealing can imitate the cries of various deer so that they come slowly through the deep shadow to within easy blow-pipe. Tayun's deer is divided according to practice: the killer's share to himself, enough for tonight and tomorrow to everyone else, the brains to old Balan (who is *his* uncle too) and odd pieces around to special friends, clamorous children—not so hungry but for fun clamorous—and ravenous dogs. The body is rough cut at the top of the ladder at first, more carefully on his part of the verandah afterwards. Heavy candles and torches of damar resin give brilliant, dithering light and push up sooty trailers which night by night tan the roof to polished ebony (and waterproof). No one need ask if meat has come into the house. The snarling, whining, shrieking, fighting curs are adequate announcers. They are hardly ever satisfied, never for long still. When things are at their most silent, between the last drink and the first cock-crow from the rafters, a pack of dogs will explode and rattle all Bario in pursuit of some glandular fantasy: no human notices (wakes for) a normality like that.

There is meat nearly every day, sometimes more than Bario can eat. The spring salt which prevents goitre is not sufficiently caustic to preserve flesh very well, but constant smoking over the fire and the cool nights can keep it a week. At the week-end the hanging strips drip maggots, giving taste. It does not really matter if there is nothing else except a few leaves to be dibbled by the fingers—only instrument of eating—out of the soup.

Each meal tends to be much like another, time after time. Until, after enough times, comes impatience with the routine. Somebody starts roasting reed stems or suddenly reveals a store of juicy barbel she has been keeping alive, fattening in a small jar. Somebody else responds by rough-baking glutinous rice. The men, bored, decide to make a mass expedition up into the cliffs in search of honey. Agan starts a snare line, fall traps at intervals along a low-cut hedge of branches; he brings in francolins, small otter, a vicious marbled cat, and one of the wonderful black and blood-red mountain partridges; all for the pot. For two or three evenings the food is exciting; then returns to routine. Periodically there are outbursts of special crops: pumpkins and marrows, water melon week, mangosteen time, and the great early burst when all the maize gardens come golden, give indigestion.

Eating plenty is important. Kelabits are always expressing amazement at how little other people eat compared with themselves. There is a certain pride in eating. There is certainly something wrong if one doesn't eat lots. To eat little as a guest at another house can easily become hurtful to the hosts.

The cooking and eating will not be done with until dark has settled and the nightjars relaxed their first nocturnal frenzy. Outside, eagle owl, screech owl, eared owl and bay owl may proclaim themselves unnoticed as the long-house simmers up towards verbal boil. While men are sharpening their knives for tomorrow (on chunks of slate specially brought from far down the Baram), women are carrying on at new mats, touch-weaving strips in and out—every now and then pressing and flattening the surface with a polished rounded pebble. This is the favourite moment for cleaner girls to go over each other's jet tresses: first with fingers hunting the head-lice, then with fine wooden combs, finally with fat to give it glisten. The cleaner bachelors prefer to de-lice in private, specialize publicly in elaborate hair trims and the minute inspection of eyelashes. If a new eyelash is growing, pull it out with tiny bone tweezers; let a girl do it, sharing desire. If hair is beginning to grow down on to manly, strong forehead, have someone scrape it off with sharpened bush-knife. Behind all sorts of sorting out of the day's fag ends, women brushing the food scraps away from the fire-places, visitors being entertained and news from afar discussed on the Chief's verandah platform, gathers a small atmosphere of restlessness, of expectancy.

*　*　*

'Atmosphere', here, is most readily measurable in the wobbles and tremors of the long-house and in non-animal sounds of high note—clinking of stoneware, pings from porcelain, liquid glugs as cold brook water is poured from carrying bamboos on to the brew stewing itself in big jars. 'Expectancy' is provided by an anticipation of the formali-ties due from the women whose rice huts were prepared this day (these huts being thought of as feminine). The three will join together to make borak for all who helped: in effect for the whole house.

There is quite a bit of messing about and getting the borak ready. The leaf binding for the jar to be taken off; more water applied to the hash, topping up on water put in about mid-day; gourds and porcelain vessels to be collected and assembled wherever the stuff is to be drunk. That point may be anywhere, either on the front verandah or along the living quarters at the back. Maybe each of the three concerned decide to give their brew separately, in agreed succession. More likely they get together beside some one fire.

Small Chinese blue-and-white bowls and dried brown gourds of odd shapes and sizes are ready around the jars, which are carried with difficulty out from the back wall. Mats are put around, gum torches trimmed, tobacco put out on leaf. Then comes the business of inviting others to participate. It is not good manners to appear eager. There may be those who do not *want* to drink or sit up, because they are tired or feeling seedy; perhaps because there is some disagreement or small dislike between the guest and one of the hosts. Complete unreadiness to join in leads to the menfolk taking over from the women in inviting; and eventually *dragging* in anyone who is stand-offish, by force. There are probably visitors from some other long-house on the verandah. These must be brought in; must equally show polite reluctance. One way and another, it takes quite a time to get everyone round the jars. Until this process is completed, it is not done for anyone to have a drink—though a point may be waived to soothe some insatiable thirst of Lawai or possibly a fast one to Tayun for providing much venison. Sitting invariably cross-legged, on the floor mats around the three jars, the day that is past is discussed, its trivial incidents recalled—especially if they are amusing. Laughter swells. These people really know how to laugh, laugh all the other places off their feet. If in the mood, the men laugh themselves crying, while the women laugh so much that they lie on their backs, beating the floor with their feet—until the house trembles and sways with hilarity.

Silly little things amuse people most. How Anyi, who is so expert a naturalist, mistook the call of a frog for that of a pheasant, so stalked with infinite care, crawling through the thorns, sharp stones and leeches up the mountainside in increasing perplexity, until he almost swallowed the little animal sitting frogging on a rotten tree stump. Anyi has already told the story against himself, and it is not necessarily true. Now it is worked up into something good by Tuan Ribu ('A Thousand White Men'), Bario's funny man—every long-house has one. Tuan Ribu's younger brother, who is well past marrying age but rather shy and still a bachelor, comes into his own as star mimic. Mimicry is a favourite pastime. It involves full-scale imitation and exaggeration of actions as well as sounds. It may border on the objectionable or rude, once the mimic gets carried away by public delight. But he is allowed plenty of scope. The old medium Pun Maran sits rather feebly grinning through a near-the-bone imitation of an old man trying to catch the fleas on his dog, when every time he catches one another flea jumps on to the dog, off him.

Farce is seldom far under the surface of highland humour; and humour gets into almost everything. A serious ceremony to propitiate spirits may be mocked, a few yards away, by children imitating, un-rebuked. Women often parody male actions, to make masculine industry and efficiency look ridiculous. If there is a good harvest, gaiety reaches its peak. Then anything goes; and extensive though improvised pantomimes involve women dressing up and behaving as men, and vice versa, with the utmost abandon.

In the now certain expectancy of some good wine soon, this store of hilarity focuses on the time between the end of the day jobs, after eating, and the beginning of drinking, before sleeping. There are also stacks of traditional funny stories to be told. In this line Lu'un Ribu ('A Thousand Rows Won') excels. Some of his stories are very long, starring the mouse-deer which is really a very stupid animal indeed. Indeed, the hunter may so confuse a mouse-deer that the little fellow actually dashes into him, to be slashed with bush knife. It doubles the irony that mouse-deer is hero in tales in which, by many subtleties, he deceives and out-matches animals far his superior in cunning and size—elephant and rhino, wild ox, crocodile, gibbon, porcupine, otter and hornbill. Such a favourite mouse-deer story is told by Lu'un Ribu any evening, to young and old:

'There was a man named Tama Nurun, who had a wife named Sina Nurun. They went walking in the jungle and came upon a tree which was heavy in fruit. So Tama Nurun climbed the tree. He plucked many fruit, both ripe and unripe. When Tama Nurun came down, he and his wife gathered the fruit on the ground and began to eat the ripe ones. After they had eaten all the flesh of the fruit, they collected the pips, intending to cook them. They made fire. Tama Nurun collected all the pips into a large bamboo and put this on the fire. Presently the bamboo was burnt black and the pips were almost cooked. Sina Nurun was blowing up the fire underneath the bamboo containing the pips when this container fell and water spilled out, scalding Sina Nurun's feet.

'Sina Nurun's feet were badly scalded and caused her so much pain that she could not walk home. Tama Nurun was very distressed. He carried his wife home on his back. On the way, they met Agan Plandok, the Noble Mouse-deer.

'Agan Plandok (the Mouse-deer) asked:

' "Why do you carry your wife?"

' "My wife's feet were scalded. She cannot walk."

' "Very sorry indeed to hear it. I want to help you, but I don't think I can. However I'll try to carry her with your assistance. May I do so?"

' "Yes, but don't let her drop, will you?"

'Agan Plandok carried her, going rather fast, so that Tama Nurun was left behind. When he was tired, he threw Sina Nurun from his back on to the ground. Sina Nurun fell heavily. Her legs were covered with mud. Now Agan Plandok wanted to kill her. But Tama Nurun came running and asked Agan Plandok why he wanted to kill his wife. Agan Plandok said he did not want to kill her. But he went on helping Tama Nurun, by carrying her again. This time he went off very fast. And when he felt tired again, he threw her off, and again attempted to kill her. But Tama Nurun came racing along and his wife was saved once again. He was very angry now and determined to kill Agan Plandok that very instant. Agan Plandok was very much afraid and ran away as fast as he could go.

'Meanwhile, Agan Plandok ran off into the jungle. After wandering in the jungle for a long time, he came to a long-house. The place was full of people; the villagers were having an *irau* feast for Tama Manalad, who was dead. Agan Plandok liked crowds. He went up into the long-house of Sina Manalad, who was mourning the death of her husband. She was sitting by the fire-place, deep in grief. Agan Plandok sat down beside her and asked when did Tama Manalad die? She said he died five days ago. "Very sad indeed," said Agan Plandok; and at the same time he pushed Sina Manalad so that she fell into the fire, burning her face severely and dying immediately.

'Agan Plandok shouted out:

' "Oh, come and see, everyone. Sina Manalad burnt herself in the fire. She said that she pined so for her husband, it was better that she die too. So she burnt herself. I tried to stop her, but too late. Alas, she is dead."

'The people came and looked at her and found that she was indeed dead. They then washed her body and wrapped it in cloth. Later they held a feast in her honour and asked Agan Plandok to beat the gong loudly. But Agan Plandok asked why should they ask him to beat the gong, as he had nothing to do with them or anybody's death? But they persisted.

'Before Agan Plandok would strike the gong, he asked them to open up a piece of planking and place a mat over the resulting hole. Only then would he agree to beat the gong, as that was his custom. The villagers did as he asked. Then Agan Plandok stood in the middle of the crowd and beat the gong, crying:

' "I came here the other day, and I have killed Sina Manalad and burnt her."

'Saying this, he dropped through the hole in the floor and ran off into the jungle. The villagers gave chase, and their dogs with them, —trying to catch Agan Plandok. They failed. He ran too fast and far.

'Some time later, Agan Plandok met Kijang (barking-deer) and told him how he had participated in a feast at a certain village and eaten all kinds of good food. Kijang said he wished to join in such a feast. Agan Plandok told him:

' "If you wish to join in, you'd better go now. Only a while ago they called for me and asked me to take rice-wine and food; I refused because my belly was already full. When you go, take along a basket. When you hear them calling 'ujuk ujuk', you must reply calling out: 'Yes, I am coming'."

'Agan Plandok then hurried on his way; for he had heard the approaching voices of the angry villagers calling to their dogs, "ujuk ujuk". On hearing this call, the barking-deer called back "I am coming," two or three times. As the people all thought this must be Agan Plandok, they immediately killed him, brought the carcase back to their village and ate it. Thus Agan Plandok once again saved himself.'

Lu'un Ribu rolls on. He tells now how, after treacherously trying to kill a bear with an eye-lotion of chilli and ginger, the Noble Mouse-deer made a mistake and fell into a big hole. When he realizes he has fallen into a deep hole, he thinks to himself: 'Certainly I will die in this hole'. He tries to find a way out; but the hole is very deep. So he stays down in the hole for quite a long time, until he becomes very thin.

'Presently there came another barking-deer (Kijang). He looked down into the hole and saw Agan Plandok.

'He said:

' "How silly you are, Agan Plandok. Why are you so silly as to fall into the hole?"

'Agan Plandok replies:

' "I am not silly. I got into this for a good reason. Perhaps you are silly yourself? You have no regard for your safety. Don't you see that the sky is about to crash down and bury us? Just look at the clouds; they are running away because they are afraid to be buried by the crashing sky."

'The barking-deer got very frightened and asked Agan Plandok how he could save himself. Agan Plandok advised him to jump into the hole too. The barking-deer did as advised.'

One after another, in the same way (as Lu'un Ribu tells it in the borak smells), Agan lured a wild boar, a big rhinoceros and a wild ox down into the hole. Then he addressed them:

' "You are all big animals and you are standing on top of me. I shall be killed by your weight. It is better if I am on the top of you all."

'He climbed on to the wild ox's back and tried to leap out of the hole; but he could not reach the top. Pretending to reach out for some grass up there, Agan Plandok said:

' "I'm trying to get some grass for you all to eat, but I cannot reach."

'He then asked the barking deer to climb on to the back of the wild ox. As soon as the barking-deer sat on the wild ox's back, Agan Plandok climbed on the the barking-deer's and again tried to get out. When the boar saw that, he said to Agan Plandok,

' "Don't you know the sky is crashing down? If you are seen at the top, we will all be buried."

'Agan Plandok said that he was only trying to get grass for them to eat. And when he felt that he could manage to leap out of the hole, he told them to keep quiet and not to move, as the sky was just about to crash down. At the moment he leaped and got clear of the hole. When he was out, he peered down and said to them all:

' "All of you are bloody fools! Where have you ever heard of the sky crashing down? You have been bluffed and tricked by me, for nothing. Now you will all die in this hole. Goodbye to you all in your hole!" '

* * *

One story ending—one of many—shows the cunning mouse-deer out-witted by an even more intelligent and deceitful fish in a race, fish under, he above water. This sort of animal story is regarded as ludicrous, but also refreshing and relevant to human follies. An excellent aperitif. Much lies in the telling. Bony, kindly, hard-living, with a great reputation as a go-between in business and other arguments, Lu'un Ribu specializes also in another sort of funny story, ridiculing ultra-foolish humans. He has made some up for himself. Simpler ones relate to homely affairs, like a fellow sawing off the branch he is sitting on. A slightly more subtle saga tells of the two brothers Palog—*Raya*, meaning large and in this case older brother, *I-it*, meaning small, the younger brother. These stories send even experienced listeners into real convulsions of (dramatized) amusement, thus:

'Palog Raya went into the forest, spending the whole day in search of the petai fruit. Eventually he came to a river. There he saw the reflection of the fruit in the water. "How lucky I am," he thought, "at last I've found them."

'Taking off his clothes and knife, he jumped into the water and dived down, looking for the fruit. Unable to find any, he climbed out of the water by the river-bank and looked again. The fruits were still there in the water. So he dived in again. He went on doing this— so many times that he became exhausted, shivering with cold.

'Coming out of the water, Palog Raya made a fire to warm himself. While warming himself by the fire, he happened to look upwards. There he saw the petai tree, with the fruit on the tree. He began to wonder how he could get at the fruit, high up there. Walking round the tree, he noticed there were ants climbing nimbly down the tree. Those coming down did so head first.

'Now he thought that he should imitate the ants, as he reasoned that human beings must climb trees in that manner as well. He began to climb with his feet up and his head facing the ground. Very slowly he climbed to a height of about ten feet. Then he slipped and fell down. Falling headlong, he knocked against the roots of the tree, hurting his head badly. He repeated the process again and again, until his head was swollen with bruises. At last he gave up trying and returned home.

'On the way home, he came across some of the petai fruits left behind by his younger brother, Palog I-it. He put them into his basket and brought them home. Approaching the house, he shouted for his father to come out and help him carry in the basket.

'He said the basket was so full that he could not carry it into the house by himself. His father was very angry when he saw the few fruits in the basket, and called him a stupid fool. Palog Raya went into the house, crying that he was exhausted from carrying the fruit all the way.

'Palog Raya then took some of the fruits to Palog I-it. When Palog I-it saw how few there were, he scolded him saying:

' "The other day I gave you plenty, you said I had got very little; and now you say plenty, when *you* have very little".'

One of the fiercest and sweetest of the Palog Sibling Saga is called

'Fishing with Mother's Ears'. It goes, in the Borneo evening relish, like this:

'Two days later Palog I-it went out tuba fishing in a river. Pounding the tuba roots, he spread the poisonous sap in the water. Many fish, stunned by the tuba sap, floated on the surface. Palog I-it caught a lot in this manner. Collecting them in his basket, he returned home and shared the fish with Palog Raya.

'Palog Raya thought that if he were to go fishing himself, he could have more. So he asked Palog I-it how he caught them. Palog I-it said that he used tuba roots to stun the fish. But Palog Raya thought that he said he used his mother's ears.

'Palog Raya went off to his mother and asked for her ears, telling her 'he wanted to use them for catching fish. When she refused, Palog Raya caught hold of her and cut them off with a knife. Having got the ears, he ran off to the river. After pounding them up thoroughly, he threw them into the water. The water was coloured by the blood; but no fish floated up as he had expected. Only one fish was killed, when he trod on it. He put this fish into his basket; but it fell out, as there was a hole in the basket. He picked it up and put it back into his basket; again it fell out.

'Again he picked it up and again the fish fell through. He kept on repeating the process so many times that he was eventually tired out. He thought he had caught many fish. And when it was evening he returned home.

'When he came home, Palog Raya went to share his fish with the village folk. But when he put his hand into his basket, he found no fish in it. He swore that all the fish he caught had fallen out of his basket. When he came to Palog I-it's house, Palog I-it scolded him saying:

' "You *are* a fool. When I gave you some fish, you said you could catch more than I could give you. Now where are the fish that you caught with your mother's ears?"

'Palog Raya could not reply.'

No one person can even pretend to remember all these different stories, telling mostly of funny or weird inhuman or unpleasant things —whereas the great sung sagas of Balang Lipang and others recall human achievement of grand behaviour, mainly. Funny stories serve as appetizers, the sagas as more solid fare, on until hang-over stuff, as the borak rice-wine runs low and ears deaden.

* * *

Everyone is gathered—including the dragged ones—presently, around the dragon jar. By the time Lian dips his dark wrist, with rounded gourd, into the wide neck of bubbling muck, everyone has thirst sharpened. The more so, because ordinarily you take no drink of any kind during the day (unless there is borak outdoors). In high heat and fatigue a hand may be dipped in some stream or pool, water flipped quickly into the mouth—as quickly rinsed and spat out again. There is no other drink but borak, unless it be the re-distilled borak dregs made into pretty-well pure spirit and drunk on its rebound, as *arak*. Arak drinking is something else again; seldom practised except at the big death feasts, then only by the hard cases, who are usually upper class— for the upper classes consider it just as important to show their industry and vitality in drinking more than anybody else or accumulating older beads. The classic statement of the borak/arak relationship, which the unselective ear is likely to hear told several times any year, cites the wife of Penghulu Puding. Penghulu Puding's good lady developed a technique at large parties. As the borak began to flow, many bowls and gourds would always be pressed upon her—as wife of a leading aristocrat, daughter of others. Not having a strong head herself, she would comply with the requirements of politeness by superficially taking each offering in her mouth, turning discreetly to one side, and ejecting same into a smaller, separate jar, thoughtfully provided for the purpose. Every now and again, as this became full, she would go out on to the verandah and put the borak through a home-made still of bamboo and tin, easily transported and assembled on the spot. This provided two or three bowlfuls of warm arak. Her good man, Puding, had a weakness for warm arak with which he was thus able to inter-sperse his heavier evenings.

This kind of conduct is not offensive; it observes the niceties. Rather it is the subject of amused and amazed admiration—that she could be so disinterested in her own amusement, so excessively painstaking and selfish (properly but not very pleasantly selfish) on behalf of her hus-band. She served him well and he died prematurely.

Borak comes bubbling into the gourd and is poured around the drinking vessels. Each drink must be offered by the hosts to all assembled in a succession at first broadly based on social position. The aristocrats will have been made to sit centrally, not without a lot of fuss and manifest humility and supposed preference for sitting at a more lowly point in the outer part of the circle. This is the only rule; and it is only roughly observed, abandoned once things get going. Still, the main hospitality is always extended rather more towards better class, good people. This is, in a way, no more than an expression of the fact that over the years they provide—through the great death feasts they make —a high proportion of the total of booze.

Men and women join at handing round. The reluctant drinker— reluctant outside the lips—is force-fed by two or three girls, with much fooling. The older men lap it up quietly. But you do not sit and sip. You take and swallow, hand back the bowl for the next man.

This borak is not very strong. A strong man can drink it all night. He will then be very gay, maybe wild, in the morning; but still on his feet (if he wishes). But women, who have not had long experience, get pretty jolly after a couple of bowls. The general all-round effect is to amplify jollity. On any ordinary Bario evening it will not go further than that. By the time the seniors have had plenty of dishes, the juniors a few, the evening's supply is exhausted; the middle of the night approaches, and people want sleep.

This is the every night function of borak; to ease up on the day, make the place go, send the house deeply asleep. Some nights there is nothing. Some years less than others, according to crops. In the year 1944 there is plenty. Special nights come up three or four times a month. Then there will be dancing and long singing as well. Dancing and singing do not depend on parties, can and do break out anywhere, indoors or out, for any or no particular reason. Kelabits are prodigious singers, once the mood has taken them. Dancing is a very secondary affair, mostly a vehicle for young men and women to show themselves off to people from other villages, on big occasions.

On a casual evening like this, if Agan or Lian happen to be feeling extra exuberant, they are more likely to do some sort of funny dance in the general tempo. A favourite one is to imitate a monkey imitating a man. The acrobatics of this performance (to the accompaniment of gongs) takes the athletic young male from a deceptively quiet opening which itself mimics the formalities of the ordinary head dance. Out of nothing flashes a leap to catch one of the cross-beams or jump sideways crashing into the back wall. This sort of monkey business is so taken for granted that the elders may not even look up from their talking to take notice.

The core of the Bario evening is all the long-house men and women —and any children that are not more amused to be somewhere else (for instance playing at cooking at a fire down the other end)—sitting around, gradually getting slightly noisier, sillier and more deafened, while they talk a bit about tomorrow, decide ahead any special jobs that need doing; what co-operation is required; analyse latest barter transactions and others in view with other villages; drink until the women are put on to hand squeeze the last drops from the slush left down in the jars; then peel off one by one—without any apology—to bed-mat and sleep.

About as long as it takes to get tiddley, the nearly ten thousand square feet of Bario, focus of hundreds of square miles of Borneo, is reduced to a nucleus in the tight night circle, shoulder to shoulder, arms readily interlocked over shoulders—regardless of sex—around dragons now shining wet below the shoulders of the ageing jars. Flickering fires, gathered now against the upland cold at night, the bright dancing flame of the resin torches, cast their multiple shadows on all the objects of Kelabit living—hung from the roof, balanced on the ceiling, slung over rafters, perched upon fireplaces, stacked against the walls, and littered (at this untidy hour) across the floor. From here, westward two slogging days' climb, ford and slither to Kubaan beyond the Tamabos; from here east an easy but hottish half-day over the plain to Pa Trap; northward for ten days if you can make your way at all between Murud and the great twin white pinnacles of Batu Lawi, Kelabit parent mountain of male and female peaks; south down into the impassable gorges of the upper Baram; over all this land, this night, no human being is.

Within the wild tangle of jungle and mountain, cleaving night wind and erratic downpour, all humanity sits secure on five mats, fifteen floor boards, three score of backsides, inside Bario. The things they are talking about are simple enough, because they nearly always know what they are talking about. The problems of life present themselves and have to be coped with in an enormous range of specializations within one common pattern. Speculation outside this pattern offers lesser enchantments. Self-expression, on the contrary, becomes a compulsion, inside the tiny circle of this equatorial interior. There is no danger of confusing Lawai with Tayun, Agan with Lian, Anyi with either pheasant or cobra. And the more we know of them, the less we can be confused. In the end, in death they will be able to express themselves differently—unless, by then, something has happened to confound these standards and overturn their monuments in stone.

*   *   *

After midnight, before yesterday is quite over, everyone is more or less asleep; the less is small, yet persistent all the same. Things that must be done in the daylight are necessarily apportioned with a moderate and sometimes rigid routine. But light of its own decides quite little.

The rhythm of light and dark is, by contrast, simplicity itself. The face of light and pace of darkness are almost the same, all the year round. This, along with big feet firmly fixed on the high ground, gives a stability and consistency which underlies the Kelabit way, even at its most winding, spiralled, or explosively erratic.

So, if Lawai's wife has a cough and cannot sleep well, she will trim and light up a gum candle to finish off the mat she was making. If Tayun feels somehow frustrated, he picks up the long wooden mandolin he made for himself earlier in the year, sits there tinkling the refrain of a sentimental song. Should he feel that way, on his own he may sing its words, more properly sung by three or four women; sometimes in fun, sometimes sadly sounding out of the sentimental temper of high youth.

When Tayun has finished singing he may be answered through the darkness, by a gentle sigh. But that would be, undoubtedly, a little forward. However, that rather depends on how used the girl is to sleeping—or going through the actions preliminary to sleeping—with him. If not used at all, yet impressed by the him behind the singing, she may send a girl friend to say something to him. (Going between is part of the complication which makes Bario life go up its everlasting spiral, always.)

More likely, though, anyone strumming or singing solitarily in this way will not be expecting any particular or immediate satisfaction; will be getting satisfaction out of what he is doing. There is not much left of courtship, and unlikely to be anyone left to court, in your own long-house, where boys and girls have grown up together in one jungle of co-education. The local boy and girl who have won each other's binding fancy will need nothing more, except the final sanction of pregnancy, to make marriage fairly definitive. It is preferable to court people from other long-houses, despite the complications as to who will live where, which invariably follow. For the rest, there is always the merry widow.

The merry widow is part and parcel of any well-organized long-house. (There is one at Bario, though—as the years will pass and turn her into something else again—it is nicer not to name her now.) She is the one who has a different idea, or for whom things did not work out quite straight. Her man jilted her; or went to another long-house on one of these trading expeditions which somehow spread over the years. More likely, she just could not settle on one fellow. And there is the widow with the least cause for merriment; she became pregnant and could not pin it on any one. For the occupational risk of upland mild promiscuity is that you are not only careless and generous, but also weak; weak in good family backing—too weak to point at a man and insist that *he* is about to be a father.

Even so, there must be something unusual about the girl's character or skill, if none will have her when she is in the family way. Generally, it is a twist of character, fundamental dissatisfaction with males; or dislike for living with one male in a society which makes little allowances for post-marital infidelity. Yet the pressures on some sort of intercourse, simply as an accepted idea of night-life, are such that whatever her feelings, only an extraordinary woman would stand out for long against the marginal, rather casual, demands of still unsettled young men. Thus the temporarily or permanently unattached older woman plays quite a role in the sexual education of boys maybe ten or fifteen years younger. No one takes any notice of that; except that she must calculate just how far she dare go, should she think seriously of 'settling down' permanently with any one ever again. In the end, however, the merry widow generally does get settled. For there is also the sad widower, the elderly man whose wife died leaving him with children; or her equivalent nervous opposite, who does not really like women, but has got to get some sort of fireplace and ricefarm permanent organization before he grows too old and cold. Such marriages of convenience, amongst those approaching middle age, are acceptable and only subject to a certain amount of behind-the-back humour in the heavier moments of Kelabit comedy-by-buttock.

As well as the graduate merry widow there is the up-and-coming eager spinster, of course. The younger woman, not yet in the family way, but emotionally less stable or undecided, unwilling to settle for any one for long. Perhaps for no longer than an hour. One local playgirl, when she feels in the mood, will gratify—one supposes—up to three men in an evening. It is not spoken of as wrong; but regarded as odd and unlikely to be in her own best interests in the long run. No really good or nice man wants to marry a girl like that. This one eventually got away with a rather indifferent permanent liaison. She says, though, in her gayer moments, that he is enough of a husband, and she had a pretty worthwhile time before him!

Settling down sexually is distinctly a desired end. On the other hand, it is considered weak, foolish, to get spliced too soon; to tie up with one girl before you have sampled many. This is mainly a masculine attitude. Girls have to be more careful. Nothing worse can happen to a girl than to be left with a fatherless baby, rare though this is.

Sex never rears its ugly head in the uplands. There is little either ugly or beautiful about it. It is there. The idea of anything other than straightforward intercourse between male and female is remote. The accentuation of esoteric tastes, all the way from masturbation to bestialism, cannot be understood by Kelabits when they hear about them from outsiders. The nervous pressures on sex are unusually slight. Pressures become largely social, physical, and connected with personality, demonstration and desire for the future as well as the present. For a young man, sexual successes with people of the same or better status—in other, and preferably far-away, communities—are boasted about in the same style as success in hunting pig or moving fast over mountains. On this scale of thought, a single brief sleeping-mat session with the daughter of the headman at Pa Bawang, three days' walk over the border, is worth one hundred of all night with the girl six doors down in the long-house, who grew up a few years behind you, but not quite in your own gang. Girls are appreciably less open in displaying their sexual emotions or comparing their successes. With them, it is more a matter of detailed and whispered discussion among special friends, usually not direct and close kin. In this, there is a good deal of comparing of notes, which results in sharing of boys recommended from mouth to ear for their virtues.

The principle virtue involved is virility. Although there is a good deal of finesse in sexual *approach*, through music, dancing, singing, dress, plucking eyelashes and delicate messages via intermediaries, this sexual relationship is basically simple. Once contact is close, the direct object of the man is to relieve himself of his desire. To a notable degree the girls are adjusted to taking their own complete satisfaction quickly, also. Exceptions to this are frequent, all the same. One notable aristocrat of the area is famed for his insatiability. And the rapid spread of the *palang*, a cross-piece driven through the male penis, has shown that behind the easy acceptance of many upland women there is a readiness to react in a more elaborate and erotic manner.

A man can easily and naturally have intercourse every night over long periods. He can as easily go without for long periods—as men and women often do, for instance when making journeys in parties with one sex, hunting, trading or whatever it may be. Often mixed parties of unmarried boys and girls will make long journeys together without any sign of fully sexual desire, let alone requirement. This is largely because sex is regarded primarily as something to do in the long-house and in the dark. It is one of the satisfactions of a settled situation. Taken out of context, into an isolated excitement of its own, there is something inoperative and almost unsatisfactory about it. Given the proper conditions, it is the ordinary thing, between the right people. The right people being those unmarried, of similar class; or those who are married to each other. Plus, at very big feasts and special occasions, certain permissible breakdowns—permissible anyway insofar as the consequences are not likely to be more than uproar, unpleasantness and possibly (for the married) a nominal fine.

The conditions of upland long-house life limit the scope for sexual frolic and complicated development. The Kelabits, like most other human beings, wish to conduct two operations in such privacy as life can permit. They copulate and defecate as inconspicuously as possible. The latter is achieved, principally before dawn from the edges of and through gaps in the floor at the back of the long-house. The former, conducted on sleeping mats for the married by the side of the fire-places; for the unmarried in the overhead galleries where the girls sleep, and less often out on the verandah where the bachelors are supposed to be sleeping. Privacy is simply obtained by rolling your two-selves entirely up inside the sleeping mat, a tubular cocoon. After that, there is not a lot of movement you can make if you wish to remain reasonably inconspicuous.

The male dress makes it easy to slip the loin-cloth to one side; she lifts her little skirt. There is a very strong feeling for the actual intimacy of bodily contact, as well as the sexual act. Embracing is comforting here. There is a tone of warm and half-sentimental affection and kindliness in so much of Kelabit sex (and friendship) which lacks, to a striking degree, the elements of tension and even cruelty so widespread among other peoples, including some of their immediate neighbours. It helps, too, that it is cold at night in the highlands! One body does not get too hot through prolonged intimacy with another.

Similarly, moderate sexuality is related to hospitality. The long-house must entertain visitors with food and drink. If they are young, acceptable and not from too far away, it will certainly be made easy for the first nighter to obtain some new sexual experience. It all assists in the search for spouses from different houses.

There is no question, here, of anyone being detailed to entertain a guest, even the important aristocratic visitor. But no sort of objection could be raised by any family with free children to such liaison with sufficiently good visitors—provided that these do not come from too far away.

Those from too far away may always find, by arrangement, with go-between, that the merry widow or eager spinster are available for this purpose, perhaps? Not that there would be any question of payment. Anything approaching prostitution is not to be thought of. But it would be quite in order—if not expected—to make some small present of beads or cloth, in this case, before leaving.

Not too far away: this is an important point. The definition of 'too farness' is that the visitor could call into account (if female) or be called into account (if male) in the event of a pregnancy. This is a highly theoretical exposition, in any circumstances. But the idea is a strong one and a protective one to the group. It is undesirable that people from more than the general area should have intercourse with your people. Along with this, the uplands are well aware that there are certain unpleasant illnesses in the lowlands arising from sexual intercourse; that these illnesses have, so far, escaped Bario and the surrounding long-houses, an oasis in the venereal populations of Asia.

It by no means always works out like this. Every now and then someone from far away becomes intimately involved. Few things lead to more trouble than such an accident of emotion. Long ago, such a thing could hardly have occurred, since war, head-hunting and the dangers of travel made the opportunities exceedingly few. Now, pushing through the barriers from the south have come men with the *palang*, to introduce a new idea. The *palang* is an idea bound to take on particularly quickly, once it has acquired, so to speak, firm footing. For there can be no doubt that plenty of women like it a lot. If they did not, it could barely survive one oestrous cycle. As a matter of fact, the first impact of a penis pierced with a *palang* in the uplands was tragedy; it would certainly have stopped anything of the kind ever again, had counterbalancing impulses not been so strong.

Not many years ago, some Kenyahs came trading for salt, from the south. One of them had an affair with a girl at Pa Main, a day away from Bario. She died soon after he had left, the following morning. It is not uncommon for Kelabit girls to go through the motions of dying in distress when a temporary lover leaves. Some rather emotional girls enjoy this sort of display. And these are no people to frown on any exaggerated display of feeling, provided it is not too deep and will not grow more violent otherwise. On enquiry, it was found, though, that this girl had really died; from the effect of the man's *palang*. This was how the matter first came to general attention in the uplands.

Latterly, a number of Kelabit men have been operated upon. Their subsequent, extensive and definitely successful pre-marital operations among the young women have caused no ill after-effects. The use of mechanical devices for this purpose must clearly be approached with some care, as they are now aware. The basic operation simply consists of driving a hole through the distal end of the penis; sometimes, for the determined, two holes at right angles. In this hole a small tube of bone, bamboo or other material can be kept, so that the hole does not grow over and close. It is of no inconvenience, once the initial pain of the operation—always done by experts in the lowlands—has been overcome.

When the device is put into use, the owner adds whatever he prefers to elaborate and accentuate its intention. A lively range of objects can be so employed—from pig's bristles and bamboo shavings to pieces of metal, seeds, beads and broken glass. The effect, of course, is to enlarge the diameter of the male organ inside the female. And so to produce accentuated points of mobile friction, quite evidently giving a peculiar sort of sexual satisfaction to the female recipient.

This is a new—and in 1944 rapidly spreading—idea. It implies, as so many new ideas here do, that often the pattern everyone has grown to regard as essential, and almost immutable, is in truth readily changeable. Change can come very swiftly, even almost unseen, in the dark.

It is necessary to add and emphasize that here there is no idea of contraception or abortion. If there were, some of the major frictions of late adolescence and near-adultery would be mightily lessened. That is not to say that there is any sacred regard for the embryo as such. Far from it. Until the time when the child is fully recognized and named, his or her life may hang on a post-umbilical thread. If there are strong other obligations—for instance at the very height of the rice harvest—his life can legitimately be put out. A woman who is having trouble with her husband, probably over the sharing of work or inheritance arrangements, and only rarely over post-marital infidelity, may use the threat of suicide against her parents obstructing her marriage. Often, it is the men who put the premium on babies. But then, they have not to have to put up with all the exasperations centred round being-about-to-have-babies, which have such a lot to do with girls growing up in the uplands.

Such, in all too brief, is that section in the wide front of the long-house night; the one which, presumably, in the end is the most essential, inevitable, as well as (ideally) the least observable in this so open society of night and day. But behind the façade of normalcy lies always the intense individuality of these mountain folk, and at times the urge to exaggerate and dramatize self out of the all-pervading propinquities of the public long-house. One expression of this is love: the attachment between boy and girl—usually strongest with the girl—which refuses to give way to the everynight facilities and will, if necessary, take on the whole society. We will encounter this emotional, or at least expressive, attitude more vigorously, presently.

*   *   *

Behind the individual noises of night—girlish, adulterous, infantile, canine, ungulate, ukelele and all—lie the regulars: Lawai's house-filling snore, a bitch scratching, the wind sighing the roof thatch, the distant chuckle of the stream pouring out of mountain onto plain, the occasional chomp of a sow, frequent half-awake stirring of grown-ups pushing with their feet on logs—to keep fires alive, as half darkness slowly grows colder before the sun's return. Long before the sun though, other sounds tell the restless or concerned how the night is passing, how long away the day. For although time is not measured and is seldom as much as a threat, it is reassuring to know where you are, casually, along the arc of its recognized movement; especially if you have a heavy day's work ahead and a slight hangover right now in bed. This passage of time is registered in accepted if evasive divisions of irregular length. There is the time when the owls stop sounding. Then there is the time when if it is quiet enough inside the house—if rain is not lashing the thatch—you can hear the whole jungle grow almost silent, as the vast part of its population which moves and feeds by night has had enough: civet cat, badger, bats of many kinds, mongoose, tiger cat, lemur, leaping tarsier, incredibly slow loris, tree frogs and flying frogs, geckos, giant toads, stag and rhinoceros beetles, crickets, cockchafers, moths, the hill otters (bigger than dogs) which roam far up the mountain sides, frogmouth, nightjar; on the plain redshank and snipe. Then comes the time when the cocks in the rafters overhead and on the cross-beams under-mat begin to wake up. Bario has its own setting of the sequences in which life growingly proclaims the growth of light still invisible to human bodies lined along the centre wall, stored between the fireplaces and snuggling on sleeping platforms, singly or entwined.

Presently from the mountainside and from the fruit trees around the long-house, a succession of wild birds announce fuller light, still barely to be detected from inside Bario. First comes the Yellow-Crowned Bulbul, producing—from a diet of tiny snails taken along the stream beds—glorious long liquid runs of high music. Next the milder stuff of Magpie-Robin, which lives close to man. By the time the vivid barbets (green, scarlet, blue, saffron) have started up their tok and chop mono-tonies—to last all day—it is light enough for a man to be getting on his feet. Well before that, back in the middle stages of cockerel waken-ing, good wife will have blown up the fire—unless she is feeling really bad. No one can go out without eating; cooking is part of the border-line dark. There is a definite feeling about getting busy *early*, if there is work to be done; even if it means going to sleep again later. The children can do as they like, though. They easily sleep far into the morning, just as they easily play being adult long into night.

Most men will have eaten and be out of the house before the sun has come out over the eastern ranges. From then on, the day is divided into a multiplicity of positions: regardless of mist, overcast cloud or storm, the sun is felt to be where it is in the sky. To make an appoint-ment, point up and fix to meet again when it is exactly 'there'.

* * *

Left behind with the very old, ill or ultra-idle are the children, often in care of the babies too. Bario mothers feel much the same as most others about their children, though they only show it less (especially anger). There is a great deal of variety, too. The conditions of life make it easy and convenient for children to bring themselves up, to an extent im-possible in many surroundings. The roomless long-house is an all-weather, all-outlet playground for gangs of all ages. The open grassland around the house is relatively safe of snakes, scorpions, centipedes, hornets and anything else worse than the painted flies which follow the fat cattle but love a fleshy human calf. Mosquitoes and sandflies are as much part of life as rain, noise, incurious eyes, rice, rice, rice, and rain again.

The great part of children's play is a direct imitation of things they will have to do from necessity later on. Far and away the favourite game for small girls is to get thick sticks and pound mud pies, as if they were their mothers preparing the rice grain into cookability.

This in no sense means that mothers do not love and fathers do not like their children. There is nothing worse than childlessness, not merely because you may need help when you grow old and *must* need help when you are dead. The people who are, anyway (in the first years of their ability), quite keen on sex, have no doubt about its eventual outcome and feel this, fairly vaguely, also as purpose. As they do not believe that a single act can cause a single baby, nine times out of ten 'marriage', however much consummated on the mat, is not really concluded until the womb is distended. If that does not occur, divorce is acceptable, so long as both sides agree. The Kelabits are conscious of the advantage they have here as compared with the other peoples living around them, whose main form of economic exchange, inheritance, and transfer of value objects is centred in the exchange of children between families on a system widely called *brian*. The Kelabits have no *brian*, instead achieve a similar purpose by the emphasis on the death rites and memorials of *irau*. This may lead to a good deal more confusion in the marriage processes; but what does that matter, when confusion, argument and inconclusion are favourite occupations of the high mind?

Adoption often fills the void, before divorce or despair. A family with several children will give one to close relatives who are childless. This child then becomes wholly a member of the new family. His true parents will preserve some special attachment, every now and then be casually mentioned as such in idle talk. But the adopted child has no further obligations to true parents, nor they to it.

Suckling babies most conspicuously expresses the difference between mothers. It would be unthinkable not to suckle your baby. It is rare not to have milk, and in that case preferable to give pulped rice milk and other concoctions which seldom leave the baby alive. But *some* women go on suckling their children for years, sometimes keeping a little milk, sometimes going on long after that is exhausted. She may do that because she likes the feel of it; or because the child insists and she does not want to upset him. Him it usually is. Boys are persistent favourites of the breast. No one notices if a boy of seven or eight (but his years will not have been counted) comes running up to his mother as she sits round the evening borak jar in a crowd: in one hand he holds a corn-cob or sugar-cane he is gnawing, in the other he takes her breast for the suck; maybe he then takes a puff at pa's small cigar. By about this time, though, the situation is beginning to be regarded as faintly ridiculous and mammy may register a mild complaint as the milk of her maternal patience runs gradually out. An enterprising youngster need not abandon hope even at this stage, however. A good-natured grandmother may be willing to provide substitute. She probably has more time to spare, anyway. At the worst, cry—something should oblige. Only when a child starts slamming his arms or legs on the floor, screaming, can we know he is being forced to face up to the larger world, where the liquid comes out of the ground instead of the bust.

*　　*　　*

For the grown-ups, ordinarily, the days out-of-doors fall into two main varieties. There are the days of big jobs, like doing the rice-huts; and days of lots of little jobs. The big ones centre around phases in the cycle of rice cultivation or the periodic (annual or less) trade journeys to distant places. Hunting may belong to this group, as well. When rhino were still numerous, a couple of months' hunt was quite usual— and during that time the party would be in entirely uninhabited country, living on wild sago and game, fungus, pork, venison, insects and grubs, bitter fruits and leaves.

Big hunting trips, long trading journeys and all the odd jobs of the year—house repairs, plank cutting, tobacco and pig food growing, visiting relatives, checking irrigation ditches, collecting and making bark clothes, forging metal tools, weaving baskets and fish traps, river poisoning for fish in bulk, salt jobbing, preparing feasts and throwing them, making trouble on a big scale—these things and many, many more, all have to fit into (and mostly *after*) the rice part of the year.

Rice does not demand attention in every month. But it requires exclusive attention during two or three, extensive during five, and some during more. Although Bario has practically never been short of rice, normally has several years' surplus in hand, it is the fundamental focus to effort in every year: harvesting for the family at least enough rice for its minimal need in that year, regardless of reserves. To fail to do this is to fail to be a person of worth (either 'good' or 'bad') in the highland community. The odd person does so fail, usually by wandering off somewhere else and not returning because of illness, indolence or adultery. A man may get away with this without losing status, once and conceivably twice in a while; not a lot more.

In the rather erratic equatorial climate of the upland basin, it is not in the least easy to be sure—at any one moment taken on its own—where one is in the year. The sun varies just enough to be detectable in different positions as it falls behind the Tamabos in different months. The length of shadow can be seen to change, also, variously with its fall overhead. The river Kayans calculate by shadow; the Muruts over in the head of the Trusan have one huge tree out in the open, which they line up with a peak towards Murud: when the sun sets along that line it is planting time—until the tree collapses.

But on the Plain of Bah the mountains build so much cloud that the sun may be unseen except as a general brightness, day after day after day. This similarly confounds the regular study of stars, which some Kenyahs favour for the checking of seasons. Bario has devised a separate system, based on the fact that an extraordinary wealth of migratory birds use this hole in high jungle as a blissful resting place on journeys further south from places almost unimaginably north. These birds, of which there are many, come in a fairly regular succession. A few have been selected as the best indicators. Around these few the Kelabit calendar is fixed.

This calendar need not be adjusted to any outside standard, any more than Kelabit character. These birds are within this world: what they do elsewhere or how they tie up with the coast is not any Kelabit's affair —which is not to say that they are not anxious about such things, believing (for instance) that some of the most numerous migrants spend the rest of the year in non-existent caves on the fabled great peak of Kinabalu, far north.

As these birds come each year on a solar rhythm and as the Kelabit is concerned with their relation to the overall 'climate' as it affects rice locally, this calendar has proved consistent and satisfactory over centuries. The object of the upland operation is to know where the year is in time-relation to the necessity for having the rice planted and germinated. The calendar does not entirely tell Pun Maran, who has the semi-final decision in these matters, when to declare the year on: that matter to be settled by mental calculation, general feeling, and his personal spiritual contacts into the invisible.

Each bird acts as check; and (as the month of each passes) as accelerator, with cumulative urgency. Within the month of each the phases of moon are minor indicators. This is so in every month, anyway. By naming each phase of the moon, it is easy to make arrangements for trade meetings or feasts ahead—though Kelabits will never trust this alone, invariably exchange knotted strings, with one knot to be undone for each night before the event due. For forgetfulness plays a fair part in upland affairs. It is a favourite source for funny stories. There are famously absent-minded characters—like Tama Labang of Pa Mada who on several occasions has arrived at Bario (and elsewhere) bringing something or other to trade, repay or present to his relatives there— only to find that, although he started out with the stuff in his carrying basket all right (under watchful family eyes), at one of the half-dozen resting points along the way he put the lot down, forgot to pick it up again (weight seventy pounds?) when he moved on after one slow cigarette.

Allowing for all the customary complications, then, birds play a key part in the year's thinking. These birds and their months are:

1. Yellow Wagtail — *Sensulit mad'ting*
2. Yellow Wagtail — *Sensulit pererang*
3. Brown Shrike — *Neropa'*
4. Japanese Sparrow-Hawk— *Kornio piting*
5. Pallid Thrush — *Padawan*

The first Yellow Wagtails seen start the year moving, in the month of their arriving (*mad'ting*); by the time they are settled in for the season (*pererang*) seed should, ideally, be in. With each passing month after that, delay increases the uncertainty of an excellent harvest, pest-free.

The bird months are calculated as one full lunar cycle after each arrival event. When Thrush month is over, there is no further calendar, except insofar as the operations of rice cultivation have, each year, their variable-in-time but unvarying-in-sequence events. But once the rice has *been* harvested, a further check is kept on the Yellow Wagtails, *sensulit*. When the last of these has *left*, two complete moon cycles are noted; on the third, it is time to *begin* to prepare the rice fields—cutting, clearing scrub, ditching and so on—to await, presently, the return of the next crop of Wagtails (none ever stay all year) and the new calendar's first point of origin.

Each calendar bird makes itself conspicuous, while here. Each is different in carriage and call from any of the resident birds of the highlands. All except the Pallid Thrush from Siberia come out into the open, to be seen soon on arrival. The thrush instead arrives in swarms of clattering noise in the scrub around the rice fields; and the only resident, related thrushes of the uplands are rare, living in deep jungle higher up. Other, more conspicuous birds do not count, either because they arrive too late to be of indicative use or because they are too irregular to be reliable. Thus the flickering, silver-white Arctic Phalaropes which descend in shoals on the surface of the rice fields by night, are so tame that before they have moved on the Bario boys have blow-piped small bellyfuls of their tiny tenderness. The three kinds of harrier which quarter the plain and help a lot with keeping down rats, come very unevenly. Ducks and terns do not come at all in some years. But when the White-winged Black Tern does turn up, this small, restless bird is admired for its mastery of the violent wind gusts and the way that it never needs to settle, very seldom does. It is called 'Ut Bario', 'The wind bird that never settles'. (The Phalarope is called 'Baby Boat'.)

There are also the munias, finch-like birds. Two sorts, the chestnut and the dusky, live and nest in the uplands. Two other kinds, the coloured and the white-bellied, arrive from the nowhere caves on half-imagined Kinabalu, in hordes descend upon the rice grain. Despite all the devices of man, woman and child, in big munia years these birds are so many, so hungry, that nothing will keep them from devastating the crops. That is the business of the bird calendar: the munias should not arrive in force until most of the grain is already garnered; that is, *if* the seed has been sown in time. Time being at best 'the month of the wagtail's arriving'—and down decreasingly good to 'the month of the thrush'. Planting as late as the month of the thrush is running things too fine, asking for munia trouble. To sow later than that is asking for it.

In the Borneo setting, it is commonplace for wide areas to be in famine and rice crops very uncertain. The birds which so conspicuously fly into Bario from as far away as Manchuria, Alaska, Formosa and

Siberia, help—or have been made to help—Bario to be almost immune from these uncertainties.

*　　*　　*

Rice is the one *essential* in Bario life which cannot come, go or grow of itself naturally. Nothing else is necessary to any meal; and nearly all the uneaten things either grow naturally—like pot-clay, rushes for matting, many fruits, resin for lighting, housing materials; or they can be obtained by fairly simple effort and (most important) at a time to be chosen by the humans concerned—as with salt, *tuba* root for poisoning fish, tobacco, leaf for wrapping rice, bamboo shoots and cassava.

The Kelabits and adjacent Muruts have carried rice cultivation to a finer craft than any other of the interior peoples. Bario has carried to it its finest perfection among the Kelabits. In this they have been assisted by the terrain, though the soil itself is by no means widely superior to that in other places. But over and above the advantages of latitude, level ground and a comparatively steady climate, the people themselves have brought to bear on the subject the keenest edges of a multiple experience incorporated in tradition, plus an experimentalism derived from individual intelligence. It is from this base, nicely supported by the natural occurrence of salt springs at the foot of the spinal range from Mount Murud south to Batu Patong (ten minutes flight for a serpent-eagle)—that the Kelabits derive both especial wealth and stability.

Bario, as the furthest west from the spinal range of the villages in the great Murud bowl, is at a disadvantage with salt: there is none in its own immediate terrain. Each long-house has a more or less accepted territory. This by no means gives exclusive ownership, only means that other long-houses should not come and cultivate there without permission. Hunting is free throughout the jungle, fishing on any water. Anybody can go and work salt—though it is polite to inform the relevant long-house and perhaps make some token gift. Bario people do go off salt-making, as many as ten at a time. But it is one of the least priority occupations. They have concentrated on rice above all else. In the occasional very bad year, Bario always has reserves in the bark bins and rat-proofed huts; these can exchange for salt and other things sufficient unto years ahead. (The price of as much rice as a man can carry is 100 small packages of salt.)

It is considered a humiliation not to have enough rice to eat three or more times a day, give generously to all comers, make all the borak anyone wants, still have a surplus into next season. To have to eat cassava tuber (*ubi kayu, manioc*) or pith from the sago palms which grow elegant and wild on every hillside, is definitely not good. This is far from the case with many Borneo peoples. Some, such as the Tagals to the north-east, cultivate cassava for preference, at times. Some Bisayas of choice and nomadic Punans of necessity, rely largely on sago. There is nothing that compels rice upon Borneo; and least of all on Bario, the highest community in Borneo, with a climate which can grow anything anyone has yet introduced. Nevertheless, for Bario rice approaches obsession.

*   *   *

The general system and cycle of rice cultivation is in part common to the whole of South-east Asia. Bario methods vary or differ at several points to such an extent that this small adult population can always command high fees over the interior, to advise Murut, Kenyah, Kayan, and other farmers—especially on the subject of irrigation, the very idea of which only came among the other peoples when the Brookes had brought relative peace, in the days when Lawai Bisarai was still a bachelor and Pun Maran not yet a grandfather.

It is dangerous, of course, to isolate single elements out of a complicated and comparatively ancient agriculture. Bario's bird calendar, for instance, is unique; and at the same time a hinge to the whole affair. With this ornithological precision in progress, the main procedures are much the same as anywhere else.

Initial procedure is to clear the ground. Even on the Plain of Bah, between the harvest and the time for beginning the cycle afresh, four to six months—depending on the weather and the weight of the harvest itself—small but thick scrub, sedge, fern, pink-flowered tea bushes, have already formed a dense tangle, which takes plenty of cleaning. This is an entirely different matter, though, from the work that faces the Kenyah or Kayan, every year felling a new patch of jungle, maybe virgin rain forest but increasingly secondary jungle which has been allowed to grow back after earlier use, often eight to twenty years ago.

Bario is one of the very few places in Borneo where land has been brought under permanent cultivation, to produce crops from the same ground year after year; all the indications are for century after century, previously for a higher population than now. As there is more than enough land for everyone, and as Kelabits are deeply restless people, it is unusual to cultivate exactly the same piece for many years in succession. It is better to leave good plots occasionally fallow. Good land relates closely to maintained irrigation ditches. These tend to run conveniently close to the long-house. Farther out on the plain, within living memory, a considerable tract has gone out of use and has now become rather bitter, feeble soil which would require extensive re-draining and care to bring it back into productivity. At present there is no point in bothering with that. Nobody is landless; nobody can be. A possible newcomer from far away will be incorporated into a family, probably will marry in. (A whole family would not come into a long-house unless they had special reasons and close relatives, who would share land use with them.)

Land ownership is not rigid. It derives from the tradition of the land which a family first occupied under rice, oblivions go. But if anyone is short of a plot to plant this year, he has a perfect right to borrow someone else's land not in use. No payment need be made on that count, unless he continues to occupy for more than a year or two, when a small rent is in order.

The land as a whole belongs to the long-house, every use of it is discussed over the evening's borak in advance. It would be impossible if it were otherwise; particularly so when the community depends for success on an elaborate system of irrigation derived from tiny streams off the Tamabos.

Irrigation is the source of Bario's prosperity. Irrigation can also be a source of maximum irritation in exceptional years of rice-growth drought. The Tamabos always provide *just* enough water. The trouble begins when the water falls perilously close to that line; when the water held at little finger's depth in the calculated labyrinth of the field comes down to little fingernail. This is a time of maximum tension, where the ties of co-operation and friendship creak under the strain of rice obsession.

Last season was one of the exceptionally dry ones. Then occurred one of these uproars. Unfortunately, there was already bad feeling between two families living on either side of the same main water ditch, tapped off the brook just below the village knoll. Otherwise it might not have gone so far. So far indeed, that Kampong Rajah ('Ruler of Villages'), brother of Chief Anyi from Pa Bengar, who had married a Bario girl and undertaken to live there (after long arguments), eventually left, returning to Pa Bengar with her and two children—of course he had been longing for an excuse to go back to his own home community all the time; and unfortunately for Bario this was it. True enough, Anyi was soon marrying back into Bario, living with Lawai's daughter to compensate. It was all very exciting and upsetting, in between other things.

These irrigation disputes are among the great affairs of upland life. Kelabits have disputes about 'everything under the Summit of Murud'. They even eagerly argue which of the death-feast clearings up at eight thousand feet there is actually the highest up: a fruitful subject, since the top is almost flat and looks different from almost any angle of approach. Quite simple exchange transactions can and do become involved in disagreement in detail; which may continue, agreeably enough, for years. But nothing else strikes so near the ear-lobe of this life, as irrigation.

In arguments of this kind, the long-house grows tormented with loyalties of kinship, friendship, and a deeper principle of what is false. In matters of irrigation the principle involved is so crucial to the community that kinship and friendship go to the bin, if the evidence is clear. But for evidence to be clear in this upland atmosphere is as rare as a pregnant rhinoceros. A man must hunt terribly close and long for either. Disagreement—when it breaks out strongly in a small community closely interwoven with ties of family, history, continuity and every-day work—becomes as clouded as the mountains that same evening; and (after the night's rain) as cold, misty and obscure as highland dawn.

In any case, there is no eventual 'solution' to this sort of disagreement. In the very unlikely circumstance that 'right' and 'wrong' are clear, it still remains for one deemed to be wrong, to be abandoned by the *whole* community, turning on him; and secondly, for *him* to *admit* the wrong. This is the hardest thing.

The case for Kampong Rajah was generally felt to be against him. Scant evidence and strong suspicion pointed most tongues at his capable hands. Quite likely as not this was not so. True or false, Kampong Rajah utterly rejected any suggestion of tampering with the water supply in his favour. As a first phase in his counter-attack against such implications, he moved his whole family out on to the long-house verandah, properly reserved for resident bachelors, visitors and travellers without intimate enough friends to draw them on to the other side of the inner wall for sleep. His family thus adequately demonstrated their dissociation in mood from the rest of Bario. They cooked on one of the small verandah fires which have no overhead frames or elaborate structures, are intended casually to keep warm a bachelor's feet or Lawai's personal piece of fat pork. The message could not then be missed by any visitor. Bario's scandal was pork and warmed feet for gossip all over the plain.

Presently, Kampong Rajah went back inside, made it up with an exchange of small pigs and small gifts between the two families. But this proud, cunning and very thoughtful man could not quite forgive— except with his body. Soon after, he went back to Pa Bengar. In doing so he had his several days of triumph over Bario. To any long-house it is an awful disturbance that someone, let alone some family, should leave them without necessity. For several days there was no work done. Everyone pleading, the men arguing, the women crying; soothing borak pouring upon the family from all sides, and in the last day an all-out borak assault in an almost successful attempt to stupefy Kampong Rajah (who likes his grog better than most) into a last-stand re-acceptance.

It could have been worse than that. Travel half a day south along the foot of the Tamabos and you come into another small valley, with plenty of signs of a past population once practising the Bario style of irrigation. Tradition has it clearly that this settlement, where the water supply is even smaller, split into two many years ago on one tremendous irrigation argument between two leading men of the long-house. No doubt this argument was little more than the peak of a long-growing division. It had the final effect of causing one-half of the people to abandon the valley and move westward over the Tamabos into Kubaan. The results were disastrous. Those who were left behind were too few effectively to carry on the complex of this cultivation. Those who moved into the Kubaan did not thrive at a lower altitude, in climate and with water conditions quite unfamiliar. Only one Kelabit remains who can trace descent from that stock. This cannot be for lack of trying to trace—a popular evening pastime throughout the interior.

What makes the irrigation so tricky, so nervy? First, it must be intelligently and cautiously used, so that if the water in the fields is not supplemented by enough direct rainfall, the brook water is kept—and so far as possible kept gently moving—from the time the rice germinates until it is ready to crop. Second, the extent of the fields in relation to the small water supply, involves a complicated system of drains and dams, which can only be made, altered as required, kept clear and day-to-day operated properly by the combined efforts of all able-bodied.

Once Bario has decided its planting programme for the season and cleared the land required, then if things have been properly worked out and everyone works together all the general irrigation preparations can be made in a few days. Major repair or alteration works are seldom necessary more than once in several years. Some of the main lines of water flow were arranged and have remained unchanged far beyond memory. But where there is no voting or counting of heads, and leadership is vested in the aristocracy only by virtue of a very general tradition plus their talking commonsense, there is always probability of individual disagreement; it is almost automatic for someone to disagree. Everybody owns land. A rich man may have one or two of the better pieces. But there is no question of rice privilege, other than that derived from personal and family effort, here and now.

In the end, what decides—or at least delimits—will be the difficulty of one person farming fruitfully outside the majority wish. The natural tendency is to farm one part of the plain at a time. That has two special advantages. The whole available water supply can be worked in one direction. And the biggest subsequent headache—repelling the upland hordes of birds, mammals, locusts and grubs which threaten the ripening grain—can be handled as one overall problem.

The ideal is to have all farms more or less together. This does not imply, for one bead on a Kelabit neck, that there is any lumping together between families. Each has its own well-defined plot and the delicate irrigation requirement within this; to make the best use of the agreed water is entirely up to the family. Often, one family will divide its rice into two plots some distance apart, largely with the idea of betting both ways. It is completely understood that industry tempered with skill is the first essential. Behind, there is the slight but constant suspicion that there lurks an influence called luck. Luck can add or subtract—and it is neither wise nor necessary to ignore this fact (any more than to ignore the fact that spirits indicate probabilities through animals or incidents).

When the ground is clear and the water running smoothly towards the selected rice plots, the third main rice process is to control the water *within* each plot. It is difficult to define or attempt to describe just how this is best done. The older men at Bario have an inward eye for ground in terms of the way water will naturally flow over it and can be made to flow over it other than naturally. In less time than it takes to strike a light from quartz on to palm pith, Lawai Bisarai or Pun Maran can map out in the mind—and shortly point out on the ground—exactly where the water should be brought in and how it should be channelled about the mind's eyed field. This may mean bringing the flow down one side, back up the centre, round again. Perhaps running the whole straight down the centre, banking up at the far end, turning back through two main channels on the outer edges, which come up the field again, sending off a score of little channels each side until the water head is exhausted before it comes back to the starting point; where it cannot thus reach on the rebound, the first centre channel to be tapped off and fed down on either side at the top.

Once the channels inside the field are determined and dug—or redug from previous use—the ground is sub-divided into hundreds of sections. These sections may, ultimately, hold anything from five to two hundred flourishing rice plants. Around each, the cleared earth is scraped and hoed, largely by hand, stick and wooden paddle, to form ridges, partitions roughly thumb high. Into and out of each partition a thumb-wide gap admits and emits water—in either direction. With a flick of big toe, either gap can be closed; or, if flow is imperfect, a new gap made.

Rice, seed selected and carefully kept from the previous season, is first germinated in a nursery at one side of the field, beside a special hut on stilts, at the edge of the farm; for this the men now supply the timber and heavy labour, the women the thatch and matting. As the rice grows and the work gathers, this farm hut becomes the centre of day-time life—leaving the very few regulars, the old and some young, to keep the big long-house 'warm' during the day. (A long-house must not get 'cold', by total desertion.) There is nothing to prevent a family spending the night in the farm hut in the height of the season; if necessary they will. To do so regularly or for more than a few nights at a time would, however, be highly unsociable.

Irrigating within the field, making the season's hut and planting the seed are strictly family matters; whereas initial clearing, like main draining, requires general co-operation. When the brilliant green rice shoots are a hand or so high, the women start bedding them out in the irrigated divisions. Already their menfolk have led the cool mountain water gently to flow through the fields and soften the hard, sandy-clay soil. Those who like to do so, plant minor vegetables along the higher banks of their main channels and around the raised borders of the field which contain its total water. Most of the finer flow preparations and divisions are made when some water is already in, the soil easier to work.

Once the rice plants are well established where they are going to grow on and die, attention now turns to protecting the plants. Each individual plant is treated as such. Every one is special. The women attend principally to keeping all other vegetation out—including during two organized and recognized periods of general weeding over all the fields together. Into this attractive, lush, watered ground a hungry flora is prepared to ascend with hurrahs of botanic joy. It is not enough for each farm to watch out lest some powerful character gets in and grows established; it is everyone's concern, lest any one farm-wife neglect her piece and bring trouble on all around. The speed of plant regeneration at Bario staggers the inexperienced. Linked with the plants, directly, the women must watch out for the several seriously threatening insects. Locusts and brilliant red and green grasshoppers do damage in three ways: by gnawing the plant, by their acid droppings, and by making orange-coloured cocoons on the rice head—which cocoons, fortunately, attract the children, because inside is as sweet as honey. Down below, large, ungainly, brown crickets damage the roots and establish their grubs inside the stems, up which they can bore to kill the whole plant long after it has apparently grown healthy. Maybe such small pests infest rice elsewhere. Nowhere else are they given such attention as here. Even so, there are years when the loss is great.

The larger perils concern mainly the men.

*　　*　　*

The inhuman life which seeks to share the rice harvest with upland man is formidable. Ruddy jungle rats emerge for the occasion to supplement the ordinary brown ones, mice, dormice. The supposedly intelligent mouse-deer are not interested; the big Sambhur much so, a stag the size of a cow can eat a lot in a night and do awful crash damage in the process. Pig, except in rare epidemic years, should be under control anywhere near the main village, where the dogs are constantly roaming, ready to bay boar or sow on scent.

Birds do less damage per head; but there are many more heads. If the bird calendar has been overrun, the heads may peck too numerous to estimate. Where planting has been in good bird-time, the rice-eager population per field should be measurable in hundreds. As well as the four sorts of munia, each smaller than a sparrow but with lively capacity (the stomach and crop of one bird may contain over one hundred rice grains), there are two kinds of dove liable to descend in swarms. Other birds interfere with the plant growth by pulling, bending or binding leaf and stem to make nests.

While the women do the weeding—and after each farm hut is completed and polished into a comfortable daylight depot—the men build up about and above the field a network of interrelated devices to contest this race for rice.

Around the field runs a fence of bamboo, supplemented with branches and thorns. This serves to repel the less determined, larger animals, including tame buffaloes. At intervals along these fences gaps are left. These inviting entrances disguise choicely placed spears and sharpened bamboo. The stag leaps gracefully over, to be helplessly impaled. Humans get in over a single notched log sloping up over the fence and tied to another leading down inside. For rats there are a variety of nooses, fall-traps, invitingly baited bamboo cones with easy way in and none out. These and more improvized bits of apparatus are placed as needed. About once every four to five years there is a serious rodent attack which calls for hundreds of traps, and ends up with the children chasing, blow-piping, spearing and sloshing rats all over the field. (Bario only has one cat.)

Bird pests demand a more detailed treatment. The basic equipment consists of scaring bridge, a shrieking windmill, and sets of cannonade clappers. On the bridge, raised just above the level of the ripe ears of rice, the family can peer into every plant on their field. As the season advances, these bridges become arteries of Bario activity. As the cold mist of dawn rises over the plain, all birds report to break their fast. The farmers already did this before daylight—to be the first in. From now until nearly full dusk, men, women and children will parade the bridges, making every sort of noise a Kelabit can make—which is saying a loud deal! This activity (in which the children naturally excel), repeated in fifteen adjacent fields, keeps the birds generally restless, developing in them (it is hoped) a feeling of guilt and erratic discomfort. To support this high-level attack, a master tactician sits all day in the hut, playing upon an orchestra of rattan vines and pulleys, with which he or she releases staccato explosions of sound from all parts of the rice, erratically. Heavy bamboos are arranged to crash on to cross-pieces; smaller combinations produce a series of maximal pops; sometimes the water can be regulated to fall through other bamboos with prolonged, irregular groans. More vine roots control pieces of matting and old cloth which posture and sway among the crops. The wind, erratic as human uproar, twirls and flutters these too; but exerts its top level on its own windmills. Two blades, each as long as a woman, work the windmill's socket and ratchet which shriek, scream, moan and groan to high heaven.

The whole tempo of life is now shrieking to its annual peak of excitement. Other peaks may be reached, as in death feasts or on journeys. This one must be climbed every year, as all the heights— Murud, Batu Lawi, unseen Kinabalu, the Tamabos—rolled upward in one.

Back at the beginning of the planting season, a sequence of planting order had been agreed between all families. Pun Maran always hoes off first. It is important that the sequence does not get scattered over many days. It is equally important that it should not be concentrated into too few. If too scattered, this will assist the birds and other attackers to pick off individual fields, one by one. If too concentrated, a good harvest cannot be gathered before it will be endangered by over-ripeness, over-wetness, over-wind. To avoid these and associated risks, the closest co-operation is required at this season. A single family could not (in this setting) anywhere near carry through a rice programme with comfort. All being well, the grain will ripen in a planned succession. In any one field, there may be two or four sets to ripen successively. Whatever the exact situation, for nearly two months the whole community is organized to work in teams along the rice sequence. Every day one, two or three farms need team attention. Each family is responsible for a minimum of one adult to help others.

This makes really hard work, at the hottest time of year. The sun blazes into the fine air of the great mountain bowl, until all but the most careless Kelabits become irritated by anxiety lest their skins go too dark.

Hard work though it feels, there is plenty of fun in fatigue. The family whose farm is being worked will provide a jar of borak in the hut, along with the usual mid-day meal of rice, gobbets of meat and a little vegetable leaf. As, day after day, more and more of the harvest is safely brought in; gaiety gathers. In the later phases, when success seems assured, the amount of borak brought to the hut rises steadily. Instead of trudging home tired in the evening, getting in at dark, eating late and drinking, you will see people staggering home, laughing and singing, barely making it up the single log ladder in the gloom; impatient for food, then falling into deep sleep, until cockrow and cookpot again.

All day long, too, as men and women work in lines across the fields, snipping the firm heads of grain—thumb-length knives worked against thumbs as hard as bone—they will be singing, joking or tirelessly leg-pulling. If one of the older women is in the mood, she may start a song to be carried on all day, unrolling the story of some tremendous hero long ago. These songs would fill many books. In a land without writing they are passed on from generation to generation in gigantic feats of memory, marathon imitation. More often, the men sing stories. Over the fields come their fragments thrown high towards the rains and ranges; as Pun Maran may readily declaim, against the background of windmill groaning, pheasant-cuckoo, bittern and cicada:

The land of Balang Lipang is Long Marong Akan Dalan.
Balang Lipang sits on the rock and works there—
He makes a sword-handle there—
He carves a pattern on the bone of the handle—
He prepares white hair for it, and a sheath—
The instruments of war
When he has finished
For a long time he sits on top of the rock—
He thinks—'Why am I so long here, and no one has called me in to eat'
He sits there a long time, then hears someone moving along the house.
The person comes to the end of the house
It is Burong Siwang, who sees his son there, and that he has work there.
He goes forward to call in his child to eat—
He comes to the door and sees his son on top of the rock; he has done
    much work.
He sees his fine son, shining so white, like the moon, his eyes like lights,
    in his ears leopard's teeth, his earrings fine ones—
Indeed he is fine-looking, his face so red,
Burong Siwang is happy to see him:

'No one under the clouds has a son like mine'
Says Burong Siwang to his son.
'Good, Balang Lipang, I have not sat with you for a long time—
Good that you sit with me
My son Balang Lipang—I want to talk with you a little.
For a while past the men have been making the rice-clearings.
If you take the dogs out into the jungle
Beware when you go into the jungle—
For many from other villages seek revenge upon me—if you go into
     the jungle you must always look out.
If you go anywhere, wherever you go, beware.
Many people want revenge for my killing.
For before I killed many from other villages—I do not lie.'
Then says Balang Lipang to Burong Siwang 'How is that, Father—do
     people now want to fight you?'
'There is one who wants to fight very much,' says Burong
Siwang, 'Tokud Udan Panit Tutub Long Midang—'
'He is the hardest one of them all,' says Burong Siwang.
Says Balang Lipang: 'Where then is his village, my father should tell
     me his village.'
Burong Siwang replies: 'Balang Lipang, if you ask me his village,
     maybe you want to go there. Do not go! He is a fearful fighter,
     no one can stand up to him. His village is very far. Do not go!'
Then Balang Lipang says: 'Truly he will fight—but I only want to try
     him. Truly my father forbids me—but I only want to go and see.'
Then Burong Siwang says: 'If you want to go, child Balang Lipang,
     I do not want you to go. I have tried him, and I was defeated—so
     I do not want you to go, I fear you will be killed.'
'Truly he may fight boldly, father. I only wish to try him a little bit,'
     says Balang Lipang. 'If I am beaten, father, it cannot be helped.'
Balang Lipang gets up from beside Burong Siwang, and fetches
     his clothes.
He takes down the skin of a leopard—
He fetches all his things, he gets his war hat.
Having gathered all his belongings, he gets his shield—
He takes his spear—
He goes along to the house to the end—
He comes to the end platform and goes down—
He goes along the level place by the house to the foot of the hill—

He starts to climb up the hill—he goes into the jungle
He enters the jungle and he coughs—he says to the omen birds
'I want to talk to you omens!
I wish to go now, for I hear news of Tokud Udan, who wants to fight
    —I want to try him, and you should help me.
If I am to defeat Tokud Udan and collect his head, you should fly
    across my path—cross to the right.'

and so on . . . and out of sight.

★   ★   ★

For the matter of that, almost any kind of sound the human voice can utter may be heard over the Plain of Bah as the rice comes in. The men have a lively, long, yodelling call, which whips up the mood in any lull moment. Everybody is looking forward to this season being over. In fact it is more than a season: it is, in the Bario sense, a year. The year that started within the month of the yellow wagtail and ends with the last harvested gold.

Before the final cropping, the dykes have been closed, water diverted back into more natural channels. This in the long run makes less work at keeping up the drainage system. The Kelabits also believe that it is bad to let the water run *continually* over the ground. It is even worse to let it lie static for any long period. The Bario system is based on belief in a quiet circulation of seasonal flow.

Bario farmers underline their current faith in their 'drying-out' method by planting, as the harvest finishes, a small blue-flowered bean. This grows vigorously and gets in before outside weeds, to give a small, sweet crop of little beans, without trouble to anyone—and with, they feel, benefit to old ground. Meanwhile, a profusion of weeds, reeds, sedges and grasses are rushing back; before long the outside eye will hardly imagine that this grey-green plain from which the warblers, harriers, egrets, bitterns, sand-pipers, wagtails, shrikes and thrushes have now departed, could a couple of moons before have shimmered with gently flowing water under vivid green plants—exactly arranged, and bending under the strain of their grain.

One or two of the older men do leave small clues to what was, so short a while before. They keep a fraction of the field under water, deepening it against a raised down-slope, to make a fish pond. The fish have of themselves flowed out of the brooks into the fields, earlier on. What the women and boys have not netted or pronged, at odd times, drift by and by into these ponds. Here the older people who will be sitting around and not travelling or hunting after the harvest, feed their fish up. They trap more and perhaps larger fish—making little expeditions down to where the river widens beyond a man's leap—to get larger kinds. These they feed up, mostly on the dregs of borak brought out from the long-house of a morning; upon these the fish thrive, as do Kelabits.

The sweetest fish, though, are not found inside the mountain bowl. These are big, juicy, eel-like catfish which come from the Kerayan, a branch of the Bawang rising across the spinal range one long walk beyond Pa Bengar. They journey in jars and can be fattened for months with success. Barter price at Pa Bengar: twenty salt per tail.

Otherwise, for a time, the plain is left to its natural plants and its much fewer resident birds. Some of the huts may be left standing in what were the fields; certainly so if it is planned to use the same land again next year. The remaining good wood, bark walls and palm thatch of others will be taken down and stored away under the long-house or rice-store huts. If the general plan is to move the whole rice operation to another part of the plain next time, then everything looks and sounds (from a distance) as if it had always belonged to the frogs, bees, grasshoppers, dragonflies and butterflies which ceaselessly proclaim their place in clamour or colour.

*　　*　　*

Happily this year is a rich one. Which can only mean: abundant rice. The first time that huge, flying bird hurls overhead, shining whiter than Batu Lawi, turning high over Murud, outroaring a thousand thousand bird scarers, the plants are as high as Tayun's knees. No one then dare predict good harvests. To do so is to threaten everything. Arrogance has many places, pride stands above all. But to boast of rice or of babies before they are harvested defies the intangible. On the contrary, just as the mother calls her fat, bubbling baby 'Dirt', or 'Droppings', so will go the answers in reply to questions which the visitor from another place should nevertheless politely ask; and to which the answers (if he is unfamiliar with local manners) can readily give him a wrong impression:

'Well, I see you have a splendid rice crop coming along this year!'

'Oh no, no, it is nothing.'

'But that splendid head of grain—you should have abundance.'

'Alas, it is impossible. The rats are everywhere at the roots, the grubs boring high up the stem.'

'I hope, all the same, you will have a very good harvest. Don't you think so?'

'I fear it is most unlikely. The sun never seems to shine this year. And the winds are the worst we have *ever* had.'

'Well, I am sure it will all turn out all right.'

'There is little hope I'm afraid. The birds are just arriving. They will certainly finish off what little is left.'

Even after the harvest is in, it would be unwise to say more than that it has been satisfactory. There is an almost invisible rat—or is it a spirit?—which gets into the bins of those who boast their rice in reverse. It is safer to say that you have barely enough for the family; you expect to be eating roots, perhaps even foraging the jungle for sago, before the next harvest. For all that, Bario is bulging (with rice). Extra storage huts will have had to be added, to take it all. Whoever has time to make borak is making it to try and keep up with the tail end of the grain, portered in load after load at the end of the day, spilling everywhere about the house; though never, carelessly, upon the way. Now the doves and the munias grow so bold they come in onto the threshing floors and into the huts; if this went on much longer, who knows they might even start getting on to the floormat to share meals?

*   *   *

The zenith of borak is after the harvest time. A sense of relief rises from the plain when the effort is over. From here on, the other half of the year can be thought about carefully, with reasonable confidence. There are so many things that *must* be done and many more that may be. Some need a general effort; these should not take up more than a couple of months, at most—unless the main structure of the long-house is due to be replaced, about one year in ten. The rest is for family and individual choice; and for parties to be formed, often from several long-houses, to travel for a couple of months out eastward to Marudi, the trading and government centre (twenty miles behind the west coast). Or along the southern trail through the Saban country into the Bahau branch of the Batang Kayan, down into the Kenyah lowlands where they make the finest metal tools and are clamorously eager to trade for the strong Kelabit tobacco or goitre-proof salt.

The world outside the mountains beckons the restless, energetic, ambitious who feel that way inclined. Plenty to do nearer home for those who feel otherwise. Some prefer to relax, making things the family need, like a new rice mortar or man-size fish-traps; equally, making things they do not need, working for days to ornament, with an antler, the handle of a knife or to finish in minute detail a little box for a beauty kit (ochre, saffron, eyebrow tweezers, de-lousing comb, fragment of mirror, lime for the skin, a tiny sharp blade). There is a sense, for a while, of less pressing obligation: relief now from the day and night association aimed at common purposes.

Among the stay-at-homes the main outdoor attraction for the men is hunting. This is an abiding love in every male belly and chest.

The women will mostly be making small vegetable gardens, attending young fruit trees, fussing about the rice huts, weaving. Indoors, any day, Bario will stink with the tangey, nose-twitching flavour of rice, husked and unhusked, being half-burnt to make borak. Sometimes the whole inner part of the long-house seems one wide ribbon of steamy, scenting mush. Between each fireplace and the back wall, the stuff is spread out on mats to cool. Instead of being concerned with keeping off the crickets and mice, housewives now engage their idler hates with dogs and chickens, descending from any angle to snatch a piece. When the stuff is cool, a white powder is sprinkled over it: this comes from cakes made from roots of a ginger, agent of fermentation. All is gathered up, rammed into the dragon jars, ready for drinking in four or five days; unless a fancy style is intended—the very best brew matures in a matter of months, after which one jar can be enough to knock out one long-house (plus *repeat* the blow, with fresh water, on the following day).

The men of Bario have an inner eye for lines of possible water-flow over land which (to other eyes) appears level, suitable only for ponds —or no water at all. By the same token, the women of Bario have an intra-muscular instinct for alcohol. More than half of them do not vastly enjoy drinking it, though all but one take it in small quantity, along with the rest. But they do feel it is part of feminine function to make good drink, just as it is part of their function to pound the rice pure white and cook it to precisely the popular degree of soft firmness, leaf wrapped. Lawai's wife is rated the best Bario brewer. But (as with almost everything) almost everybody can brew satisfactorily. There are refinements; and after the harvest is the time for them. The alcohol sense enables drink of varying strengths to be adduced with almost equal ease from pineapple (which is not very popular otherwise), bananas (grown on the hillsides in many varieties, from the size of a girl's forearm to the size of rice-mouse), cassava, sugar cane, ripe cobs of maize. Cassava beer is considered second-rate, as is eating cassava direct. Cassava beer tastes more bitter. Taken in quantity it produces a virulent hang-over—absent as after-effect of borak properly prepared from rice. Sugar-cane borak is fierce—and unpopular. As an occasional joke, drink may be made from the varieties of rice which give a black or red grain, a liquid like blood. The occasion for presenting blood-like borak needs choosing properly to avoid giving offence or causing alarm. It should never, for example, be done at a death-feast, should rather cap a time of utmost harvest hilarity.

★　★　★

Men do not help to make *borak* and women do not go hunting (except for their husbands or fish). There are passionate hunters like Tayun and Anyi. No man can not be a hunter, however. The idea of hunting is the idea of being man. Only age or imbecility can excuse the in-ability to spend and to enjoy long spells far out in the jungle, living without the every-night long-house comforts, feminine aid, commerce with visitors, borak.

The hunter sets off in simplicity. He carries his blowpipe with spear bound to the end; a bamboo quiver of darts, poisoned and plain—perhaps with two sorts of poison, the one kind that kills very quickly by nerve shock and the other which stops the heart; basket slung on his back, with uncooked rice and a spare loin-cloth rolled in a small, plain sleeping mat; of course a haired sheath bush-knife round the thighs, a piece of sharpening slate tied on to the dart quiver, and another smaller bamboo container for tobacco and fire-making kit.

If the hunter is out only for the day, he will likely go on his own. A long trip (as befits the time after the harvest) is best carried out by four. One, either a boy or the least active, to act as cook, and attend the meat during the day: the others to work over a wide sweep of jungle separately, in touch, with four or five dogs. All four make the night's lone shelter of leaf, with a few sticks just off the ground as floor. All chop up the day's meat, help to clean and strip it for drying. Of it they eat all they can, sleeping at night regardless of mosquito and sand-fly (kept out of the long-house or hut by smoke for ever in the enclosed space, but eager in hordes here in the jungle). These hunting trips, if successful, are as much devoted to giving the hunters an orgy of meat-eating for themselves as to bringing back meat for the long-house. If the hunt goes on long, only the last few days of meat can be brought back. Beyond this, the point is to be out there, to move through the multiple interests of the wild; as men, without women.

Hunting tries all of men's patience. On the plain or in the long-house, patience is not necessarily conspicuous. In the jungle nothing may be won unless one can stand still for much of a day, regardless of fire ants walking over feet, leeches crawling up legs, biting flies buzzing behind, mosquitoes humming both ears. It is easy to travel through Borneo jungle without seeing anything of its enormously varied and numerous life. This is partly because a very large part of it is either nocturnal or moving high in the forest canopy overhead. Very many insects, birds, squirrels, do not come out by day or rarely come down from the light top layers into the shadow and dank of the greens and browns beneath. If anything strange enters the forest, calls of approach travel ahead along a hundred different lines of alert. Many of these messages cannot be detected by man; only the crudest can be interpreted by those untrained (which includes all women). Further, man stands higher than any other form of life in Borneo, though he is not so *long* as rhinoceros, buffalo, wild ox and the larger deer.

The hunter needs, therefore, to move with extreme caution; if possible to get into his selected area at the first streak of light, before the brighter rhythm has got under way. Once there, he must be prepared to crouch hidden and let nature run its course, over, under and through him, hoping something good will come within range of the blowpipe —or, possibly, the spearblade always lashed onto the blowpipe's end. He is aided, in this intricate bide-and-seek, by all he knows of jungle sounds, from the noise a party of black-and-white leaf monkeys make when they spot a tree-leopard or the peculiar quick squishy thump made when a big flying squirrel lands on an opposite treetrunk at the end of its glide, through to the whistle of a crested partridge calling its covey and the distant *whoosh* of a hornbill flying towards some mountainside fig tree. He will study fruit trees, scores of varieties in the jungle, which may ripen at different times, and differently attract their customers on branch or ground below *or both*. As the whole terrain, once off the plain, is rugged with ravines, moulded in hills and jagged with cliff or rock, an exact knowledge of the ground is essential. If the target is on the ground only, it may be best to be in a tree. But Kelabits, although they always sleep off the ground, have a distinct though vague dislike of getting their feet far off it for long out of doors. Any man can climb almost any tree. The risks taken after honey on cliffs result, every now and again, in one broken neck. But by and large, to hunt is to move, stand or squat on the ground. Whatever the position, the right hand—only one man is left-handed in Bario—holds the smoothly polished blowpipe.

* * *

Few Kelabits (or people anywhere) can make a blowpipe. It is one of the few true specialisms. It is easy enough to begin, another matter altogether to finish by making a more than man-height hole come out straight at both ends of one piece of hardwood. A block of wood is set in a rough clamp on the long-house verandah, worked on with a very long piece of iron. The craft is to force the iron in evenly, constantly, wetly, through. To some extent the grain of the strong wood helps keep the point along the line; one lasting mishit can offset that. The wood is bored rough, then polished and shaped, the width of an eye when complete. It is then something to last generations.

A master blowpiper can hit a monkey in a treetop, provided the foliage is not too dense. He can shoot further sideways, level, than any sizeable target is ever likely to be distinguishable and tree-free in the underscrub.

Hold the stem with the left hand cupped under and the right just behind it (also under and interlocked), right back at the base end, balancing the length of wood with the wrist. Aim on the upper knot of the binding which lashes the spear to the other end and sticks up slightly on the top side (the spear pointing below); this gives a slight tilt. Slightly bite the circle of the pith which enfolds the dart shaft, so that this fits tight and close into the hole. Now blow, not hard but with a quick, sharp, quiet-as-possible pouft . . . and the dart should rip out, sibilant . . . to strike with sharpened head into flesh for the eating.

What does it matter to miss, anyhow? The thin sliver of wood slides past the squirrel unnoticed; shoot another, and improve. In this it is superior vastly to any introduced weapon.

Treeshrews, mongoose, bulbuls, green lizards, leafnosed bat fall to a plain dart, one handspan long; which is long enough to get in the way and obstruct any escape. Larger prey demand poison. Bario relies largely on a single giant upas tree over at Pa Bengar, where Anyi's father introduced it as a seedling from the lowlands. Anyi is the expert at tapping the gummy sap, then dried to a black cake, later wetted and smeared on the dart point or on added, barbed head. Otherwise, poison is traded with neighbouring peoples. Fairly fresh (this year's?) poison, strongly applied, should stagger a monkey before it can travel three trees—provided the dart hit hard, went well in. Fairly strike a barking-deer in the belly with a thickly smeared dart, and relax. Light and smoke a leaf cigarette; then go further up the track until you come to the sound of thrashings in agony. Lawai's great-great uncle is said, once, to have killed a rhino this way. . . ?

The meat is not spoiled by the poison. Cut out the flesh round the hit, though; then the dart can be used over again.

* * *

When there are plenty of pig about, no one bothers much with any other way. But pigs are puzzling creatures, very mobile, sometimes suddenly moving away even over the mountains into other valleys after better fruit there—or for no particular reason man can define. When pig are scarce, some strain is put on the comfort of Kelabit life. There are plenty of small fish if caught sparingly and conserved; with enough over for an occasional orgy of *tuba* root poisoning by two or three long-houses at once, killing fish down many meanders.

The domestic animals are entirely required for special occasions; a buffalo, ox, fat pig or goat is not to be killed except for a large feast, almost invariably a death ceremony, while fowl are reserved for smaller occasions (but principally to lay eggs required for the regular pro-pitiations of ominous spirits). It becomes important then, both physically and mentally, to hunt effectively under any conditions; preferably for pork.

The hunting trip may well overlap a jungle produce trip; hunters are always looking out for good places from which to obtain the resin of damar, wild rubber, big rattan vines, camphor and a few lesser vegetable things which are so highly valued at the coast that it is a worthwhile proposition to porter them over the mountains into the lowlands. A proposition out of the question with anything Bario *grows*; although Bario knows that between one year's visit to Marudi and the next the damar that was worth so much last time may now be worth only quarter, whereas the wild rubber which no one would look at before is now in clamorous demand.

But hunting is a definite outlet in its own right. Hunters go out for a day or a moon, feeling near elation. It strikes one of the strongest chords in Kelabitry. It does not really matter much if the results are unimpressive. A man may come back loaded with game and have to send the rest of the village, even the women, back to get what they could not carry in from last night's camp. To come back empty-handed is awful. From the point of view of the long-house—where those who did not go are waiting ready with fireside criticism—only pork, venison and other big meat count in the hand. If those who return do so without any such solid fare, they will have to sit, that evening, over the borak through a prolonged session of wisecracks and facetious advice to which they will surely give as good as they get, raking up the past of other previous endeavours. But success pleases everyone. When there is plenty of meat in, all eat as much as stomachs can take, plus. There may be little more of it for quite a while.

Hunting for food channels some strong passions. The full flow in that channel is the hunt for big game no one dares to eat. And this is the only sort of hunting where the hunter carries a spear on its own shaft, not a blowpipe. Or if, within the possible of Kelabit never, he does, then this is the start of something too terrible, 'inhuman'.

* * *

Since Lawai was a young man and Pun Maran a father, head-hunting has become no longer respectable and regular. Yet the feel of it lies close below the surface of Bario. The arrival of the Japanese entirely disturbed the old order of benign but determined Brooke rule, which —although it only touched the Kelabits gently, at several removes— imposed upon Sarawak and all the western side of the spinal range a mood of peace and fear of bloodshed, unless with the Rajah's authority.

Twice the Rajah *had* given direct authority. On one of these occasions the Kelabits led down-river Kenyahs and Kayans on an expedition, unsupervised by government, against the people of the north and east who had been crossing the border and raiding the Baram watershed. The Kenyahs and Kayahs who move almost everywhere by canoe were already weary by the time they reached the Plain of Bah—the first time these people had ever seen the irrigated uplands. The idea of travelling on across the spinal range and for days towards the actual trouble-makers was altogether too much for Tama Balan, Tama Uding, Balan Ding and the other great lowland warrior chiefs. After long discussion with the leading Kelabits (supported by suitable omen propitiations and spirit ceremonials) they decided to simplify the issue by substituting the much nearer and more available people of the Bawang, only two days' trek further on, with only one severe mountain climb involved. They (nearly a thousand men armed with rifles and shot guns) therefore fell upon the unexpectant Kelabit cousins in the lovely, open, irrigated and densely populated plain at the east foot of Mount Murud. Scores were killed, with negligible loss from the Sarawak side. The main booty consisted of heads of the slain, live captured boys and girls and valuable old jars. This vast prize was divided broadly so that the Kayans had most of the heads which they needed ceremonially at that time; the Kenyahs most of the kids; the Kelabits the jars (too awkward to porter over the ranges). Although few of the active participants in this affair are still alive—for it is rare to live into very old age—Bawang, from the non-Rajah side of the ranges, keeps up a steady complaint. Every few years they put up a demonstration demanding retribution; and although they permit the Kelabits to go there and trade, only selected Bawang people (without relatives concerned) come westward in return.

All the time, vengeance and head-hunting feeling underlie. It is not a separate feeling in any sense. It is a kind of quintessence of the urge towards dynamic action and dramatic self-expression found among so many warm-blooded people and subject to such particular impulses among the Kelabits, who quite often ache for adventure, dream daring. If there were tigers or elephants in the uplands—and if this same drive had not already made the rhinoceros so scarce and shy, near extinction (or even if the jungle was more difficult to control in order to win good rice crops)—such outlets might be more available.

The only *permanent* furniture of the long-house is the circle of skulls hanging on a wicker frame from the rafters over the centre of Lawai's verandah, at the centre point and axis of Bario. It is time to focus on this. Each head had its bloody story. In a bunch, they are not thought of like that; but rather as a negative, anonymous, ultra-metaphysical, over-and-done-with (but highly poignant) story. Their presence at Lawai's place reflects the especial association, among the Kelabits, of head hunting with aristocracy and leadership. It is up to the upper class to be foremost in industry, enterprise and initiative in *all* things. This applies to head hunting just as well as to rice planting or bargaining for beads. The aristocracy must also *lead*. Smaller social fry give essential support. But it would be improper for them to push forward on occasions of danger and potential prestige. On very rare occasions, a lower class person might take a lead or head; and if he did this under circumstances which could give no offence and which deprive no one senior of privilege, this would add largely to his prestige and assist the family to climb socially (an essential social mobility).

In the uplands, head hunting never got out of control in relation to ordinary life. This was not necessarily due to any particular self-restraint among the people themselves, except insofar as everyone realized their interdependence in an area where there were no water communications and where all interruption of interchange of commodities (salt, iron, pots, mats, cattle, girls) between villages soon becomes highly inconvenient, presently intolerable. More of the credit must go to the mountains and rivers, the twisted and tormented geography of the far interior, which makes protracted expeditions—on which total caution, silence, non-disturbance of game or anything else in 'enemy' territory—far more difficult than the ebullient mass sorties to be undertaken by river or through lowland swamp.

Before something is said of the actual methods employed in the complicated business of head hunting, its purpose needs to be appreciated.

* * *

The stated intentions of head-hunting vary very widely among different peoples. Why not? So much so, that evidently many modern usages have developed as local specializations and in a sense as rationalizations, some aberrations. Along this line the Kelabits have perhaps developed further than any other peoples—and perhaps largely because of the special difficulties of head-hunting among the mountains, on foot, in great jungle, with cold nights and difficult ways once one leaves the established tracks—along these a head-hunting party dare not move. Thus, in ways easier to experience than to describe, the great feasts for the dead so much tied up with heads, mark a half-considered move to substitute the sacrifice of buffaloes for the killing of humans in the struggle for invisible reassurance and perpetual life-strength. This association cannot (in the Bario context) be written off as simply traditional and historical. Everything suggests that the people came onto the Plain of Bah from the south and south-east. No one in that direction has cattle; and there are clear records in local song and tradition that the beasts were brought by barter (long after stone monuments were widely established) from Brunei Bay, a month's buffalo leading to the north.

Heads or tails, however, the fact is that here head-hunting has seldom become obsession. Instead (and partly because it has not been enjoyed in large quantity) to chop off other people's tops is a trifle refined. The action gains in validity through being relatively discriminating, deliberative and rare. The effort of achievement then becomes, to a considerable extent, more significant than the result: the dripping head, which is sometimes in danger of ending up as almost a joke, an anti-climax, and in actual fact a football when it gets back to the long-house verandah, in consummation of its journey from the life of another community to engender new pep inside Bario.

The head is substantial evidence, also. Among people who exaggerate by tradition and boast for fun (or to stimulate others), skeletal evidence is desirable to back up the speeches and songs of the brave telling so well their own heroisms, sung, orated or chanted, as in the familiar Bario saga:

Tokud Udan now rushed at Balang Lipang and caught hold of him; they wrestled again.

Tokud Udan pushed Balang Lipang and sent him a tree's length. Balang Lipang came back at him, and rushed Tokud Udan. He made himself strong, and stronger than Tokud Udan (a little).

Tokud Udan got on top of Balang Lipang, then Balang Lipang got on top; they rolled over and over, one on top and then the other. Balang Lipang now tied him up again. Then he was amazed and said: 'How did I manage to get him like this. My sword was broken on him, he is exceedingly tough—how did I manage to get him like this?' says Balang Lipang.

Balang Lipang thinks to himself—'How can I wound him, his body is so hard? And my sword is broken?' Then he saw a small knife in Tokud Udan's belt. 'Oh, I'll try that,' he says, and he takes it out and stabs Tokud Udan. The knife enters.

Then Tokud Udan cried out loudly: 'Perhaps I am dying. Before this I have fought with many men—and never was I defeated. Now, I think maybe Balang Lipang has beaten me.' And the blood spurted out of his body like water.

Then Balang Lipang pulled out the knife and he cut off the head of Tokud Udan.

When Balang Lipang had taken the head of Tokud Udan—

'What do I think after that? My heart in my body thinks it will go home.'

He thought he would return to the house of his father, Burong Siwang at Long Marong Akan Dalan.

And so he does, with head, bleeding.

Boasting is splendidly supported by tradition. To all but the most interested listeners, some of the sagas of past Kelabit heroes can grow, by the second night or so, tedious in repetition of battles fought with incredible, ancient, but ultra-repetitive valour. These songs generally tell of two men, both with 'bodies like iron', enormous size, super-montane jumpers, who battle for days with spear, sword, sometimes additional club; they battle for months at a time. Less frequent are those which sing of two brothers who revenged offence to their parents (while they were still children) by slaughtering a whole long-house— usually by surprise and cunning device (this latter closely paralleling the methods of Mouse-deer in the funny animal stories as told by Lu'un Ribu, already heard). This second kind of story is closer to the Kelabit ideal of attack than pitched battle, with open challenge and incidental acts of chivalry which would seem to belong to a more graceful yet fiercer age, in another climate of the killer mind. Deliberately to fight a pitched battle makes no sense nowadays. By report, it did once upon a year, though.

Latterly it grew sufficient—and sufficiently dangerous—to kill, on proper occasion, anyone outside your own group and get away with his or her head and your own. So sufficient that the head of a little boy, surprised while bathing alone, proves every bit as good as his father's.

The idea of daring combined with cunning replaces the need for open man-to-man challenge; though if it comes to this it can quite well be done in that way, too. But the object of head-hunting is to *hunt*, get and *bring back* one or more heads; normally one per operation. The Kelabit view has not required that this should be an individual achievement by ordinary citizens. They also know that a good deal of the head talk of other people is boasting; but that these people are not so good at detecting and penetrating boasting so that they impress themselves and others with feats above the actual. Indeed—as the talk is likely to point out while it drifts that way some evening—if all these others really did what they said, there would soon be no heads left, in the lowlands.

Within the uplands, there are only three ordinary, fairly simple reasons for head hunting expeditions:

First: because times have been bad generally and there is a feeling for renewing the vitality of the long-house and land; in sorties of this sort it is necessary to take the head from a long distance away and at the same time to take earth from under the fallen corpse and bring this back also;

Second: as an expression of hatred and insult to another community, with whom some disagreement has arisen not able to be settled by go-betweens, exchange of gifts and other means; this is in fact an act of war, against which the others must retaliate—in the case of the first kind of foray, it may well be that the long-house which lost its head either does not at once discover who took it or cannot penetrate the mountains to get at Bario (who had it);

Third: as an act of individual protest, most often by an upper class man who feels humiliated through some failure or alleged failure of his own in his ordinary activities—especially if his wife publicly rebukes and/or privately nags him for some inadequacy.

Each of these incentives is achieved within recognized limits. For instance, you do not naturally take a head within your own community or from closely associated long-houses. You should take one (for need) from far away. You only take a head among Kelabit and adjacent people for hate reasons of the second sort; and you do not do this without previous negotiation and breakdown. Inevitably, there are exceptions; people break the rules. These exceptions are so rare that they are recorded in stories, the effect of which is to represent irregular actions as deplorable—the reverse of the emphasis in the long sagas which, however boring they may sound, elevate personal courage as the most desirable of qualities (after steady industry)—and the saga battles themselves are marathons of industrious slaughter (sometimes two men battle one year). The favourite straight stories are those which tell of the individual explosions.

It is many years since a man so indulged himself from Bario. The latest of these significant demonstrations took place at the next door long-house, Pa Main, south-east across the plain and over the Libbun (the uppermost branch of the Baram which rises from Mount Murud) by a suspension bridge made of bamboo and vine slung between long trees leaning over the water. Precarious though this bridge can seem— especially to women heavily laden—it is preferable to swimming this swift water. Only last year a young man, on his way back from getting salt at Pa Main, swam across, and in clutching at a branch to secure himself on the Bario side, clutched also a snake; he just managed to reach the outermost farm at Bario; was carried up to the long-house, there died. No one knows what sort of snake it was. Most likely a hamadryad, king cobra, most deadly of snakes and the only one which will sometimes attack a man unprovoked. A hamadryad's bite ought to work more quickly than that, though; perhaps it was one of the tree snakes; a kind that only occurs up in the highlands and about which nothing else is known.

The Pa Main character of record courted death deliberately in the formal direction. He was—he has since died—the father of Belalang, distinguished as one of the strongest Kelabits. He was of the upper crust, owner of a valuable old jar and much else. He was also possessed of a persistent-minded wife with a loud voice. His wife's elder brother was also more than somewhat on the drunken side.

One way and another, Belalang's father came into dispute with his in-laws over the question of inheriting a share in their parents' estate; and in allocating an allegedly inappropriate portion of this to the expenses of the necessary death feasts for these, his parents-in-law. His wife nagged him, on and on.

One night, seemingly interminable argument came to head. She drunk, and long after midnight—when lots of people were in the same state—leapt to her feet, started shouting that he was no man thus to be put upon by her brothers. Then she dashed to the family fireplace, and began battering the floor with the large, rounded stones used to keep the fire in and the embers scarlet.

The shame of this fell fully upon Belalang's father. He slept on the verandah that night; and for the next three nights on his farm, avoiding her altogether. On the fourth day he reappeared in the long-house surprisingly, after dark. To move by night is critical. He walked into the circle of men, women and children and dogs supping round the wine jar, his high shadow fading into the roof top thatch, his face tense, drawn, pale gold in the fluttering torchlight. No one spoke for a bowl or so until the noises from the teeming night life outside embarrassed the sensational silence within. Then he sat down as if nothing had happened. Drink was poured at him; he carefully drank too much, too quickly. To ease tension water was hastily added to other jarlets; even if not quite ready for drinking, they would do at this pinch. His own closest friends had already restrained his wife and taken her, under guard, to lie down at the far end. The elders sat with the now apparently relaxed husband, drinking through cockcrow to cooking. Dizzy with drink in the dim light, he went to his fireplace, took a spear, parang knife from a basket, some rice and tobacco, long bark coat; he put an axe in the basket as well, without saying a word walked along the verandah down the ladder east towards the dawn.

That was all anyone knew—they had all been too sozzled and sleepy to register much—for more than a month. In that month the lonely traveller's humiliation seethed as he worked, avoiding all tracks, through the dense jungle and over the difficult ranges. He had to go slowly, eating as best he could; he ate, among other things, birds' eggs and frogs' legs, goat-moth caterpillars, fat crickets, toadstools, orchid pods, camphor bark, nuts, rose-apples, water vine, wet moss, horse-shoe bats, eleven partridge chicks caught in one lot; and gloriously an old, sterile sow which he sprang upon as she slept in a nest which she had all too cleverly made of branches and leaves, proof against flies (herself against boars?), heat and this human's scent. All the time, there was something more than murder in that heart: his burning desire, the overwhelming need, to silence the bitter tongue and affirm manhood. All the way, he was working, most indirectly, to get round the head waters of the Kerayan into the mid-river terrain of the Milau people who live between the eastern Kelabits and the down-river Kayans. To cut his long agony short, eventually he got there undetected. After laying up for three nights in a clump of bamboo overlooking a newly-made fish weir, he saw a boy (not yet full-grown) come down early in the morning to inspect the big bamboo canes set in the weir to take fish—at dusk there had been heavy rain, raising then dropping the water level to push the fish conewards.

With one tremendous scream and leap, he cleared the bank and fell upon the boy in the water. Surprise overwhelmed the boy. The shriek was to fortify the man in his last moment of hope. Two full-arm slashes with his knife, and the boy—with a spear thrust clear through the spine—got beheaded. The shriek served a second purpose; it at first over-alarmed the boy's father nearby. Soon, with long shouts and then beating on gongs, everyone had been warned, a chase was on. By now, though, he knew, from careful study, his way back into the safety of the border ranges. He could not know this jungle as well as they, for all that. And this is *the* main hazard head-hunting must face: the job of bringing yourself back alive. Only with exceptional luck would you ever find a place, a person and a time to take a head without a general alarm soon after. It is an almost instinctive precaution inland, that no one ordinarily moves in complete isolation; and this is not merely because of head-hunting, but equally because there are many accidents that may happen to an individual (falling tree, honey bear, snake-bite, twisted ankle, toe cut off felling timber), when immediate help will be needed.

But Belalang's father came home. He reached the comparative safety of the higher mountains (his heart-land) after three days in which he was hunted by hundreds of furious men with hungry dogs. There is nothing to say about that style of experience; everyone knows how the jungle can be; and lying up, moving with utmost care and stealth, day after day, is the familiar pattern of serious hunting anywhere, from rhino to mouse-deer.

Long after he had been given up for lost, Belalang's father re-emerged at Pa Main. It needed no torchlight now to throw the shadow he was of himself. Emaciated (not only from hunger but innumerable leech bites), covered with thorn scratches and jungle sores, hair matted, filthy and uncombed, eyebrows and eyelashes sprouting—it is a wife's job to pull these out for her husband—he staggered into the open grazing land beside the river, spearless (the spear had been left in the boy's carcase, in the rush) and naked (thorn, creeper, sting and stone had long torn bark cloth to tatters). He managed to summon up one last tremulous yodel; and thereby to shatter all within earshot. Shatter . . . because he made the long, lilting, up-curved cry of a warrior party returning with head. The long-house looked and sounded likely to fall apart as the people inside rushed to the eastern ladder in. It was true enough, though. He who was now to be hero had, tied by the hair round his waist, boy Milau head to show.

From this day forward, no one could think to say this man was not one. Least of all his wife, before whom he dropped the head on the floor—as she had flung down the fire stones two months before. This was more than her answer. She was never heard to speak of him (or to him) again with other than the courtesy custom does like. And when she had had plenty to drink, every now and then, she would be first to get up on her broad, corny feet and proclaim his superlative manhood. Who else had dared like he? Who else sitting here had taken a head alone and so far? Said she!

*　　*　　*

The impulse of individual outburst is double-edged. On one side, the individual can avenge himself by bringing back a head, thereby stopping all mouths and removing any stain (imagined or otherwise) upon his fair name—which he will now (of course) change, to record this personal triumph. On the other blade, if he fails he will never return: he dies in the jungle or he is caught and killed (probably with excruciating slowness) by those he sought to slay. Worst: no one can hold his death rites. Suicide and murder—if the thing can be so simplified—are thus equalized. These are the antidotes, when matters move beyond the power of words. Great though this power is at Bario or Pa Main, it cannot always suffice. When the same sort of piled up, angry distress develops between long-houses instead of between individuals, it is no longer necessary wildly to imperil oneself. In this situation, the antidote is attack by one long-house on the other—not with a view to exterminating the other, but with the intention of taking a (any) head from it, therewith reducing them terribly, elevating and strengthening ourselves tremendously.

Suicide rather easily comes near, less often to, the surface in the upland atmosphere, too. The masculine method is the head-hunting ego. Women cannot take that way out. Nature and custom offer a substitute which has proved satisfying to many, even if, in the event, suicidal to few.

Pretty, soft, pale yellow, the convolvuloid flowers grow on the plain and at the edge of recent clearings before the full jungle takes over again. The leaves of this climber are large, strong, deep green and heart-shaped. This is *lemuan,* the way out for women. It is generally accepted that between one and four of these leaves, sickeningly chewed (the juice must be swallowed) will cause death without undue delay—the traditional method of self-destruction for females, who cannot dramatize this wish in the more exhilarating gesture of head-hunt. The act is not lacking in drama, for all that. Nearly all remembered cases where a woman has done this thing to herself, she has done it with an amplitude of public relations, previous announcements and some choice of moment. To some extent this is simply due to the tremendous importance associated with the incidence of death; also, the value set on individuality and strong personality. But the propaganda side of what might (elsewhere) be a fairly simple operation, reflects here the primary function of suicide: which is *not* to commit it, but threaten it, before there is nothing else left.

The *threat* of suicide is arrived at as the last but one stage, when all other forms of argument have failed. In no case within recent knowledge has anyone wished to kill themselves—just like that. If they did, the leaves would grow all over the place in abundance, so that anybody can gulp down twenty and be finished with. This is not the idea. Instead, the leaves are the last course, held against opposition to some underlying urge on the part and in the heart of the heroine.

She cannot get her way any other way. In a setting of sound where words are so used that it may become difficult indeed to judge just how much strongly expressed feelings are truly felt, and where the processes of argument are elongated and complicated to wind around the crisis, hasty decision or binding defeat, there comes a special need to draw the line somewhere and show (as well as say): '*Thus long and no longer.*'

Lemuan is the graphic example, on the feminine side, of this emotional equation. There are girls who run a kind of progressive suicidal trend, starting by near-eating one, then stocking up with a couple more, to increase the margin of terror. Without going into too much detail, it will be simpler to take one woman at work in this way.

The trouble started because she wanted to marry a man who was noticeably of 'bad' family, without property and with a reputation for carelessness, even laziness, at work. Worse than that, he refused to come and live at Bario; and she was determined to go and live in his house, to the east. As well as her family, everybody in Bario was against this arrangement. This opposition, which would soon suppress some Kelabit girls, in others of more obstinate individuality only increases determination; and so it was with her. Of course, behind this was some-

Ia   Within Borneo, above the cloud and jungle, seen from Mt Dulit,
1932. (*See pp. 6 and 152*)

Ib   Borneo, forest and mountain, rice clearing in centre foreground.
(*See p. 6*)

II The long-house at Bario under the Tamabo Mountains. (*See p.* 9)

IIIa Bario with secondary scrub behind, grassland plain in foreground, and virgin jungle reaching away to the mountain tops out of sight. (*See p. 5*)

IIIb Family fire inside the long-house. (*See p. 23*)

IV Tayun, a young Kelabit, wearing very valuable ancient glass beads and leopard's teeth in his ears. (*See p.* 10 *on*)

V Anyi, one of the best Kelabit craftsmen, wearing hornbill ear-rings he has carved and hat from leopard he has speared. (*See p.* 44 *on*)

VIa   Man carved in stone relief from a boulder high in the mountains on the Sarawak border. (*See pp.* 109-120)

VIb   Kelabit girl of marriageable age; she is wearing valuable glass beads in her necklace and very valuable orange-coloured small beads in the front of her skull cap. (*See p.* 11)

VIIa Women working in irrigated rice fields at Bario, November.
(*See p. 70*)

VIIb Women fishing with hand nets in the Bario stream at 4,000 ft. Fish, shrimps and water insects are popped into the gourds slung from their ears.
(*See p. 31*)

VIIIa   Woman making Kelabit pottery at Pa Trap

VIIIb   Man in Swatow ware bath weighing about 100 lbs at Pa Dali in the far uplands

thing more than her feeling—strong though that was—for this attractive and amusing young man, splendid dancer, and himself with a reputation for commonsense and hard work away from the bad name of some of his relatives at the far end of their long-house. For she was the youngest in a family of five; she stood to inherit little of the family wealth; and she did not get on at all with her two elder sisters, both married and bossing her about night before day.

Months passed and a harvest, with her sitting, obstinate and alone, at first under reasoned argument, gradually more and more violent, ending up with sisterly blows. Meanwhile, at the other end of the tension, her lover's people were now publicly (but probably no more than that) antagonistic too. They were saying:

'Who are these Bario people who think they are so wonderful? We don't want one of their girls coming here, however good they make out she may be. They are always like that—think they're too good for anyone else. As far as we know, they are certainly not a bit better than we are. Our son can have one of twenty wives. Why should we bother any longer with that noisy, boastful crowd at Bario? That tatty girl?'

Village pride whips up, at their end, in response. Every long-house looks down on every other, at the best of times. In the middle of hullabaloo she and he grow more determined than ever. Especially she. But under such circumstances it simply is impracticable for two young people to live together (in peace) against *both* public opinions.

The lad is out on a limb at this point. His manhood is not in dispute; merely his family's status. As what the girl's relatives say is substantially correct, all he and his people can do about it is proclaim the louder, exchange added abuse through intermediaries, who easily find excuses to go to and fro between the two houses—for the affair has now got past the stage of recognized go-betweens trying to arrange some settlement, compensation in property for the Bario family before they let the girl go: everybody is agent now.

The girl is left with her last resort. Working herself up wildly, she rushes out of the house crying that she will eat the dread leaves. Other women run to restrain her. But she plucks some and starts to chew. With infuriated strength in her already so strong, big-breasted, young body, she takes it in before they finally get her down in the mud with a frenzy of pleading, crying, hair and nose-pulling (not ear).

She is carried kicking back, up the knoll, into the house. Big gongs are beaten. Everybody hurries home, dropping whatever they are doing for the day. She is in a bad way. But they force rice water down her throat in large quantity, put hot stones on her stomach, cut her forehead and shoulders to make the blood flow. She is a very sick girl that night. But she doesn't die.

After this, the atmosphere changes. No one is quite sure how far she meant it. But she has served notice on her people that if they insist in opposition, she must take it to mean that they seek to stop all that she wishes to live for. If they want to kill her, the deed is on them; next time she will make sure of her own finish—and let her spirit haunt the lot of them, as she (through they) will.

After which—much more discussion and suitable face-saving—both families give way. The agreement is that they marry; but he must come to live at Bario. He will take her from the fire shared by her two elder sisters, to occupy one side, vacant, of uncle's fireplace further along the house. So it is done.

Sure enough, also, so it is presently undone. After two harvests during which the husband works quietly hard to help his brothers-in-law in their rice fields, the couple (now with a baby, and now on good terms with everyone again) go off to 'visit his parents'. They do not come back. Every time anyone from Bario goes there, they raise the matter and are reassured with soft words, more or less. Perhaps, later on in life, they *will* go back again—it is likely. Until then, he thinks with relief, some sunny mornings, that he does not have to go out and work on the back-aching irrigation ditches in the open grassland; and she, while enjoying the sweet fish which he catches further downriver, thinks with longing of her lifelong girl friends and that somehow especially soothed evening borak back at rice-rich Bario.

* * *

Suicide attempts have outnumbered conclusive suicides by something like twenty to one. One or two famous cases have grown into Kelabit tradition and song. The most famous is an exceptional suicide pact. This happened down in the south, half way between Batu Patong and the Kenyah river people. The daughter of a good aristocrat fell in love with a Kenyah slave boy, who had come up the Baram with his master on a trading trip into the Saban-Kelabit land. A marriage of this sort was inconceivable; even temporary liaison annoying. But the girl cared. Her very good father thought to fix his only child by declaring that if she went on with this, she must have no more to do with him or his. The more practical Kenyah chief decided the only way to deal with the presumption of his slave was to slay him—and for this purpose presented the youth, in a cage, to the enraged Kelabit father, to do away with as he saw most fit. At this critical point, by full night, girl let boy out and both crept out of the long-house, vanishing into the jungle. They were not missed until morning. A wide search was organized by the local Kelabits and the large party of travelling Kenyahs. They found the lovers the following evening. She had swallowed the poison leaves; he had stabbed himself with a poison dart from his blow-pipe. They had died together, embraced, convulsed, in separate agonies.

It was held that only a slave man would behave so badly—in abducting the girl and then in killing himself like this. But the lovers had the last word. Treated in the customary way, their suicided corpses were left where they lay, to the awful indignity of pig, blowfly and ant. Before that conquest of flesh could be accomplished, however, the two turned into stone. To this day, the traveller may see this lovers' stone; and he will hear, coming from down the hillside where it lies, an unceasing, melancholy lament of falling tears.

*   *   *

Sudden death in any form strokes fear into Bario. Worse even than suicide is that one of her people should lose the head. Bario is in such a remote position, so difficult to approach over the mountains and again to surprise across the plain that in four generations no head has gone away. Others have been much less fortunate. This is vital; because the skull itself is the substance of extensive later funeral ceremonies—first a year or more's interment, sealed in a coffin on the long-house verandah, followed by removal of the bones and re-burial away in the jungle inside a stoneware jar or vat of stone. Exactly how the body works is not of much concern. In sickness the sufferer is treated as one whole; a cure will seldom be limited to one part of the person.

He who is seriously ill must be patient indeed. Near relatives will devote most of the day and night to guarding against the grave danger that the spirit of the sick might depart from the body. There are many minor remedies, palliatives, leaf medicines, intestinal mixtures from animals, slittings and bleedings; but the principal treatment applied to anything serious is both dual and invariable:

(i) Compel the patient to eat *bubor*. Bubor is a watery soup made by over-boiling white rice, so that the grains collapse and almost jellify. Piping hot, this semi-fluid is poured into the mouth—if necessary forced open—at frequent intervals, spaced just sufficiently to avoid causing the sick one to be actually sick (or explode). No other food should be given during the critical illness, unless the patient discloses a craving for something special—a cigar, sugar-cane, eel, chicken?

(ii) Noise, preferably uproar. Never let the patient relax for a moment. Do that and he will soon lose the will to live, to fight against the outside pulling at him. If he goes into a coma, shake and shout him out of it. If he appears to be actually expiring, bellow in both ears, breathe and blow fiercely into his mouth. Never let him have a moment's peace until he seems out of danger.

When you have done that you have done all that you can on the body. Simultaneously, the spirits will be being dealt with separately by Pun Maran and the old women. In the last resort, bang the trying-to-die's head up and down upon its small wooden pillow.

The head—which sees, eats, speaks, hears and smells, in that order of importance—is the one indispensable. In a sense, it is everything. A head can exist without a body, where a body cannot persist without a head. The head of the dead—taken nearly always by stealth from another people—receives lavish attention as the highest prize, the strongest separate and external force that can come into the long-house. Before this power can enter, protective measures are needful to make sure that the power is not too great for the place; and to prove that the good qualities (which go with the head) alone get in, shedding anything bad, including everything to do with the body and the alien spirits attached to another community.

When a head-hunting party returns successfully, purification, washing of them and the heads, propitiation of spirits, must be first carried out on the ground below. At the same time the women will develop, with song and gong and repeated movement, sobbing, beating sticks, stamping into swooning, self-hypnotized dancing with and around dead head. The process is repeated, on a larger scale, indoors. Days will be spent in visiting and welcoming a new head. The man who actually got it—properly an aristocrat—will come first in songs, processions and dancing all one night, leading a line of dancers moving without rest through every part of the long-house; he led by the head, held out. Those who went with him on the expedition are favoured, prized, made the subject of song after song improvised by excited women.

After several days of visiting, drinking, dancing and general pleasure, the new head has been taken in adequately and is placed in a rack hung on the verandah. This particular head then becomes a centre for important spirit offerings and prayers, for the time being. The longer a head has been around, the less its febrile power is felt to be. Thus in any *severe* run of ill-fortune, grave accidents, or inexplicable disasters, a new head offers hope of retrieving the situation and preventing further misfortunes. A disaster is no isolated incident; it is rather a warning that something is wrong somewhere and everyone had better attend to the atmosphere smartly. The same idea is conversely expressed by all the hunters taking new names; and if the success has been a great one, or the need for a new head long and strongly felt, every man, woman and child in the long-house may take a new proud name. It doesn't deeply matter if the head is male or female, young or old. It is not desirable, however, that it should be that of an aristocrat.

The quality innate in any head from outside the group is such that there is no need to add the qualities of the head's original owner, personally. If head-hunting parties start killing aristocrats—who are the most important people and the minority in any community—another sort of disturbance may set in. The loss of the head of a middle-class girl is dreadful; something will have to be done about it, definitely. But the distress and humiliation does not much affect the balance of the community as a whole or the interests of valuable property, three-quarters or more of which is held by the few rich. When, usually by mistake but sometimes by deliberate viciousness, a chief or important person is killed, the repercussions will upset the uplands for many a day, if not a year; there is no question of letting things simmer along: it is war. War is a thing that Kelabits have only wanted in their wildest or most drunken moments; have over the centuries learnt to avoid at almost all costs—and regret at every.

Ordinarily, even in the sort of head-hunting raid designed to humiliate or retaliate against another long-house or group, it is never the purpose of the operation to decapitate a specified person—although it may well be that one particular person on that side has caused all the trouble. The big idea is to get one head from them. Once that is done, our side is satisfied. It is hardly to be expected that the other side, down one, will feel the same. Their concern, from now on, is to answer back and correct this deplorable imbalance. Consequently, the 'winning' lot live—perhaps for years—in a state of constant uncertainty, expecting reprisal. That is the pay-off, price of this lethal achievement. It is really most inconvenient to be in this position of negative defence. And it answers nothing to burst out of it and again assault the opposition. That will only protract our own uncertainties: for now the other fellows have two dead to recapture.

Ever since legend can remember, there has been fighting of a kind. There is always a certain amount of uncertainty, since a sudden attack is daily possibility. But in these far uplands, there can be a feeling of more safety than is possible elsewhere. Only when some fairly adjacent people have a known score to pay, is everyday life seriously disturbed. Night life is not affected; that is one of the things that the long-house is under one roof for; an entrance ladder at each end only, the top pulled up indoors after dark. But in these danger times all outdoor activity is upset. Women dare not go down to the brook for water separately. Children cannot be let to roam unwatched over the plain. The rice fields must be put in one concentration, else those working far apart become easy targets. Prolonged, this becomes tedious beyond words; while the facts of life, even the size of crops, are affected.

It is wise also to keep up certain broad defensive devices. The main paths must be blocked, hidden diversions made: not that an attacking party will come along the main track, far from it; but they would like to dash along a main track in the subsequent get-away, so that they can keep together, move much more quickly than is possible in the jungle uncut. Deception by false outgoing trails along the line of expected retreat has several times been engineered with good result. But the most effective defence weapon is a highly sharpened bamboo stake buried with just the needle point at the surface under a leaf. This will go through the horniest foot, with crippling effect. Beds of these foot daggers are set about the house, paths, field and other approaches; only the residents knowing the places. All this is troublesome. Sooner or later someone forgets; a child is wounded, or a buffalo.

Should things drag on too tiresomely, an alternative offers. The side that is one up may offer the other side compensation. After all, we have had our triumph, we have made our point, we have gained in power as well as prestige. We can afford to be generous; we really cannot afford to go on anyhow else. A human life is more or less equivalent to one good quality old jar, plus the odd buffalo, fat boar and salt to top up.

To give up an old jar is another matter altogether. It requires not only the agreement of one of the few aristocrat owners—in the public interest—but also that all put in shares and equalize out the jar value. If it cannot be settled by stoneware, there is still another way: settlement by slave.

A slave is worth an old jar, just like anyone else. But he or she is expendable, unlike the jar. Especially if it is an elderly she, past outdoor work. Moreover, these slaves are, by definition, persons without kin or close affinity. The slave class is composed of descendants of prisoners of war or occasional strays from far away communities who drift—lost, insane, outcast, or runaways—into the uplands. Slaves are only allowed to marry slaves. They are not considered a class at all. They are not spoken of as 'bad' in that sense. They are spoken of as nothing; strictly, as nobodies. Nevertheless, they have heads. The sacrifice of one of these heads will satisfy the repressions of the one-down, who have failed—as yet—to avenge.

There are well-known stories of peace being made by these means—including one, recently, to stop a protracted period of unsettlement between Bario and Pa Dali. This dispute originated over an old jar, and was principally between the family of Lawai Bisarai and his opposite number in greatness to the south, the father of the southern chief Rajah Omong ('He Who can Defeat any Rajah'). Bario people still cry easily as they tell again the story of how the old woman was handed over at a great meeting place on the fringe of the grassland along the track to Pa Main. There, the enraged and hitherto frustrated recipients speared her, one by one, delicately, to death, every man stabbing selectively—as is the custom in deliberate execution throughout the interior. The old woman had no idea what was coming to her that day, suddenly, then very slowly, in the driving cold mountain rain.

★　　★　　★

Death in the long-house, whatever the cause, appreciably upsets the place for a day or two. It produces a feeling of uncertainty inside everything. A man may be prepared for death, the necessary rites completed to his satisfaction; indirectly this somehow underlines the impending event.

How is it that—when all is done to carry the living beyond—one need do anything more; need die? The need is that death should come slow rather than sudden. Even to fall stricken on a head-hunt raid is little compensation and less of glory. Those who come back are the heroes. Those who do not have failed—and (further than that) have reduced their community, even had heads taken off. Deaths in rapid succession inside Bario—or anywhere else—build up more serious alarm. Maybe there is something badly wrong underneath this living? The feeling is *cold*. This is the word—*cold*—to describe the process; applied equally to cold in the bodily feeling, cold in the guts. The long-house is growing slowly cold. Someone charged with sitting at home by day has let every fire utterly out. Warmth and goodness have leaked away.

Ever present is a mild yet underlying preoccupation with the possible growth of coldness. The creeping terror of failing warmth should lead duly to outburst, in endeavour to offset this peril. Poised in the air over Murud and in the soul (so to speak) of human-kind, it can be that this coldness already moves beyond remedy. The only other thing to do then is to abandon the long-house and build another—as has often been done. Beyond that, again, the last resort is to abandon the river and all the land it waters below the long-house—as also has happened, more rarely.

Beyond and behind that, again, and again, lies fate and despair, there where nothing more can be done, by man against the inexplicable. The end of this torturing climate, expressed in repeated death, drought, locust plague, rat and rice race, munia and other misfortune—is petrification. The ultimate Kelabit disaster: to be turned into stone.

These suicide lovers, chief's daughter and slave boy, turned into stone in unique departures. Most records of petrification are mass catastrophes which fall upon separate long-houses—usually as the direct result of a single, stupid, casual, individual act.

* * *

The Plain of Bah and those to the east of the spinal range are supposed to be the soil deposits left by great lakes which eventually broke out through the gorges otherwise containing the highlands, which now carry the flow of more than a thousand head waters roaring into the low country, wide rivers and canoe people of the Baram from Bario, the Sesayap from Bawang and Kerayan, the Batang Kayan by the Bahau, to the north the Trusan and Limbang.

This plain soil is sandy clay mixed with vegetable deposit. Even where streams have cut fathoms down into the flat land, there is seldom stone. Such rocks as occur are few and far between, scattered in evident random.

There are, in fact, two regular ways in which stone can come into position. The Kelabits (or their shadow ancestors) may have placed them. Or they may have been there 'always', no Kelabit can see how, in human terms.

The existence of stone, on its own, irrespective of man, is admitted. The towering cliffs of the Tamabos behind Bario stand, lit by sunset, testimony enough. The rocks in the mountainside rivers, before they come out on to the plains, belong to the same class as flower-peckers, broadbills, swallow-tails, fig trees, mountain badgers, rhododendrons in the moss forest, flying lemurs. They belong. They may require close attention and study; they require no precise explanation; they are. In the mountain streams, or lower down larger rivers, stones of selected shapes and sizes are further studied and noted by men for future use. Occasionally, the river changes its course; new rocks may be exposed. If any of these are particularly desirable for Kelabit purposes the finder may reserve his discovery, announcing the fact in the long-house that evening.

The way in which rivers do deeply change course is a matter of high interest; to Bario people perhaps more than to any others, but to a considerable extent to all. This is part of the sense of water among people who get into or travel upon water less than any others in the inland. The old waterways are for ever extending their meanders, until these become so looped that the distance between the start and the finish of one is short enough to be readily broken through by an exceptional flood—or by man. Upland experiment shows that the soil in a left dried-out ox bow from a diverted meander gives greatly increased rice crops for many years, so long as it is properly treated. Man therefore goes to a deal of trouble to watch waterways and see when a cut can be made (at some great death rite).

When a possible cut has been determined, the actual operation will require the co-operation of many. The convenient occasion for conducting this operation is when people from all the surrounding long-houses come together, after a good harvest, for a death feast. The making of such a cut—as of any major new irrigational project—counts as an ancestral memorial. Only thus can it be financed. A cut in the ground is exactly the same in quality as a cut across the skyline on the mountain top, or a cut across the path on a ridge; these are equivalent to making a stone bridge over a cut, shaping a stone seat, erecting a monolith, dolmen, seat or the stone mound of monster demonstration for the permanent disinheritance. All are basic interferences in the nature of earth and rock.

*　*　*

A quick look at one of these mounds will clear the mind for the last and most complicated side of Bario life: death and property diffusion.

The great death difficulty arises when there are no direct or near heirs. Usually, parents will adopt a child. Boy! is there manoeuvring within the family as to who should be adopted if there is an old jar or many valuable beads at stake? But sometimes a couple will be obstinate about this, in a kind of reverse, frustrated spite—though in Kelabit terms it does not seem like spite so much as self-respect, the individual right. Hardest of all is the case of a childless widower or a confirmed bachelor who is rich. About one in every two or three hundred Kelabit men does not marry. This will always be of his own choosing. Even the deaf-mute moron at P'Umur has a wife, though no children. Sometimes a man does not marry, for physical reasons; but there are also odd men who dislike women, sometimes who treasure their individuality and inner personality too much to share any piece of it with another person.

The Kelabits have devised a solution for this problem; it aims to preclude the most violent source of argument, the permanent property in old beads and jars, by simply destroying it all, in a big way. What happens is this . . .

'I am in middle age, a wealthy aristocrat. My possessions are un-challengeably mine as the only heir and I having performed all the necessary measures for my father's and mother's departure and monuments. I possess five buffaloes, sundry other cattle and pigs, most of which are not in my possession but owed to me in my own and three adjacent long-houses; also I am owed a buffalo, two fatted pigs and two hundred salt which I invested by contributing to the death feasts of kins, and which they must repay me or my heirs for my own. But I have no direct heirs. And I can only see trouble if my nephews and nieces get into this. There are many of them. They have all been *most* kind. But I do not really want to be dependent on any of them, can support my old age with a few ordinary jars and cattle if I live too long to work (which I doubt I will). If I go they will merely fight if I leave it to some, inheriting only ill will.

'I have one very fine old jar, red earth, three dragons, six ears with only one chipped, also eleven other lesser jars, four of them valuable, five of them modern; several good plates, and two fine blue and white bowls hanging in frames on the wall for use on special occasions. I have a great many beads from my mother, including an excellent cap with more than three hundred orange cane beads, as well as two necklaces of rounded green glass ones of the kind we know to be oldest of all. Two good gongs, a set of full-size cooking pans for salt making, two fine parang knives from the Batang Kayan; all the planks and boards for my part of the house and a lot more I have lent to Tama Labang these recent years. Two blow-pipes, a dancing cloak of hornbill feathers, two huts full of rice and all the other usual things.

'As my further future seems somewhat uncertain, I had better settle the matter myself while I am still active and entirely alive. I will put aside the planks and boards, three of the lesser jars and some of the animals. The whole of the perishable rest, salt, rice, pigs, buffalo as well as many other things to purchase, like tobacco, betel nut, eels and labour, I will expend with due notice at a mighty feast after the next rice harvest. I am in a position to give a very big feast. Hundreds of people will come, including my relatives over in the Kerayan and Bawang to the east and as far as Pa Tik beyond Kubaan to the west. It will be a splendid amusement, tremendous exchange.

'On the last day I will declare my monument. All my imperishable property is to be collected in a heap on the ground over there, a dart's flight from the long-house ladder. Every man present will come out when it has stopped raining and form a line from the fine old dragon jar in the centre of the slope down to the shingle bank in the stream bed. Along this living chain, from hand to hand, should pass first the small surface stones and gradually, as the work goes down, larger stones and then boulders. All this will travel from the river bed up the bank on to the little knoll above flood level, slowly shaping a pile of stone. Presently this will grow into a mound higher than the long-house is off the ground, and twice the width anyone can leap. All mine.

'Thus will my belongings be secured for ever. Thus my own memory will stand to eternity. It will be larger than any ordinary man's can be, because so many come to my feast and are so well entertained—since I have nothing to keep and pass on, I can, I will spend the lot in one great final display; and in consequence make a mighty effort to do well by me, piling rock upon boulder upon pebble upon stone.'

There are nine of these impressive stone mounds round and about the Plain of Bah. Others no doubt have gradually vanished, as the all-powerful jungle has submerged them from above and undermined them with groping roots from below. As usual there is a snag, a snag on the short view too. Some parts of the highlands, including Bario itself, are situated on such small streams and in such stoneless ground that these mounds cannot be made. After all, this quite suits Bario. Inheritance is half the battle of higher living, after all.

*　　*　　*

Even cutting the river knot, straightening the bend as a memorial, has its considerable complexities. Very many people must be brought together to a great feast, which can only be supported by aristocrats prepared to dispense a considerable share of their inheritance and a share for the benefit of their family honour and future memory.

On the working day of the canal-cutting burial feast, at the height of the jollities, two hundred or so men will take off for the chosen spot —at which they will find ready food and drink in plenty to refresh their labours. The labour may be large, according to the length of cut required, which can be anything from five to thirty or forty fathoms. But on this sort of occasion, everyone sets to with tremendous energy and strength.

This cut then becomes known by the name of the person memorialized therein. The cut itself is seldom intended to cause the immediate diversion of the stream. The objective is to prepare an easy way for the next big flood to break through and close the U, beheading the meander. At least once a year there is likely to be a period of intense rainfall in the high mountain rivers, to send belting out on to the plain and pouring down the gorges a lesser mountain of water which, submerging everything for days, may break through and leave an oxbow. There are nevertheless odd cases where cuts made in a previous generation have still not come off. This does not diminish the value as a memorial; it irritates so that, probably, presently, another attempt will be made.

It is an insult for one village to be able to say of another that its rivers are needlessly crooked. It is an appropriate and frequent boast: 'our rivers are straight'. Kelabits travelling in the lowlands are provoked by what they regard as the slothfulness of Kenyahs and Kayans in this respect; indeed they look down on the river people as wretched agriculturists and experimenters—both careless and lazy, they say.

A great wonder happened in the headwaters of the Akar, on the border of Kelabit country, recently. The river changed course on its own. In the middle of the new river bed was an enormous boulder, the top of it carved with a spread-eagled human figure complete with head-dress, extended ear lobes, loin cloth and leg bangles. This rock carving was (and is) not unlike other ancient ones; but instead of being executed in high relief is incised into the stone surface. It differs also in having feet which swirl into fin shapes; the hands show ordinary fingers, though only four.

This revealed stone brought excitement and many sightseers. With so close an interest in stones as things to be moved, erected, and carved, it is no wonder that the big, isolated boulders, which outcrop at sudden and separate points about the plain, also excite curiosity. How on earth did they get there? Anyi, Tayun, Lawai and Pun Maran are natural scientists. Although they take for granted the existence of resident forms of life and structure in the normal run, they mostly concern themselves in knowing as much about as many of these as possible. Nevertheless, the oddities never fail to attract not only attention but puzzled discussion. For example, the way a tarsier can turn its head in a complete half-circle to look behind as well as in front; the repellant stink emitted by black and white badgers, and the curious localization of this stinker only on the east side of the Libbun river around Pa Main and P'Umur; the sporadic appearance of armies of hairy caterpillars marching in column. Nothing stimulates more curiosity than big, isolated stones, on flat land, and projecting higher than a man above ground. There are not many. Where they occur, conspicuously, the conclusion the natural scientists have reached is that they are the result of petrification. No other explanation satisfies the conditions. *Balio*, —must be . . .

*   *   *

Balio means petrification; and something more than that. Turning into stone is mixed up with the cold end of everything, although not verbally clarified or 'worked out' to that extent. Balio is the finish of a people, their domestic animals, belongings and buildings. It never happens to wild animals. It only happens to humans through their own 'fault'. It is the end of growing old-cold. It *could* happen suddenly; but the procedures causing petrification are hardly likely to occur except in a community which is losing its standards of proper Kelabitry anyway.

The principal causes of petrification are these:

Most often—ridiculing wild animals.

Often associated with this—harshness or lack of hospitality to orphan children looked after by grandmothers, who, in secret fury, put the rest of the long-house on the spot by presenting them with a wild animal in a ridiculous situation, so that they all laugh.

Very rarely (and rather uncertainly)—incest between father and daughter or some other extraordinary act; but as the petrification follows immediately upon the act, which in this kind of case will be secret, it is far from certain what is the cause, except in cases of animal ridicule, where there is usually at least one survivor (grandmother and orphan always survive, and by incestuous inference then renew the line).

The records of petrification are not preserved in song, but strictly in spoken stories; these are numerous. Stone stories tend to follow one pattern closely. Before hearing one of these curious stories—which always arouse interest whenever they are told for the benefit of children and strangers—a word on the process.

Petrification begins immediately after the act which triggers it. As this act may have been performed away from the long-house, during the day, the first warning most people get is a sudden drop in temperature. This is quickly followed by raging wind, hurling down freezing cold lumps of rain, hail, which is also Balio. Hail is extremely infrequent (snow unknown), even in this the highest settlement in Borneo. Its appearance justifies near-panic Three things must be done at once. Everybody must get indoors. Every gong in the long-house must be beaten as loudly as possible. And at least one of the two doors out from the verandah must be blocked with the most valuable, aristocratic and oldest dragon jar in the place.

The clamour of gongs, accompanied by wailing and crying, must continue as long as the hail. It is possible that this alone will prevent the long-house slowly turning into stone. But if that does happen all those who got safely in have now a second chance. For when once the hail has stopped and the petrification settled, everything is sealed in an enormous rock *except* that the venerable stone-ware jar cannot be conquered by stone. It is stronger than anything else anywhere. So when all other hope is lost and the people trapped, the owner of the jar shall smash it. Where it was fixed in the small square doorway, there is now a round hole as wide as the jar at its widest. Through this all may crawl out into the open and safety. Everything else they possess will have been lost. They cannot go back again; that night the hole will probably be blocked by fallen stone, anyway, leaving only a crack or mark to show future generations the way of that escape.

A long-house which is so lacking in high aristocracy that it has no sufficiently old jar has had it in any such event. Jar or not, more often the hail comes too quickly for any precautions, and everyone perishes. Those people and cattle who have got into or under the house are petrified where they cower, smaller stones dotted around.

With the hail comes a tearing wind, roaring thunder, searing lightning. After it, days and nights of continuous rain, which threatens to flood the whole land. Thunder always causes some concern in consequence. The proper thing to do, when it starts to thunder, is to make small-scale thunder and echo noises yourself, crouched down, keeping still, hands over face. Which makes quite an inside din, in a storm.

Tradition tells of disastrous floods separate from petrification, but also caused by human acts. These have seldom been so serious; while the acts have always been corporate. Every Kelabit long-house has suffered at one time or another in its remembered history from an occasion where some sort of man-eating monster, tiger, or gigantic snake was slain and eaten. This beast lived in a hole, among rocks on the mountain side or in the bed of a river. From this hole it would emerge and stealthily gobble up first children and then grown-ups, gradually over months gnawing deep at the population. No one knew quite what to do, until some cunning young man thought of a trick to make it leave a trail—charcoal attached to live bait usually (the live bait always being recovered alive in the end). The monster was thus finally trailed and slain in its lair, usually with fire and smoke supported by spears. The killing of one of these monsters is commemorated on a big sloping boulder in the bed of the main Baram river, below the junction of the Libbun near Pa Dali. This dragon, incised in the stone, has the body of a bulging crocodile magnified, the head of a dog, eyes the size of big blue-and-white drinking bowls.

Flood troubles were not directly due to any killing of man-eaters. Unfortunately on several of these occasions, the delighted killers celebrated their vengeance by deigning to eat the corpse. The body, almost as long as the long-house, was cut up and shared out by fire-places. While the flesh bubbled in earthenware pots all along the house, the water boiling in the pots whispered this message:

'Beware, beware, you boil me here as your share. I have eaten you and you would now eat me. But if you do, you die. Beware, beware, beware.'

Only one hears this message; one family, poor people at the far end of the long-house (who have in some way been almost outcast). These heed the warning and escape swiftly into the hills or up river, before the feast begins and disaster falls upon the rest. Thus only the slaves are saved to start the social cycle again!

Somewhere in all these dreadful happenings, unnatural behaviour towards living natural objects always comes in. One everynight style of petrification story goes:

'There was a great feast on in the long-house. But in all the fun and hospitality, no one remembered the old grandmother and her little orphan grandchild. They were left out of things. And indeed someone, drunkenly, made a joke about the old woman. The drunk gave her a piece of sugarcane, amusingly saying this was her share in the buffalo flesh and seeing of course that she had no teeth left strong enough to chew such stuff.

'Inside, the old woman went cold. So she told her little grandson to go down to the riverbank to find a nice, fat frog. He brought several back, she chose the largest. Then she took a tiny piece of cloth and wrapped it round its middle. She took two tiny bells and tied them round its feet; and another round its neck.

'She took a small brown jar, of the kind occasional borak or strong arak are stored in. She dumped the frog into the empty jar, tied a piece of banana leaf over the top, as if there was a drink inside. She waited a while until the festivities had reached the height of frolic, levity, shouting, singing, dancing, arguing.

'Then, very humbly, she came forward into the centre and offered this tiny jar—where the long-house was oozing with the drinks of big ones—as her poor contribution to the feast. Her gesture was treated with some pleasure and laughter and all the rest. She gave it, as one can 'give' a jar to a particular person (who must presently reciprocate) to the man who had hurt her before.

'Soon he undid the leaftop, taking a gourd-spoon to ladle out the drink. Instead, out hopped the frog. The frog hopped across the floor looking ridiculous in its miniature skirt and bells. At the sight and sound everyone fell to laughing, cheering, all sorts of wisecracks.

'While this was going on, the woman quickly carried her grand-child out of the house, and away into the mountains.

'She was just in time. For the ridiculing of the frog came a tremen-dous sudden tempest. And before anyone could even think to place one old stone-jar in one of the house-doors the whole place was turned to stone.

'Not that it would have been much good anyway, since all jars were wet with borak, and that is no antidote.

'If you pass that way by the great rock you can still hear, deep inside, the sounds of hollow laughter (if you listen hard enough).'

So it is that stone, which now has little importance in the everyday essential routines of Bario life, in one way and another sandwiches that life, between undertone fear and overtone ambition. At one side of this sandwich, petrification; at the other, those memorials for death which are the outstanding and distinctive characteristic of these people and the focus of most of the surplus energy, property and intelligence.

*　　*　　*

It could be that the rich plain set in the far folds of high mountain is somehow very slowly turning more and more into stone; or, that the human proportion here is under steady push from that direction. It is not simply coincidence that among the labyrinth of ideas which intertwine in intelligence, the two which have evidently long been of exceptional strength and intricacy, connect up a general theory of stone formed from human wrong-doing on the one side and a practice of carrying stones long distances, arranging or carving them for the respectable dead, on the other: the two lines of thought running in parallel zig-zag. These ideas intertwine with the general idea of nature and its relationship to human life, which is serious. Further, with the idea that in the past animals have been hostile to humanity on a big scale—and even in defeat have brought disaster when treated with contempt (cooked): treated properly, they also can stay memorialized in stone.

Aristocrats who have reached a reasonable age, and preserved—and by their industry maybe enlarged—their property, will ordinarily be memorialized either in stone or in those alternatives of a cut in the ground or river or through the forest across the crest of a mountain. The particular design followed depends on several things—including: the stated preference of the person directly concerned; the wishes of the family; the size of the feast to be given and the number of guests (equals potential labour force) to be expected; any particular needs of the community in that year; fashion, recent trends among other families of similar status; fashion, the urge to do the same but more; offsetting fashion, the desire to do something different; indications, conveyed to the experts through omens and dreams; weather at the time of the feast.

The scale of such enterprise can be measured crudely by the memorials which survive rain and flood, landslide, jungle growth and general decay. There must be nearly a thousand still recognizable within a day's walk of Bario. Nearly a hundred of these can still be associated with some definite persons. If everybody could afford to throw sufficiently large feasts, there would, clearly, be many more memorials. But to command the labour to carry and erect a monolith or climb the ranges to cut among the clouds, falls within the spending power of few. It is not that the labour has to be paid. It is simply that the feast must be big enough first to attract many guests and second to entertain them so well that they feel obligated—without feeling grateful—to do well by the host for one of the three or four days a big feast should last.

A big feast thrown by one aristocratic family as principal is likely to include and incorporate death rites due by less well-off families in the same long-house, simultaneously. These will contribute as they can. They will memorialize their dead more simply, that's all.

Bario does not bury its dead, unless for special reason. The proper procedure falls into two main parts. First, at death the deceased is laid out and keened over all through the night. This keening should continue without break until relatives from other long-houses have been summoned and see the cadaver. The sounds of grieving pour out across the plain. But they do not preclude a measure of festivity. Directly at death the family have asked friends of neighbouring fireplaces to start preparing several big jars of borak in aid of the second phase.

The second phase coffins the body, which cannot well be kept out any longer in this climate. The principal mourner has commissioned others to prepare a coffin, the head and tail of which are carved (usually) with antlered figures, the whole shape something like a boat with a lid. When this is ready—worked in softwood, it can be done quickly—the dead one is put in, with appropriate additional uproar. The coffin is laid on the verandah; in front of the family fireplace on the other side of the centre dividing wall.

Here it will rest for at least a year. In the early stages the aroma is sufficiently conspicuous to the visitor. It has to be taken as breathed by the residents, finding its natural level among the many mixed scents of the long-house, where cockroaches inside and pigs below act as effective scavengers, an unending chain of refuse disposal—with the advantage that the refuse also fattens the pigs for the death feasts.

To circumvent the smell so far as is possible, a long bamboo drains from the bottom of the coffin into the ground below the house. The coffin, if decently finished, fits tightly above. But when there are—for some reason, such as an epidemic—several dead in the long-house together, conditions do become pretty fierce for a while. Pun Maran notices it. However, to remove the dead from the house at this stage is not on. It would expose him or her to dereliction; and the living to haunting anxieties—perhaps to growing colder, even.

The third stage of the journey of the dead on earth: removal out of the long-house, away from everyday human activity. One of the functions of death feasts is to facilitate this spiritually tricky transfer, and to ensure that it has no spiritual repercussions of an undesirable kind.

There are a number of different ways of placing the remains at the end of the affair. By now the coffin on the verandah will contain nothing more than dry bones, beads and other personal ornament. These are removed and placed in a basket or jar, usually. If in a basket, to be placed in among rocks, or in stone vats and other arrangements.

With all due rites of spirit propitiation and proper lamentation, the bones are carried to the common place for final burial. It is not in the least compulsory to use this place, though. One Bario family keeps a private lean-to shelter, on the hillside nearer the long-house, for the bones of its departed kept in a special dragon jar (of Siamese origin). There are many variations. The common factor is a distinction between the whole body and then decomposition into skull and bones—the former inside the long-house, in the continued line beyond living; the latter away in the wild, with the living tie severed by extensive acts to reassure death (and deathliness).

These extensive acts are on such a scale that they form the hub of the non-rice year, a great outlet for social, family, and enemy relationships throughout the interior. Bario cannot have one of these feasts annually. No one could! This would put devastating strain upon the economy and energy of the community. All being well, anyway, someone need not die in the year—no one of importance, surely. And one occasion can do the deaths of five years (much more at a pinch). When someone of much importance has died, this is the time for others to attach themselves and carry out a combined operation, planned to be completed after the next or next below following rice harvest with the removed bones; provided, of course, that the harvests are good, everyone relaxed, abundant food and drink available.

* * *

Stone may be able to move by itself or arrive from the clouds. Humans only move it with efforts and purpose, some of the maximum effort of upland activity. It stands to Kelabit reason, therefore, that round these efforts centre the optimum intellectual organization of the people.

The system of stone and related memorials derives from property, class, occasion and inheritance. With people who do not write, inheritance is always liable to become complicated. In addition to the ordinary complications, Bario invites these:

—The wealthy have a great deal of property.

—Kinship and marriage rules are very considerably elastic.

—No kinship contract is entirely binding.

—All other contracts are variable and through intermediaries.

—The essence of upland character is to complicate, vary, and adumbrate.

—Property is only partly kept by its supposed owners and largely invested in loans to others; repayable with interest on demand.

—There is no marriage settlement of the *brian* type so widely used to adjust property between husband and wife sides of the family.

—There is no last will and testament—nor any other final and definitive statement on anything whatever at Bario.

The great death feasts are the Kelabit attempts periodically to clarify this situation, define heirs and inheritance, and circulate property (at interest) as widely as possible. No one can fully understand all the ramifications even of any one such activity, but every one thinks they know a lot about some. Each and every such occasion provides the opportunity for immediate or subsequent—sometimes generations subsequent—argument.

* * *

This is not to say that disputes over inheritance are regular. Nine times out of ten there will be no trouble. The tenth, the jackpot, however, should make enough noise to keep everyone talking about it for nights over years.

Conscious of this difficulty, the Kelabits have devised methods of circumventing likely conflict in families like that of Bario's chief Lawai Bisarai—famous for their violence in this field. One way of getting round the difficulty is to celebrate death feasts for your parents (and spouse's parents-in-law) while these are still alive. Many elderly people welcome this measure.

When a rich man may participate in the funerary redistribution of his own fortune in public festivities, it is reassuring. For there is the constant undertone of anxiety: that after I am dead, my heirs may not be able to appear to do the right thing by me in a big way—a way big enough to elevate, expedite and glorify my departed spirit in full accord with my own living status there on the plain.

If there is only one child in the family, it is relatively simple: the question, then, is will he or she possibly exploit this *unchallenged* situation to be sparing in the share of the estate he expends for the ceremonies?

A large expenditure does not necessarily mean any material reduction in eventual total estate. This largely depends on the ingenuity and shrewdness of the individual. There are many ways in which he can put others under obligation to him in conducting the affair. When he uses large quantities of rice to feed hundreds of people for days, he may not be using his own rice at all but the whole long-house's—because in the past and for generations his family has contributed to the death feasts of others extensively. The buffaloes he sacrifices may be owed to his father from years back; in killing these he simply recognizes that even in the uplands neither debts nor domestic animals are immortal. More of this later. . . . The immediate concern is the scope for uncertainty regarding family property. Where there are several brothers and sisters, living in different long-houses, long walks apart, complications increase. In particular, it is thereby hard for one member of the family to know exactly what another is doing. It is possible for a go-getter to build up a big death set-up, gambling on future inheritance by borrowing on a large scale in order to collect the many things needed on these great occasions. In this way he can establish a large claim on the estate, on the rough assumption—and rough is the word—that the more he spends the more he is entitled to. Where there is an old jar involved, the whole question becomes: who shall acquire the jar? No amount of other property can compensate for not getting this. In theory, 'according to custom', the eldest male has the first claim. But the eldest male may be lacking in drive and intrigue compared with his sister's husband; or he may be unfortunate in a sick wife, so that his rice and other results have been poor, and there are no children of his own to help in the innumerable jobs of highland life; or he may have married away, so that the jar in question is in substance in the hands of other members of the family—who, for sure, will do everything they possibly can to avoid letting it go further from them than the tip of a long bamboo.

The lengths to which people will go to avoid parting with valued property have lately been demonstrated at Kubaan. Here, as well as our old Balan's jar troubles which led him to transfer himself (with jar) to Bario, there is another old jar in a family with two older sisters, both aristocrats married to strongly opinionated aristocrats—plus their much younger brother, Ma'at, unmarried and slightly mild in temperament. The sisters made big death feasts and generally got control of the family situation while the boy was small. Both the husbands, though aristocrats, are not in the highest bracket—they own no old jars, passionately want them. The sisters, both strong-minded women with theme lines in vituperation (inherited, without dispute from their ma) have fallen out violently as to who should have the best jar. Their fireplaces are adjacent. The jars hover uncertainly tied to the back wall, at the borderline of the two domestic territories. Every time there is a big party, the dispute breaks out afresh. If they do not bring it up themselves, there will always be someone else to start that fun going!

Once things reached such a pass that the younger sister starting beating the jar with the stem of the big river lily. This would not break it. She was threatening, though, to smash rather than let her sister have it. This debate continues. . . .

*   *   *

With such tremendous vested interests involved, it is clear that anything goes, where an old jar is concerned. In this setting, it is easy to see how, even after husband and wife have become implicated in inheritance by sprouting heirs behind them, in-laws also form two potentially divided interests of ownership, jealous of each other's present possessions and future avowals. So Belalang is driven to his personal head-hunting saga. So the loving girl, engulfed in unemotional complications she as yet barely understands, protests her right to the boy of her brown bosom by nibbling the poisonous vine-leaves.

There can, then, be no difficulty in appreciating why there is not one of these *irau* feasts every year. There is sure, though, to be one somewhere in the vicinity. That is the essential lubricant of highland living, of the extra quality in life over and above the rice cycle itself. Whoever is making *irau* will invite all the rest.

Invitations are sent out by runners with knotted strings enumerating the nights before the party starts. Runners fan out in all directions. If the feast is going to be on a generous scale, they will go as far west as Pa Tik beyond Kubaan, as far east as the Bawang and as far south as the Saban Kelabit villages above the beginning of the Kenyah country. Invitations on this scale cover some thousands of people. Often, a long-house makes a point of putting on a big feast in a year when it alone has an exceptionally good rice crop and others have *not* had nearly such a good one. This practically guarantees that invitations will be taken up, from all around, to attend this opportunity for eating, drinking and enjoyment at a high level; that is worth even a long climb and jungle trail. And all those people will thereafter be under obligation to this house.

It is the intention of the hosts to put on the biggest show possible. Once they have decided to hold an *irau*, with ample rice in stock, then back and brain goes into making this a rip-roaring success. It is almost as if an obsession towards material suicide comes over the place. A people traditionally and naturally hospitable, proud and competitive between communities, now become engrossed in out-doing all others, thus making their name for the year (and other years to come). There is plenty of calculation along with all this. *Irau* is more than a bringing together of people in mass enjoyment. It is just as much a centralizing of business, barter, bad and good debt, unsettled argument and uncertain inheritance, an economic occasion of such complexity that no one observer could ever hope to take in all that goes on as between groups and their go-betweens, sitting sipping, sucking buffalo meat and pork fat in great lumps, in among dancing, singing, boozing, wrestling and all the rest—including, always, at least one fight.

The tone of the *irau* is set as the guests arrive—this year at Bario, already famous for the richness of its performance, firmly based on the rich regularity of irrigated rice. Thus, guests who approach from the west must come over by one pass of Pungga Pawan—avenued by cuts in the jungle and another ditch cut in the ground and a broken big jar —down the steep track across a further series of cuts made on the crest of the knife-edge ridge which cascades into Bario from behind. The only other line of approach, from north, east and south, is across the open plain where all tracks join at the far edge. Either way, before the guests (moving in large parties by long-houses) approach Bario itself, they halt to bathe with great care in the narrow, muddy brook. They are hot from the journey, dirty from the mud picked up on the plain —where the buffaloes now roam at random since the season's farms are no longer fenced, indeed are barely distinguishable any longer.

Some of the incoming men will be carrying fat pigs slung on poles. These are contributions to the menu to come. They serve one useful purpose by ensuring that there is more than enough. Bario, having once entered into this, cannot afford any gesture which does not indicate unlimited hospitality. Gift pigs have to be accepted, included in the feast, throats cut before the present is over. There is no Kelabit way of looking a gift pig or cow in the mouth. All you can do is kill it, eat it and lump it.

The lump it part of it means: whichever of the co-hosts was given this particular pig, hereafter owes that pig in return. He cannot, however, pay it back as soon as he wishes—in the unlikely event of his being able to pay back anything for two or three years after an *irau*. On the contrary, he will be expected to pay the pig back when the donor himself makes an *irau*. This pig has been brought along with that purpose in view. In this way, a long-house which is planning to *irau* a few years ahead, makes a point of going to parties and putting pigs upon them, thus disposing of pigs which would otherwise be over-mature later on, while at the same time freeing their own pig potential to feed up more fat boars.

Some beasts brought in will have been asked for by the hosts on loan; or, will be the rewards of their own past planning in this same manner. Salt and all sorts of other commodities to be used in the *irau*, may similarly be brought in to repay (or indebt) Bario.

The great thing now, though, is to get clean and look nice before coming up that ladder! A certain amount of reserve is advisable, at this point, all the same. Girls can be seen giving their best loin-cloths to an older woman, to be put on indoors; she follows behind the main party as it comes up. As well as this, there is a lot of hanging about going on. No one wishes to be first to arrive. It is polite to be last, as long as you are not too late. A long-house party which has, through some miscalculation, arrived in the middle of the afternoon, may hang about washing, combing, de-lousing and preening, more or less out of sight below the stream bank and among the pink tea-bushes—until others have arrived to reassure their approach. When this is all sorted out, each group approaches, the most important man walking in front, in single line winding along the foot of the slight spur which runs out from the Tamabos and towards Bario's burial ground to the south.

The first welcome—as the guests reach the top of the ladder and bend to come in through the single low door—is distinctly lukewarm. For at this point some of the younger and livelier Bario citizens are arranged in the rafters, under the palm thatch, holding big bamboos of mud-water mixed with soot, charcoal and oddments. These they now generously discharge on the new arrivals, the younger and livelier of whom retaliate by climbing up after and pulling down their attackers in general scrimmage. Once this is survived and the tempo set, the newcomers settle down on the verandah to exchange the essential polite greetings with their hosts before being asked through the wall into the families there to complete make-up, ready for the party proper.

There will always be one small group who do not dress up at all in advance and, having approached, do not climb the ladder. Instead, they huddle, looking miserable, in the mud under the edge of the entrance platform. They mean to look miserable. Soon they make their presence felt, above the gathering din within, by ululating lamentation to seep up through the groaning floorboards overhead. This quickly demands attention. At first Bario will send a senior guest as go-between, to find out what goes on. They know in advance but naturally cannot show so.

Before long the go-between comes back and reports that these are visitors from the Bawang houses which were attacked in the famed raid of Kelabits, Kenyahs and Kayans armed by the Second Rajah. By and by it develops—also as everybody knew—that they are actually from other houses, sent themselves as go-betweens. After the promise of a fine knife and a pig for the time being, they are eventually prevailed upon—before the dark grows misty, wet and coldly miserable out of doors—to come on up and join in the fun. The pig, which turns out to be a piglet, is killed in front of them on the verandah, put into the common pot. After a further show of reluctance this little group is prevailed upon to come in back; eat, drink and soon be merry. One day that argument may come to be settled. This is not the day and—as Bario insists—the matter concerns many more than they.

The excuse that they were then acting under orders cannot be adduced for this purpose. It can and often is adduced during the *irau* itself. Anything that happens during the *irau* is the responsibility of those making it, and this applies throughout Kelabit hospitality customs. If a visitor gets helplessly drunk on your borak, it is up to you to see that he comes to no harm. Should he fall out of the house or through the floor boards, or on to the fire, he can rightly claim according to his hurt, anything from a small pig to a large buffalo. It is therefore desirable, in generous but well organized entertainment, that the strong young sons and daughters, nephews and nieces of the hosts shall be moderate themselves, so that they may attend their elders and betters from elsewhere.

The party gathers rather slowly, at first. It is not done to rush things. All the guests do not arrive together; some will not arrive until the following day, including those who wish to show themselves a little stand-offish or to give the impression (hopefully false) that they are in no way beholden to Bario. Close relatives from other places tend to come early; but this is no more than a tendency, since long-house loyalties frequently supersede those of kinship, and the sometimes painful processes of relationship tied up with property are specially likely to become acute during *irau*, directly connected with the redistribution of wealth.

The second day, things really get going. Those who have not a care in the world—mostly the young—settle down to the protracted fun, fooling, mockery, mimicry, leg-pulling and mild practical joking in which Kelabits excel. The older people take their share in this. A good many of them will be more or less preoccupied with more serious matters—which become increasingly serious as the feast goes on, temperaments rise with the level of borak falling in perhaps a hundred jars, and impatience accelerates with tiredness and the irritation, which continuous noise and crowds can produce even among people used to a great deal of both. Some of the elders will have returned to the verandah, there to adopt the same sort of attitude as the Bawang people before they came up; that is, they will sit and sulk, refuse to eat or drink until some debt owing from Bario is settled.

The creditor squats on the verandah, opposite the inside fireplace of his debtor. Through the small door in the wall between, the go-betweens shuttle to and fro, carrying reply to question, argument and rebuttal, offer plus protest, then minus. Plenty of pressures are put on. A special small pot of best brew—or claimed to be so—is sent out to the verandah as balm. A charming niece—better keep daughter out of the picture for the present—is sent out to wheedle the Pa Main man into taking a bowl. If he can be got to do that, something is won. It depends on the size of the debt; whether it was imposed, voluntarily incurred or otherwise acquired (maybe by inheritance); on how much the creditor really does want to be paid at all at that time; how much the debtor can pay or promise to pay in what time; the temperament and temper of both parties, enlivened with alcohol; and to what extent either or both of them feel that they may wish to carry out other transactions with goodwill later on. It may come to the stage where the creditor's demands, if frustrated, become so aroused that he kicks over the small pot of wine without drinking. Almost anything can happen, for the matter of that.

The debtor can only take the defensive, or negative, if unready or unable to agree the transaction. Or he can claim that the whole thing is false—in which case, elders from other villages will be brought in to arbitrate, a big discussion builds, in which anyone from anywhere gives evidence; and which is unlikely to be finished until, at the earliest, the next *irau* but two.

* * *

The clearing of debts continues alongside and in among all the lighter activities of *irau*. Nine times out of ten the transaction is semi-satisfactorily settled before the guests depart—on the third or fourth day, according to their number and the host's supplies. Plenty of other transactions will also be carried through; not only debt repayment but new barter or debt involvement, between Bario residents and selected men—persuasive, quick-witted and with memories capable of surviving much drink—sent as go-betweens representing families or whole long-houses and concerned to trade in cattle, tobacco, salt, pottery, metal or whatever else it may be.

Every plank, mat and rafter of Bario seems to be occupied by cheerful (or temporarily sulky) humans; so many that for once the dogs are driven out in defeat from multiple kicks, curses and whacks. One big group will be spending most of its time in Chief Lawai's inner section and on his centre part of the verandah. At times everyone will be summoned there. But there is continuous movement, each family inviting friends and visitors from afar to its fire; and the principal hosts summoning one and all to eat of the beasts they have killed, as these are cooked on the verandah in huge containers by elderly men with meaty reputations. A general plan of campaign has been agreed by the men and women of Bario before the *irau* begins in earnest.

But no plan can survive the hundreds of human links which are refreshed or freshly developed in this great meeting of far and near. This is the occasion to strengthen bonds of affection, for the young to enter into new entanglements. As the party develops, a great deal of sexual promiscuity is permissible among the unmarried, at night at the far ends of the verandah, up in the rafters or elsewhere out of brilliant view. This is one of the best chances young people get of meeting persons of the opposite sex and their own age from outside their own, so well-known and often very limited, long-house selection. In this the *irau* serves a third subsidiary (but important) function—in addition to the functions of rebalancing physical death and perennial indebtedness. The elder brothers and sisters of Bario boys and girls will be at great pains to perform as go-betweens with those whom they consider suitable possible mates from other villages. If they do not do so—perhaps because they fear losing one of the family in case he or she should marry elsewhere—other young people will readily serve. Nor is the process in any way confined to Bario. Many Kelabit affairs begin in this way; a fair proportion of eventual and lasting marriages result.

There is no space in night and word, here to describe all of the very many things that can occur at an *irau*. Special dances are brought out, or thought up, for the occasion. A rather general pattern is for men to dance as women—particularly the beautiful dance of the lowland Kenyahs, imitated by Kelabit men in semi-caricature and semi-seriousness. In this dance, the women barely move their bodies, except for slight stamping of the feet, in a complicated, very slow rhythm which is primarily set by the hands. In each hand is held a fan of shining black-and-white hornbill feathers, spreading outwards from the end of the fingers. The dance is done with these hands, fingers, feathers—fluttering and intertwining with utmost delicacy. The effect is deeply heightened by a flickering light; this is not a dance to try in the daytime. In the same sort of mood, men will dress up as girls, by putting gourds—in the absence of the ideally suitable coconut not found in the uplands—as false breasts.

Sometimes, a wild man at a party, such as oldish Ngewelan Ribu of Pa Mada, will do a dance representing the exaggerated act of copulation itself. Anything (or nearly) goes.

And on the other foot, the *rules* are extremely unmarked. There is no chance, indeed no exact performance or moment, that *must* be done during the *irau* necessarily, excepting only the memorial piece of work (which is its outward expression in time), and the final definitive killing of the beast (which points the material, temporary and economic spear or finger).

Games of all sorts can equally merge off into dances, mimes or stray sexy activities. A dance particularly associated with the time after the harvest, but also very popular in an *irau,* is the dance between the rice-pounding poles. These beautifully shaped lengths of wood are made by the men, used by the women, for pounding the unhusked padi rice in the double-holed mortars which line the back of the verandah in the long-house and dehusking their own pattern of salivary music as the women work at preparing the rice polished for cooking, before dusk. Two persons, of either sex, hold each in either hand one end of such a pole. The poles are brought together and apart again a few inches off the ground, to make a loud, sharp, smart cracking sound. The dancer waits his moment and leaps nimbly (he or she hopes) between the poles as they open; leaps swiftly out again, before they close upon an ankle painfully. One foot should be used; the polished performer jumps in on right ankle, turns and goes out on left, turns and comes back again on left, out again on right—and continuing thus as long as he or she can survive. That won't be long, because Bario variety is the antidote to regularity. The two handlers will get faster and faster and faster, cracking, clicking, opening, shutting, to match the quickest effort of anyone. Then, the dancer sideways falls, or shouts and bumps off or jumps at one of the handlers, screaming with laughter. And the next person takes a turn. . . .

In the hubbub it takes an experienced ear to detect or distinguish music and song and frolic, which may break out anywhere, in any style. At one fireplace, a group of people are singing an old head song. At another, Tayun is stamping a sword dance, dressed in feather cloak and leopard hat, twirling a goat's hair shield and handsome, spiral-cut sword-handle, for the edification of a small group of newcomer girls. Further along, Lu'un Ribu is telling a funny story to kids and grown-ups alike. At one end of the verandah, visitors from Pa Mada and Pa Dali are engaged in exhaustive tests of strength—elbow-bending, standing throws, weight lifting, bear hugs—with some of the Bario quality. At the other end someone, unidentifiable in the smoke, steam and scrum, is playing a high, wailing dirge on bag-pipes made from six bamboos blown into a gourd. Gongs are beaten with roots, floor boards with dancing feet, shields with dancing swords, the strings of three plucked mandolins by the right hands of three boys from Pa Main playing in harmony. Some hostess—overworked, underslept, bag-eyed—may even for once beat her small boy's behind, sacrosanct in better times.

Sleep is there for those that want it. Lifetimes of training ensure that the tired can lie in any corner—or up in the ceiling—and sleep in peace. It is highly improbable that they will be left in peace, however. It is one of the jobs of young hostesses to keep on bidding guests to the feast. As the feast has more than one centre inside the house and new food and drink are insistently being brought forward, there is a lively contest among hostesses, each wishing to have as nearly as possible everyone—and especially 'everyone that counts'—at her piece of feast. People of good family have little hope of long rest. Why worry? This is not what you came to Bario for. On the way home, the day after tomorrow, once you have managed to get across the sunlit plain, there is plenty of sleep to be had beside the trail in the jungle shade; never mind mosquitoes, leeches, sandflies, serpents, ticks.

*   *   *

Before the *irau* guests do finally depart, two things must be done. First of course is to fulfill whatever the task set for this *irau* is. The other, and (in its way) separate climax of the affair is the sacrifice of one or more of the largest beasts in the feast, which must be done out of doors, ceremonially.

The task was set for the *irau* night (as we know) by the erection of almost any kind of monument in stone or its equivalent in a range of alternatives from a ditch cut across the path up into the Tamabos, a channel through the bend of a river, an irrigation project extended upon a plain, or a spectacular cut through the trees on the crest of some dominating ridge. Ordinarily, the affair is probably celebrated by the erection of a single large sandstone block, not shaped in any way, but carried by many men, slung on poles—maybe for two or three miles from the place where it had been discovered, pinpointed and reserved for just this occasion. If something really special is required, three stones can be erected as feet, upon which a much larger one is balanced, either a flat slab forming a table or—but these are very rare—an enormous round stone placed to make a spectacular dolmen. More difficult still, and seldom done within memory, memorializing by carving in relief or by pitting on the surface of a large rock in its natural position. The latest of these, a few years since, was made for the late father of Rajah Omong (otherwise known as Penghulu Miri), the senior family of the southern Kelabits. This was carved by Anyi (who then lived in Pa Bengar and now in Bario), with the aid of several other people over a long period, to represent a buffalo and some more subtle symbols.

Whatever the nature of the monument, only the virile male guests will participate, under the direction of one or two members of the family directly concerned. The peak occasion, from the point of view of everyone present, is the ceremonial killing of the largest possible buffalo.

This peak of an *irau* is conducted outdoors, close to the long-house, in a setting of seats, carved logs, finely decorated with frills and loops and spirals, forming a kind of amphitheatre around the point of the kill.

The buffalo is thoroughly secured to a post, the top of which is carved into a spear shape. Upon this 'spear', a quite valuable jar may be placed, and left there as a second perpetuation of the occasion. In this sort of thing, much depends on the richness and the desire for display by those making the *irau* on the occasion. Similarly, if they are big people, really 'good' and wanting to be even better, they may line up many other beasts kept to this end of the feast. There are always shifting tendencies of this kind. At the moment, the big families are competing heavily with each other in killing more and more very large, specially fattened, castrated boars. Tama Bulan of P'Umur last year killed ten of these, putting him well ahead—for the moment.

With all the usual reluctances and demurs, as the crowd is gradually gathered in the prepared arena, four to six big jars, good ones, of borak are brought out into the centre. For this everyone except those engaged in essential cooking and other works within, must come out and participate. When all are assembled, with a deal of fuss—fierce attacks to drag deep sleepers and dissatisfied creditors—the chief person making the *irau* summons someone of equal status from another long-house to spear the buffalo sacrificially. This is, as ever, something more than the spiritual consummation of *irau*. It expresses the commercial and competitive character. The man who has been made to perform the final sacrifice is usually one who is behind in his own death feast affairs. By distinguishing him in this marked manner, the host is pointing the same spear at him: that he shall make *irau* and reverse the compliment. Or else he himself is catching up!

That evening is the last—maybe the fourth or fifth—of the party's life. Traditionally it is the big night for the older folks. They are showing the strain less than the young, by now. Years of experience and late nights of lesser indulgence count.

This is the night when the fully-grown and the outblown play the rice game. Set off by Lawai, boasting channels into remembered sex. The triumphs of premarital forays are raked out and put on the mat afresh. Each in his or her turn, according to boast, declaring in loud voice every adolescent achievement, at the same time kneading a little pyramid of wet dregs from the bottom of a used jar of borak. As the pyramids increase in faintly arranged lines of ten, comment, laughter, criticism, encouragement and rebuttal gather into gales of highest amusement. Lun Aran has got to 27 when he declares:

'This one is Dayang Agong.'

Dayang Agong, newly a grandmother, vigorously rejects the suggestion. She shouts, sing song, that she never had him, refused all his
importunings and go-betweens. Vivid argument uproars. All take
sides. But Lun Aran, after a barrage of bawdy abuse and reply, carries
on to 46. When he's just about reached the bottom of the barrel, he
scrapes out a nomadic Punan girl he once had while out hunting. He
doesn't remember her name. This provokes some scathing comment:
'To go so low as a nomad, even less than a slave.' 'You can't count that,
damn it all.'

He rests, then, at 46. The next fellow tries for 47, fails. The wife goes:
20 only; weak memory? But presently 46 is exceeded. Everything
always will be, can one somehow be sure. 62? And what more?

The last token gifts are over and distributed, last debts incurred (or
rejected). After dawn, the *irau* is over. Going home is not going to be
nearly so much fun. Never mind; sleep on the way, bathe in the Libbun,
muse that headache, sing as you go, take one last one for the path! . . .
for the path that is winding over the Tamabos or across the now
muddied, angle-deep plain, where, for the moment, only a smart
Pied Harrier, floating along alert for a rat, gives vigour beyond the buzz
in poor Bario's overhung brain—while, as it ricochets the thinking,
there comes a roaring from the world without, four vast engines
ranging far over Mount Murud.

II

STARTING EX 'Z'

'The vulture passed, a shadow on the fire,
And the dark hills were loud with dreadful cries.'

G. K. Chesterton (*The Curse*).

'What have we here?' I asked, inspecting the tray.

'Kippered herrings, sir.'

'And I shouldn't wonder,' I said, for I was in thoughtful mood, 'if even herrings haven't troubles of their own.'

'Quite possibly, sir.'

'I mean, apart from getting kippered.'

'Yes, sir.'

'And so it goes on, Jeeves, so it goes on.'

P. G. Wodehouse (*Very Good, Jeeves*).

'Thou whoreson, zed! thou unnecessary letter!'

Shakespeare (*King Lear*).

STARTING EX 'Z' SPECIAL

1932-44 . . . Melbourne to Manila (via Mass-Observation)

A CLEAN white mist lay placid, a great blanket of cotton wool, stretching from Mount Murud away fifty miles to the south, eiderdown. Through a few stray gaps in this gently inviting cover, patches of almost black green could sometimes, for a few moments, be seen; and just at one place, pinpoints of lighter green blending to yellow, from the big plane roaring at ten thousand feet.

No one in the plane could possibly have known, on their own, that there was really a plain below. One plain, a hole in the dark tall jungle, inviting human bodies to come on down in comfort and ease. Even less was there the faintest suspicion of human life. Instead, thousands of white fluffy cloudlets left range after range of mountains, handsome, rigid and coldly unpromising, so that the heart of Borneo beat in a myriad capillaries—or an archipelago of island peaks set in a silent and sunless sea of white.

The sun began to throw its first pale platinum shafts into a somehow impossibly remote dawn.

The plane circled, seeking a brighter, paler gap insofar as the daring —and dead before dusk for that quality—pilot could manoeuvre the big four-engined bomber with any sense of safety alongside the toothed Tamabo cliffs on one side and on the other the border ranges, a few cloud puffs away.

Nothing could properly be said to be visible to the standard of dropping routine. But this was the third dropping sortie, the thirty-second hour of flying over Japanese-held territory, in my final effort to get in. If it was ever to be done, this must surely be it. For worse or for better, after two circling searches, four bodies shot through the Liberator's camera hatch in quick succession and joined their gently falling parachutes to the general pattern of downy blobs drifting with softness over the Plain of Bah.

In a few minutes these had fallen through the cloud and materialized upon the Kelabit earth, as the bodies of three Australians and an Englishman. I was the Englishman, with the doubtful privilege of being the first white man to touch down and thus to return after the years of Japanese occupation.

This first renewal of western impact was achieved—as in all my previous and subsequent para-activities—by my backside. All four of us, in fact, landed with splendid squelches at the edge of the plain, in swamp. In so doing, we were about to upset—to an extent which, if any of us had thought of it, we should have put aside under these circumstances of war—one of the last places in the world where life was still lived relatively unaffected by and fundamentally independent of, industrial, mechanized or moneyed civilization. But at this wet moment (the wet unexpectedly cold), not even in contact with each other, sploshing about in swamp and mist, the questions sounded as simple as this:

   (i) Was this hole in the jungle the only one in the interior; and was it sufficiently good landing ground to build up as a base?

   (ii) Had we landed anywhere near where we intended anyway?

   (iii) Were there people living anywhere near enough for us to find them in time to survive?

   (iv) If so, would they help us—or take our heads instead?

   (v) Where were the Japs?

My own view, grown since I had started working on the problem nearly a year before, was that we should not lose our heads; and that far the best way of beginning intelligence and guerrilla operations prior to organized landings in Borneo, would be to work from the far interior *outwards*, from heart to skin. I had continued to hold (and push) these views under opposition from both colleagues and seniors. As there was virtually no existing intelligence from the area (and what little we were given in advance proved dangerously wrong), I had to go on three lines of study and thought: first, a feeling about these sort of so-called 'primitive' people and their basic attitudes largely based on elsewhere; second, research into the literature available in Australia, during delightful weeks in a private room in the admirable Melbourne Public Library; third, previous flights over and sights of the interior, starting as soon as aircraft were available to reach that far out from Pacific bases, but before it was practicable to fly in, circle, and drop men and supplies with precision and persistence.

Evidence of this character is inevitably open to argument and alternative interpretation. My case was in no way assisted by a reputation for strong self-opinionation and a general reluctance to concede to opposition.

Now, above the knees in foul mud, surrounded by tussocks of rushes higher than I—and somewhere amongst which I blasphemously hoped that Sergeant Sanderson, Staff Sergeant Bower and Sergeant Barry were equally floundering (keeping silence in accordance with our only too apparently misplaced but rigorously indoctrinated landing drill) ... now, unless all continued not to go according to plan, was the time when this tripartite thesis should be experimentally tested. If we did not contact Darwin, Australia, by radio—where on God's earth had that storepedo dropped to?—in forty-eight hours, other theories could come into their patient owns. It was nearly as simple as that.

*　*　*

I had first seen a fleeting glimmer of the Plain of Bah towards the end of 1944. At this stage in the Pacific war, General MacArthur's policy was to make a bold series of jumps, starting from New Guinea, to en-arc Japan from south and east. It was not until the Americans had a fully established air-base in the Halmaheras that there was any possibility of flying over Borneo at all. Alternative—and in some ways better situated—bases for the same purpose became available after the next big hop into the Southern Philippines. On this, the first air drop into Borneo, we had in fact flown from the Philippines, after two hideously boring and disheartening attempts starting in the Halmaheras and requiring, each time, thirteen hours to and fro over antagonistic land or unsympathetic ocean.

Our difficulty was to find a way into the tormented land mass. The maps at that time were grossly inadequate—for instance, repeating Mount Murud twice with different spellings twenty miles apart. Most of the interior map was blank; and we did not then realize that by taking off at midnight in order to get over the land at first light, we were making it as difficult as possible for ourselves. The day's cloud routine is absolute in the interior. The unvarying saturation of humidity means that every night, as the temperature falls, the mist gathers into cloud. It takes at least two hours of direct sunlight, ordinarily, to raise this cloud out of the valley bottoms. And it takes a good half-hour for the sun to be high enough, after the dawn, to get into the deep valleys. The time to aim for is three hours after dawn; but not much later, or a new and more dangerous set of clouds will be building up in billowing banks of cumulus thousands of feet about the mountain tops. We were working, at first, in complete ignorance of conditions which had not been at all studied, because they had not previously concerned anybody from the world outside.

Had we known as much then as we did by the time of Hiroshima, the point of view of mere parachutists might well have been outweighed by the greater anxieties of air forces. The air crews were concerned with getting back as well as with getting us there; and there was still enough kick in the Japs to try and prevent them, especially if they both came in and went out during full day.

General MacArthur had two other ideas about the Pacific war which affected us. One was that he should return to Manila in triumph; the other that he should personally receive Japan's surrender. He was motivated, on an immense and constructive scale, by much the same sort of drive to reverse past events and more than restore his own ego, as was the heart and head in this vastly lesser body which bumped so soundly into the swamp. The effect of the General's dynamic urges was seldom helpful to the non-American elements in the Far East war. The Americans were not really interested in anything off their main line of leaping advance. Borneo was out of their big picture, matter for the British and the Dutch. The Dutch had not done (and in the event proved that they never determined to do) much—which is one crude reason why, in Borneo anyway, there now are no Dutch. For the British, Borneo presented particular difficulties, complex priorities.

Admiral Lord Mountbatten's command operated from thousands of miles to the west and fell short of Borneo. It was still bogged down in Burma. During 1944, cloak-and-dagger links had been established with Freddie Spencer Chapman and others, who had hung on or been put into Malaya, with Force 136. But Borneo, another great overlap east, was out of range for any western-based proposition; and by this stage in the war, tip and run sabotage was ceasing to work out as worth while. Established set-ups, watching posts, embryo re-occupation groups were becoming the need—as the ultimate defeat of the Japs grew certain and closer.

Borneo therefore fell, or rather wavered, somewhere between two stools. It was too far for Mountbatten; it was near enough to Mac-

Arthur for him to keep control over it, without wanting to do much about it directly. In the end, it thus fell to the Australians, under American High Command, to deal with the matter. By now, they were quite used to doing the dirtiest work and the oddest jobs. But Australian Field-Marshal Blamey had at all times to conform with MacArthur's over-all plans. In these, Borneo was given a lowish priority. (See Map A.)

This over-simplified summary does, nevertheless, substantially set the position in which those interested in a (European) return to Borneo and the *positive* throwout of the Japanese—rather than ignominious after-victory return to old *status quo*—found themselves in 1944. It seemed, to the British, of importance to come back fighting as soon as possible everywhere where they had previously been respected in the east. This view, sent down from War Cabinet level, was fully justified by events. But how, for British Borneo—as one of those places of concern—to set about it? In particular, how to set about it for the most distant and the most tricky of the three British territories, Sarawak, at the north-west corner of the island.

Sarawak, biggest territory of the three, presented unique problems in Asia. Foremost of these problems was the status of the independent white Rajah Brookes, the centenary of whose extraordinary rule had been celebrated only two years before the Japanese arrived to intern or to murder every senior Brooke officer who stayed at his post (as directed). Sarawak was thought to be particularly delicate ground; here the problem was not simply to get back; but also who or what to *put* back.

While these high matters were pursued, usually wisely, but sometimes (mainly at the middle levels of interpretation) with staggering stupidity, it was left to a small unit, largely officered by Englishmen, to consider and implement such action as might usefully be taken in Sarawak and other surrounding territories on the borderlands between MacArthur disinterest and Mountbatten's intelligence.

* * *

There were several units responsible for what are nowadays known as cloak-and-dagger works in this theatre. True to the mood of the business, the secrecy they valued above all other was among themselves. Each unit appeared more concerned with preventing its 'operatives' from knowing about or being in contact with any other unit, than anything else. It was heinous sin to be found in possession of knowledge of or contact with a closely related body operating in parallel with you —or, often, in conflict. One of the ultimate effects of this was that units with the best salesmanship, warmanship and political savvy tended to get the plum jobs, on a system of competitive tendering which sometimes staked claims, took risks and even made statements of fact for which there was little (or no) substance behind the cloak. A further and perhaps more important effect—for the lives of volunteers sacrificed to a group loyalty or colonel's ambition can hardly be counted in these war years—was that a lot of things which should have been done never got done properly; through lack of liaison, because no one unit was fully equipped to do it, and because (with very few exceptions) no two units were ever allowed to work together.

This arrangement was to trouble me long before the moment of squelching into Borneo. And even then, in my pack, when I emplaned for the operation, I had very stupidly carried a paper with a special code devised between myself and another unit (British of course—even I would not have dared *know* about the American and Dutch) which held in its bondage some Brooke officers who had been on leave or escaped from Sarawak, and were now available. An elaborate system had been worked out by which they should intercept any messages I could send through a common link which at this time, curiously enough, took radio for both units—though, of course, in separate codes. At the last minute before take-off we were ignominiously searched; stripped even of signet rings (as well as the ordinary identifications). This amateurish enterprise of mine was therefore detected. Fortunately for me, not until I was half-way to Borneo, already, where no court martial on earth could now hook me out to answer the awful charge of a double-loyalty. But though not much harm was done, it did mean that both organizations increased every precaution. So none of these available Brooke or other government officers took any active part. People like myself were presently left to re-establish administration, over vast territories, absolutely without experienced advice, let alone experience.

As regards our own unit, taken on its own merits, we operatives could have little cause for complaint. We were fortunate in having at its head an Englishman whose appearance of indolence, even foppishness, helped to deceive both Australians and Americans into thinking that there was not likely to be a great deal of trouble if they passed jobs (or bucks) to him. Tall, cool, handsome, Colonel John Chapman-Walker, in peace a Conservative politician and Bond Street solicitor, was not exactly a lovable man from below. But until he was finally side-tracked out of our command—a fate which commonly befell the heads of cloak-and-dagger units in this theatre, once they appeared to be firmly established—he did handsomely in pushing, with great skill, the peculiar spear-head of 'Z's' interests forward; it was he who eventually put 'Z' at the top of its class, the dagger pack.★

For 'Z' we were, and proudly. I am, alas, unable here to pay tribute to the genius who thought of cloaking this dagger with such a staggeringly simple *nom de plume*. To make sure that the mystery should not be missed, the word 'Special' was added. Members of our gang moved about Australia and the Pacific bearing, therefore, the charming imprint:

'Z' SPECIAL UNIT

I once got off the train from Melbourne at Sydney's thronged station. The Provost Sergeant at the barrier checked my papers; the gay uniform of a Green Howard with a commando beret (my dash) and paratroop badge (just to make sure no one noticed Major Secret Agent) was then unusual in that part of the world. With a good Queensland bellow, he roared at the surrounding troops:

'God Almighty, here's a pommy officer from that overpaid bunch of "Z" Special bastards. Make for the boozer, all of you. *He* can stand it.'

In a more retiring mood we were also called 'SRD'. Here security was effective indeed, because no one ever told us what it meant. It was mildly argued, wherever we were, if we were Special Research Department, Special Reconnaissance Detachment or Services Reconnaissance Detail? Whatever the answer, it was the 'Z' which buzzed for us. To be a 'Z' specialist was something to be proud about. We were the last letter in the army alphabet, a corps elite.

The prohibition on knowing about other units extended to knowing

★ John Chapman-Walker, who in later years became a close friend, died untimely in 1958. Obituary notices are in *The Times* of March 3 and 4, 1958.

about other sub-units within our own, all of which—though necessary —made for a lot of confusion, especially if an officer was trying to generalize or to inveigh. These arrangements further led at times to contradictory duplication or delay. All the same, it can fairly be said that 'Z' Special was one of the toughest, quickest, most intelligent and least red-taped of any, in any field of allied activity, in the war. That at least is my considered opinion, having been—by then—with widely different civil, military, naval and air outfits; and having studied many more.

But whatever the drive and efficiency which came down from John Chapman-Walker (who had direct access to Field-Marshal Blamey) little could get round the handicap of working under the Americans and not being American. This was accentuated, in the case of a few of us, by the inevitable lack of Australians who knew anything about Asia—which has only become of much interest to Australia very recently. It was impossible to find Australian officers to act in senior roles—planning, intelligence or operational—where Sarawak and British Borneo generally were concerned. Pommies thus had to demand facilities from Australian command; and the sort of facilities we needed were difficult ones, like submarines, long range seaplanes and secret radio bases. Pommies had to be in command of Australians in the field on this type of 'subversive operation'. The delicacy of this situation— with a nation which has a high idea of its own he-manism and often a profound belief in the feebleness of the English—needs no emphasis.

In the early stages our concern was relatively simple, some of these issues did not arise. Australians, British and Dutch alike were faced at all times with the American domination, necessary, inevitable, but sometimes humiliating. With our particular Borneo operation, remote both in place and at this stage in apparent practicability, American dis-interest (bordering on dislike for what seemed to them likely to be wasteful) was acute. For me, trying to devise and draw others with me, the greatest difficulty at first was the mere physical feat of keeping head above water in the wake of MacArthur's supermarine roller-coaster.

No one high up in the American command was interested in deviating anything further west, unless it was to bomb concentrations of Japanese shipping. It was important for the Americans to concentrate every thought on the great undertakings which still lay ahead. It was, from their own point of view, short term, sound psychology to think of nothing else. This did not mean that they sought to stop others thinking otherwise. But the frame of mind was so instilled into every rank, that even when a general said you could have a lieutenant, you somehow never got the lieutenant. Getting the lieutenant became, for the tiny major that was then me, the all-absorbing concern, the equivalent personal return.

It is too painful, and also uninteresting, to recall now the aching months spent trying to probe a physical way into Borneo from without. For the first point on which to satisfy the senior 'Z' specialists (and the Higher Command for whom they strong-armed) was clearly: to demonstrate that there *were* places in the interior of Borneo which could be used satisfactorily for parachuting operations. If this could be demonstrated, the other and bigger questions of policy, strategy and security would then be worth examining closely. Otherwise, the whole thing was off before it could get properly on.

It should be realized that at this time there was very little know-how in any army or air force, about dropping into equatorial jungle in this theatre of war. There had been individual experiments (generally unintentional) in jungle dropping, most of them disastrous. But the war, so far, had only reached into countries where there were open spaces, grassland and scrub; and where map and advance intelligence information made pin-pointing for return, contact and dropping a reasonable proposition in planning. Borneo presents the largest area of virgin jungle and rain forest anywhere outside South America. The island— and particularly the British parts of it to the north and west—is sparsely populated by eastern standards. Away from the immediate coastline, the only clearings (which show as light patches from the air) are the result of the shifting system of rice cultivation practised by everyone, except the then barely known upland Kelabits. These open places are really a mass of tree stumps and tree trunks only partially felled and burnt out of jungle in the annual shift of slash and burn rice agriculture. Deceptively beckoning from the air, under that pleasant green lies every sort of snare and spear for the body falling from air. That at least was the theory to which everyone then subscribed. The first thing, therefore, was to find at least one permanent inland clearing safe to land on, safe to drop bodies and stores on, if possible to be made into an airfield later on, and above all a natural part of the landscape—any special close felling and clearing would inevitably be noticed by Japanese aircraft and intelligence.

I held the same view as everyone else in this matter. We were all wrong; at least we were too fussy and finicky, too impressed by that drab word 'jungle', too timid of dangers which still can always defeat.

All the same, it was commonsense to start at the beginning and reduce the initial difficulties to a plain minimum. Here the general line of argument continued: that the whole of the interior was impracticable for parachuting—therefore a parachute operation in the interior was impracticable. It was simply up to me to show if this were not so: to get somehow over Borneo and bring back evidence, photographic if possible, that there was at least one worthwhile Dropping Zone up there inside. Thus, over these aching months, I tagged along in the sweating trail of every smile from any MacArthur lieutenant. This trail led into many strange corners of war, from the Solomon Islands and New Guinea, through the Admiralties, Hollandia, Morotai in Halmahera to Mindoro, Mindanao, and eventually (on the rebound) to Manila itself, smoking in shambled destruction.

I need only remember the steaming days when I socially climbed the great hill at Hollandia, in the north of Dutch New Guinea. The Americans had done one of their seemingly incredible jobs at Hollandia, which for a time was MacArthur's main base in his vast project. A whole mountainside had been moved out of millenial jungle, into a gently graded hill of grassland, a monstrous Bario carrying thousands of men and a hundred women in every conceivable aspect of house from long to Long Island. On the pinnacle of this bewildering peak sat the moderate palace of General MacArthur. Below this, the mountainside was contoured with sweeping radius. Below MacArthur came lieutenant- and major-generals, then brigadiers and colonels, finally on into the bottom of the valley was a camp of Australians. At suitable intervals downwards, were messes, PX shopping centres, and the other facilities of different grades. Out in the valley a great aerodrome. Beyond this the wide pale lake upon which black woolly-haired Papuans fished on in their dug-out canoes. I worked—or more exactly wormed—my way up this mountain of human achievement, from the good Australian base into the lower skyline of colonels and brigadiers. The price of this achievement was to grow calmly accustomed to having my gold buttons and shoulder badges roughly but warmly recognized thus: 'Gee, a British officer! I didn't know you guys were in this thing.'

For MacArthur's worry was another worry altogether. The only way to get even a sneak-hold in it was to subscribe. One great advantage was to be the only British officer thereabouts at the time. Another was the possession of a kitbag full of Smith and Webley revolvers. You could buy your way up into almost anything American in the Pacific, then, with an honest-to-goodness revolver, six chambers going round. The Yanks had chambered automatics; but of course they were all, in this tropical context, exaggeratedly pioneers, waggoners and cowboys at heart. A pukka *revolver* does something to a full blooded American boy.

To cut a long climb short, in this and other devious ways, Squadron-Leader Cook (RAAF) and I at long last—and with the patience of our superiors almost exhausted—found a plane which would take us over Borneo for the first time. The misfortunes of others gives a chance, in war. American naval planes had been bombing Japanese shipping concentrations off Labuan Island which lies north of the Borneo mainland; any such shipping always felt like a flanking threat to the Americans, naturally enough. Many of these planes had been lost—and presently we were to reap some of their human harvest. Immediately, a Liberator of the United States Navy Search was going out to look for one of their planes which had failed to return the previous day. At maximum invisibility, we won a permission to use some of the plane's search time and fly back across the middle of Borneo, instead of direct to Halmahera base. It was, further, most fortunate that this was the crew's last flight in their operational tour. The eight lads were excited, speaking wildly careless if feeling specially cautious. Tomorrow they'd be heading for leave States-side; today was a kind of throw-away—and they did us proud with it indeed.

★   ★   ★

To fly *into* Borneo is always difficult, and was more so in 1944, when we knew so little of the ground and of the climate. On this first flight, lying head down in the bomb aimer's glass bay forward, the strain of both excitement and concentration threatened to explode this precarious blister. Beneath the four zooming propellers and the plane's shining silver cigar, for three hours we bored west across the lingering fringes of the Pacific Ocean and into the South China Sea.

From the American base on Morotai, the northernmost of the Halmaheras—still infested with Japs, suicide troops crawling into American mess tents to explode artillery shells—we flew nearly a thousand miles northwest, through the scattered Sulu Archipelago, the tail of the Philippines, to the north tip of Borneo. This is one of the marvellous landfalls anywhere. From far far away you see, standing out in its own unique kind of majesty the overwhelming pinnacles of Mount Kinabalu, highest mountain in South-East Asia. Kinabalu has long been accurately calculated at 13,454 feet. However often you see it, it is hardly possible to believe that it is not a lot more. The magnificent assemblage of separate peaks rises from about two miles of sheer black granite. The top two thousand feet is pure bare rock, scooped and twisted into weird fingers, grotesque pinnacles and deep crests which stand tormented, each separate and yet all intertwined, to consummate the huge mass of the mountain below. To the south and west the mountain rises in a stupendous series of slopes, clothed in dense, perpetual green vegetation. To the east and north, some of the highest sheer cliffs in the world carved straight up into the crowning peaks.

Rising straight out of the lowlands and not from a slow build-up of foothills, the effect on the eye is to magnify. This, with the utterly barren rock and the peaks never touched by plant (or snow) is to subject, through the eye, the whole mind to a bombardment of strangeness. My feelings about this wonderful mountain have not been diluted in the thousands of times I have seen and the hundreds of hours I have climbed on Kinabalu, since that morning from the American Naval Search plane's nose. It was a shattering introduction to Borneo under the Japanese.

Kinabalu—the name is variously interpreted, but I like best 'The Black Widow'—made American air-navigation comparatively easy insofar as Borneo concerned them. It impressed the American pilots immensely also. So much so, that before long they had convinced themselves that the pre-war survey height could not be right. The crew-cut, blond lieutenant piloting us put it like this:

'Say, that goddam thing cannot be *thirteen* thousand. Why, that's nothing. It must be near as high as Mount Everest. These Borneo maps are all to hell anyway.'

Sure enough, by the end of the year *all* maps used in this theatre promoted Kinabalu, with a large black over-stamp, elevating the highest pinnacle to 19,000 feet. This soothed all inferiority feelings—though increasing the consumption of oxygen among pilots flying above a theoretical fifteen thousand and mechanics correcting altimeters obviously registering too low.

From Kinabalu the Liberator turned southwest, so that dawn came on to glitter-wings shadowed by the dark monstrous rock and softly creeping, weeping, cloudy mist around the summit of the Black Widow. From here on, well in among Japanese fighter range, our job was to search for yesterday's bomber which had not returned.

The sun came up and the South China Sea grew a slow blue, where it washed with long white combers spraying far below on to the exquisite coral islands which line the west coast from Kudat down to Jesselton and over the wide Bay of Brunei to the bigger island of Labuan. We kept away from that, the main Jap naval and air base, and the only serious concern remaining to the Americans on their western flank, thus far. It seemed likely (from signals) that the bomber had come down along a line directly east of Brunei Bay. We searched wide and daringly low that day without finding it.

As we searched behind Brunei Bay we were passing close (or a week's travel on the ground) to precisely where I wanted to go. At this limit of flying, with the plane carrying no bomb or other load, we could spend up to an hour over Borneo, before being compelled to make back for Morotai base. When the pilot and navigator had satisfied themselves that they were not going to find anything (one never did by this method), they handed over to me. From now I steered the plane. Already from the coast, with Kinabalu almost out of sight to the north, another, much smaller but in a way even more startling landmark had come into my view. Two white pinnacles, close together and joined by a saddle, which I could not then identify on any map but which became our landmark into the interior on all subsequent flights. We provisionally named this magnificent double peak about six thousand feet, but standing out on its own in the interior jungle, Mount 200, for the flight number of the special wing in the Royal Australian Air Force soon to be formed to carry 'Z' Special's droppings. Its proper name had to be learnt on the ground: Batu Lawi, its pinnacles the male and female symbols of all upland people (whose very existence the couple traditionally saved by defeating the mountain of fire, Batu Apoi, all aflame to consume them).

From the twin pinnacles we aimed a little south of east and then ran slap across the island. Looked at from this angle, going at this speed, the chaos and illogic of the ground seemed insoluble. Nothing agreed with the available maps. Everything seemed to be peak, cliff, landslide, river torrent, unmitigated rain forest jungle. From this blasted blister all Borneo looked like a dying lump of coral, overgrown with fungus; and when we went lower, the unyielding forest canopy, tree-top touching tree-top, leaving no trace of ground beneath, was as featureless and far less friendly than an old bath sponge. Each two hundred foot tree elbowed each other, a million, billion, trillion green pimples without one tiny trace of individual touch. Everywhere, the mountains alongside and the gorges below were fierce and splendid; but these offered no promise for us. Yet in among it all we did rather uncertainly see patches of paler and brighter colour and what looked like small ponds, a few minutes' flying south-east of those twin white pinnacles. And again, after crossing an impressive double range east again, suddenly several miles of open grassland in a very deep, steep mountain valley.

My colleague, the RAAF Squadron-Leader, doing the photography, could not succeed in getting anything very clear until this grassland valley. By now the pilot was growing nervous, lest we abuse our fuel reserve. By now I was beginning to understand and get something of the feel of this at first bewildering, depressing and superficially inhuman terrain. We just had to turn back, though. Tantalized at the edge of precision, we nevertheless had won a single negative which showed square miles of ground without a single tree or tree stump. This fitted into nothing I or anybody else had expected, read about, hoped for or guessed at. There was simply no record, map indication or other trace of such a place existing. We erroneously concluded that this was in 'the Kelabit country', the uplands of Sarawak on the border of Dutch Borneo. We were quite wrong, as it turned out. But fortunately, before we decided to drop there, we learnt better—and it was left to me to satisfy my curiosity about this extraordinary (and, in Borneo, unique) landscape by descending upon it from another plane, very much the worse for wear, later on (after the war) on my thirty-fourth birthday. The great thing was that, for the moment, we had got one proof of *a place* where it would be reasonably safe from the physical point of view to drop people; and reasonably practicable for planes to return to the same DZ and find a drop there again and again, if and as initial operations succeeded and could be built up.

The negative established our very first positive. It was no longer possible to say that we could not find a way into the middle of Borneo. We had sought for a hole in the jungle and found a gaping wound. Had we in fact used that one, at that time, this book would not have begun. It was much too far out of the central heart, the ground only grass because of complete erosion and poverty, the population a pitiful relic of past greater years in that great river, the Bahau branch of the Batang Kayan which reaches the sea opposite the Tarakan oilfields.

Happily, however, encouraged by this initial positive, the project now gained more prestige and somewhat higher priority. This meant that I was able, not long after, to make a second flight. This time, by good luck, the early morning cloud was much thinner than usual and I was able to see—though not on this occasion to photograph—several large clear places, *flat* (unlike the Navy Search find) and clearly under extensive cultivation. It was into that flat (nearest our Mount 200) that we were first dropped through the dark morning cloud. And this was the Plain of Bah.

*　　*　　*

The Navy Search Liberator boomed back over the active volcano of Halmahera, to Morotai. The crew cascaded on to the tarmac, laughing, singing, bunny-hugging each other and us. Sad as it was to fail to find their missing friends, this was the end of the tour for them. For me it was near the beginning. For both parties, cause for celebration. I just do not remember how Cook and I got back through New Guinea and Queensland to the Commercial Travellers' skyscraper in Melbourne (where I was living, sporadical and high).

The results, so far, were pleasing. It had been pleasing too (as we flew towards our grassland find), to see, way out on the right, formations which I actually recognized from twelve years before: another and quieter twin peak with saddle, Mount Kalulong; a long, flat-topped range, Mount Dulit; the tortuous gleaming River Baram, with its big tributary, the Tinjar, which I particularly knew. This way was too accessible from the coast, and too rough of itself, for our supposed dropping needs; it was not considered of significance in our early plans. Plenty was known about it, including that the rice crops were often inadequate and the people intensely superstitious—factors which counted in any plan involving large scale local support. But these people came into the bigger picture and part of my own argument— that we should be well received, if not better than that; certainly not betrayed or beheaded—based on knowledge gained during six months on and about Mount Dulit and the Tinjar, winding brown round its sandstone feet.

In 1932 I organized and part-led an Oxford University Expedition to Mount Dulit on the Tinjar. This was the first expedition on a large scale which the Rajah Brookes had allowed into the country during many years. It was one of a series of Oxford Expeditions, of which I took an active part in three (though I went to Cambridge, Pembroke College).

I spent my twenty-first birthday studying birds on top of Mount Dulit. As I described it in an address to the Royal Geographical Society (Evening Meeting of June 12, 1933):

'The high camp (at 4,000 feet) was placed at the cliff edge in a small clearing made for the purpose. The view from this site at certain times in the morning and evening was beyond description—you could see for more than 100 miles across the whole of Northern Sarawak and miles and miles of very little known country to the perfect mass of Mulu, the double-peaked Kalulong, to the Kalabit country, the Hose mountains, the dome of Batu Song, and on perfect days even to the extraordinary knife-edge of Batu Lawi—all standing as islands in a sea of white cloud.'

I did not then suppose that before I had doubled my age I should have made Batu Lawi a friend and—in a small way—memorial, to the faults of war; let alone lived with and loved some whom I then called 'Kalabit'. These highlands were divided from Dulit by uncounted ranges and rivers, weeks of harsh trekking apart. But from the cloud-lands of Dulit's moss forest and montane avifauna I looked long and often across this imposing barrier to that 'Kalabit country', of which the lowland people of the Tinjar spoke as of a lost tribe, another world—fabled for its big men, sexy women, cold nights, rich harvests, irrigation, inaccessibility, cattle and goats. No one from the Tinjar had then been there; but everyone talked of the high, rich land where other plants and animals thrived and beyond whom again lay men said to be tailed.

The scientific results of that Oxford Expedition by now total fifty odd original papers and theses. More quickly, something appeared by the local leader, appointed by the Rajah to collaborate with me. He was Mr E. Banks, Curator of the Sarawak Museum, a man with a great knowledge of and love for Sarawak, who shared with all Brooke officers (and the whole Brooke set-up) an immediate suspicion of outsiders, especially those coming into the country for a short time and no doubt going away to cash in—exactly as we did.

Mr Banks and I, from the moment we met on the messy Kuching wharf, did not see eye to eye. His eyes are brightly grey and mine a dreary shade of goat: the wonder is that all four were not regularly black, the way we went on. It must have been intolerable to him to have to work in his own country alongside a highly egocentric undergraduate, in approximate charge of more. The arrangement was absurd in the first place; it could not work nicely. But under Mr Banks —as I think (without malice), after all these years, while I sit in a much improved version of the chair he once occupied in Sarawak—made the worst of a bad job, from the start. Among other things, he perpetuated his abiding anger in the Annual Report of the Sarawak Museum for 1932; he wrote:

'Members of the Expedition included Graduates and Undergraduates of Oxford and Cambridge *as well as outsiders,* their ages ranging apparently from about eighteen to twenty-four, and it cannot be considered a good thing to have chosen, even for the sake of gaining experience, the entire party of young men; inevitably their inexperience left on those who did not appreciate this an impression unfavourable to the Members themselves and to their Club and University, a proportion of older experienced people being necessary to any Expedition depending so much on European and native assistance, lest the inexperience and irresponsibility of younger men in everyday affairs create undue misunderstanding and extra work for others who are helping, and promote consequent ill-feeling. Every bit as important as selecting technical ability is the *rejecting of men lacking normal manners, uncouth in appearance or unpleasant in personality, characters admittedly in only a small proportion, yet doing much to antagonize both European and native against the Expedition's better interest.'*

People like me do tend to decide, if in doubt, that the nasty crack is made at them. This one was meant to be for me and the other pushful member of the party, Eddie Shackleton, all right. Us he truly hated, up to the point where we began to fear he might suffer a heart attack or brain burst. Shackleton even had the bad manners to insist on climbing Mount Mulu, then thought to be the highest peak in Sarawak at eight thousand feet—and hitherto unattempted by Brookeians.

The thing was distressing. It continued to rankle in my mind. When I read what Banks wrote in the Museum's Annual Report, I made up my mind that this one should not pass. It was just a little too bad. For on this expedition I fell for Sarawak in a very big way. I also learnt, for the first time, to appreciate an entirely different kind of people, the native pagan people of the Tinjar and Baram rivers. And they seemed to appreciate me, too. I found in these people something I had been looking for without success in the west. Answers to an unhappiness which I had not yet learnt to analyse and offset on my own. . . .

Banks's few printed words rankled deep indeed. It would be absurd to say that I remembered them constantly. They came to mind every now and then—especially when my self-satisfaction suffered some sort of relapse (which was frequently enough). There was only one other thing that could rate alongside it in my life: my father's refusal to believe that I could live on my own efforts—exploring, brains, birds and writing —without toeing the line of his business routine. My father, a fine man, but narrow, was able to write me off with a much more devastating document than Mr Banks. He simply left me out of his will. His handsome estate went, through the banks, to my younger brother, obedient Bill.

But neither father nor Curator could have the best of me as easily as that. There is nothing to be proud of when I say that it is hardly an over-simplification—if I look at two of the conscious impulses running through the adult life I came of age into on September 26, 1932, at the top of Mount Dulit—to define: (i) prove that I myself (it was already too late to prove it to my father) not only that I could do my own things and keep my independence, but also that I could do his own things too (e.g. winning the DSO); (ii) that I could prove in a more local way, that coming to Borneo as an outsider was not a mere flash in the pan; and that even such an undesirable character as Mr Banks had made me out to be might, in truth, prove no more unpleasant than he (e.g. as his successor, Curator of the Sarawak Museum). I hope I may be forgiven for introducing this somewhat unattractive note at this stage in this story. It will not be necessary to harp on it hereafter.

*　　*　　*

Eddie Shackleton, later to play a worthwhile part in the air war as Parliamentary Secretary to the Secretary of State for Air and much*

* Sworn as a Life Peer, Lord Shackleton; House of Lords, 22 October, 1958.

else, went from Borneo to lead the Oxford University Ellesmere Expedition in the following year. In the introduction to his *Arctic Journeys* (London; Travel Book Club, 1937) he wrote:

'The Oxford University Expedition to Borneo in 1932 spent four months doing biological and survey work under E. Banks and T. H. Harrisson, and penetrated into unexplored areas of Sarawak. In 1933 three expeditions were in the field, those of Wilfred Thesiger in Abyssinia, Dr John R. Baker in the New Hebrides and A. R. Glen in Spitzbergen.'

For by the time he was in the Arctic (where I had already been on my first Oxford Expedition) I was sweltering with John Baker in Melanesia—which is in every way hotter, wetter, uglier and nastier, on aggregate, than the worst bits of Borneo. The New Hebrides were really rather hell.

In the interval between Sarawak in Borneo and Malekula in the New Hebrides, I had quit Cambridge, which grew to be unbearable after the wide view from Mount Dulit and the narrower one in father's eyes. My going down was the last straw with the latter, who abandoned hope for and direct interest in me thereafter. I left two regrets behind at Cambridge, my kind friend Louis Clarke (to whom this book is dedicated) and Tom Manning. Tom and Reynold Bray had been at Harrow together and we there started a club to make Harrow boys take more enterprising holidays and find out about other sorts of people. This was an early experiment in that field and attracted much public attention. At Cambridge, Tom and I continued in the same way, re-energizing a defunct club called 'The Wayfarers' out of which has since grown much of the extensive exploration and adventure vacation activities of undergraduates. Tom and Reynold had practised as they preached also; by crossing Arctic Lapland in winter, proceeding without authority into the Soviet Arctic, ending up in a Leningrad prison as a *cause célèbre* of the day.

I greatly regretted leaving Tom's almost silent but awfully (in the strict sense) impressive company behind in Cambridge. But I now shifted the balance of power to Reynold in Oxford, which I infested until the next expedition took off. It seems queer now that I could have done some of the things that I did. But in those days you could do a lot in Oxford—more than in Cambridge. For instance, I regularly walked the city not only barefoot but with red toenails. The first part of this fetish has proved useful ever since, in laying the foundation of two tough feet on which I have often been able to travel where shoes are a nuisance or have long since worn to pulp.

By this time the goings on in Reynold's quarters had become unbearable even to the patience of Balliol. He quit; and we established ourselves at what was then a beautiful little pub by the canal, 'The Rose Revived'. Presently we moved to a cottage at Wyck Rissington beyond Burford in the Cotswolds. Our wretched landlord soon found his garden gate decorated with a new nameplate:

'The Trobriands'.

For in those days we had all been stimulated by the anthropological researches of the chinless wonder Pole, Professor Bronislaw Malinowski, whose methods have stamped themselves with such reduced but deadening effect upon the London School of Economics and much else in British social anthropology. The change of name was a little pretentious —rather in the Kelabit manner. But there certainly were some goings on in the erratic and almost invariably inadequate emotionalism of the early thirties. Perhaps it is better not to remember some of the people who came and stayed at 'The Trobriands'.

As a result of irregularities in and about Oxford, the Professor of Zoology directed (by telegram from Java) that I be expelled from his department, where I was engaged in working out results of the Oxford Arctic Expedition under Charles Elton (who is still in the department, a Fellow of the Royal Society; and who greatly helped me to organize my mind in observing nature during the months we shared a tent of continuous daylight). Anyway, it was now time to go with another zoology don, John Baker, who is also still at Oxford, bless his heart.*

*　*　*

The people of the New Hebrides proved, on the whole, tougher propositions than Oxford undergraduates or Borneo head-hunters. I learnt, there, to be a cannibal in feeling almost more than in fact. Or I thought I did; so that the difference did not matter (to me). The idea in my mind—started by Mount Dulit experience—was to get to understand, as far as possible, people as different as possible from me as myself. My line, which got me on to whatever expeditions I wanted, was zoology in general, ornithology in particular. By this time I was a well-known birdman, had written original papers and a small book.

* In 1958 John Baker was elected a Fellow of the Royal Society, too.

For the first year in the New Hebrides I worked the whole time on zoological problems; mainly the breeding cycles of birds, mammals and reptiles. The New Hebrides had been selected as having as nearly as possible a similar tropical (and, for humans, lousy) climate in every month of the year. So that to a large extent the influence of climate on breeding seasons could be ignored. The Royal Society, Percy Sladen Trust, British Museum, Royal Geographical Society and University bodies sponsored this and similar expedition projects with which I was concerned. When the Bakers and Terence Bird went home, I was joined by A. J. Marshall. We worked together to complete a detailed programme on breeding, including collection and dissection of monthly quotas of selected animals, daily meteorological records, observation of animal habits, flowering plants, etc. Jock Marshall was a zoologist from Sydney University. With his one arm below curly hair and pugnacious jaw, he could dissect a flower-pecker with tissue paper skin—and skill. We had a good time, in a tough kind of way; and I was very thoroughly indoctrinated into the major masculine neuroses of the Australian people when faced with Englishmen, an experience which later proved of great value for the 'Z' Specialist—as we may presently see . . . ?

*   *   *

When our zoological work was up, I forgot about birds and devoted my energy to these extraordinary New Hebrideans, still living in their own way inside the big islands. This second year was the hardest but the most fulfilling so far. Birds and bats were clearly not enough. It was impossible to be satisfied with anything else than the stuff which made humans tick. I moved firmly away from parrots and mice, to men who could also explain themselves away and refute, while being studied.

I only managed to tear myself away from my cannibal-friends of Malekula because the elder Douglas Fairbanks sent his one hundred foot yacht to fetch me back to Hollywood and make a film: about him and these cannibals. Happily, I had the sense to take a fair chunk of his money—I had to part earn it by being polite to (Lady) Sylvia Ashley (later Mrs Fairbanks)—and abandon ship when we called at Tahiti. I lived in a Tahitian hut, thus adding some understanding of another people to my slowly growing gain.

What a people! Our favourite game was to sit on the grass under the palms and play cards. The recipe for this sort of Polynesian civilization (in 1935):

Take five—or eight—packs of cards. Shuffle and mix them all up together. Sit on the ground in a loose circle. Somebody start dealing; it doesn't matter who. Deal each card slowly. If someone is dealt a low card, everybody instinctively expresses regret, sympathy, bad luck. When, happily, anyone gets a high card, all exclaim with pleasure. Cheer. Congratulate the happy one. Continue like this until all the cards are exhausted. Then start again. . . .

*   *   *

During more than two years in the Pacific I did not read a newspaper or hear a radio. I came slowly back from Tahiti on a French cargo boat to Marseilles. It was an excellent way to get the full impact of the west and re-balance that wonder of human diversity. I had lost touch with almost everybody—which had vaguely been what I intended in staying half-lost so long. Reynold Bray and Tom Manning were together again in the Arctic. Before long, Reynold vanished into the frozen sea, carried off on a break-away ice floe. Tom has been up that way ever since.

Britain, by 1936, was quite bewildering enough to anyone, let alone a de-tribalized young man without any visible means of support beyond a pair of by now rock-hard feet. It seemed to me that I had spent quite a long time learning how to live among cannibals and so-called primitive people. I had acquired a good deal of information potentially acceptable as of anthropological validity. But now, with the shock of clarity that absence and return can refresh, I saw that most of the things I had been studying and methods I had been using, both in ornithology and gradually in ethnology, arose just as much as problems among my 'own' people. All over the world people like me were going out to study other civilizations on a scale of intimacy and detail which had not yet been applied in our 'civilized' societies. I myself, for instance. Although I had made conscious efforts to get to know more about England than I otherwise would—spent three school holidays in the East End of London, two others tramping (and that meant something then) Scotland and Wales—yet I knew pitifully little about the every day and night life of the mass of the people. Why not study the cannibals of Lancashire, the head-hunters of Stepney?

This was more or less my state of mind after a few months back in London, during which I soon found I could make a moderate income working a few hours a day, lecturing, broadcasting, writing about what I had been doing in the previous years. Reassured in this, I took off for my next expedition.

* * *

Next morning I arrived at Bolton in Lancashire. There I lived for the next three years, mostly in one of a row of workmen's houses on cobbled Davenport Street. I began painstaking efforts at enlarging human understanding, along a line that was so broad that I could hardly lose it through all the doubts and confusions that were bound to arise in trying to study objectively a society in which one was so deeply involved, subjectively. All the time, Borneo whispered in my right ear, Malekula my left, while my head buzzed in the shifting stresses of excitement and despair, the ache to be sincere and simple, the urge to succeed and some impatience to lead in a new field.

The one and only thing which I could find that affected the lives of people in all the places I had been to everywhere in the world was the Unilever Combine. Even the cannibals in the mountains of Melanesia were touched by the tentacles of this colossus, buying copra, selling soap. Unilever stemmed directly from William Lever. He was born and started business in Bolton. So I followed there. I began by finding out everything I could about the first Lord Leverhulme, his family, his work and then the organizations in the area which had developed from these. And *did* I take it seriously! At various stages I got jobs as lorry driver, shop assistant, labourer, cotton operative, ice-cream man and reporter in firms in or to do with Unilever. The evenings, necessarily sprinkled with eau de cologne, I sat at the fireside of prosperous Lever relatives, feeling slightly guilty but softly elated. For the first discovery that I made (for myself) in Bolton, was that it came just as easy to penetrate other kinds of western society, as societies in which you are from the start in 'stranger situation' (e.g. cannibal). This was in those days still a significant discovery for the sociologist; and in recent years it has been widely lost sight of again.

What excited me most of all was to find that when I took a job in a cotton-mill there was no point in my trying to disguise my 'educated accent' or anything else. Unless I did something silly, none of the men and women starting work before daylight that winter, finishing after dark, would for a moment imagine that anybody came in to this heat, uproar and mechanical risk unless they absolutely had to earn £3 10s 0d a week (which was what I got). They simply thought I came from another part of the country. British good manners being what they are, all I needed was the mildest cover story, should anyone ask politely.

Since then the European war has demonstrated the same point again and again and again. That is what cloak-and-dagger organizations are dependent upon. Then it was an exciting methodological result.

One day in the winter of 1937 I got back to my room through the slushy industrial snow, worn out after a day lifting the big 'beams' of cotton for the jolly girls—particularly a red-faced Rose from West Houghton. From being a beamer, I was transformed back into being a cannibal of parts by a letter from Victor Gollancz; he said that the book I had written about the New Hebrides was out and proving a success. I had written this, *Savage Civilization*, before I came north, shed it before this next stage. In it I had tried hard to say what I so far knew about these cannibal people being in many ways as, and in some ways more, civilized than the Europeans in the same part of the world. This was not a new approach; but nor was it as familiar then as it is now.

I was now, age 26, as far away from Borneo as I had been. It looked as if Bolton must take up the rest of my working life. In the north of England in 1937: gathering assurance, the whole business of living (and being happy as well) for a while seemed to be growing clearer and clearer. The necessity for avoiding familiar relationships and for making a sort of search for truth in more difficult places, seemed to be dwindling. There was enough of the stuff right there on the cobbled street. . . .

* * *

None of the phenomena which I was noticing in Bolton = 'Worktown' were confined to that salubrious and self-satisfied city. The divorce between ordinary *public* opinion and *published* opinion was becoming, there as everywhere, so apparent that a particular need for machinery to bring the two particles together was beginning to be widely felt. The *Daily Mirror*—in its way the cleverest newspaper organization in the world—then carried among its shrewdest reporters Charles Madge, also known as a poet of glacial distinction (most of the iceberg did not show). Charles Madge, with documentary film-man Humphrey Jennings (whose obsessive brilliance gloriously vanished as he stepped back, arms waving and whole body explaining the next sequence, over a cliff-edge in Greece), Stuart Legge, poets David Gascoyne and Ruthven Todd, got the idea of setting up a nation-wide network of people who would write in as direct, candid, private reporters on whatever subjects were put to them. This idea was befogged by all sorts of side issues, such as Humphrey's theory of validity by co-incidence, and Charles's hope that such reportage would breed a new kind of mass literature. That was the way it was with all of us in those days—as Hitler became gigantic, implications intolerable for the young.

Out of a union of Charles's delightful big house on the edge of Blackheath and my bug-ridden Bolton slum was borne the thing called Mass-Observation. Mass-Observation became something of a sensation at once. We met with immediate response from hundreds of voluntary correspondents; and presently from many ready to spend holidays and even throw up their jobs to do whole-time study.

The quick and wide repercussions of what we few had begun took us by surprise, and were in some ways unfortunate. Mass-Observation seemed to get at once under an enormous number of skins.

Professor Malinowski, though he can hardly have known how we had flattered him with 'The Trobriands' renamed at Wyck Rissington, gave—from his position of supreme eminence in the pre-war anthropological field—a boost, forty pages of support, during which he said:

'In all this I speak mostly as an honest (I trust), though perhaps slightly sophisticated (I am afraid), Mass-Observer, who naturally "observes" himself first. Rumour and legend had made me acquainted with the names of Tom Harrisson and Charles Madge some time before I met them. I was prejudiced. Worse, I was inclined to make fun of what I knew was a serious movement, whether as a danger or a constructive force in society.

'The first time I met the two leaders of the movement, one of them (Tom Harrisson) read a paper at the Institute of Sociology. He started with the time-honoured abuse of things and men academic. My prejudice did not melt. Then he came to the point. I was puzzled, at times irritated, but realized more and more that I had to become acquainted at first hand with the movement. After a careful perusal of the published results I veered round in my opinion almost completely. I found that the movement was in no way a caucus or cabal, but a scientific undertaking, in the sense that everything was being done above board. An occasional *boutade* or joke apart, the workers were keen to work hand in hand with academic interests and institutions.'

And in closing he expressed what was then the troubled mood of nearly all men in the democracies:

'Mass-Observation, alas! is inconceivable in any of the totalitarian communities. This in itself and symptomatically is a high testimony in its favour. Yet in the countries where democracy is still at work, Mass-Observation may not only be a useful instrument of scientific research, but it may become an extremely important practical contribution towards the maintenance of human civilization where it still survives.'

Mass-Observation, alas, did not achieve anything like this. And today it continues as a respectable, successful and exceptionally intelligent research organization, working for business and advertising mostly. But what Mass-Observation did do in the thirties was to start —or rather to stimulate and bring out—a novel approach, for a time at least, both in social science and in broader socio-political thinking. I still keep on meeting people who, to this day, have been powerfully influenced by our *idea*. Though Mass-Observation has only published about fifteen books and full-length reports, there is a steady stream of stuff by one-time observers writing about it.*

We truly tried to bridge a gap, left achingly void, between the working street in Worktown and the sanitube, clean, skitofax, deodorant, Ginnsbergerized layers of LSE sociology, so called. Between, too, Worktown, Melanesia and Borneo. In that time of European squalor, 1937-9, M-O at least did throb; and *felt* undefeated. Perhaps that was its peculiar contribution—and why so many people who were young and tortured then still think of it kindly today.

*   *   *

The war, which started slowly in 1939, brought Mass-Observation into its own sort of own. Although other organizations had by now sprung up to study public opinion, we could offer a then unique service

---

* Two amusing recent ones with chapters on M-O: *Into the Dangerous World* by Woodrow Wyatt, and *Indigo Days* by Julian Trevelyan.

for the study of *private* opinion and the interpretation of broad trends: those amorphous marshlands of the mind which in war-time are dubbed 'morale'. Morale was meat, drink and regular salaries for all in Mass-Observation. It meant leaving Worktown and establishing a new headquarters in London, 'in touch'. The pace soon became tremendous, the organization prosperous, the original intentions more and more distorted by the pressures of war, the bugs of 'security' and state.

I found myself plunging into problems ranging from shop steward influence and air raid precautions, 'Arm White in the Black Out', saving and non-, government advertising and the anxieties of submarine crews, Dublin opinion on Belfast. . . . Everything had to be done in a hurry, reported upon at once; often subsequently enlarged upon to a sympathetic recipient or defended against a furious one who felt criticized. Some of our reports naturally reached up to the highest level—since we were applying a novel approach to problems of importance to the conduct of a new-scale war.

Presently, too, I found myself, night after night, being bombed in a different city. That was the hardest work of all. We were commissioned to write a series of official reports on morale aspects of the great German air-raids. This meant that for a period of some months, the telephone might go any evening soon after dark, warning where the blitz was starting up that night. With elegant Humphrey Pease as an unvaryingly patient (and unpaid) chauffeur, a select unit would head off to Hull, Liverpool, Plymouth, Southampton, Glasgow, Greenock, Portsmouth, Tyneside: we did the lot. Fortunately—for us!—the Germans usually made a series of raids on one town on successive nights, so that more often than not we were on the spot when things were at their most difficult for the civilian population and the multiple organizations set up to cope; as the most acute problems developed in the days following the raids when the ordinary social services had been crippled or collapsed. I fancy that if anyone was to claim records for the number of bombs he had been within half-mile of, George Hutchinson, Humphrey and I would have sure chances of places.

* * *

It was all too bad to last really. The pace was growing unbearable. At the same time the pressure from on top was getting tougher. I was on some Secret Special Reserve List, under the personal protection of powerful lads. But no one was more powerful in this realm of human manipulation than Ernest Bevin. A good many of our reports touched upon his elephantine interests. He was one who lunged at a pin-prick and thought it a spear. (I sometimes think of him now as I aim a blow-pipe dart at a tree-shrew.) The atmosphere was beginning to stink in my vicinity. More and more of the things I was being asked to do were moving over the borderline of objective description and honest analysis towards provocative partisanship or actual espionage—of the latter I did one deplorably 'effective' job.

After the glamour, excitement and financial stability had worn off, the Mass-Observation approach had been proved effective (in its way) over a wide range of conditions. There was not much more worth while left to do, at the moment, needing me. A person with energy, impatience and high opinion of self, could hardly feel good if he stood outside the fuller consequences of war indefinitely. Personally I had come to the end of the Bolton-Blackheath road, for the time being anyhow. Round the bend—though as yet I could not see it—lay again Borneo's green jungle and gay, brown, crowded long-house people.

* * *

I seldom was more miserable than the first day at Newport, Isle of Wight. My initiation into the wonders of the British Army was conducted by a captain who gave me a verbal questionnaire—one was presumed to be illiterate until proved otherwise—and just asked me if I was single, married or divorced. Sweating profusely, I muttered that I was all three.

This first six weeks of automation went like that all the way. Just as the new trick of Mass-Observation had been called in to study civilian morale, so the psychiatrists and psychologists were having their first major field day in The Forces. We spent a good deal of our time at Newport being tested, which was much nicer than being drilled or peeling potatoes. It was nicer still because the galaxy of faces familiar from the Psychological Congresses (which I had regularly disturbed with my views in earlier years) now lay shadowed under high-officer hats showing strain. This was a testing time for them, too; and some of them were not at all sure if they were doing right, either.

I did extremely well in the intelligence tests; my frame of mind was

the same as the testers'. I held a Major spellbound by my facility with
word-associations which he had evidently devised himself. We had
just shared the experience—but I did not so fully share his bewilderment at it—of the cockney lad one before me on the production line,
selecting his associations. The problems with which we were presented
went something like this:

'Put these four words into two natural pairs—
    BLACK   TIGER
    LION   WHITE'

My predecessor had elected for 'White Lion' and 'Black Tiger'.
Challenged by the startled examiner, he explained adequately that
the White Lion was his corner pub; and Tiger Black was an all-in
wrestler of repute. It was suggested to him, with something like
diffidence, that a better association might be Black and White. He
accepted this, a little doubtfully, on the understanding that the officer
meant drink.

When it came to 'aptitude tests', the story was different indeed.
Again the production line moved, foot by foot, number by number,
through the mill of educated sergeants supervised by officers with
D.Phils. Little bays contained different jig-saw puzzles and pieces of
simple machinery, to be put together or taken apart. I sweated again,
with all the anxiety of non-mechanic snob. I was right to do so.
Presented with a bicycle pump which had been taken to pieces—the
trick cyclist trick in classico—I succeeded in re-assembling this so that
it was not only unworkable but could not be taken to pieces again.
In the panic search for a substitute pump the whole human flow of
testees was stalled. I reaped my reward at the passing-out parade.

These were the days—how infinitely remote they now seem—when
the army was getting itself 'fully mechanized'. It still had a long way to
go! Meanwhile it was seeking everywhere for engineers, technicians,
machine craftsmen, anyone with an idea in such matters. The rest
could go walk, dig and shoot. As the adjutant detailed, by name and
number, each one of the hundreds now milled into potential troops, it
was borne in upon a gypsy, a moron, the fat boy and I, that we formed
a unique quartet, the four not selected for any of the fully mechanized
or newly formed arms. As adjutants have to be kind at heart, ours
came over and spoke to this pitiful detail:

'You are going to the KRR's, the old 60th, chaps. A wonderful regiment. And don't think they are mere infantry. They are *motorized* infantry now.'

Motorized or otherwise, within twenty-four hours we were learning to march at a hundred and twenty paces a minute, the Light Infantry step of the rifleman going for his life.

After the physical and nervous strain of two years as a pseudo-civilian, to sink into the cypher-life of a King's Royal Rifleman was sheer delight. Is there a duller-looking place in the world than Strensall Camp in Yorkshire? But here, for nearly a year, I repeated, at a different tempo, the first Worktown training again. This time there was no question of going to Lever Tillotson's for sherry before dinner, however. Some thirty cockneys and two public school boys shared a barrack room by night and eleven hours of disciplined movement by day; and there was nothing else to do. In this way it was almost as fresh as living with cannibals in Malekula. No half-measures were possible. Total absorption was the only smooth way to success and satisfaction.

*   *   *

And what savages we were!

We lived in wooden huts, the atmosphere pullulating with nicotine, saliva and smutty language. You could taste our barrack room as you came in; and it tasted like pea soup that had been running warm through the gutters of the Mile End Road. A rectangular, bare barn with sixteen double-tiered bunks, one table and two benches. In this, we riflemen made our own, exquisitely rich, private slum, within all the sanctions of army hygiene and discipline, and daily order.

This slum was largely of the taste and of the mind. We never discussed an idea, wrote anything or spoke a sentence without swear words and more. I did manage, somehow, to keep up my weekly Radio Critic Column in the *Observer*; but this was an extra-mural activity, involving an evening or two a week in the only room with radio (invariably empty except for me) in this huge camp—behind the canteen. The doing of it merely underlined the other, all-the-time life which mattered. Indeed, while I was in the ranks I *had* to keep on with this column, for the good of my wife and sons; in those days the weekly pay of a rifleman was under forty shillings. (As a matter of record, I continued my weekly column through Sandhurst and my early days as officer; when I went east, an Astor kindly agreed that I should continue to be paid a retainer so that, if desirable, I could take up the job again on my return. For years, the *Observer* continued to pay me a weekly fee, while I was mucking around in the middle of Borneo and for more than a year after the war until I came home.)

Do not let it, for a stripe, be thought that I look back on Strensall and our private slum with anything other than steaming affection. I have lived in some strange communities, before and since, ranging from the nomadic to the cannibal, teeming long-house to American General's Mess. Nowhere else have I met anything quite to beat the peculiar sort of vitality, mixed with underlying generosity and outflaring animosity, which made our little Bedlam tick.

We lived our lives as riflemen completely divorced from any contact with or knowledge of (or feeling for) our officers, most of them boys from Eton, Harrow, Rugby or Winchester, who had come straight from school to commissions, through various special wangles. Naïve, gentlemanly, well-meaning, gallant, educated enough, they valued all the qualities which were least admired among us, their troops. Extraordinary ideas about these officers prevailed among us; dreadful libels were perpetrated about only too innocent boys. That was part of the game which kept us going and contented. And, in another way, it was part of the pattern of separateness and social ignorance which had already so much intrigued in other places, with Mass-Observation as on Mount Dulit.

In this human jungle of the underprivileged and well-satisfied, perhaps the outstanding character was Jackie. Jackie was unmistakably an east-ender, by sound, taste or sight. He was the sharpest in a very sharp bunch of operators, among whom neither Humphrey Brooke nor I—the only two with post-primary education—stood out, except that we were the two with bodies built up to best capacity from having enough to eat *every* day since delivery. One day, Jackie asked me what I was up to, always writing in a corner. I told him I wrote a piece for a paper every week, commenting on radio programmes. He instantly digested and regurgitated this information, which dealt with something outside his province of mind hitherto. He had never read a newspaper, he had not heard of the *Observer,* and he could not believe that anyone could conceivably get paid for writing about broadcasts *after* they had happened. (At that time, before television, actually very few papers had radio critics.)

Two nights later, I came into the barrack room, climbed on my bunk—I had the top one of a pair (Humphrey below)—and found it occupied by a large typewriter. I had not been using a typewriter, because I did not want this particular fraction of my life to be too conspicuous and possibly antagonize the others. Jackie's gift—for it was him, of course—was a sort of sanction. It was nice of him to have remembered me as he was leaving the office he had burgled that evening in York.

Our second burglar was less intelligent. He was known as 'Flannel Foot', because of his way of padding about with a mousy and some-times malicious quietness. Indeed he could be a dangerous man, the back alley cut-throat on the cheap. Physically, he was the weakest man of the troop, the evident results of years of malnutrition in youth. He exploited this weakness with shrewdness, in all kinds of ways. One way was to go and madden the largest, clumsiest and most simply animal man among us, always known as 'The Whip'. 'The Whip' was a great, big, burly, surly brute, who would move in one direction at once and continue along it until he encountered something to direct him else-where. 'The Whip' distinguished himself, at one stage, by responding to a call for volunteers for the paratroops. This was greeted, virtually, as an act of disloyalty and almost evil, from the rest of the troop who would have overlooked arson, incest or rape. 'Flannel Foot' made hell out of it, representing 'The Whip' as merely getting out of this unit so that he could be nearer London, better fed, closer to a girl or even away from him. Unfortunately for 'The Whip', within a fortnight he was back in the unit, having been thrown out of the paratroops already. But the thing he most feared was FF. He could have killed him with his bare hands; but the FF's of this life are not for that kind of killing. It is difficult, nowadays, in the Welfare State, to realize how many people—even two decades ago—were shockingly affected by a back-ground of poverty, inadequate diet and insufficient medical attention. This set of defects in fact let FF down, by and by. He burgled the house of a Vet (also in York) one Saturday night. Made a hash of it and was caught, failing to escape over the back wall. Several envied him his transfer to less exacting conditions.

At least five of our thirty odd bodies spent a lot of their time (and everyone else's) in trying to devise ways of getting out of the army altogether. There were several desertions. But these never seemed to come off, and the Glass-House at Aldershot had a fabulous reputation as the living hell of a prison for the recaptured.

The most persistent advocate of a return to civilian life the quick way was an unattractive youth called Rex. He put up a brilliant approach, though I have a sinking suspicion that after he was removed from our midst, he may have been put in the Education Corps for his pains. His speciality was to sleep in the top bunk by the door. This spot was the least desired during that bitter winter, because whenever anybody opened the door some eighty cubic feet of icy air blasted in from concrete lavatories without. As somebody was always deserting or being arrested or going sick, the lower bunk by the door was regularly vacant; and every few days was filled again by some hesitant new-comer. His initiation came from above, during the night. It was always awaited with warm tension, by the whole of the rest of the barrack. It must have been puzzling for a new arrival to guess at first what all the jokes were about, why he was being treated both as a kind of holy animal for the evening and as a subject of such intense amusement, even by cockney standards. Anyway, during the middle watches of the night he would inevitably receive a powerful shower of urine from gentleman Rex overhead.

Wetting your bed is—or was in those days, before psychologists were fully organized—regarded as a serious crime in the army. The bed-wetter was regularly up on a charge for it, and cumulatively built up the idea that this was a major, uncontrollable neurosis, with him for life.

A more sensational ploy of this kind was devised and finely developed by another intelligent cockney. The first indications of his awakening genius were borne upon our never very boring routine—there was always something extraordinary happening—one morning on full parade. This chap reversed a series of orders, so that whatever the troop did, he did the opposite. Brought before the company commander, who was said to be and certainly looked like a champion boxer (but the theories we had about these officers were often completely false), he suddenly sat on a table. This was the beginning of his version of schizophrenia. He resisted every sort of punishment and kept up the act with the crude virtuosity of the true psychotic. He presently came to me (as the supposedly clever guy) for additional briefing; I was able to dig out some quite good stuff on schizophrenia from the local library. Provided he kept on like that, wherever he went when he, too, left us, he probably acted himself into Broadmoor. His departure made way for one new recipient of the upper bunk's golden accolade.

It is barely possible to exaggerate the variety in this life at Strensall. Nor was this by any means confined to the other ranks. One of our senior officers invariably came on parade accompanied by two fine Chow dogs. On certain hand-signals from him, these dogs were trained to relieve themselves upon the legs of the soldiery. If they did this wrong, selected the person whom the loving owner had *not* indicated, he would then and there shout for the Sergeant-Major and put one or both 'on a charge'. This sort of thing was completely in keeping with our own approach to the problems of military life in the earlier part of the war, in Yorkshire!

Our star turn indoors was an Italian barber, useful with his hands and a passionate exhibitionist with some of the rest of his body. What he had to offer in this field was repulsive. He took pleasure in detailing the causes of the various kinds of sores, scars, laminations and patina adorning his tawny, rather deadly, strong young body. He was a vicious man in a fight, too. There were not many of these; but the few were nasty.

For a while, I made up my mind to stay with this unit all through the war. It would be fascinating to see how each individual worked out, especially when in danger of something more than the regimental Chows. I wanted so badly to see how different they could be in different places, lesser discomforts, greater dangers. But by now, psychologists were catching up with us again, as their war rolled on also. Also, I must admit, the companionship was growing somewhat monotonous. When one knows the language very well from the start, the amount of purely masculine company one can stand for months on end in a confined space is more limited than with quite other people, thinking in different symbols altogether and speaking words which must be learned afresh from the beginning. But my memory of the last months as a rifleman is somewhat dim. So I asked my friend Humphrey Brooke, who is now Secretary of the Royal Academy at Burlington House, to read what I have remembered and comment. He comments as follows:

'I have always wondered how our military "Ernie" (Bevin) managed to jumble together such a high proportion of eccentrics in one platoon. It was certainly something of a freak and you have pin-pointed (with accuracy) only a few of its odder characters.

'The picture you paint of yourself does not strike me as quite so true. As I remember, you were a figure of awe to every rifleman. You looked fairly untidy, but were tough, efficient and a master of repartee, known to "work your loaf" to a super-degree. Your mail was enormous (I believe you were still directing Mass-Observation) and you dealt with most of this, as well as drafting your weekly *Observer* articles, during periods of instruction in the barracks. But I never remember the surprise question catching you out in these preoccupations. Altogether a thoroughly independent figure, who made no secret of the fact that a "riflemanly" career in the army, even as an officer, was not your ambition.

'I believe that you felt that "the 60th" was slightly old-fashioned in outlook and that a unit in which one of the officers habitually brought his dogs onto parade (and even put them on a charge) was scarcely in harmony with the kind of modern scientific warfare which you wished to pursue.'

Well, I suppose you are right, my dear fellow? In any case, for their better or our worse at this stage, both Humphrey and I were removed elsewhere—he to end up the war as a Colonel in Germany, I back inside Borneo.

* * *

The War Office Selection Board, to which we were sent without the option, was a psychological picnic. Instead of bicycle pumps there were contrived situations to test leadership, decision, 'quick thinking' and other supposedly 'officerial qualities'. As these were conducted in the pleasant Cheshire countryside, far from the faintest suggestion of lethal reality, I was able to bulldoze myself into the highest possible rating, which proved useful all the rest of my army life—for 'A1' gives a sort of halo of lunatic fringe capacity to those arrogant enough to display instant decision, automatic fearlessness and ruthless devotion to death among the marigolds, cuckoospit, daisies and hay.

For most of another year it was satisfying to learn about things previously unsuspected; and especially to find that a long-standing inferiority feeling about manual and mechanical aptitude was just that, a feeling. Tanks and armoured cars, long-range radio and morse code, artillery, cross-country motor cycling, proved as easy as assault courses and battle drills in the well devised and nearly always well executed system of training at Sandhurst. Though I cannot remember a single letter in the morse code, and once more shudder at the thought of touching a carburetter, it is good to think that once upon a time dismantling the engine of a Daimler Armoured Car made an enjoyable afternoon.

Sandhurst was enlivened by the presence of Frank Owen, who had been jerked out of his editorial chair on the *Evening Standard* in the same wild rush of old bull Bevin to which the head of Mass-Observation had demi-willingly succumbed. There was much leisure at Sandhurst. Frank seemingly employed the whole of his spare energy, which was then enormous, on London night life. After a few of these sorties—which for some reason always started in the buttery at the Berkeley—I found it impossible to appear on early morning parade in a state that would pass the eye of the Grenadier adjutant. Frank kept it up splendidly. I satisfied myself, subsequently, by thinking that if he had not quit Sandhurst half-way through, to join Mountbatten's staff in Burma, he would have cracked up in the end, somewhere between Ciro's and Camberley.

By now I knew most of the tricks of army examinations, which are simple. Unfortunately this time I was too clever for myself, and passed out top. The adjutant had arranged to have me posted into the Brigade of Guards. But the Recce Corps, still in its infancy, would not give up the body of one who had travelled so far from the bicycle shame of Newport, Isle of Wight; they insisted I must now be sent as 'the first fully-trained Recce officer' to a regiment newly converted to this corps.

Even if I had been a tactful and quiet person, this spearhead role would probably have been extremely unpleasant. The Green Howards, then stationed at Ballymena in Northern Ireland, were properly proud of their position as an Armoured Car Regiment. They deeply resented being converted to Recce. I was the first strictly Recce body to arrive—a rather sloppy-looking, over-age, second lieutenant. As 'the expert' I soon succeeded in littering Ulster with bogged or crashed Bren gun carriers and scout cars. While I dashed at the peat, the old hands stuck to the roads and prayed for better days to come. They did not come, and after the Normandy landings an exceptional proportion of these fine fellows died trying to push out in front—as, by then, I sincerely trust they had been better taught to do in those ungainly, sad vehicles.

For the one and only time in the British army, I felt in a round hole. I was saved by a gong, which rang out from Northumberland Avenue, SW1. This time the Colonel was not sending for me in loathing and scorn: better for him and me than that, he was sending me on an un-specified secret mission, out of the unit.

In the relics of a Northumberland Avenue hotel, I was interviewed by Colonel Egerton-Mott. It took some time to understand what he was talking about. He seemed to be under the impression that I was a Com-munist. At that moment this was a good thing to be in his eyes, for it was Allied policy to work with and encourage Communist Chinese as guerrillas against the Japanese inside South-East Asia. As far as I can make out, the original idea was that we should repeat elsewhere in Asia this technique which was already proving so successful, in the very short-run, in Malaya. I had difficulty in clearing this up.

Years later I came upon Egerton-Mott again, bowler-hatted, an important official in the Colonial Development Corporation. He told me that MI5 had mixed up my life with another person of the same name (only one 's'), a well-known left-winger in Spain and so on. (I was, at the time, Parliamentary Liberal Candidate for Watford, Herts.)

Anyway, Mott offered me Borneo in the end, adding that I was about the last of their hopes. They had already (he said) asked everyone with any conceivable knowledge of the country, including my colleagues of the 1932 Oxford expedition. When I practically leapt at the offer, he shed his cavalry veneer of calm for a second in pleased evident relief. For, in a tiny way, the British Services at that moment badly needed to find a few men to go back into Borneo and try to save some of the face, chin-up, lost to the Japanese.

For the next few weeks my lately softening feet hardly felt ground. Special Operations Executive, 'SOE', the British centre of cloak-and-dagger, was a most efficient organization, in a different class from the ordinary army or civilian services. Parachuting, coding, disguise, hiding, searching, tailing, burglaring, stealing trains, blowing up railway bridges, shamming deafness, passing on syphilis, resisting pain, firing from the hip, forgery and the interception of mail, were some things one could learn in intense concentration. None of them would be of much use in the east. But the acquisition of so much criminal and lethal knowledge gave a kick of self-confidence. I particularly remember the lessons in poaching which we received at Beaulieu, Hants, from a portly captain said to have been a Royal gamekeeper at Sandringham before he took the pips. I even learnt a way of setting a snare which (as it turned out) had not been thought of by the Kelabits.

* * *

It was quite something to fly to Australia early in 1944. One did the journey in two-engine Dakotas, pleasantly reliable, unpleasantly seated on aluminium benches. There were interludes in North Africa, five days' breakdown in Palestine, three weeks' wait in Ceylon. From Ceylon, the Japanese lay in a deep belt eastwards. The only way of getting on was in a Catalina two-engine seaplane, specially equipped with extra tanks and therefore ordinarily capable of taking only two passengers. As we took off before dawn from Galle in the south of Ceylon, we saw the sun rise over the Indian Ocean. We saw the sun rise again as we came in towards Swan Lake in Western Australia, after more than a day non-stop, without seeing land anywhere on the way.

I arrived at Perth under such secret auspices that no one expected me. I knew no one to expect. I asked a taxi driver to take me to the nearest available military headquarters. He elected to drive me to the Officers' Club in town, refusing a fare from the freshly arrived 'pommy'.

I walked into this unattractive but throbbing club, with the unvarying pitch of the seaplane still drumming my daze. The captain who approached me to ask if he could help was the first of many fortunate finds in Australia. He was Ernest Beaurepaire; his eldest brother, Sir Frank, had been various sorts of swimming champion (including Olympic) and was Lord Mayor of Melbourne. Ern proved to be quite a lad in his own right, at that, with a character and interests almost diametrically opposed to my own, so that he proved a delightful companion in Perth—and years later elsewhere, including Europe as far as the Arctic Circle.

Ern urged that my first job was to become 'acclimatized' to his marvellous continent and its good people. This suggestion was acceptable enough after an elaborate journey. When the first pleasures of West Australia's extreme free-and-easiness were wearing off—and when I had been shown Swan Park fifteen times by different kind people, usually male—my friends put me on a freight plane for Melbourne.

In Melbourne, I was at first faced with much the same problem. Where was my unit, and how should I approach something so secret? It seemed to have been assumed, when I started out from Baker Street, W1, that the all-seeing eyes behind the cloak would pin-point and gather me into the fold on arrival. Far from it. When I did eventually find the right place and person, I was received with a sense of shock. Guessing that this would be so after the Perth experience, I put in a delightful first few days at the Military Club in Melbourne, perhaps the best club in Australia. The overwhelming hospitality with which I was greeted by elderly generals and the Australian MacArthurs was accentuated by the discovery of a large stock of Pernod in the bar. The origin of this was uncertain; and no one else knew how to drink it. It took nearly a week to demonstrate.

Alas, all daggers must some day find sheath or shoulder blade. And I was duly received into SRD='Z' Special Unit, near the Botanical Hotel in Melbourne. An extraordinary assembly here gathered. Most of them can only be remembered either for their conceits or their eccentricities, which were no less in variety but more limited in intensity than those of Rex, Jackie, Flannel Foot, and the rest of the King's Royal Riflemen. But here we lived in style with virtually unlimited expense accounts, allowances, leaves, and no-questions-asked about anything (except security) when we were not wanted for something.

There was early on a discouraging idea of training the first trickle of British officers who now began to arrive from Europe. Major N. G. P. Combe—who had held (and has since held again) senior administrative posts in the Government of North Borneo, neighbour to Sarawak and proud owner of Mount Kinabalu on its crest—and I were sent to a Special Commando School on Great Sandy Island at the south end of the Great Barrier Reef. But tough as they may be, Australian commandos had nothing to teach us ordinary English army products. We made such a fuss that they soon set us free. But the period was of much value to me because I shared a tent with Nick Combe, who made me speak all the time in Malay. Although I had not spoken this—the *lingua franca* of Borneo—since 1932, it soon came back; and my patient tutor enlarged my knowledge enormously.

Combe's operational interests were parallel with mine. But he was concerned with North Borneo, I with Sarawak. The North Borneo operation was called, in code, *Agas*, which is Malay for a sandfly. The Sarawak operation was to be named *Semut*—Malay for an ant. We were to be biting ants. In accordance with 'Z' Special procedures, there was no operational or intelligence contact between the ants and the sandflies in the field, and I regrettably had no more to do with Nick until long after the war was over—when the peace-time Governments of North Borneo and Sarawak obliquely adopted a somewhat similar approach towards intelligent co-operation and shared intelligence! I believe that in the event Agas suffered more than Semut from the security block between us. Certainly, their results, despite brilliant early beginnings with the late Colonel Gort Chester, the advantage of Nick Combe's great knowledge of the country and administrative experience there, and a piece of Australian dynamite called Rex Blow (of whom more) turned out less satisfactory, and in some ways unsatisfactory.

There were three headquarters officers who were particularly concerned with Semut. Colonel Jack Finlay (nowadays Commissioner of HM Board of Customs), a Camberley trained General Staff Officer, was the Director of Plans, and easily the most intelligent, consistent and helpful man in a unit which did not necessarily value these three qualities (particularly the second one) above all others. Jumbo Courtney, already richly decorated for work in the Mediterranean, including the insertion of General Mark Clark into and the extraction of General Giraud out of North Africa, was the enthusiastic GSO2. Kindly George Crowther, in civil life an oil-fields surveyor, was GSO3 and a sort of Daddy to Semut, which soon became a little army of extremely seething, sometimes biting, ants to worry him. Without his attention to detail, none of these ants could have lived to milk another aphid.

Semut, at this stage, comprised two persons. The other was Major G. C. (Toby) Carter, a colleague of George Crowther in prewar oil-field survey, who had worked especially in the Baram-Tinjar river basin, which our Oxford Expedition had also traversed in 1932. He was a New Zealander and was in the New Guinea campaign with an army unit, before acquiring his 'Z'. He had naturally arrived in Melbourne before me. I found that Captain Crowther and he had already cooked up a considerable plan for West Borneo, eagerly.

★   ★   ★

The first plan was, roughly, to 'make initial penetration' by submarine. This presented one enormous advantage. At any time Borneo was within submarine range of Australia, hazardous though the journey through Japanese patrolled seas might be. A submarine could carry large quantities of stores, and deliver personnel immediately. The only other conceivable method of getting in at that moment was by the use of the same kind of seaplane on which Qantas presented me with the Order of the Double Sunrise (on vellum) for the trip between Galle and Beaurepaire. But Sarawak in Borneo is very poorly provided with lakes to land upon inland; and to land at sea was clearly inferior to approaching the shore by submarine. The idea of landing on Lake Bunut in the lower Baram was toyed with, but it would have been almost certain suicide, plane and all; for it is nearly always far too shallow. Catalinas are conspicuously slow, the chances of the plane getting there and back over hostile territory consequently slender. The disadvantages of a submarine op at extreme range were evident. Apart altogether from the difficult straits to be threaded in order to get round to the west coast of Borneo, the shore line of Sarawak presented its own snags. Either the approach must be over dangerous coral rock or —for at least nine-tenths of the coast—over very slow shelving mud.

This would mean that the submarine must stay far out, personnel and stores to be taken in rubber dinghies long distances in particularly unreliable seas and very strong double tides. That particular difficulty was not so strong in North Borneo, but both territories offered a second difficulty, which eventually became a major handicap to the development of Agas. This was simply that the Japanese were concentrated along the coast. This was the only thing we did know from intelligence; because every now and again a Malay or Chinese fishing vessel would drift or steal away from Borneo and be picked up at sea off Australia or New Guinea. In any case, it *could* only be so, as all the towns and significant trading posts of Sarawak are on the coast or within the tidal reaches of the great rivers.

The coastal people were bound, therefore, to be under much closer supervision than those further inland. In addition the temperament of these people, particularly the Malays, did not lead any of the informed observers available to suggest that we could expect any immediate, enthusiastic and positive support from that source. But no one could conceive that we could make a coastal landing undetected. The beaches are the main roads of coastal Sarawak, there are no others. Every mile of offshore sea is worked by fishermen day and night.

Submarines appealed, however, in Australia. Several successful operations had already been conducted elsewhere. Parachute activities were as yet little understood in this field, and there was so far no parachute and dropping organization with skill and experience set up within the framework of 'Z'. (What other units may have owned I do not know.)

Parachuting powerfully appealed to the Australian male character.

It seemed tough. They had devised a system of training paratroops for their regular units which (alas for them) went right through the war without seeing real action—tougher training than anything of the kind elsewhere. Nick Combe and I had been through the lightning course at Ringway, near Manchester, in England, to emerge fully winged with five jumps in three days—man, woman and child. As neurotics, hypochondriacs, physical cowards, amiable fat men, virgins and some grandmothers make some of the best subversive agents, this free-for-all quickie method proved indispensable in Europe. To suggest it to the Australians was to threaten their ideal of manhood. This was a definite obstacle from our point of view. No one was to be allowed to qualify as a paratrooper without doing the full, the over-brimmingly full, course that they laid on for a muscle-racking month, at Richmond, New South Wales.

Toby Carter himself had a physical and psychological repugnance for parachuting. He actually started the Richmond course but was compelled (indeed, ordered) to give up—as at least three-quarters of the agents dropped into France or Greece would have been, no doubt. Inevitably, this affected his line of thought, and favoured the submarine approach, whatever the disadvantages.

The submarine approach appalled me, as soon as George Crowther was satisfied that I was who I was and could be taken into his SRD confidence. I had no deep prejudice against submarines; I had already had to do with them in connection with problems of civilian and service morale, and with the psychological difficulties certain technicians encountered when working underwater. But it seemed (to me) that even if a party survived a coastal landing, they could never get from there into a position of reasonable security and extend into well-established, long-term and possibly large-scale operations enough to inform and augment subsequent landings by regular troops in Borneo.

*　　*　　*

In submarine approach—inshore topography, tides and beach transport apart—the human problem was likely to remain as grave as or graver than any, if the party were safely ashore. In this terrain and set-up, lateral movement along the shore line would be out of the question. The only alternative (in West Borneo) would be to go up one of the large rivers. This could not fail to be extremely conspicuous, in an area where the Japanese were bound to be most numerous, their administration, intelligence and intercommunication best organized.

The coastal people were bound to be more under Japanese eyes, were almost entirely Chinese or Mohammedan Malays. The pagans, the head-hunter types, lived inland, roughly from the upper limits of the tidal reaches. The record of the past century or so did not suggest that these coastal people would readily act with the same toughness as the inlanders, for they had been long peaceable and closely administered. Surely, the difficulties of establishing even an elementary intelligence system in these surroundings would be fraught with danger—to such an extent that the mere job of keeping alive would be likely to preoccupy operatives, at the expense of objective estimates and co-ordinated achievements.

How could it fail to be both safer and easier to move from the inside outwards? *Down* the rivers, starting in areas of known toughness, with communications so slender that incisive action on arrival could probably control and restrict these and prevent quick leakage out towards the Japanese?

But what counted most, in my subjective estimate, was the character of the inland peoples whom I had met during the Oxford Expedition of 1932; and whom I could compare, in contemplation, with the love-loving Tahitians, the cannibals of Malekula and the cotton operatives of Lancashire. These strong-energetic, warm-hearted, generous minded Borneo people possessed a *positive* affection for the symbols of power and a comparatively small regard for personal comfort or absolute safety. The Kenyahs and Kayans of the Tinjar and Baram had clearly been devoted to, even loving towards, white men, through the goodwill built up in a century of White Rajah Brooke rule. Further inland the rumoured Kelabits might well be even more 'unspoiled', dynamic and warm—or deadly?

* * *

The laws of protocol were necessarily strict in 'Z' Special. Toby arrived first on the scene. So he was the senior officer in Semut. As I arrived second, I was second-in-command. Bill Sochon arrived a few weeks later, from being superior of some English prison; so he was third. But 'Z' Special was also, like all operational subversion, inherently also a soviet. Bill felt rather like me, having pulled his great weight through

Ringway's hoops and equally emerged a parachutist! Our two votes had some influence, and it was now passed over to me to *prove* my contention that an approach by parachute from the interior was feasible in the first place and preferable in the second—despite the delay in time which must arise before we could get within dropping range.

Fortified by feelings left from 1932 and by the years of subsequent experience in Malekula, Bolton, Strensall and Papeete, I set to work to convince myself—at least—that the thing could be done and was worth doing, my way. My ego could hardly be kept out of this. When I had accepted Colonel Egerton-Mott's shady overtures in Northumberland Avenue I had been given to understand that I should be on my own. No doubt this is the impression wittingly given to every visibly egocentric candidate for this sort of skullduggery. The attractions of working under somebody else—especially one of a gentler and nicer character —did not seduce. I must not disguise the point, therefore: my energies were now expended not only in proving the parachute approach feasible, but in claiming the privilege, if this plan were agreed, that I go in first (whoever commanded).

Sustained with this not even sneaking ambition, and supported by the tireless hospitality of Melbourne relatives and friends, I spent some of my happiest weeks on library research. It is worth very briefly summarizing the basic results, in so far as they did illuminate what was then known about the far interior—and especially the Kelabit peoples of the high uplands.

I had heard of the Kelabits and looked into the country (as we have seen) from the top of Mount Dulit. I knew no more than that: vague report; exciting fable. At first I drew a library blank, though the efficient Melbourne people got me in books from all over. None dealt with the interior terrain, open spaces, food supplies and other matters which must concern us. The principal Borneo writers of fact, such as Hugh Low, Alfred Russell Wallace, Spencer St John, or the first and second Rajahs Brooke, had not been interested or observant of such affairs. They were also much out of date; and none of them had been into the far interior areas which seemed the most promising for para-operations outwards, in antithesis to the submarine's inward approach. When I had exhausted the books—and incidentally established a general foundation of literary knowledge about Borneo which has been useful ever since—I started in on periodicals. Here I presently hit pay-dirt with a journal which was, in fact, then extinct.

The *Sarawak Museum Journal* (edited by the Curator) had been allowed to fold up by Curator Banks in 1937, on its thirteenth issue since the first in 1911. In that first 1911 issue was the first good clue.

Under the title 'An Expedition to the Bah Country', was a twelve-page article by R. O. Douglas, first white man to penetrate the hinterland. This was the first account of the uplands I had been able to find anywhere—and it was encouraging.

To start off with, it clearly referred to the people I had heard about when I was on Mount Dulit; for Douglas wrote:

'The expedition was directed against some tribes of Kalabits, living right in the very centre of Borneo, in a sort of no-man's land on the borders of Sarawak and Dutch territory. These had been raiding and killing Sarawak subjects for some years past as they had refused to listen to the peaceful arguments of various ambassadors. . . .'

The explorer tells of his long and exhausting journey up towards the uplands until on the seventeenth day he reaches and crosses the great Tamabo Range. As I went on, with him, from there it became perfectly exciting.

'In front of and below us was stretched out the plain of the Kalabit country. This great plain is bounded on three sides by the great mountain ranges of Pamabo, Murud, and Apo Rewat, which in places run up to 8,000 feet in height, whilst on the fourth side lie the head waters of the Baram River. These mountains are much higher above the plain on their outer face than on the inner, and I should think that this enclosed tableland must be between two and three thousand feet above sea level. It was a magnificent sight. . . .

'From here we descended into the plain, which near-by had been thoroughly irrigated and was covered with crops of rice in various stages of ripeness. It is strange that these Kalabits, *the wildest and furthest from civilization of all the tribes in Borneo*, should be the *only* interior people to irrigate their fields, and therefore, are able to obtain *two crops of rice in the year*.'

And as Douglas came down from the mountain top, I went with him, in the rather dark, pleasantly musty Melbourne Library room, out into what must surely (I felt) prove to be the Dropping Zone of 'Z' dreams—or (otherwise) all nightmare.

The last of what Douglas had to say was mostly about his own adventures, wars and peaces, head-hunting and ritual. But he emphasized one point again and heavily:

'All the tribes beyond the Pamabo Range are *entirely self-supporting*, growing their own rice by irrigation, making their own cloth out of bark, and as I have related making their own salt, which they trade to obtain steel for making their weapons of offence.'

I did not like so much the way he said:

'They have a name for being treacherous.'

Clearly, this *Sarawak Museum Journal* paper put the whole theme on a better footing. No one in Australia had even suspected an upland plain, let alone irrigated rice fields and independent people living in para-troop country, right inside Borneo.

Within a few months I was to be hearing direct of Douglas's epic three month journey, from the Kelabit end. The Kelabits love to detail the names of all white men who have ever come among them, though they cannot get the names right, any more than the white men got their names right in the first place. Douglas was the first to print the name 'Kalabit'. But Hose who preceded him as Senior Officer in the Baram, probably initiated the name. Their version of how they came to be called Kalabit (Kelabit latterly) goes like this:

The first man from the far uplands to visit the Government Station near the mouth of the Baram (?1900) could not speak any language known down there.

Hose: 'What race of people are these?'

Semi-interpreter: 'They are Pa Labid people.'

Hose: 'Ah: Kalabit.'

So Kalabit, latter Kelabit, they became on the subsequent records through an accident of the first contact being made with people from the Labid river (Pa), now uninhabited. The Kelabits make great fun of this and many other stories of contact with Europeans. They do not think of themselves as Kelabits at all, among themselves. It is only Europeans who group them in such formations.

While reading Hose, Douglas and the rest, I slid into the same attitude and it presently took trying time to get out of it again. The results of this attitude can be quite bewildering when you are trying to conduct para-military operations. The people of Bario, for example, will tell you—if you are stupid enough to ask them in the wrong way—that the Kelabit people stretch right across Borneo to the east coast and number millions. What they really mean is that these are all the people to whom the Brooke Government did not give their names—such as Kenyah, Kayan or Iban—either because they were in the hinterland or because they were not in Brooke territory at all. By the same token, Lawai Bisarai of Bario, initially implied, in proper upland fashion, that he was the head of all the Kelabits; and therefore my erroneous and excited early conclusion—that with great fortune I had fallen upon the leader of a million men! In Sarawak the word has acquired such currency, however, that it has to be used. And as the people called Kelabits in Sarawak are only a small section of a much larger language and culture group over the border to the east, no serious damage is done to ethnological conscience.

Douglas has passed into Kelabit folklore as *'Tuan Sandinglut'* (the end taken very fast, and the whole being derived from 'Resident Douglas'). The terrible occasion on which an elderly female slave was ritually put to death at the edge of the Bario plain, as the only way to stop a protracted head-hunting feud, almost corresponded with Douglas's visit. When he heard of it, he fined the parties concerned—their first and for a long time almost their last experience of outside administration in practice.

In the '20s and '30s individual Brooke officers visited the Kelabit country. But no accounts of these journeys were available.

Happily, the *Sarawak Museum Journal* provided a second and more recent account, in its dying 1937 issue, from no less a master than my old colleague of 1932, E. Banks. Mr Banks was a skilful and determined traveller; this side of his journeys excelled rather than his powers of accurately recording, in intelligible terms, what he saw and heard. As Curator of the Sarawak Museum he had, under the Third White Rajah, unique facilities for travelling throughout the country, in consequence an incomparable knowledge of the Brooke parts of Borneo.

Banks had visited the Kelabit country partly as a result of a report from an administrative officer who had noticed the megalithic monuments peculiar to these highlands, but who had allowed amazement to go to his head and produce a highly coloured exaggeration of the Atlantis 'Lost Tribe' type. In the *Museum Journal* for 1937 Banks wrote of the same plain Douglas had first seen:

'Undoubtedly the most striking feature is the view from Pungga Pawan 5,500 feet high on the top of the Tama Abo mountains when taking the Tutoh route, overlooking the wide flat plain between three and four thousand feet high where the people of the village of Lam Bah have broken up the plain into irrigated rice fields. . . .

'Lam Bah is a small village of perhaps not more than fifty people, intensely rich in this world's goods thanks to their situation. The plain itself is *as flat as a board,* covered with long grass or scrub vegetation where not cultivated. Situated in two parts, that recently cultivated is about three miles long and sometimes as much as half a mile broad. I can scarcely imagine a more ideal spot for European occupation *if only more* accessible.'

It was delightful, sitting there in bright brass buttons in the quiet room the Melbourne Library people had put at my disposal, to be studying my old opponent in words and treasuring every sentence of his otherwise unattractive prose style, to be memorized, analysed and rearranged to support arguments in favour of an interior approach. Douglas's account was too old to stand on its own in this affair. Banks gave weight of later date.

* * *

These were the pearls which I cast before my seniors of 'Z' Special. While Banks was languishing in the bitter miseries of Japanese internment outside Kuching (the capital of Sarawak) thanks to Banks, George Crowther, Jumbo Courtney and Jack Finlay now began to take Harrisson seriously. Hitherto, we had been discussing the heart of Borneo as if it were a closed book. Now began glimmers of light, encouragingly.

What we still lacked was any information about the much larger area of the Dutch Borneo interior. Here there was no museum or journal to help out. And the Dutch themselves were unable (or unwilling?) to give any help. But here I had a stroke of luck. I had been spending some extra-curricula time earning a few half-honest pounds by writing a series of articles in the *Melbourne Argus,* describing Australia as seen through pommy eyes, and purporting to be by Colonel I. M. English. These bomblets caused quite a stir and also brought me into friendly association with the editor, Brigadier-General Knox, who had previously been Director of Military Intelligence in the Australian army. One day I took a chance and told him a little bit of what I was up to, with special reference to Dutch Borneo difficulties. Largely as a result of this, a document was unearthed in the files of the Shell Company Head Offices, which proved of the highest value both to my argument and subsequent enterprise.

This document was a long report by Dr W. F. Schneeberger, a top oil geologist, who had explored the north-west interior of Dutch Borneo for the Company just before the war. Schneeberger spent the better part of a year in the Dutch interior and eventually nearly died on the lower reaches of the Sesayap River, which rises as the Bawang from the most easterly toe of Mount Murud, at Pa Bawang. Of first importance, to us, was his description of a series of plains, comparable to the Plain of Bah as described by Douglas and Banks, but between twenty and fifty miles further east, across the border. The report was illustrated by some photographs showing beautiful, fertile, flat valley bottoms, clearly densely populated and cultivated. These were the first photos to give support.

These three rather obscure sources provided the ammunition sufficient to establish a case for at least *thinking* in terms of parachute entry, as a possible alternative to submarine sneaks.

By the time I emerged from my library studentship, it was becoming clear that somewhere there in the middle of Borneo, although not marked on our maps, there existed:

   (i) Plenty of pagan people.

   (ii) Plenty of potential food supply on the spot, especially rice.

   (iii) Several large tracts of open and flat grassland, swamp or rice.

   (iv) Practicable, though difficult and trying, land communications by jungle tracks leading *out* of the interior in several directions.

   (v) But very little knowledge and virtually no direct contact from the coast (at least until 1937) to the upland plains.

Thus armed, I worked my way through New Guinea, scaled the social pinnacles of Hollandia, and flew with the lads from Morotai to confirm with the eye and the camera, as will be described.

The submarine project was dropped. Toby Carter and the others generously agreed that my indoor efforts should be rewarded; that I could be first in the field.

By one of the feats of organization in which 'Z' Special did excel and the Shell Company still do, a few hours before my plane—now a Royal Australian Air Force Liberator of the newly formed 'Z' Special Flight 200—took off from Queensland for New Guinea, Dr Schneeberger was delivered unto me in person, fresh from New York in a topmost secretist package. This delightful neutral gave all sorts of additional information which had had no place in his oil report but which greatly increased my confidence; we were on the right lines. He also confirmed my suspicion that we could not conduct any operations from the interior unless, in the end, we disregarded the distinctions between Sarawak and the adjacent territories of North and Dutch Borneo. He also fired my imagination with descriptions of the eastern valleys, their rich, friendly and forceful peoples.

The final message from Schneeberger was on a currency note. Money was of no use. The best thing to take in bulk, he suggested, would be needles and fish hooks. This conversation was conducted in the secretive setting of an aerodrome far out on the Darling Downs a hundred miles west of Brisbane. It was late. We were due to take off at dusk. This was the type of situation which always brought out the worst in 'Z' Special. Not to put too fine a point on it, the fantastic furniture of our first landing at Bario included fifty thousand fish hooks and a quarter of a million needles. After we had produced a situation of advanced steel inflation throughout the interior, the needles found a second function. Ingeniously arranged, set in bamboo, they made reassuring palisades, hidden in the ground around jungle camps at night.

*　　*　　*

Flight 200 was commanded by Squadron Leader Graham Pockley, DSO, DFC, who earlier in the war had gained fame flying Sunderland RAF seaplanes against submarines from south-west England, a bit of which had for a while been nicknamed 'Pockley's Corner'. He was basically a happy man. But lying in the warm sand on the beach at Mindanao, amidst the carnage of the American Philippine landing, he admitted he was less happy flying Liberators than Sunderlands. It was one o'clock on a marvellous moonlight morning. In a few minutes we would wander over to the American met. station on the edge of the airfield, get reasonably good weather (in this monsoon season) confirmed, determined to end the long misery, since we left Darling Downs —of weather delays and failed attempts to find a way through cloud down into a jungle hole, when we had actually got over the interior of Borneo all ready to drop.

We lay and talked in the blistering moonlight, baring only far hopes and the slower aches. I remember the conversation with sadness and because of this sadness. Also because it was the last conversation of the kind that I held in peaceful and pleasant surroundings with another person of my own race (even if he was an Aussie!) for a long time to come.

I verbally visualized the end of this journey, coming back out of Borneo. To Graham I explained, sprawling unashamed in the shadow, my intentions of returning to Mass-Observation and Lancashire with a new dedication. I must not, I must not (I said) let myself get caught up again in the whirl of ambition, publicity, money, and facile prestige which had seemed to be wished upon me against my own better sense. With unusual clarity I defined to him (I think) the difficulty which had infested a good deal of my life and which, this shining morning, could be looked at coolly with the promise that part of the dilemma must be solved for a time if we survived in the middle of Borneo.

What I adored in myself was an unquenchable curiosity and an apparently endless, tireless urge to record what I saw, plus a certain ability to dissociate myself from violent feelings about it. The thing which makes science tick and threaten humanity, ticked in me until I wanted no other. The burning search for some sort of final satisfaction in knowledge, regardless of power. How easy it was to say, in the sweet air of the Philippine bay, ignoring wrecked landing craft, a smashed fuselage and the battered-in helmet, my pillow of the mood. How satisfying to segregate, in this solitude, the other side of Harrisson's equation—the apparently insatiable ego, the drive to do whatever I had to do or wanted to do, either *before* or *better* than anyone else (preferably both).

And how unpleasant all success did seem. Was it not awful to falter for comfort's sake, to make concessions for acclamation, and so on and so on? I would refresh my spirit and purify my heart by returning only to the simple ways.

My Australian friend fell into this mood and talked of his own post-war dream. He would buy two islands off the Great Barrier Reef. On one he would build a simple but very comfortable hotel with attached bungalows, offering the visual wonders of these rainbow coral bays. On the other he would build with his own hands—a wooden house, from which he would manage the hotel.

We settled at that and with soothed subconsciouses strolled over to the Met. Officer. By noon I was drunk and he—along with the others of his crew and a delightful major from Leicester, Everard Ellis, an SOE man out from London to study our para methods—sunk in the South China Sea.

MAP B

BORNEO AT WAR: FEBRUARY-NOVEMBER, 1945

The island of Borneo was the subject of several sporadic efforts by 'Z' Special. The two which developed and survived were Agas *(Sandfly) in North Borneo, as shown on the map opposite; and* Semut *(Ant) to the south, which eventually operated in all four of the Borneo territories—the south-west corner of North Borneo, Brunei, a large part of interior Sarawak and what was the then Dutch Borneo.*

The Roman numbers indicate the Semut area as eventually divided between Semut I (Harrisson), II (Carter) and III (Sochon; see page 229).

Allied landings subsequent to the establishment of Semut occurred successively at Tarakan, Labuan Island and later around Brunei Bay, and in the south-east on Balikpapan (where there was no organized hinterland, intelligence or other support).

III

THE MOUNTAINED HEART

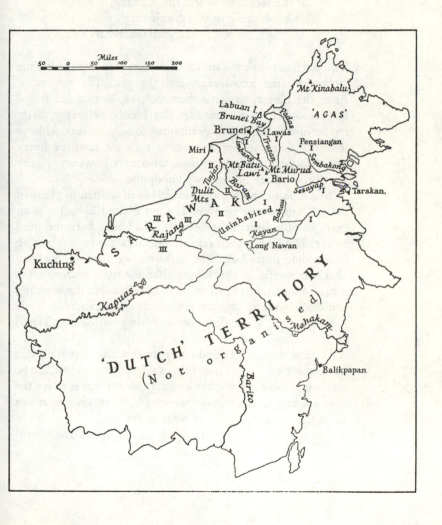

Miles
50 0 50 100 150 200

Mt Kinabalu

Labuan I.
Brunei Bay
Brunei
Miri

Padas

'AGAS'

Lawas

Pensiangan

Sembakong

Limbang
Trusan
Tinjar
Baram
Mt Batu
Lawi
Dulit
Mts
Rajang

Mt Murud
Bario

Sesayap

Tarakan

S A R A W A K

Uninhabited

Bahau

Kayan

Long Nawan

Kuching

Kapuas

'DUTCH' TERRITORY
(Not organised)

Mahakam

Barito

Balikpapan

'Soon he soothed his soul to pleasure.
War, he sung, is toil and trouble;
Honour but an empty bubble.
Never ending, still beginning,
Fighting still, and still destroying,
If the world be worth the winning,
Think, oh think, it worth enjoying'.

Dryden (*Alexander's Feast*)

'I should like to ask the advice of any kind reader who has the inclination, the knowledge, and the pen. The subject is, Ants; the object, to wipe them out, or, as our old friend Roget would have it, to murder, slay, nullify, neutralize, do in, render moribund, put to death intentionally, or sink without trace; so that not one survives to ruin the lawn or hurry across the table at breakfast-time, when ants, however worthy their mission, are notoriously unpopular.

'Much, some think too much, has been written in praise of the ant, emmet, or pismire. The ant is cited by bores as an example of industry. Far better if it had been born too tired to live. The ant has been admired by romantics for celebrating its wedding in mid-air. The husbands, we are told, die soon after this nuptial flight, having, like the male spiders, some sort of dislike taken to them by their wives. For the wedding and the funeral no separate invitations are necessary.'

R. C. Robertson-Glasgow (*Sunday Times*)

'Of course there are a good many times when there is no war just as there are a good many times when there is a war. To be sure when there is a war the years are longer that is to say the days are longer the months are longer are much longer but the weeks are shorter that is what makes war'.

Gertrude Stein (*Wars I Have Seen*)

IMPACT OF ANTS

1945 . . . Bario, from 5,000 ft.

Dropping out of a four-engine Liberator bomber is roughly comparable to water-skiing behind a speed boat; or bob-sleighing. But it also has something more. There is one moment in this kind of parachuting which (although I have done it often enough) has never ceased to hold a magic not quite to be met with any other way.

To start with, jumping out of a Liberator is—or was, as 'Z' had it arranged—easier than any other despatch. It required minimum acts of volition and decision as compared with the effort of jumping through the square hole in the floor of a Whitley (seeing the land below, remembering not to jump too hard and hit your head the other side); or out of the door of a Douglas (with harness trappings and one eye on the tail plane). All that we had to do in Libs was swing legs over a sort of an aluminium toboggan slide, fitted forward of the camera hatch in the tail. It was back in the nursery stuff. You could not see anything out of the camera hatch, let alone anything below. You did not have to do a thing but just sit there, wait for the word, let go your hands, slide smoothly down on your backside and parachute pack.

As in some dream of boyish whoopee, you shot out legs first into 200 miles an hour of slip stream, under the fat bomb belly of the plane. For one delicious moment this pulsing current held head back, feet up, as if lying in dreaming semi-sleep on air. Once the trick was learned, I could keep my head back and watch for that ecstatic second when the static line connecting the pack on my back with the hook inside the plane ran right out. Then: flick, and the marvellous silken unfolding of the giant parasol; life. For by this time the feet were falling, the illusion of everlasting peace shading away back into the faint scent of mortality.

The rest was less easy, and much less interesting. On this Borneo morning, it was even useless to play boats by manipulating the multiplicity of ropes connecting the parachute panels with the tight body belt. There was no point in trying to sail with air against the wind blowing. Also, the morning cloud gathered and obscured everything, and in a few seconds sucked in the parachute too. That was a nasty half-minute, swishing and swaying down without being able to see ground or tree, unable to balance the muscles and prepare for the saucy roll-over which the simplest parachute training insisted upon. As I always hit the ground wrong anyhow, it was actually a relief on this occasion not to have to think about trying to please the spirits of past instructors or possible critics.

*   *   *

The Liberator roared away, following the white fingers of Batu Lawi, 'Mt 200', which could still guide them. Unfortunately, on the way back, they decided to shoot up what looked like a harmless motor-vessel but proved to be camouflaged ack-ack.

It was some months before this news saddened us. It taught me one lesson though—a lesson I had already begun to suspect I ought to learn through the tensions of our false flights in the previous weeks. I have since made it iron principle always to jump out of any plane I got into intending to jump from; whatever the conditions, never to be carried home.

The effect of silence, by comparison, lay shatteringly upon the plain for a minute or two, before ears re-attuned to the ceaseless insect thrum of Borneo.

You could almost touch the woolly cloud, dank overhead. Under foot, deep brown mud sogged and swooshed at the least movement. Nothing to be seen but great tussocks of rush and sedge close around, in a moment of entire loneliness, nearly of non-existence. One might have been a ghost, so impossible seemed the sudden transition from bomber to Borneo, from ambition to nowhere known.

But there was more to be done than masturbate the mind. I broke disciplined silence with a queezy shout which echoed back from the Tamabo cliffs and was, in its way, to ricochet through the interior and away to the sea, sounding a new age for the unexpectant far high interior. From nearby came reassuring replies. Following me out of the hatch had shot (in a sequence which I have now forgotten, but remember there was fierce competition about) Staff Sergeant Sanderson, Staff Sergeant Bower and Sergeant Barry. These three, and four more to follow, had been selected out of all the personnel available in 'Z' Special and—as a special privilege for this operation—from the ranks of the regular paratroop organizations also. I had selected the three in my immediate party each for a special role:

Sanderson—for a previous knowledge of the east (though not Borneo); a facility for languages; high quality of courage already proved; quick intelligence; disregard for personal comfort. His special responsibility: to make the earliest possible contact with one or more local persons so that we could immediately obtain help to gather up the several tons of stores dropped after us; or, if the initial contact was unsatisfactory, to take measures to organize against possible hostility.

Bower—a well qualified radio operator and mechanic; of even temperament, with great willingness to tackle anything. His immediate concern: to recover the radio-set dropped with us in a special marked container (storepedo), reassemble this, contact Darwin in Australia quickly.

Barry—in civilian life a surveyor, was also an experienced soldier and competent organizer. Small, very strong, and even stronger-minded; physically and mentally nimble. His first job was to organize the collection of stores dropped.

Sanderson without needing any orders (he never did) had taken off on his quest. The other three of us thrashed around, anxiety and irritation swamping elation—we were rather exhausted even before landing—feebly attempting to find wireless, weapons and stores (including needles). Very slowly the mist lifted. The first faint shaft of eastern sunlight filtered on to the plain. It began to smell something like everyday day again. I heard Bower cursing in the fluent, Victorian way. We were around that bend, all right! We wallowed on, happily unaware that this swamp was the favourite resort of a very large King Cobra which had killed six buffaloes not long before; and of tiny ticks which carry Scrub Typhus (later acquired).

Into this disorganization, so wildly contrary to the disciplined landing and immediate action which we had devised and rehearsed over and over again on the open Queensland downs, there suddenly obtruded a white flag. A small square of white cloth—one of the only pieces of cloth in the area at the time—appeared bobbing up and down, some tussocks away. We made all the encouraging sounds in all the languages we knew, without moving ourselves (or its manipulator). As it would not budge, we squelched to encircle it, presently to discover a shivery fellow, olive-skinned, with splendid black hair flowing down below his yellow bark loin-cloth. The white cloth was tied to the spear end of a long, polished blow-pipe. Thus after years of Japanese occupation, Bornean pagan and Anglo-Australian Christian man met in peace once more.

The son-in-law of Chief Lawai Bisarai was shivery with cold as much as with fear. For some months past the occasional planes—in which I had been probing inland—had caused increasing alarm. On this day, we had circled so closely that although the Bario people were not certain anything had dropped out of the planes, their men had fanned out across the plain to try to find out what went on, each Kelabit with a small piece of the one white cloth, ordinarily reserved for spirit propitiation ceremonies. They knew vaguely that aeroplanes were artifacts (containing people); but had no idea that people could *drop* out of them *deliberately* and the planes continue on. And although markedly less suspicious than most groups of humans, they felt it possible, if not probable, that spirits were mixed up in all this. If these spirits were going so far as to *return* to the plain itself, this was something new. It was also, according to deductions to be drawn from Kelabit sagas, likely that under these circumstances those returning would be friendly, or, at the worst, subject to propitiation, susceptible to amiable protestations plus adequate supplies of borak, rice, pork and women. If this were not so, petrification would have long since set in, the dreadful *balio* conversion.

I had given up smoking while in the KRR's, back at Strensall where I found that if I gave my cigarette ration to the Sergeant he let me off early morning parade before breakfast, which I never ate anyway. But my two Australians performed a conjuring trick on the tense Kelabit face by offering fags and real live matches. As our man dragged and so evidently eased his anxieties, I plied him with questions which I had constructed and memorized *ad nauseam*. We had concluded, correctly as it turned out, that we would be very unlikely to contact anyone who could speak Malay straight away. These people were remote; it was not to be supposed that even the *lingua franca* of the lowland pagans would have penetrated and proved useful up here. Banks had implied the greatest difficulty in making himself understood.

And in fact a good deal of what he reported was inaccurate for this reason. Douglas, earlier, had recorded a short vocabulary of words. I had spent weary days filling this out with other vocabularies from the *Sarawak Museum Journal* file at Melbourne, hoping some of the words would correspond in other pagan languages.

The effect of my verbal attempts upon the good man were entirely negative. Indeed, less than that. For instance:

Me: 'Kita Kelabit?'

He: . . . .?

Me: (tapping his chest and looking winsome) 'Kelabit—Kau Kelabit?'

He: 'Ekor?' (meaning 'You').

Me: (getting over-excited, thumping him and pointing all round) 'Kelabit? Kelabit? KELABIT?'

He: 'Bah!'

We had a lot of that Bah, which I could not grasp was attached to several words; to mean the long-house in which he lived, the plain on which we stood, the people around. For we had indeed dropped at Banks's Lam Bah, Bario. The problem of who *he* was did not present itself to *him* in this context—let alone the problem of what group he was supposed to belong to. Only the chiefs and the sophisticates of outside contact had to be aware of being something more than them.

This exercise in linguistics got us nowhere. Apart from the inadequacy of the original vocabulary and the absurdities I had added by trying to graft in outside (though adjacent) languages, Kelabit is spoken with a series of tones, glottal catches and stresses which are difficult to express in written words and put it (as spoken) in the same class, muscularly, as Chinese. Soon we resorted to simple devices, hand signs, eyebrow work, with particular emphasis on pointing into our mouths. Long after, when we could talk to each other, Amat explained that he thought we were rebuking him for not having brought any borak to drink; he had felt terribly ashamed.

Leaving Bower to continue the search for radio and other stores, our first contact—soon joined by two more—led Barry and me out of the swamp and quickly into delightful, clean grassland, white at this season with tall, spiky orchids, and loud with the calls of Sedge and Reed Warblers wintering here from the far north. We did not realize that a lot of the ground we were walking over had, a few weeks ago, been golden with a particularly early and rich rice harvest, luckily for us. The fields had been drained; the fences, bridges, clappers, scarecrows and windmills taken down and stored for next season. But as the sun edged well over the eastern ranges, warming into the valley, we could see that we were in a magnificent setting. At this hour of the day the mountains to the west gain an exaggerated altitude, and the tremendous cliffs obstructing a view of Batu Lawi to the north-west grow into monstrosity as they catch their first shafts of sunlight.

Round a twist, through low bushes with pretty pink flowers, and there—smoke black and looking rather like a long, leafy model of itself—sat a long-house (echo, for me, of 1932) snug on the knoll at the edge of the plain and the foot of steep mountain slopes, densely covered in dulling jungle. We still weren't sure where we were. But at the top of the notched pole, welcoming us as we crawled up into the house, was clearly a great man. He had put on all his best clothes, was magnificent in leopard skin hat, hornbill feathers, old beads, brass ear-rings, a tattered khaki coat (Brooke relic of rank), leg bangles, sword in embroidered sheath, and all the rest.

Lawai Bisarai was more familiar with outside ways than was his newly nicotined son-in-law. The most white-influenced of all the upland people, he had done time as gardener to the Administrative Officer down in the lower Baram, as penalty for killing a man (already described).★

This middle-aged 'murderer' at once put my doubts at rest. He welcomed us into the long-house. There people crowded around. Things became fearfully confused. The main over-all reaction was bewilderment, amazement, coupled with dreadful efforts to ask questions from both sides about things which, on each other side, were not of immediate interest—or worth explaining even had that been prac-ticable. The first things the Kelabits wanted to know were: were we humans? and how did we get out of the aeroplane? The first things we wanted to know were: were there any Japs in the immediate vicinity? and would these people help us—at first simply hide and feed us? For although we had brought some food supplies, my argument as to local availability had been only too readily accepted (by HQ) in favour of using our available weight balance for technical equipment and arms.

Our welcome by Lawai had already been prepared by the skill with which Sanderson had found his way towards the long-house and separately contacted their people; he was already inside and had succeeded in explaining, mostly by signs, that we had a lot of stores,

★ If all this had been nowadays, that act would have cost Lawai his life, by hanging.

IX   Penghulu Lawai, BEM, at Bario, 1958. (*See p. 196*)

XIa Penghulu Miri (with belt of silver dollars) and other southern Kelabits in 1945. The man on the left of Penghulu Miri is wearing his sergeant-major's insignia on his left wrist. (*See p. 205*)

XIb 'Sarongs from Heaven': Kelabit women in new clothes celebrating a war-time occasion. (*See p. 104*)

XIIa and XIIb Views of the final ceremonies and communal drinking outdoors in an *irau* feast at Bario. (*See pp.* 129-133)

XIII Bario man with blowpipe and some less formidable quarry of those days. (*See p.* 88)

XIV   Senghir, the top aristocrat of Balawit, holding one of the most valu-able jars in the interior; Senghir was second only to Penghulu Lasong Piri as a war-time leader in North-West Dutch Borneo. (*See pp.* 25, 34, 46, 115)

XV The path westward to the lowlands crosses the Kubaan river.
(*See pp.* 19 *and* 227)

XVIa Kelabit making canoe paddle for use once arrived in the lowlands. (See p. 21)

XVIb The type of long-house commonly made by Kenyahs and Kayans in the lowlands in the Baram river. (See pp. 22 and 318)

which we hoped were to be found, out on the plain. Now that a welcome of sorts had been given—and clearly there were no Japs threatening right on the spot—all efforts were expended in getting every man, woman and child out to hunt for our dropped storepedoes. The idea sank in; the response was adequate. But before the operation could begin there was an exasperating period in which we were compelled to drink borak. As the others had never had it before, and as it can be much stronger than it smells, our weary brains now battled, in addition, with alcohol.

Never mind. Soon enough Barry and Bower had about fifty people out searching. Meanwhile, Sanderson and I sat swilling with the seniors. Gradually Lawai revealed that he could understand a good deal and speak a little Malay, learnt during his murder sentence. But it was hard going.

We got across, though, the general idea that we were here to stay; to oppose the Japs; and as prelude to a mass return of white people. This was received well; but clearly with doubt. We could not then know that over-stating the case and wildly boasting are taken for granted as human attitudes at Bario, and therefore plain statement tends to be discounted.

All the same, within an hour of first meeting me Lawai Bisarai had in effect, over borak, pledged himself to our side. This was a brave thing to do. The Japanese had been squeezing the whole island in a reign of terror which had penetrated into every corner of it. Their actions and propaganda had put across the idea that the white men were finished for ever. Our reappearance—for once the spirit thing had been sorted out, we were readily identified as relatives of Banks and Douglas —was all the propaganda we needed except for one thing. This one thing was: the few guns owned under the Brookes had been confiscated by the Japs.

If Lawai supported us, could we back him up against the Japanese with arms? We got it across, more or less, that we could and would, rapidly and with vim. But all this hung in doubt, and almost as much in my mind as his, while we sat on the mats and drank, the sun climbing outside to scorch down on Barry and Bower.

I was having difficulty, in general, in focusing now on what on earth it was all about, why were we here, what for? Dizzingly, the directives for operation *Semut I*, the First Ants, echoed:

(i) To establish initial contact with the native inhabitants and see if they are friendly, and to prepare the way for *Semut II* anyway.

(ii) If friendly, to find out where the Japanese are and set up an intelligence system to radio back full details of all enemy depositions, strengths and movements prior to Allied landings planned on both sides of Borneo's coast in the near future.

(iii) If possible, further, to train and deploy the local population as guerrilla troops and attack the enemy and dislocate his communication from the rear, co-ordinating with (but not ahead of) the aforesaid Allied landings.

(iv) Meanwhile and immediately to take such steps as are practicable to dislocate enemy supplies, communications and help without being detected.

(v) Further, as later Allied Forces intend to occupy the coastal areas only, to build up an organization to deal with all enemy forces likely to fall back inland and, unless dealt with, remain a menace.

(vi) To make urgent enquiries as to the whereabouts of surviving Australian, English, Dutch and other Civilian and escaped Prisoners-of-War, believed to be in the interior, as well as bailed out American bomber crews; and to take immediate steps to secure and evacuate any such.

No, it was really a bit too much for just now. I took another long pull at the rice borak, on the floor, by the dragon jar.

★　　★　　★

In all this haze and heating confusion I had nearly but not completely lost sight of the fact that my second-in-command and three other chaps were absent from this mountain scene. They had been in a second Liberator following behind ours. We had seen this circling and heard it overhead after our landing. But in the unsatisfactory cloud conditions and with security restrictions on radio inter-communication, I was not at all sure that their lot knew that I had jumped or if they had jumped themselves. This uncertainty was balanced in favour of *no*, when there was no sign of them upon the plain; and none of the Bario people had registered them. Still, Sanderson got it across that a special party must go and search further afield. I don't suppose he got it across much, because such a search, if the party were lost, would probably have been hopeless any way.

Immediately behind the plain the mountains were so tangled, the jungle so complicated, that when (a few weeks later) a Liberator mis-dropped arms on us, with an error of under a mile, into the head of the next but uninhabited valley, it was more than three years before Tayun discovered the first storepedo relics, torn to pieces by honey-bears. The other point—which needed no putting across—was to send runners and bring in people from all around as soon as possible.

So, there were plenty of questions buzzing about the Plain of Bah and my reeling head. Where were the storepedoes dropped after us—if they had been dropped at all? Where were the other four? There was not yet time to start worrying seriously about where were the Japs, or any other enemies. These would be answers to seek and send directly we had something to send with, assembled, and on the air.

Before long, the first storepedo was found out in the scrub. These storepedoes were admirably suited for their purpose. A cylinder of very hard cardboard reinforced with metal bands, long enough to hold a man, carried a conical and hollow cardboard head. The object, which looked something like a fat torpedo, was secured at the rear end to a strong, khaki cloth parachute. After ejection, the parachute unfurled and swung so that the conical head pointed down. The nose struck the ground first, and took up a great part of the shock. It was therefore possible to land delicate apparatus in this way. In this and the following months we received tons of radio and radar equipment, medical supplies, explosives, grenades, ammunition and fire-arms, with prac-tically no damage. We only lost about twenty per cent of all drops because of planes dropping them into jungles, rivers, gorges and God knows where.

It took eight or nine lusty Kelabits to carry in each storepedo. When we gave the rough cloth panels to the first four, the acceleration seemed to turn the plain's mud into dust. Dr Schneeberger and the rest of us had overlooked the parachutes themselves. These immediately became a new sort of internal currency, at a time when all ordinary traffic with the coast had come to a standstill. The Japanese had been unable to keep up imports and the whole interior had slid back into bark cloth, which makes less comfortable and lasting garments (and long before this, had grown to be regarded as an inferior type of clothing, the sack-cloth of Borneo habit). The several miles of parachute cord involved in any drop also acquired high value—not only for binding, making nets and traps; but also, unwound, stripped, respun and woven on hand looms into excellent waistcoats, skirts and sarongs.

The whole tempo began to speed up. The amount of anxiety, silence and shyness to dwindle rapidly away, replaced by the noisiness, 'heartiness' and voluble laughter we soon came to learn—and sometimes to hate—as the true sounds of upland living. By dusk, the whole affair had taken on the quality of an enormous picnic. The short grass on the knoll beside the long-house was covered with laid-out stores, now being unpacked, by quick and eager Kelabit fingers, and classified by Barry. After the initial mistake of giving away a parachute, the others were laid out to be distributed carefully, our currency.

By dusk, too, the uneasy though not unexciting feeling that the four of us were unexpectedly left on our own, was resolved by the appearance of the other four. Their arrival was heralded with vast shouts and long yodelling yells, as their guide-rescuers brought them in from the far southern side of the plain. They had not needed any rescue in fact; the guiding, however, had come in handy. It was grand to see them again—and even better when we found that their storepedoes had curiously been dropped correctly on to the plain, where they had not.

Eric Edmeades had seen me jump and, of course, determined to do the same, even though he, his pilot and the despatcher—without the advantage of the knowledge of terrain I had acquired on previous flights—had very little idea where they were. So his stick of four had shot through the hatch and the cloud, to end up crashing into the jungle canopy about three miles off 'DZ'. Fortunately, there had been old cultivation here and the jungle was not more than fifty years old, the trees less than one hundred feet high. Two of them had crashed straight through, the other two extricated themselves, somehow, from the tree tops and got down with the use of harness and lines. Once down it had taken them two hours to assemble. They then navigated by compass on the basis of a rough sketch of the valley conformation which I had boldly devised, largely from imagination, beforehand. But it was mainly by Eric's jungle sense and his quick detection of human indications that his party managed to find a way so quickly.

There are few things simpler than getting lost anywhere in the interior of Borneo. Step two paces off the track, turn round, not notice a mark—and that may well be the last anyone hears of you.

A word, before I go on, about Eric Edmeades. I had been allowed, in good old 'Z' Special style, to select *anyone* I liked as second-in-command of this advance party of Operation *Semut*. As Ant No. 2 I had chosen Eric because he differed from me in important respects: he believed in toughness for its own sake; he took risks for fun; he looked nice, blond, clear-eyed, strong chinned, fine shouldered, most athletic; he was not primarily interested in ideas or principles, yet had a firm moral base from missionary parents in India; although in the Australian army, he was a New Zealander and had those slight differences of outlook which sometimes make the New Zealander more English than the English, while they remain more easily acceptable to the Australians than an ordinary pommy, as leader. I correctly anticipated that at one time or another my Australian subordinates would get difficult, especially when they got far away from my direct control, spread out in operations over a wide field. I also estimated that in such cases Eric would be an ideal trouble shooter to sort them out. He had a further advantage in this beginning. When I chose him, he was a senior instructor in the Australian Parachute School and had done more jumps than anyone else in the continent. This gave a sort of halo of respectability to our phase of the operation, a sophistication and polish of theoretical performance which no one who had seen me bumping out of aircraft could conceivably award to Ant No 1. I could not have made a better decision, for once. Without Eric, everything would have been twice as difficult, some of it impossible. He literally did not accept the word impossible. It may be taken for granted, in all this story, that whatever he did, he did twice as fast and well as could be expected.

Eric's party included the second wireless operator, Sergeant Hallam, who was immediately pressed into service with Bower, assembling the first of our 'Boston' portable radio-transmitters.

Staff Sergeant J. Tredrea, Ant No. 7, was the medical orderly. He launched his warm heart at the terrifying panorama of ulcers, yaws, skin diseases and other troubles always present in remote places, but now accentuated by several years of Japanese occupation and the consequent dislocation of the minimum commerce and contact outward.

Warrant-Officer Cusack, a tall, cool, quiet Queenslander, had been included as quartermaster. He was now put in charge of the stores and security side of things, while we got organized and established.

*   *   *

By dark, then, a good part of our stores and all of us were assembled on the groaning boards of the long-house verandah at Bario. It was painfully noticeable that these eight white Ants, all set to eat their way into Borneo, failed to meet any of the specifications set down thirteen years before by Mr Banks when he discussed the undesirable characters of the energetic eight-man Oxford Expedition of 1932 (page 153). He had written that four men were enough, four months time enough. We already exceeded the former and were due to exceed the latter standard. Apart from myself (thirty-three) the average age of the party was twenty-one. Several of us were already—and all about to become—'uncouth in appearance'; and the object of the operation was to be, in certain directions, as 'unpleasant in personality' as possible.

But young or older, we were too tired by now—and mostly too full—to care more for the moment. We only had to look at the faces around us, listen to the singing and laughter, to be assured that we were among friends. The idea that any of these people could think to betray us, steal from us or mislead us (seriously), seemed inconceivable. And for once in inland life, things were exactly set for our purposes; the rest would come out in the wash long after the war was over—some of it, not yet . . . ?

I can only remember two things from that hilarious evening: one, that in response to numerous songs of welcome in our honour, the only one we could all eight find in common and sing in unison was 'Three Blind Mice'. With Barry's sense of the dramatic and Sanderson's of the ridiculous, plus some of Edmeades's exuberant gymnastics, this proved an overwhelming success and almost brought the long-house down (literally). Second, the dogs. This was our first experience of the appalling clamour with which Kelabit dogs decorate the gamut of darkness. If they are kept in the long-house, they spend the night dashing about in packs, scratching and fighting around and across the sleeping humans. If they are kept out, they yowl and shriek, bay the moon, bark the owl, chase the pigs, infuriate the buffaloes beneath your plank. This first night, they were left in. Several of us lost valued army boots in consequence. (Poor Cusack last saw his self-winding wrist-watch disappear with a dog chewing the strap.)

Perhaps I have not done justice to the occasion which, after all, deserves some note. After years of complete Japanese domination and a cruel control—during which the white man was shown to be gone beyond recall—here were eight whites dying of sleep in the snug, smoky, torch-flickering long-house, furthest, highest in the land. But if in this odd situation we felt the Japs offered no threat to us, could we feel that we offered any threat to them? Yes, we already could—and did—so long as we and our friends felt this was a *beginning* and so long as the Japs themselves should not become aware of our presence before we were strong enough and ready. Such was the power of the impression we got from these remote people that first night.

Eric Edmeades lives just across the Sarawak River, nowadays—in the peacetime capital, Kuching. I only have to dial Constabulary Headquarters and ask for his office, Commanding Officer, Field Force. So I dialled Eric to write down what he remembered of that first Bario evening; he responded:

'*I shall never forget my first evening in Bario.* Over the years I have spent many nights in long-houses scattered all over the interior. But the sense of wonderment, the dreamlike quality of that first night, will never be recaptured.

'The reaction after months of training and disappointments, the excitement of our quick transition from Australia to the tropics, the thrill of floating down through the clouds all combined to make the evening memorable.

'It seemed hard to believe, sitting there in the smoky, dimly lit long-house surrounded by the flat, brown smiling faces of our hosts that we were in Borneo. There was no question that we were amongst friends, but where were the Japanese?

'After two or three hours of Kelabit hospitality I personally couldn't have cared less. All my security training seemed awash with "borak" and I remember remarking to someone else in our party "*What a wonderful way to go to war*".'

Next morning the tempo stepped up again. The two wireless operators had got an aerial slung high on the knoll overlooking the long-house and were beginning to pump out our code sign on the reserved frequency where Darwin were keeping a twenty-four hour watch.

Edmeades, with Sanderson's aid, was primarily concerned with finding out everything possible about routes west, farther into Sarawak. Once established with reasonable short-term security, my next local tasks—as well as the big ones of the basic directive—were fourfold:

(i) To reconnoitre a way *west* into the main Baram for Carter and Sochon to follow after they had been dropped into Bario at the earliest possible date; and as far as possible to ensure their good reception by the Kenyahs and Kayans in the upper reaches of the Baram.

(ii) To reconnoitre *eastward* and find out more about the possibilities of the otherwise unknown areas, clearly of potential importance if operations were to extend rapidly.

(iii) To reconnoitre a way *northward* into Brunei Bay with special reference to gaining rapid intelligence on Japanese forces there.

(iv) If moving in the *easterly* direction—as under (ii)—proved practicable, to obtain immediate intelligence on Japanese positions on the mainland opposite Tarakan Island, east coast, and first Allied landing objective.

Before leaving Australia, we had been given reports of large numbers of Australian, Dutch and other prisoners-of-war believed to have escaped into, and survived in, the interior. I was to make special efforts to locate, report and rescue any such. One intelligence report referred to over a thousand Australians surviving somewhere in the hills between Tarakan and the Sarawak-Dutch border. My intention was to send Tredrea and Cusack in that direction as soon as possible; Sanderson towards Brunei Bay; Edmeades and Barry westward on the Baram recce for Semut Phase Two (Carter).

This last was the urgent local need. Within forty-eight hours of landing this first recce party left to climb the Tamabos, make the long descent on the outerside of the mountain bowl to Kubaan; and then through the great uninhabited belt surrounding the uplands, to hoped-for contact with the river people on the Akar tributary of the main Baram. The others I could not yet spare, there was so much to do.

Just how much there was to do became increasingly clear as the sun climbed over the plain on this our second morning in Borneo, now again newly at war. The deputations from surrounding long-houses began to arrive in force. Every few minutes the plain dotted with people approaching. They always stopped to bathe in the brook, to put on their best cloth and to approach ceremonially. As they came up, they all had to be greeted with polite formulae. These functions of politeness showed no sign of strain; only these mobile faces registered astonishment, anticipation and some anxiety. From this morning onward, for days on end, I never had a waking hour in which I was not introduced to somebody new. Often I was awakened to meet someone more. With the first wave of visitors came one who spoke fluent Malay.

*   *   *

Penghulu Miri had taken his name when he was made, under the Brookes, Chief (Penghulu) of the southern Kelabits. Miri was the first great oil centre in British Borneo, the metropolitan centre of the known outside universe. His name, therefore, firmly implied that he was chief not only of the southern Kelabits but also as far afield as the Miri oilfields and administration headquarters on the west coast. He adopted this name change from his previous one, Rajah Omong ('Above All Other Rajahs').

Penghulu Miri had learnt his Malay to out-smart everyone else in the far interior. He could speak seven other Borneo languages—or out-wrestle any other man over twenty. He lived (and lives) at Pa Dali. He had gone out of his way, on visits to the lowlands, to study the occasional white man. One of the first things he did, on reaching Bario, was completely to reorganize the long-house, arrange a sleeping platform for our party, fence off the dogs and do a lot of other things which I had wished but not liked, as yet, to ask for lest we upset the mood. He also produced, from local ingredients, delicious coffee served with honey, followed by pancakes mysteriously made out of cassava root. Into his two words of English he put more feeling than one could have believed possible. His first 'Good morning', delivered in high equatorial afternoon, was the final assurance that we had arrived.

With Penghulu Miri, Sanderson and I were at last able to get somewhere by interrogation. We were now reasonably clear that although no Japanese had actually been to Bario, patrols had been active through the interior and several had recently come up from Brunei Bay and closely covered the peoples living just over the border range. We amassed and noted information on the routes they had taken and the routes we could take. Virtually all of this later turned out to be unreliable.

Not in any way due to deliberate misinformation, but to Kelabit experience of the few Europeans who had visited their country. This experience led them to define, for our benefit, a day's walk as the distance it would take an average local to cover in only a couple of hours. When Eric and others demonstrated that they could, when determined, walk as fast as anyone, the picture was radically altered. Distances that at first seemed far, shrunk to the practical, before long became part of our everyday walking.

Penghulu Miri was emphatic that there were no Europeans left anywhere in the interior and that there was no substance for the intelligence reports given us to investigate. This seemed to make sense to me, too. I took a chance on it and stopped thinking about that part of my task at all. Penghulu Miri was right.

On the other hand, he reported that there were a number of later-coming white men scattered about the interior—some alive, some as taken heads, some dying. These were all, he said, men who had crashed in planes in or behind Brunei Bay and escaped inland. None had come this way; he believed there were several away to the east. When we asked if they were Americans, he no more knew that word than Australian.

Penghulu Miri also urged that before we decided on our headquarters, we should come south and inspect his territory; at least make an alternative headquarters there in case the Japs got on our track. Cusack was put in charge of this, as soon as stores were straightened out in Bario. We established an emergency jungle camp near Pa Dali with a reserve set of stores, radio and the rest, as a fall-back point and rendezvous in case of extreme emergency.

Finally, Penghulu Miri urged that we should not make our base to the east but stay in *Sarawak* which, through its loyalty to the Brookes, now pledged itself utterly unto us. Along with this, he asked that our 'doctor', Tredrea, should as soon as possible tour all the local long-houses, where there were many cases in need of urgent attention. The halo of magic around the word 'doctor' had already spread throughout Borneo. This was the first white one anyone had heard of and Jackie, with his golden hair, charming smile and infinite patience, was the dream doctor of their wish—and remains so in memory to this day. I agreed to this for the time being, and so it was done.

Apart from the more ordinary moods inspiring Penghulu Miri, he could see at once that a lot of prestige was coming to his class rival, Lawai Bisarai, if we remained at Bario. Also material riches. Beside these considerations, the Japanese risks paled into the insignificance of an imitation dragon jar or modern bead. Despite my innocence of the inner workings, these social tensions began to impinge a little upon me on our second evening. Bario would not be nearly enough, clearly.

The second evening, after dark, radio conditions grew rather good. Bower got through to Darwin. This really was something. It made us feel doubly secure. And, clearly, it meant that we were not to be an isolated operation but only the beginning of something bigger following on to and from us, as planned. By establishing first contact with Darwin we ceased to feel isolation; just as we had ceased to feel uncertainty the evening before. This also gave Edmeades and Barry a good background with which to start out into the hazards of the lowland people, days (by Penghulu Miri, weeks) over the mountains away. There was no radio or operator to spare. But now there were plenty of willing volunteers, gunners and runners, to go with them. For Cusack had been unpacking the rifles, carbines, Sten guns, Bren guns, hand grenades, sub-machine guns and high explosives with which 'Z' Special had providently supplied us.

The very sight of these weapons acted with compulsive force upon every able-bodied Kelabit male. The girls could now have the parachute cloth as their share. All that any ordinary man wanted was to be allocated some lethal weapon on charge. The idea of levelling it at all was madly exciting; a mood we sharply exploited by fire-arms practice upon the plain. The idea that white men might actually sanction a *return* to arms for murderous purposes seemed almost as marvellous as the para-facts of our appearance. The promised opportunity of shooting, at a later date, at the Japanese (who had confiscated their own shot guns and compelled them to bring down and sell products for little or nothing, as taxation) produced an enthusiasm which must—even at this great distance—have stirred uneasily all the ghosts of Strensall and Sandhurst.

As the borak spread its added courage into the cockles of these bold hearts, I began to realize that one of my big problems was going to be damping down over-enthusiasm and keeping control over the urge to kill. Not that this was a problem of tomorrow. There were nowhere near enough guns to go round even those present, yet. But, according to all reports, soon thousands of people would be swarming upon me. Every one of them would be asking for a gun. There could be no mistake about that.

Great discussions boomed and banged through Bario on our second evening. As well as Penghulu Miri, other great uplanders had come in, notably Aran Tuan of Pa Trap, Tama Bulan of P'Umur and Ngomong Sakai of Pa Main, who with Penghulu Miri and Lawai Bisarai formed the top five of the high aristocracy. They talked among themselves in Kelabit. We could only guess. There was evidently plenty of disagreement in detail, inside general support.

Penghulu Miri (as the recognized expert on white men) gradually dominated proceedings—not at all an easy thing to do in this sort of setting. Through the uproar, I eventually fell asleep, entirely weary again. I woke, later on, to hear Barry arguing Marxism with Sanderson. This was too much of midnight madness, at 3,500 feet, near the equator. I told them to shut up. With mutterings of a kind unknown among English sergeants—but merely bordering on subservience when emanating from Australians—they obliged. Then I could lie and listen in peace, to the foul dogs and the restless fowls and the distant owls and, at the far end of the house, to which he had thoughtfully ordered all the Kelabits and remaining drink, Penghulu Miri proclaiming the new order. This new order included a revised hierarchy for military purposes, of the Kelabit aristocracy.

I woke up to find myself a Rajah.

* * *

I woke up to find myself a Rajah; worldly-wise Penghulu Miri had estimated me as such. And not simply as one of the many Kelabits using this title to rise above all others: 'Long-house Rajah', 'Rajah of the Great Past', 'A Thousand Rajahs', 'Rajah Above All' or Miri's own earlier name, 'Above All Other Rajahs' (Rajah Omong). I was *The* Rajah. Plain and flatly that—though I was slow to realize it!

This honour was conferred upon me, because when I dropped I was wearing a cloth jungle cap (see Frontispiece), bartered somewhere along the line of Pacific campaign. I disliked wearing shoulder pips; and it seemed a smart idea to be able to pose as a private in a few seconds, by smartly discarding the cap. So I put an ordinary English major's gold crown in the peak. Rajah Omong (and all the other rajahs) concluded that this crown meant I was at last a proper one.

Most Kelabits realized that the third of their Rajah Brookes was an old man. It was expected, in Sarawak, that his nephew would succeed him as Brooke IV. I am not quite such a handsome fellow as Mr Anthony Brooke, but we share a common age and weakness of chin. I was taken to be either him or his spiritual equivalent. It is not a Kelabit way to ask direct questions on this sort of subject. No need to tell a lie. The golden accolade was, once really impressed, far too precious to deny. My position in their eyes was further accentuated because they saw seven other *white* men doing (at times!) what *I* told *them*. No situation of this kind had previously arisen among them, or would normally arise in public anywhere in Brooke Sarawak.

Finally, my golden boyhood was sanctioned by golden sovereigns. Based perhaps on cloak and dagger experience in Europe, 'Z' Special had decided (before we met Dr Schneeberger) that we should need gold as currency. It was correctly deduced that paper currency would be devalued. In fact, the Japs had forced everyone to exchange all previous money for their own. Within a few days of our arrival we succeeded in making this not worth the paper it was printed on; and within a few weeks this total devaluation had spread over a huge area, with disastrous effects on urgent Japanese efforts to 'purchase', through agents, large quantities of rice and other supplies inland from the coast. These they desperately needed as Allied bombing severed sea-lanes.

The Kelabits and other inland peoples had never heard of gold as *money*. They valued it highly, for one reason only. The habit of chewing betel nut, which spread into the interior in comparatively recent times, damages the teeth eventually. In the interior there are of course no dentists; while methods of cooking and many items of diet require strong teeth. So, since the interior came into regular and direct contact with the coast, far and away the most important reason for collecting jungle produce and carrying it out, with enormous labour, has been the urge to protect these front teeth with gold caps. As well as this the show of gold in the mouth is regarded as attractive in itself. It some time ago replaced the earlier habit of blacking the front teeth, for beauty. A set of gold caps, prepared and placed by a Chinese 'dentist' at Marudi, down on the coastal plain of the Baram, cost about £10 before the war—a big sum, involving saving and much effort for these people.

During the Japanese occupation, gold had gone the way of so many things; the supply had ceased, ownership was illegal. My bags of gold sovereigns were tooth caps from heaven—although I had not the faintest idea of this at the time. As it was at once apparent that they would have no ordinary currency value, that money currency was not thought of and much better not introduced at this stage, I used the sovereigns as meretricious gifts to all important men and to anyone else I liked the look of. The stuff was far too heavy to carry about anyway. By the time I was lighter by some hundreds of pounds my status as aeroplane and gun owner, magic controller of wireless—for no radio had been here before—and dispenser of casual gold, was even beginning to make Penghulu Miri wonder if I was not something *more* than a Rajah Brooke.

For myself, this particular piece of calculated exhibitionism has left a rankling irritation. After the war, when a sovereign was worth a tiny fortune and my son longed for one in his private museum, I could not obtain one in the whole of Borneo, either for love or a buffalo. The whole lot had been turned into teeth. The upland smiles of today therefore shimmer, for me, in a very 'Z' Special way.

*　　*　　*

One of the first acts of Borneo's newly appointed—and in borak anointed—Rajah was to see Captain Edmeades and Sergeant Barry off on their long way west over the Tamabos, towards Kenyah and Kayan country below. These two had five main jobs to do:

(i) To extend our existing friendly relations westward to the outer fringes of the Kelabit country at Kubaan and Pa Tik, two days away.

(ii) To ascertain the best way of getting westward beyond the Kelabit country into the Sarawak lowlands and provide detailed information on camp sites, food supplies, security problems, etc.

(iii) To move into the lowlands beyond Pa Tik with special care, make initial contact with the riverine people and establish first friendly relations with these if possible.

(iv) To select one or more suitable dropping zones for storepedoes carrying the supplies in for the second (Carter-Sochon) phase, Semut II. (Personnel of Semut II were for safety to be dropped on to me at Bario, supplies on to Barry wherever the recce party selected.)

(v) To get some preliminary intelligence of Japanese positions further down the Baram. (I had already decided to ignore making further enquiries about supposedly surviving white civilians or escaped prisoners; for the time being, on that side.)

My second-in-command must therefore hasten down and return to report these matters in detail personally, bringing with him guides and contacts from the lowlands to take Carter's next party out and down there quickly and safely next time. The delivery of phase II was not planned until this information was to hand, confirmed by radio from Bario to Australia.

The principal jobs of the remaining six I allocated as follows:

Bower and Hallam: establishing really good radio contact and keeping it up, with regular night and day schedules.

Cusack: distribution of stores, general administration; then consolidate an alternative emergency camp in Penghulu Miri's territory.

Tredrea: maximum medical goodwill, including a tour of adjacent houses, as soon as possible extending further afield.

Sanderson: to concentrate on obtaining and recording all sorts of information about adjacent peoples, personalities, potential battle leaders, routes, hide-outs, coastal approaches, etc. etc.

All of us also to become proficient in languages and quick movement in this difficult country, and to learn every possible trick from living off it, independent of extra porterage and personal stores.

The radio was causing most concern. After the initial triumph of contacting Darwin so quickly—more quickly than they had anticipated —the operators ran into all sorts of trouble. Some of the trouble was due to geography. Set deep in the splendid Plain of Bah, the knoll from which we were operating did not give good clearance over the great surrounding bowl of mountains. This could be readily remedied and was. As soon as we were sorted out and the Baram recce party for phase II away, the radio station moved on to a dramatic ridge half a mile in from the long-house, under the Tamabo cliffs which run on out of sight towards Batu Lawi. With these cliffs behind and a clear run eastward over the border range (which is not so high along the Darwin bearing, almost due south-east), we soon had much stronger signals, though the frequent storm disturbance from the mountains gave a good deal of incidental trouble.

Far more troublesome was the code we had been given—and told to use under pain of death by disaster. This code was so secure, so intricate, elaborate and contrived, that it was almost too much for the best wireless operators, living and working under these conditions. It was a major operation to encode or decode a message, involving two large volumes—and usually involving the wretched major himself, in the end. This code was so arranged, in five-letter groups, that presumably no one in the world could ever crack it. By the same token, a trivial mistake in a message could readily make the whole thing meaningless. What with errors of cyphering, transmission atmospherics and the distances we were working (enormous on such simple, portable equipment) no wonder that at times we almost cracked up ourselves with this superbly 'Z'-worthy cypher. But there was no alternative, other than to come up in clear. This clearly would have been folly; practically treachery too.

From an aerial strung between the jungle trees, in a radio hut of leaf well hidden from surprise eyes on the plain below or in the air above, the operators—and whoever else could be spared—poured anxious minds and muscles into this dreadful machine. Mosquitoes, sand-flies, leeches, ants and biting flies abounded upon the hillside; each in their separate, purposive way, adored us. Much of the time we were enveloped in mountain cloud. All the time we were on the air we had to pedal or crank the portable generator—not until later could we train Kelabits to do this work with the necessary sustained effort required for a purely mechanical routine quite outside their varied experience.

Though we had excellent communications on paper (so to speak) the information which we succeeded in communicating was far less satisfactory either in quantity or quality. This soon became a matter of great concern. It was all very nice for Australia to know we were alive and well. But there was almost everything else under the Borneo sun that they wanted to know as well. And we very quickly began to get information of direct and immediate importance to Australia—for instance, about the positions of the Japanese around Brunei Bay and on the east coast, directly affecting the planning of air attack and the details of landings from the sea by the Australians at Labuan and Tarakan. We felt elated by the amount of valuable information we were obtaining, yet horribly frustrated when time and again this failed to get through: our signals had to be repeated; and repeated in reply to queries already distorted. These were some of the worst hours ever. Some nights I spent entirely with the code books and a hurricane lamp, probably only adding to the confusion in a type of mental exercise which is no more my metier than crosswords, mental arithmetic, chess or bridge (all of which I abhor).

We simply battered away at the ionosphere, up and down, wireless wave after wireless wait, sometimes in despair, occasionally ecstatic. We probably would have felt a great deal worse, had we known or even imagined that our messages were being received at the other end with so much confusion and uncertainty that it was seriously suggested we had been compromised.

To be 'compromised' was the worst thing that could happen to a 'Z' Specialist. Nobody minded who you went to bed with; few among our superior officers were in a position to criticize on that count! In our language 'compromised' meant that the Japs had jumped you. Worse than that: it implied that one or more of the members of your party had played traitor or been tortured into disclosing the code and how it worked in transmission—for each operator had secret, personal, identifications outside the cypher itself. There had already been at least one occasion—according to our private, illegal and insecure operators' grape-vine—where a party in Timor had been caught by the Japs, who for months had successfully operated their radio and had 'Z' supply them regularly not only with stores but also with counter-information. This possibility was always a gnawing anxiety in the minds of the officers responsible down in Melbourne HQ.

Our main camp was below the wireless ridge, on a lesser ridge just inside the jungle, above the edge of the plain half a mile behind the long-house of Bario. It would not have been suitable to stay in the long-house, when we had technical problems, a lot of edible (for the dogs) equipment and, as yet, insufficient training in the arts of sleeping amidst uproar and living without a moment's privacy. More particularly, after the first general discussions and decisions, I needed to be able to talk to people of all kinds without being overheard. I wanted to start selecting special people as individual agents, runners, personal assistants to my direct subordinates and so on. More than that, I wanted people to tell me freely about other people, including other people who might be unreliable, possibly treacherous. As news fanned out like the extinct and legendary flames of Mount Batu Apoi fighting Batu Lawi through the interior, this consideration grew. Very soon, people began to come in who had never been here before. Some, in the past, had been at war with the Kelabits. Many held exaggerated or fantastic views of who and what the Kelabits were; thought they would be poisoned, beheaded or swallowed up by long-legged monsters of the uplands. Such people much preferred to come and see me direct and not to go to the long-house until sanctioned by 'the Rajah' and accompanied by his men. Included in this group were many of the Bawang people who had been falsely and fiercely treated by a Brooke Punitive Expedition years before.

These Bawang people emerged as of first importance to our plans, Sanderson's enquiries showed that the best way down into Brunei

Bay must lead through their territory. This way had been closed to the Kelabits for decades past. With the mass of Mount Murud blocking due north, the only alternative route was a ten-day diversion by way of Kubaan over into the headwaters of the Limbang; or otherwise to explore and make a new way of our own, which hardly seemed feasible then (though it has been attempted, with poor results, since).

Lawai Bisarai and all our other Bario friends showed distress when we moved from under their roof. It was something of a slight on their hospitality. But these are eminently reasonable people, and my explanations were accepted. Up to a point they were accepted with mild relief. For with each passing night, the possibility—slowly growing into probability—of the Japanese coming to hear of our presence, must surely increase. No one was in any doubt of what that could mean in terms of reprisals and most savage punishment. To meet this inevitable doubt —and danger—I had from the start insisted that should the Japanese get into the picture, before we could properly arm and mobilize the interior, the people were at perfect liberty to state and swear that we had landed upon them without encouragement and compelled their co-operation by coercion; that they had insisted that we should not live in their long-house or associate with them in any way. This formula did not make much difference to most people, but had a certain value in reassuring the half-hearted and so dangerous few.

One of our special pieces of equipment was a kind of jungle hammock, an ingenious thing. This could be quickly slung between two trees. It had a waterproof fly cover, mosquito curtained sides. It was thus an all-weather, anti-malaria, one-man mobile camp. Apart from lean-to's for the radio and for cooking, this was all the camp we needed. On alarm we could flit mighty quick.

We slept scattered about in this way, and it was very melancholy. It is fun to sleep in the deep jungle, three or four of you snug in line under a good thick leaf thatch, feet warmed by a bulging fire, pork and venison drying in the smoke—which also offsets mosquitoes. But when you have to be alone and inconspicuous, the jungle at night is almost too much. Too much for me, certainly; and too much actually for most Kelabits. It is not so much the several hundred different kinds of insect and other sounds that are bothersome. The nastier noises are the creekings, scrapings and miserable groanings, sometimes from very far away, where branches overlap or tree trunks seek to snap. When a tree does finally snap and crash—maybe ripping down half an acre around in the process—it is a relief. Ordinarily, sounds of this kind, irregular and hard to identify, tend to exercise a slow and persistent strain on the nerves, where eyes cannot see and there is no other escape except sleep.

But the nastiest noise of the jungle night is the one that isn't. I mean the suspicion or expectation or feeling of something moving; but you cannot be sure whether what moves is a thing more than pure imagination. Although, heaven knows, the Borneo jungle is already sufficiently populated with movement and noise, day and night, somehow this never adds up to be quite enough. It can feel nearly queer that there is *not* some one extra noise, some sound which approaches you closely, me, ego, into innermost mind. Can a centipede not be silently crawling along the hammock rope? That microswish must be a bat; and about to tear into the netting? Perhaps because of some curious experience when landing in the swamp, I developed the absurd fantasy of a large Sambhur deer stalking through the forest and accidentally pronging me with its antlers from underneath. But I did not like to sling my hammock any lower down, in case a civet cat jumped on to it!

Waking, half, from jungle sleep, it was fearfully easy to feel suddenly surrounded by *human* noise, by the breath of man. And who else would this be but Japanese? To anyone with even the subtlest shadow of paranoia, these conditions were trying. Anyone without a good deal more than a subtle shadow of paranoia can never make a good subversive operator, secret agent, 'Z' Special type. So there we were . . . oscillating in falsely infinite uncertainties of darkness. Or do I exaggerate?

* * *

We did not, in any case, stay thus for long. Sufficient had got through the air to Australia, for my masters to send in a special supply drop ahead of the original schedule of Semut II personnel. This drop consisted almost entirely of firearms. By now the clamour for these could practically be heard in Brunei Bay, if not Tokyo. Had we been forced to delay much longer, we would—despite an embryo army of blow-pipes—have been in danger of passing the peak of *positive* courage and giving some sanction to those who might feel that even the Rajah From Above was just as much a vain boaster as anyone else—only feebler at the words of boast, also.

This was the sort of opportunity to which our unit rose handsomely. The drop was not a good one; a good deal of it was lost. What mattered most was the proof that we had further support. Above all, to them striking proof that I could say we would bring a plane with guns next day, then tell them what time it would come over. After all, the Kelabits did not judge the inadequacies of radio cypher in quite the way that John Chapman-Walker and Jack Finlay, back at HQ, did.

This further demonstration—of our good faith and continuing enterprise rather than, so far, of actual strength—clinched things in the interior. Farther away groups who had remained on the outskirts, in doubt, now pressed in and proclaimed themselves valiant. Two of these were men of outstanding capacity and courage, who made an immediate and intense impression upon me and played a large part in our activities almost from the beginning.

The first of these men was Penghulu Badak ('Great Rhinoceros'), chief of the Kelabits, Muruts, Tabuns and related people living in the upper reaches of the Limbang way to the north-west, and within relatively easy river-way reach of Brunei Town, the seat of the powerful Sultan of Brunei and centre of the state of that name. The other was Lasong Piri, chief of the Bawang and all the related people lying adjacent to the east—one of the most influential inside Borneo. After a good deal of trouble sorting out temporarily the aged disagreements between Bawang and Bario—which I insisted *must* be dropped in the present emergency—Lasong Piri made the way open to all. This immediately made it much easier for Penghulu Badak to get into the Limbang around Mount Murud, instead of the arduous way he had come by, all along the ranges lying to the west, round through Kubaan and over the Tamabos again into Bario.

The guaranteed loyalty of Lasong Piri and Badak opened up a new promise at an unexpectedly early stage. The prospects were so bright that although I could ill spare Sanderson, I determined to send him at once, round through the Bawang and then on into Limbang. He left next day. And from that day to this I have never seen him again—though no other human being has caused me so much trouble, deserved so well of me or (since the war) kept up such an informative correspondence—from Australia, where he now owns a fruit farm in New South Wales.

I shall inevitably and fortunately have to come back to Fred Sanderson again presently. Immediately I must say something more about Penghulu Badak and Lasong Piri.

Two more different people of closely similar origins it would be difficult to meet. At least, difficult for an outsider, particularly a white man, to meet. At the fringes of different dialects of the same language, Badak and Lasong Piri could well understand each other after a few minutes manoeuvring with diphthong tones and glottal catches. Both were of the highest aristocracy and closely similar in physique. Rather shorter than the average for inland people, squat, but strong and with the large heads and emphatic chins which often go, here, with aristocracy. Badak was a Tabun, a branch of the Kelabits who originally lived in the Tabun tributary of the uppermost Limbang which flows directly under Batu Lawi. The Tabuns moved in later days down into the Limbang and a safer atmosphere from the extreme isolation of their hinterland, in which they had taken refuge from the expanding Kayan movements of the early nineteenth century, and where they left some splendid stone monuments to proclaim in the present-day barrier of uninhabited and now tremendous jungle, the past existence there of people who thought highly of the dead.

Penghulu Badak married a Bisaya, a people who live in the middle reaches of the Limbang river behind Brunei, and have a marvellous reputation as magicians and poisoners. Badak, as the highest representative of the old culture from the interior, commanded sufficient respect in the up-river lowlands to be regarded by all as their social superior. This tough, smiling, little man had a heart of a lion rather than a rhinoceros. He was the first man from the outer fringes, the lowland edges, who boldly came forward—having walked thirteen days through the mountains—to proclaim himself for us. Although he lived far up the Limbang river, nevertheless his long-house could be approached directly by river, by the Japanese. Thus he was the first man within easy Japanese contact who openly declared himself. In the following months, partly through his deliberate boldness and partly through accidents of war (which we shall presently pursue), he and his people suffered more than any others in all Borneo from Japanese depredations. He remained an unflinching ally, a true king within his tiny empire of the brave. Also, a man without tiresomeness and of unusual patience, gentle unless it was needful to be harsh, a wonderful naturalist even by Borneo measure, and a listener in the land of the outspoken and verbally impatient.

Lasong Piri looked not at all unlike Badak, though he was in fact quite a different cup of borak. A good deal of the difference lay in the accident that he lived over the border in (then) Dutch Borneo. Little could be more different than the Brooke and the Dutch approaches to the inland peoples. The Brookes did what they could—once the people had ceased to be (by their standards) obstreperous, lethal and opposed to paying half a crown a year per family door tax—to leave their inland people undisturbed by outside influences. Mohammedan and Christian missionaries, traders, self-seeking Chinese or Europeans, legislators, policemen, magistrates and above all lawyers, were excluded altogether from the interior. The people were encouraged to keep their own ways of life, provided only that they kept the peace.

The Dutch had their part of Borneo highly organized. They did not esteem the people so much for themselves, but as enumerated persons associated in larger organizations; and in particular as persons who had some rather vaguely defined duty either to exploit or export from their country and produce 'revenue'—or allow others to do it in their stead.

Lasong Piri was a trained exponent of this Dutch point of view, up to a point. However, the Dutch showed a startling ineptitude in putting across this point of view completely in depth; largely because they were incapable of allowing *enough* for the pride and dignity of people who were not, by birth, either from the Netherlands or of a Netherlands father. As compared with Sarawak, the equivalent remote inland territories across the border in Dutch Borneo were far more, far 'better' administered (before 1945). There were embryo educational services, crude medical facilities, even iron-wire bridges over rivers and chasms, undreamed of to the west. Administrative Officers probed far inland. There was a police and native officer depot at Long Bawang, a day from the border and spinal range—the nearest equivalent westward in Sarawak was more than a week away. In every way, the Dutch did their large share of Borneo organization. Basically, though, it was organized *for* the Dutch. Sarawak was disorganized by comparison. This disorganization was almost entirely in favour of the resident peoples and to a large extent to the disadvantage of the few Britons who ran—or crawled—the country, usually casually.

Lasong Piri, in consequence, was a much more difficult person to deal with than Badak. Badak treated me as an equal, and added to that a respected superior—provided I lived up to his rajah expectations. Lasong Piri treated me as an overtly respected superior and only presently, with great difficulty, came to like me as approaching an equal (when he lived up to my expectations). They were both fine men. But though I could never like Lasong Piri as I loved Badak, he made the greater effort and was, in his complicated fashion, estimable. He could not help calculating who he was, who we were; whereas Badak was able to take these calculations for granted, then disregard them. At any moment Lasong Piri felt that an Englishman or Australian might start behaving like a Dutchman. But in intervals when he forgot about this, he was the bold master of thousands of willing men who obeyed him even though they disliked him—after all, few aristocrats are likeable when you live with them at very close range, on rice.

Some of my subordinates later found Lasong Piri 'unreliable', 'two-faced', 'too smooth'. That was not it at all, actually. They made him behave in a manner unfamiliar to his other ego, a sullen thing they stirred. Badak suffered under no such inhibitions when facing paler skinned fellows.

The difference between the two was, in simple terms, the difference between Brooke and more ordinary colonial outlooks; it contained most of the conflicts of today in Asia. Perhaps if Sarawak had been a full-scale British colony *before* the Japanese occupation, 'we would have lost' it as utterly as the Dutch lost their part of Borneo, flatly humiliated. As it happened, all three British territories—Sarawak, Brunei and North Borneo—were none of them then run on ordinary British colonial lines. But the Dutch, who in East Borneo carried colonialism to its logical conclusion, lost out the moment the Japanese blew the powerful gaff. Their rule was based not on affection but on discipline. Discipline in the western sense is irrelevant to the Asian way of life. There is already sufficient of that as determined by nature, superstition, monsoon, wagtail and belief.

I am not digressing on to irrelevant issues. This kind of complex about Europeans was a *major* factor in grappling with characters to the eastward, of whom Lasong Piri was largest. One did *not* need to *think* like that when dealing with westerly people inside Sarawak. Badak never raised one problem, one difficulty, one hesitation, from the moment he pledged himself. This does not necessarily make him any more brave than Lasong Piri, tormented by doubt and latent dislike— but who, for example, brought in presently more than 1,000 volunteers to build an airfield on his own land, with the hot breath of the Japanese blowing up the wide Trusan and prosperous Bawang straight into his alertly shifting eyes and hawklike, imperious, sweeping limbs of multiple gesture.

* * *

Farewell, then, to Sanderson. With Badak and him went also Jack Tredrea, whose mission was to leave them and fan out east—while Sanderson went from the Bawang north-west into Badak's Limbang, handsome Jack Tredrea I charged not only with spreading our goodwill eastward into Dutch territory—which I had not yet seen (except in the Schneeberger photographs)—but also to look for further clues of the airmen reported still alive over that way. (Cusack was to join him later.)

This brought our original eight Ants down to four—Bower and Hallam on the everlasting treadmill of radio, sturdy Rod Cusack and myself. Leaving the lads to their own cypher hell, Cusack and I took off for a quick tour of the southern Kelabits, in aid of the ego of Penghulu Miri, who certainly had helped a very great deal that second evening of obscure balance. It happened to rain monumentally. We waded up to our chins three days, into Ra Mudoh and Pa Dali. It was worth doing, though. Re-orientated from Bario, it gave a wider idea of the sort of people we were dealing with. More than that: it really sewed up the loyalty of the immediate surrounding villages. We went unarmed, carrying our own personal baggage—something unheard of for any previous European—and to an unnecessary extent sought to express our wish to be one and the same as all the people we had already implicated in this initially precarious enterprise.

* * *

As we moved south, splashing through deep muddy waters, emissaries from afar, and farther, pursued us until there seemed no limit to the willingness of inland loyalty. By the end of the third week, something like 100,000 people had voluntarily become involved in following, to some extent, Semut. This was more than enough for immediate need. More and more, I became concerned with the operation's security. Could we prevent the Japs learning that we were here, when *they* were regularly moving through the interior and had frequently visited Bawang, ascended the Trusan, and so on? This would not matter so much when Semut II had got in and moved over westward into the Baram. But to endanger our initial mountain-head before that would be inexcusable.

Despite this anxiety I could not help but feel that all these people were to be utterly relied upon. Even if they might not have had much to do with the Brookes or maybe did dislike the Dutch, there were three things which tipped the scales too strongly in our favour. First, the Japanese had behaved with almost incredible stupidity, particularly in showing even more contempt towards inland people than had the coastal Malays in earlier days, or the Dutch latterly. Second, Japanese ignorance—rather than deliberate interference—had brought much of the commerce and interchange of the island to standstill, when the inland people depended on such ebb and flow (even at Bario) for their vitality. Thirdly, under the skin of administration, all these hillmen were fundamentally fighting men still. They admired boldness, the urge to fight and kill. The total impact of their history, song, ritual, spiritual belief and observances honoured physical bravery in combat; and this had been denied them for many years past. Denied them with their consent, indeed approval. But the sad history of human bloodshed is largely that such self-denial in the long run hurts the fingertips, the tongue tip and those twitching secret muscles of the darkling nightmare before first cockcrow.

*　　*　　*

I must admit that at this stage the upland response to their new and unwitting Rajah had begun, slightly, to overwhelm him. Four outsiders were too few to irrigate the flood waters of a vast and gathering enthusiasm. Happily, at this hour, my irrepressible second-in-command reappeared. Eric Edmeades, earning the local name 'Lightning', came steadily panting down the mountainside, into camp. He had established contact with the great chief of the lowlands, Tama Weng Ajang, through the Kenyahs and Kayans on the Akar. They had shown a readiness almost as immediate as Lawai Bisarai's. He had arranged a 'dropping zone' and left Barry in charge there. He had plotted and detailed practicable travel routes. He was enthusiastic about what the Ministry of Information used to call 'morale'. He felt (rightly) sure that the Kenyahs, in particular, would give the next phase, Semut II, with Toby Carter, unflinching support.

We were ready, it seemed, for Semut II.

* * *

Semut II were not quite so ready for us. They were worried about our radio signals. Were we compromised? And there were all the other usual intricacies which follow the first flush of apparent success, the most thoughtful seconds of essential consolidation. The tedium of waiting had by now become an accepted entry in the catalogue of our numerous uncertainties. Before too long, Semut II did come in. In so doing, they supplied the final sanction. The first eight ants were not casuals. Everybody now recognized that I had been telling the truth when I said that we were the first in a private but gathering army of biting tiger-ants.

There are big satisfactions in seeing one's friends descend upon one through the clouds. This morning over the Plain of Bah, conditions were happier than those we had earlier enjoyed, although our distorted signals still had not prevailed upon HQ to delay dropping until long after dawn when the cloud lifts from a deep valley.

The two Liberators came over and dropped like clockwork. First run four men; second run twelve storepedoes; third run, of the other plane, four men; fourth run their storepedoes. I sat on the knoll beside the long-house and watched each one of them with the super field-glasses which 'Z' Special had specially manufactured in (I believe) Tasmania—I still have a pair, unsurpassable.

To the two senior men in this drop, the experience had a particular piquancy; at least, below I felt it so. Toby Carter had never dropped before. He had (for reasons I have already explained)* been unable to complete the grotesquely he-masculine course required at Richmond, New South Wales. He also had an allergy to this type of activity. His dream had always been the submarine. There was no way of detecting this, though, as he fell until the loving, boggy, rich ground of Bario claimed him, with a squelch. He landed perfectly, perfectly relieved.

Bill Sochon was another kettle of fish. Bill belonged to the hearty school, though not in his heart nearly so hearty as he likes most people to note. Toby Carter had been a senior Shell surveyor immediately before the war, happened to be on leave when the Japanese arrived, so that his secondment to 'Z' Special was natural if not inevitable—

* See page 178.

provided only that he volunteered for it (as so few did!). Bill Sochon had been in the Sarawak Government under the Brookes, as a policeman. The Brookes were arbitrary in their methods of employing and of dismissing personnel. This particularly applied to the Third Rajah, subject to favouritisms and hostilities sometimes inexplicable by any objective interpretation of justice at present available. Bill Sochon was politely but firmly transferred out of the Sarawak service some years before the war. He returned to Sarawak in something of the same mood as I. Though he had made a good way for himself in the world afterwards, he never felt that the regime had done him right; instead he felt he had been rather meanly handled—as, on a smaller scale, I had felt about the Oxford University Expedition of 1932 and the attitude expressed in print by the Curator of the Sarawak Museum, Mr Banks.

But Bill was in a very different position from me. For me, to join SRD ('Z' Special) had got me out of a regiment I disliked and a piece of the war I distrusted; this blew me back to a country that I already loved and long had wished to revisit. But Bill went straight into cloak-and-dagger, as an over-age civilian from an established job in a prison. He was too old, heavy, and potentially lazy—on paper—ever to make a parachute operator. But Colonel Egerton-Mott and the other cavalry figures whose smart shadows fell from Northumberland Avenue unto Baker Street had grown so desperately short of volunteers that after combing through and reaching me, they had then come upon the true blue list of Brookeiana, which included Bill.

Watching Bill drop was something special again. One of the more delightful decisions of Australian parachutism at this time (when they had never been operative) was presumably based on the anger which the regular units felt at the way things were favouring us irregulars, to the exclusion of their own so much desired (and alas never achieved) dropping. Be that as it may, it was a decision, imposed upon 'Z' Special—who had not got as far as having a complete parachute making, assembling and packing unit of its own—that no parachute should be used in actual operations unless it had already been used at least *one hundred* times for training purposes. The theory, presumably, being that it was a waste to drop a good parachute in conditions where it was unlikely to be recoverable.

Even in Semut we had ants in our pants a few times, at the things happening to the 'chutes as we tore out into our individual slipstreams.

Bill Sochon—much the heaviest man to be dropped into this part of the world—provided a better proof that our semi-fears had not been unfounded. As he descended upon the plain, the panels of his 'chute began to peel off one by one. He was nearly half a mile away from me across the grassland. It was pretty to watch the cloth streaming up as he came down; and after the necessary distance delay, to hear the high ping, orchestrated by his own powerful-lunged vocabulary. Faster and faster came old Bill down. If he had not landed into the swamp not far from the bogs we had earlier plumped, he must have been crushed into pentonvillion pulp!

Some fruity signals followed on the subject of one hundred drop 'chutes. I do not know if they were ever correctly deciphered; but after that we did get brand-new 'chutes in all operations. These were beautiful, clean, coloured silk. Their currency value exceeded that of the ordinary 'chutes, with which we had landed, ten times over, thus materially easing our interior currency problems.

*　　*　　*

I asked Bill Sochon to write his memory of this thing; he wrote:

'We were called at 2 a.m. and after a most eerie early breakfast, proceeded to the landing ground and boarded our planes and took off at scheduled time. With me travelled WO Horsnell, Abu Kassim and Sgt Long. Horsnell was our machine-gun expert, and it was his responsibility to look after the one package which contained our Bren gun, and as he was dropping fourth, it would immediately follow him; he vowed and declared that once that package was in the air he would follow it all over the sky if necessary. With extra gear which had been made up into packages, two waist machine guns and their gunners, parachute gear, and the big steel chute from which we were to make our exit through the camera hatch, it did not leave much room for us to get comfortable, but nevertheless we managed to get in about one-and-a-half hour's sleep. At first light we found ourselves flying over British North Borneo.

'It was an impressive sight when we found ourselves flying along-side Mount Kinabalu. At 13,000 feet we were more or less level with the summit of this mountain and being early in the morning with the amount of low lying cloud which was about, made the scene an indelible picture on one's mind. We realized by this time that unless the sky cleared to a certain extent it would be very difficult indeed to find our objective, as we were flying through nine-tenths cloud, white billowing masses, which gave one the impression of a vast field of cotton wool. By seven o'clock, local time, we were over our stores DZ which was approximately at a distance of sixty miles to the southward of our personnel DZ—this part of our plan had been arranged so as to avoid the unnecessary humping of stores from the personnel DZ down towards our first objective which was Long Akah.

'The reason for this being that the country was very mountainous and we were not in a position to know whether it would be possible to obtain the assistance of the local natives. We had gathered from Tom Harrisson (radio), that the natives were friendly disposed towards us, but it was a matter of uncertainty whether their service could be obtained. Previous arrangements had been made with Harrisson for two of his party to proceed to Long Lelang, our stores Dropping Zone, and it was with great trepidation that, on making the circuit, we wondered whether we would find smoke signals giving us the assurance that the coast was clear for dropping. This part of the project, of course, had not been confirmed, as their party had no wireless equipment with them yet at Long Lelang.

'Again, the dense cloud created a difficulty, but it was with a feeling of relief that we saw smoke rising from the selected area. We circled again, made our run, and the stores were dropped, trusting in all the faiths that they would land close together in a safe area and not be tied up in trees or finish in the river which flowed close to the site. The pilot then set his course for Bario which was our personnel DZ. Each one of us was carrying sufficient equipment to keep him fully armed for forty-eight hours' fighting, together with emergency feed packs, and first aid kits: I would say that each man was carrying approximately 40 lbs to 50 lbs on his person. As we had no para overalls, we had, before leaving, smartly commandeered some boiler suits, off which we cut the legs and sleeves and slipped them on top of our equipment, thereby reducing the risk of getting ourselves tied up with our rigging lines on dropping. Each man also carried a 50-foot length of rope, which in the event of making a tree landing, would enable him to make some effort to extricate himself from the tree. It was at this time that we really felt that the job had at last come, although we were dubious owing to the cloud, whether we could make the jump or whether it would be an abortive flight and we'd have to come back the next day. About fifteen minutes later, after our harnesses had been checked, release boxes tested, our static lines checked and the hooks were properly secure, we really felt that it was a question of seconds waiting for the red light to give its intermittent flicker calling for action stations. This, I should say, was one of the most anxious periods of the whole operation, knowing that the ground should be fairly safe, but still not completely certain, having had no contact with Harrisson for nearly forty-eight hours. May be that he had to leave his area on account of Jap activity; but this was a risk which had to be taken in such operations as this. Everybody, needless to say, offered up a little prayer hoping against hope that the landing was going to be successful.

'As I was jumping No 1, the period between action stations and the red light warning to jump into the steel chute seemed an eternity. But eventually the red light came on, then the green, and out. The feeling during this period was one which cannot really be described —the mind was a complete blank and it was just a question of self-discipline and training whereby your thoughts were only concentrated on those two lights. The four of us were out of the plane within three seconds, the plane having slowed to approximately 230 miles per hour. Knowing that it could not keep at this speed for longer than five seconds, owing to the possibility of stalling, it had to be a quick jump. We realized before jumping that we were at a fair height, a height far greater than we had ever jumped before, and on questioning Carter, who was in the leading plane, on landing, he told us that the pilot had informed him that it would be impossible to get lower than 3,000 feet above ground level (8,500 feet up), owing to the cloud.

'My own experience on coming out of the plane on this occasion was a black-out for a second or so, then lying on my back seeing the plane slowly sailing away from me, and realizing then that contact with the outside world was completely cut off. It was with a feeling of relief that I felt the gentle jerk on my back, realizing that my 'chute had opened—this I imagine, to any parachutist, is the most comforting feeling, knowing again one is safe until the landing is made. I looked up to see that my 'chute was properly opened and that I had not developed twists or that my rigging lines were not caught up, when to my horror I discovered that *seven* of my parachute panels were ripped from top to bottom and as I gradually fell through the sky, I could see more panels gradually splitting until eventually, on my landing, *fourteen* panels in all were ripped from top to bottom. It was during this period that Horsnell carried out his promise that he would chase his Bren gun all over the sky if necessary. This created quite a diversion, and kept my mind, to a certain extent, off the predicament I was in; and I shall never forget the sight—he stood about 5 ft 4 in—as a very small body, legs kicking, endeavouring to control his 'chute to take him where he required it, literally chasing his Bren gun over the sky. He eventually finished up about a mile from the main party, but his Bren gun was safely in his hands.

'By the time we landed we were in an exhausted state owing to the amount of control which we had to use with our 'chutes directing them on to the Dropping Zone, but fortunately we all landed safely without injury, and the party quickly re-formed. Tom was there to meet us with two other members of the party and we immediately made for the Kelabit long-house, which was in the centre of our DZ. The Kelabits were very pleased to see us and did everything in their power to assist in collecting the storepedoes which had been dropped here by No 1 and No 2 planes.

'That day was spent in conference by Harrisson, Carter and myself and it was decided that I, WO Horsnell and Sgt Kassim, should leave first thing next morning, April 17, for Long Lelang to check up on our stores. Carter would remain a further twenty-four hours to talk more and then proceed with the remainder of the party. Needless to say, that night was spent with a certain amount of celebration with Tom and the Kelabits. They produced a marvellous brew of *borak*, and entertained us most freely, with smoked pig, rice, and liquid refreshment.

'The following morning my party moved off for Kubaan. The first day's walk consisted of climbing Tamabo range, to about 5,500 ft. Which causes the most exertion I do not know, either climbing up step by step, or sliding down the other side. The following day's journey was one of the most depressing I have made—dense jungle, endless brown fallen leaves, the awful smell of dankness, and (what appeared to be on every leaf) a leech of some inches long, sitting up and just waiting to get his bloody suckers on to you . . .'

* * *

So Bill Sochon and Toby Carter, bloody but unbowed, moved with effort out of the control area of Semut I and both went on to form in due course other wide guerrilla zones, Semut II and III, Second and Third Armies of Ants. They left me slightly down, in one respect.

The immediate (acting) Rajah, alas, suffered from this otherwise successful drop. Both Toby Carter and Bill Sochon were then Majors, as I was. They were also more orthodox guys. They, therefore, each had a crown on *each* shoulder. The appearance of two double rajahs confounded the scholarship of Penghulu Miri. The difficulty was politely passed over. I did everything I could to disguise the dilemma. Bill obligingly took his crowns off. Toby—who was, after all, officially commanding officer of Semut—could not see his way to do that. With almost indecent haste, therefore, I organized him forward, up the mountain and over the Tamabos to the positions already prepared, five (Edmeades') days away to the west, and held there by Sergeant Barry.

That was the last I saw of Toby for quite a long time, though far from the last I *heard* of him. The position was already a bit embarrassing. By now I had achieved a large scale organization and a limited but deep prestige. In brief, I was being *treated* like a rajah. This did not necessarily mean that I was behaving like some of the less satisfactory despots of Asian states. At this stage, there was not the slightest question of being autocratic, acquiring wealth, wives, or any sort of wantonness beyond the overnight demands of borak normality. But Toby (who was automatically out of this picture) was visibly displeased with the atmosphere of relaxed tension and aggressive exuberance which he fell into at 3,500 feet above New Zealand's sea level. Well within his rights, he criticized several of my arrangements within the hour. This was distressful indeed.

Within two days, I had delivered him unto the mountains and he was away. As the radio had by now become the greatest worry of Semut I sent with him Sergeant Hallam, who already had a month's experience battling with the 'Boston' at Bario. In exchange he gave me another sergeant, Long. This was about the best deal I made in my life. After the acquisition of Long, our radio difficulties steadily reduced; within a few weeks they were negligible. Long was able to adapt himself to any environment. He could concentrate the whole of himself upon radio, with the additional and invaluable capacity of forgetting all about it when he was not doing it. He really enjoyed himself climbing a tree, shooting at finches or playing with babies (several of which he adopted during the following months).

Radio continued for a while, however, to spoil this part of our lives. A week later, Toby reached Barry on the Baram. But the drop there had not been fully successful; he lacked a good pedal generator to work his main set. He could barely contact me across the Tamabos, could not contact Australia direct. I therefore had to pass all his messages to and fro. As commanding officer of Semut, he properly claimed priority. Meanwhile, urgent intelligence information was pouring into us which could not under these conditions be sent out. Finally, my CO (him) ordered me to send my own equipment to him. This meant going off the air myself; and all of us going off the air for *at least* a week. Regretfully, I could not comply; I took the unusual step of referring his order to higher command. I was ordered to stay on the air and not send him anything.

You can easily imagine the miserable atmosphere of two or three days while this was going on, between two people who had a common purpose and strong affection. The outcome was happy all the same. Immediate extensive supply drops were made to Semut II on the Baram; and it was realized that the original idea of controlling the intricate whole of the interior under one officer would never do. The response from the people had been much greater than higher command dared to anticipate; instead of creeping in and crawling up, the ants were swarming on the march. The distances were great and the numbers of people involved already so large, that it would evidently be better to set up separate organizations to cope, as conditions required.

Within a few days, therefore, I was appointed commander of the uplands and all the country northward into Brunei Bay and eastward (if I could go there), ill-defined, to the coast behind Tarakan, Toby was to be in separate command of all the country *west* of the Tamabos in the Sarawak lowlands. And presently, as Bill Sochon separated from Toby and forced his way with tremendous marches beyond the Baram watershed into the great Rejang river system further south, he was appointed to a third separate command, Semut III.

* * *

Semut II (Carter) and embryo Semut III (Sochon) had now secured my vulnerable western flanks. The run that way was now 'over to them'. I could concentrate attention towards the remote east coast behind Tarakan; and north and north-westward towards the very important problems of Brunei Bay and Labuan Island lying within it. From this time forward, I had no further concern to the west except when this impinged upon me (as, for instance, it later did when large Japanese forces came through from that direction into my zone of command). Grappling with the huge geography of a still largely unmapped country is something of a headache, even to someone like myself, intensely interested in shapes. It was a big help not to have to think to the west, any more.

A first step eastward was to move base camp and wireless station across the plain to Pa Main. This was the first of several hops within a short period, bringing us soon over the border range, into the more densely populated and all round accessible country in the north-west corner of what was then Dutch (and is now Indonesian) Borneo.

By this time, there were suspicions that the Japanese were beginning to have an idea we were there. These suspicions were in fact unfounded. From beginning to end, until we deliberately struck at the Japs after allied landings, they had no direct confirmation of our existence. So far as I know, there was not one traitor among 100,000 people, any one of whom would have earned a rich reward for his treachery (or loyalty, if looked at that way). Naturally enough, the Japanese were beginning to feel the first *effects* of our presence, mild though these still were. Within a short time of our arrival, the whole attitude of the inland people had altered. They no longer complied with orders from the coast. The supplies of rice, buffaloes, iodized salt, jungle produce and conscripted labour which had been flowing down the Trusan, the Limbang, the Baram and the Bawang ceased almost overnight. Unable to diagnose the cause, the Japanese nevertheless felt the consequences of these defaults, upon an economy already wilting under American air attacks and other general stagnation in the last phases of their war.

Every day there were rumours of large forces coming in to discipline the interior. We were confident that before long we would be able to deal with these. In the interval, it was necessary to safeguard our friends by measures to prevent visibly identifying any peoples with us, should a really powerful Japanese force appear before we were sufficiently supplied, armed and trained to eject them.

A minor by-product of this phase was my order that all European personnel moving around long-houses under wet weather conditions, where footsteps could be identified, must remove their boots. The only footwear in the interior was, of course, worn by us. Everyone else always went barefoot—until one day someone dropped 1,000 x No 10 boots. It would have been, at first, impossible for any community to deny our presence in the face of enemy surprise, with tell-tale hobnails or rubber boots upon the long-house ladders or adjacent earth.

This order seemed simple enough. But by now we had acquired a pukka doctor. Jack Tredrea was already operating eastward on his medical mission of goodwill and probe. Toby Carter's party included a doctor whom he agreed to lend to me for a fortnight, as he did not want to take too many people over the mountains on his first move. This estimable and highly qualified medico flatly refused to comply with my footloose order. He said that as a professional medical man, he could not agree to expose himself—or permit other personnel to be exposed—to the dangers of hook worm and other diseases attacking through the soles of the feet. There followed one of the most macabre military arguments. Fortunately, Eric Edmeades was available and, as ever, I handed over coping with Australoid obstinacy to him. But for an hour or two it was a question whether or not I should shoot this gentleman, quietly, in the jungle?

Eric worked out a better solution. After he had gone to bed, we confiscated all footwear. I then ordered the doctor to proceed elsewhere.

*　　*　　*

Jumping the spinal range eastward from Pa Main landed us next in Pa Kabak, accompanied by a horde of Sarawak Kelabits on this, our first, probe into Dutch Borneo. It was necessary to spend two nights at Pa Kabak because here I intercepted large deputations on their way to me from much further east, who had themselves been intercepted by the accident of a huge *irau* death feast in process at this small but prosperous long-house set in a tiny, beautiful parkland of cattle grazing, with some imposing megalithic monuments nearby.

My memory of this, the first of many *irau* in the highlands, is distinctly dim. But I must have done all right; the chiefs and warriors who had come to meet me turned aside to follow, and became some of our best. I do distinctly remember the headman at Pa Kabak becoming most tiresome as the wine wore on. He insisted that I had now been in the interior long enough (months) to take a wife. This view was universally supported. These good people could not understand how we white men had not raised the matter earlier, outsiders though we were.

It was difficult to resist this and related suggestions, which I felt to be improper under the circumstances. Indeed, throughout this period—and until after the war was over—I felt no interest in the opposite sex. This was not through lack of opportunity or innate inclination; and for once it was possible to be certain that it had nothing to do with secret drugs supposedly inserted into the diet by the alleged machinations of military medicos. All the machinations in these war months worked in the opposite direction. For although it is considered a very bad thing for a girl to have anything to do with a man from another group visiting or met casually, our method of arrival and subsequent effort made the people feel that we were one with them in many more respects than any outsiders before us.

Kelabit women themselves are seldom nearly beautiful by western standards: their broad faces, extended ear-lobes, extraordinary tattooing and often blackened teeth. But they have fine bodies, strong breasts, lovely hair, warm thighs and full laughter. They are straightforward, tough, generous, good-hearted, extrovert women who have not allowed hard work, indoors and out, to blunt the attributes of femininity, frequently identical with those displayed (more artificially) by western ladies. But there was something about the tension—or excitement and satisfaction—of this for us new way of life which for a while put all the emphasis on what we conceived to be masculine attributes. Chastity and war—or to be more exact, delayed concupiscence in the smell of action—do seem to go together in many sorts of pre-civilized war contexts. The Kelabits themselves had strict observances, exclusive of the female, before going on head-hunting parties and during these.

Fortunately, for me, this phenomenon was not confined to me. One of my few anxieties about the tough Australian paratroopers of 'Z' Special was that they might cause trouble with the women. That is to say, make advances in an improper way or to the wrong women (married ones). For, as with all things inland, there are ways of making a pass at a Borneo girl nicely and nastily. I need not have worried. To the best of my belief, from the beginning to the end of the whole of our operations—eventually involving many rugged Australians out of my direct control in this sort of respect—there was no incident to cause undue disturbance of the female bosom or husband's heart. The lads were not only innocent of making passes nastily. Few made any. In all the years since I never heard a suggestion of the kind—though I have heard plenty such about other Europeans who entered the interior, before and since!

* * *

Having dodged the matchmakers and potential embracers of Pa Kabak, a short march took the gathering gang on to Lembudut. Lembudut had already been reconnoitred by Tredrea on medical and general patrol moving east. He had sent a good report of this large community, set in a lush irrigated plain, richer even than Bario. In consequence, now that Semut II was well away and secure behind us to the west, I asked that the next build-up for Semut I should be sent in here; dropped at Lembudut, where Tredrea waited to receive me.

Our wireless communications were now much better. In general, also, we felt free to move about more openly and rapidly, with an assurance of ample warning before any enemy approach. However good the radio communications, there was always the slip between set and drop. On the third day after the drop was due, two Liberators came over our handsomely prepared ground signals, our dropping sign, orange and magenta smoke flares for OK. It was a honey for the eight new men and mass of arms now eagerly expected below.

The plane then headed smartly north, to our bewilderment. I picked up the borak party begun at Pa Kabak, with an extra brew offered by the otherwise somewhat disagreeable chief of the Lembudut people. Nothing more could happen until next day, at best. Enormous bonfires were built, with coloured flares attached, to make sure of no further mistake. In the middle of a jolly time with everybody shouting war— but these occasions were very useful in bringing out information, ideas, antagonisms—arrived a panting runner. He carried a message which I am sure I can reconstruct reasonably correctly, as it was so well in the 'Z' Special manner:

'Sir—I have to inform you that I led my party correctly as ordered and that I await your further orders now. I was surprised to find nothing prepared and no-one who could speak to us at Lembedoet where I now await you.

(signed) Geoffrey Westley (Lt)'

When an Australian rose to this pitch of literacy (and disrespect), it was every-day stuff in 'Z'. Never mind that. Where was Lt Westley? I am not likely to forget the answer to that. We set out in a gruelling afternoon sun to cross the low divide north of Lembudut and marched for hours over eroded scrubland, past cultivation without a flicker of shade, the surface soil of scintillating white weathered sandstone reflecting each ray, frying out drop by drop of borak in the blood. At long last we came out upon another of the glorious open rice plains of the far uplands; the finest of them all, it runs from the very head of the Bawang under Mount Murud for miles eastward to Balawit, and on past the rich mineral springs of Pa Potok.

Westley and seven men, surrounded by some thousands of well-wishers, were already established in one of the many long-houses which dot this plain. All his stores had been easily recovered, were already being got into some sort of order. After the necessary geographical revaluations it was evident that the accident had done good. This was a bigger and more prosperous plain, an ideal dropping zone where no plane *could* go wrong; and cursory inspection suggested that an air-strip could easily be built at one of several dry flats round about. This was the plain shown in Schneeberger's photographs, which had inspired me on the Shell file back in Melbourne. The reality was even better. From this time on, the Bawang valley in general, Balawit in particular, became the centre of all Semut I operations.

It had been right to drop into Bario in Sarawak in the first place. I doubt if we could possibly have kept security and our secret from the Japs if we had gone straight into the Bawang, which was under frequent Japanese patrol and with a large population in constant communication with the east coast—and a population *initially* less sympathetic to the white man than the related groups over the border in Brooke Sarawak. But by now, all the interior peoples were in our Semut mood and behind us. Westley's mistaken jump at Balawit further strengthened this mood.

The Balawit drop was the first in a series which sent me people I had not always selected and trained personally in Australia. Despite the over-lucid arguments which I had drawn from the bowels of the Melbourne Library, my superiors had not visualized any extensive operations at least for months ahead. Our rapid first success was, for them, definitely worth following up as fully as possible. Very soon we were short of trained and suitable bodies, not only in Semut I but in Carter's Semut II and Semut III.

I was worried, once more, about the sort of trouble some of these new boys might get themselves, or others, into. Most of them, when they hit the Borneo deck, could not speak a word of any language other than Australian. One or two of them could not knit their sentences together to make much written sense If we were to develop quickly and efficiently I must now send such men to range widely through the country and extend swiftly towards the coasts—both eastward towards Tarakan and north-westward into Brunei Bay,—before the Allied landings in these sectors. These places were many days' march away over the mountains; and there were not enough qualified wireless operators suitable for this work to supply each sub-unit with a radio from the beginning. Demands on individual initiative, steadiness and concentration need not be underlined here.

To try to cope with this difficulty, I borrowed a leaf from the pages of Ringway, Beaulieu and the other SOE streamlined training courses back in Britain. I devised a two-day indoctrination course in the Bawang. On the third day, each party of eight was sent off in four pairs, on missions involving their further separation, as individuals, roughly a fortnight later, on receipt of their first reports and return confirmation from me by runner.

These runners covered prodigious distances. Until we had a fully run radio network (covering 20,000 square miles) they were the life blood of a highly thrombotic vascular system. On one occasion a Murut-Kelabit from one of the Trusan villages travelled with an urgent message from Eric (encamped just behind the Japanese at Lawas in Brunei Bay) to my Bawang headquarters in a day and a night and a part of next morning; the fastest Eric was able to do this journey on foot was three days; and I once managed it in just over that, too – the normal peace-time journey takes the people who live on the Trusan seven to eleven days, solid plugging.

*　　*　　*

Goodness knows what some of the warrant officers, sergeants and corporals did about language at first. But this became easier quickly.

Previously, there had been no big impetus for any of the local people to learn Malay—or in many cases for more than a minority from each group to travel widely among other groups. We were turning the interior into a seething circus of to and fro, with urgencies of speed and sanctions of power which over-rode all the ordinary obstacles of ancient conflict, current convention, customary manners, sweaty climbing, omens, superstitions and propitiations. These people accepted the new conditions as requiring the temporary rejection of any beliefs which would interfere with what I could reasonably explain as necessary measures, in preparation for the return of white men *en masse* and the molestation (not forgetting decapitation) of Japanese meanwhile. There had already been some Christian missionary activity, most effectively from the Dutch side, before the Japanese occupation. But the great majority of inland people were much too afraid of the past to overthrow old superstitions. It was one of the inevitable and in some ways saddest repercussions of our sudden appearance that, almost overnight, these traditions had to be reconsidered and revaluated as so often in so-called total war—especially where total war has not been before. I suppose I was one of the last people in the western world who wished to upset and alter other people's beliefs as such. But it would have been impossible to have conducted any operation had we followed local observances and determined the movements of our runners—or our aeroplanes—by the position of the first barking deer to sound off on the track in the morning, or the direction in which an eagle was last seen to be soaring over the mountains at sunset.

Malay can be rapidly picked up and learned as a local *lingua franca*. The few inlanders who could speak it well, like Penghulu Miri, started (with my active encouragement) classes to spread the knowledge. The inland people are remarkably quick at languages. Malay is the easiest language in the world. It is ever so much easier than Spanish, Esperanto, Basic English or any other of the new things. The basis of Malay is logical pronunciation, simple grammar, a small essential vocabulary to begin with, but a wealth of additional words available; and, above all, a flow, a rhythm based on short words and syllables which can be strung together and sounded in simple, straight, yet felicitous and lilting melody by anyone with any idea of sound at all.

My Queenslanders knew the sound of sheep, kookaburras and the things that go on around billabong trees. These provided sufficient audible experience, when stimulated by eagerness, lack of alternative and an element of risk for the underinformed. I soon found that all I had to do was send a chap out with a dozen or twenty hill people, one or two of them speaking some Malay. Within a fortnight the peace-time shearer, coal-miner or tractor driver would be making himself sufficiently well understood to give orders, see that they were carried out; and to send back information at least of sufficient standard to indicate whether or not it should be followed up. As well as Malay, some of these excellent fellows became first-class in local dialects otherwise unknown beyond the mountains.

This, then, became the usual pattern: after an accelerated initiation, to send out parties on a ratio of one white to ten or twenty brown; to extend in a certain direction, and be responsible for an area which might start from one hundred to five hundred square miles. Once I had made the thoroughly pommy gesture of shaking the chap by the hand as graduation blessing, usually I did not see him again, ever. I am not ashamed to say that I do not remember the names of most of these men, whom I only saw once or twice at most. Among other things they got a code name when they left. And having learnt, from the bitter experience of our over-codified wireless, I coded each man by some characteristic about him which most struck me at once and which I then distorted (politely) into a letter and a number—to avoid giving offence.

Areas, localities and camps were also simply coded, just in case a runner ran into something wrong. We soon began using these codes in clear English—and in flagrant disregard of 'Z' orders—in most inter-communications over the growing radio set-up, based on Sergeant Long—now aplomb at Balawit in the Bawang—and with Staff Sergeant Bower as its extreme northward prong far away, probing behind the Crocker Ranges east of Brunei Bay.

Coding camp names was particularly easy. Every particle of the middle of Borneo has its unpleasant insect. For ecological reasons (which need not here detain us) the dominant insect varies, strikingly, bitingly, from place to place. Thus, anyone who ever camped at Lembudut will remember it for the exquisite, transparent-winged, blue and orange painted flies which raised their half-crown lumps on any exposed daylight surface of flesh. Pa Main then excelled in the tiny sand-fly, Bario in the malaria mosquito, and other places in specialities ranging from buffalo-leech, tiger-ant, poisonous spider, sweat bee, hornet, wasp, deer-fly, all the way round and through to the vicious striped tiger-leech and the very nasty tiger-hornet. Each place was named for its special pest.

* * *

Bario had seemed magnificent, wild, and—in its way—out of this world. It was something of a relief to shed it, for the time being— though not for nearly as long as I then expected; to move into a similar but more extensive, expansive upland countryside. Maybe I could recapitulate here, from a geographical survey I later wrote (as published by the Royal Geographical Society):

'The principal flat, rich lands are around Bario and in the head-waters of the Libbun; at Bah Kalalan in the head of the Trusan; at Bawang and Balawit; and again at Lembudut and Pa Koerid farther south on tributaries of the Kerayan; and along the main Kerayan in the district of Benoeang. All lie within a narrow rectangle about thirty miles north and south, fifteen east and west, and over 3,000 feet above sea-level, mainly in Dutch territory.

'In all, these pockets of tableland cover little over a thousand square miles. But they are richly different from anything else in the interior, a difference striking not only to the outsider but to native mentality in general. The shock of pleasure when emerging into one of these tablelands after a long jungle spell is best recaptured from my diary:

' "After weeks with an horizon of not more than thirty yards, the sun always obscured by the forest canopy, I feel literally faint on coming out into the open, the clear sunlight, the perspective of distance, flatness, intense fertility, still water, colours other than green, a complete view of clouds or stars, and the rain pushing straight into you instead of dripping down your back off the branches. Above all, the conviction that you can walk twenty paces without collecting another leech." '

Food supplies were, for effective purposes, limitless. Labour was abundant, energetic and bold. The labour was also more and more in demand. As assurance grew and personnel spread over more than a semi-circle, from the Limbang and Trusan rivers down over the Kerayan head-waters into the Batang Kayan to the south (Lt Westley's particular appointment presently)—I began to tackle bigger, longer-term propositions. Among these, priorities were given to the general improvement of the very poor, narrow, winding jungle tracks, hitherto the only communications in the interior and unsuitable for our speedy purposes; the improvement of medical facilities, including the establishment of a good hospital in the Bawang valley; and the preparation of an airfield.

The airfield occupied a lot of attention in its time. There were two reasons for giving this urgency, even before there was any possibility of anything landing on it—for even in my best moments I do not think I sent a signal to HQ suggesting we build an airfield big enough for four-engine bombers in the middle of Borneo, in 1945. But we anticipated, intelligently enough, that allied landings on the coast would benefit from being able to contact us direct inland. And how much more would such contact benefit us!

Sanderson on his way round Mount Murud, to turn north-west with Penghulu Badak into the Limbang, and Tredrea pushing on east after Lembudut towards Tarakan, sent back specific confirmation of the presence of shot down American airmen, of whom we had heard more vaguely in the first Bario evenings. I had already sent runners with messages to their supposed positions. Now we located some of them Tredrea dropped everything else to go to their aid. Initial reports were alarming. Several of them were in dreadful condition, evidently dying. I made a levy of all available clothing and comforts (things we were not worrying much about) and sent these off. Gradually, with a great deal of trouble, we managed to bring thirteen of these Americans back into life and, slowly—some of them carried all the way over the mountains—to the Bawang valley, where we could properly nurse and secure them. In the absence of any of the expected surviving British or Australian prisoners of war, this gave some outlet to those of Semut I short on pituitary discharges. What a business it was, though!

The unshakeable strength of the average American is his inability to see the other race's point of view. This, coupled with an innate sense of superiority and fearless insistence on personal (American) rights, brought these Yanks—none of whom had ever been in jungle before—through under circumstances few could have endured.

Poor lads, they took so much for granted. The first one to arrive asked me why we had not sent him Chesterfield cigarettes and American newspapers. By the time four had arrived, nothing was nearer my heart than completion of an airstrip. By the time all of them had arrived, and most of them had recovered their natural virility by consuming special rations and comforts, they felt like 3,000, not thirteen.

As they were all airmen and Americans, each one of them felt he could and must improve on my own ideas of building an airfield. These ideas (which I worked out with proper 'Z' Special abandon) involved a certain amount of my time when not engaged in sending and receiving messages and deputations; a little more of Sergeant Long's, when he was not glued to the main radio; and the all-day vigorous drive of tough little Penghulu Lasong Piri as head of a labour force which some days numbered thousands. The Americans were appalled to find that we had no tools, in their sense of the word. The ground was being broken with sticks, ditches being trampled out by foot, earth carried and levelled by hand.

First go, I fell for their line, feebly. I radioed for an urgent drop of equipment to 'perfect an airfield'. On that basis, the Australians were able to swing it on to the American Air Force. Within forty-eight hours one of the long-houses on the plain had been heartily dive-bombed. By good fortune nothing more than a goat was killed by the avalanche of spades, mattocks, pick-axes, hoes, rakes, graders and other things which showered in metallic rain, as if to more than petrify all Bawang and Balawit.

No one would *use* any of these instruments. We went back to the good old ways and in ten more days had an excellent strip on one sandy side of the plain, surrounded by the irrigated rice fields and egrets. The Bawang people do not drain their fields after the harvest, like the Bario people do. So the airfield was an exquisite island, beside which I set Sergeant Long and his gradually elaborating radio and radar station, with bulky Private Bob Griffiths as Air Port Officer, i/c! I made my headquarters 600 yards away on the edge of the plain, beside several big long-houses, at the foot of a shady grove of rich old fruit trees, mango, mangosteen, jack fruit, pomelo, pawpaw, orange and lime. Sergeant Long and I chatted by walkie-talkie, signalling to come up on the air with three carbine shots across the glittering meadows.

* * *

The danger of this airfield being detected by the Japanese was now outweighed both by the strength we felt as a growing force and by the strength of my longing to be politely rid of my trans-Pacific guests.

Some of these were survivors of the same plane which had been shot down the day before my own first flight over Borneo. The American plane which had first taught me the splendour of Batu Lawi, shown the first glinting hope of a hole in the jungle far inland, had been from the same Navy squadron, searching for these very boys. Their plane had crash-landed just behind Brunei Bay in a swamp. This highly armed bomber had been shot down by a single Japanese fighter, out of the blue. The pilot, a naval lieutenant-commander, staggered out (they said) into the swamp declaiming:

'Gee, I didn't know the Japs were *that* good.'

The crew could not agree on the best thing to do. So they split up. Four headed inland and got into the Murut-Kelabit country on the Trusan in north Sarawak after great tribulations. The Japanese were hunting them, at times hot on the trail. But the Trusan people, although anxious to pass them on and away as quickly as possible, fed and led them further and further inland, never gave them away. Several Sarawak Muruts were brought down to the coast and interrogated by the Japanese on this account. At least three of these were cruelly put to death by torture, without giving their own people or the Americans away. This Trusan-American party continued up from village to village, 'very very slowly', mostly hiding out in the jungle. By early 1945 they were scattered about in the remoter valleys of the interior, where the people continued to look after them as best they could, individually, at enormous risk.

The other half of this crew unhappily elected to cross north-east from the Trusan in Sarawak over the Crocker Range into the Padas river valley in the territory of North Borneo. Here, before very long, they were betrayed by the Tagal people, who sold them to the Japanese. As well as the reward, the Tagals were allowed to keep their heads. Every group in Borneo has its peculiarities. A North Borneo Tagal peculiarity is that head-hunting rites often do not require the possession of a whole head. When new head material is required for any ceremony or circumstances, a small *fresh* piece frequently suffices. The heads of these American airmen were divided out and distributed over a large area of North Borneo for this purpose. (After the war I met a kindly American Colonel, one of several nationalities going round ghoulishly recovering the bodies of their dead, in order to re-inter them in symmetrical cemeteries accessible to official openings by Field Marshals or Ministers of War. I never heard what he made of the report I gave him about these, four, subdivided by then into four score.)

Another of our American boys was the sole survivor of a plane that had caught fire on the way back from bombing the Japanese naval base at Labuan. He had landed by parachute in the jungle 'somewhere' no-one knows where. After living off roots, grubs, lice and mice for, he thinks, fourteen days, he met a man who brought him to a village about twenty miles east of the Bawang. Here he was hidden and slowly nursed into recovery. When we found him, he was a morass of ulcers and fantasies. He also had practically perfect command of the language of the Kemaloh people, among whom he was living.

The opportunity of helping these lads was a pleasant relief, up to its point. To this was added a touch of deeper emotion, when at too long last it came to the time we could see them go. For then one of them volunteered to stay and help us. This was Dan Illerich, a radio operator —and the only one who had volunteered to help us in our sore need. This offer created something of a sensation throughout High Command and was approved in a glowing message from the highest level. But it was not fair to Dan, things then being still pretty uncertain. It was worth helping the others, though, to be helped by him—and to hear from him every now and again, from the USA, to this day. Dan Illerich, 2601 W. Street, Apt. 8, Sacremento 16, California, USA.

*   *   *

The moment for peanut-manic departure came with the arrival of the first Australian Auster flown in by Lt Cheyney from Tarakan. By now a Brigade, an Australian Task Force had landed on Tarakan, on May 1, 1945. Enough importance was attached to our intelligence and other information for an Auster wing to be detailed to establish contact via our strip; which, of course, I had been praising to the skies for this reason. Tarakan lay just about 200 miles due east of Balawit and the Bawang, across uncharted miasmas of cloud and storm, without one possible place for emergency landing between island and coast. An Auster could make this, refuelling from supplies dropped to us.

The first landing was perfect. The pilot was a bit doubtful about the take-off length. I reassured him. And to prove the point to my extremely critical Yank friends, I took off with him on the first flight. We narrowly missed Sergeant Long's radio station, careered through the suddenly blessed lakes of the rice fields, gave a buffalo cow a miscarriage, turned neatly nose up in the mud.

Those things happened in those days, though. Within three days, Lasong Piri's strong-arm-and-tongue methods had lengthened the strip another hundred yards. We resurfaced the whole with thousands of giant bamboos, which grow in splendid groves around the edges of the Bawang plain. Each bamboo was split longitudinally, laid out with the inside paramount. The internode sections along the bamboo's length served as long lines of little sprockets or pegs which helped slow incoming aircraft after this. (Outgoing aircraft kept their wheels between these lines). A relief plane came in, repairs were done, and we were again a going concern in the air as well as on the track. Within a few more days pilots were acclaiming this field as better than Tarakan, which was constantly flooding. It was, I believe, the only all bamboo surface strip ever, at that.

* * *

Contact with regular forces at Tarakan opened up new horizons and responsibilities. It was gratifying, too, to be warmly received by Brigadier D. (Torpy) Whitehead, of Desert Rat fame in the Middle East. Whitehead was the oldest and at first least impressive of the senior Australian officers who from now on began to appear on the Borneo stage. A lawyer in civil life, he had a dry mind and a peculiar sense of humour. I remember vividly, that evening, when one of his colonels had just received news that he had received the DSO recommended by his Brigadier for action during the Tarakan landings. The colonel somehow just hadn't seemed able to get over it. In Torpy's tent, the three of us drank a good deal, and the colonel kept on reiterating: 'Why, Sir, I don't know how you do it—I thought you didn't even like me. . . .'

Apart from the Divisional Commander, Lt-General Sir Leslie Morshead, there was something oddly aggressive in a petty way, about the others. Only Whitehead seemed able to think—or any way to talk —of wider issues than the immediate; to take seriously subjects like the possible effects of present actions on the peoples of Borneo and their future behaviour in days of declared peace. The other top soldiers appeared to be too concerned with matters of interest to the Australians only—and usually in a rather restricted way, without thinking much beyond the affairs of their own units.

* * *

The information we had sent out had been helpful in the landings, supplemented by some daring reconnaissance on Tarakan Island itself (which lies just off the east coast of Borneo), undertaken by Dave Prentice, an Australian captain in 'Z'. It was encouraging to find that our ant-heap of the far interior was being treated seriously by old soldiers of stricter sort, too.

The first Australian days of Tarakan were not particularly pleasant. There were lots of Japanese around the small Australian bridgehead. These Japanese specialized in crawling into the camp by the night and putting hitherto unexploded shells under mess and staff tents, suitably time-fused. But my one evening there I was not in the right place for such eroticism.

My sudden emergence on the coast also produced some unusual enthusiasm from the 'Z' Special's staff end. An aeroplane was sent to Tarakan to fly me back to Morotai, in the Halmaheras, for cross-examination and policy discussion. Morotai had, in the short interval, grown into a great city of troops, cinemas, sports grounds, snobbisms and disputes. 'Z' Special had established forward headquarters there, now under the charge of Colonel Jock Campbell, florid, rotund, misleadingly giving one the impression that there was a wide difference between what he said he would do and what he would actually do when it came to the point (as he saw it). Happily, Jack Finlay and Jumbo Courtney were both up here, as well as George Crowther; and we were now allowed a direct wireless link Borneo/Morotai. My visit sewed up loose ends, put things on a firmer basis of liaison and inter-communication for the next phase of our proposed operations.

'Z' had also brought forward to Morotai some picked men ready to be dropped anywhere at short notice. I claimed the right to take seven of these back with me next day. I was allowed to choose this string (including one captain) to be in charge of our rapidly expanding eastward movements, leaving Eric Edmeades, as second-in-command, to concentrate and become more fully implicated with our extensions to the north and north-west, now of pressing urgency because of pending and larger scale Australian landings on Labuan. I was now allowed to know the exact date of these landings—June 10—and their proposed extensions on to the mainland, though these were to be strictly limited, most of the mainland being left as our own hunting ground.

My luck with captains held. I chose Captain Jack Blondeel,

Flemish—and the only one of his kind we saw in the field.* Blondeel had escaped from Holland during the war and became one of the best secret agents of SOE operating from England. He was the first of a series of officers with European experience who now came into my picture. He was also the only one who was much use; the only one not so obsessed by previous successes as to come to this new field with over-confidence and also with a kind of cruelty and harshness. Ruthlessness went well with many European cloak-and-dagger activities, but did not at all automatically fit in to our role among head-hunters. Blondeel, from the minute he clawed his way out of a mud and water landing in the Bawang, was a major asset to Semut.

Before dawn on my second morning on Morotai, we took off in two Liberators again. As well as seven good new men I carried masses of new arms and ammunition, now a hot need. Thousands of hill people were clamouring to be armed. Apart from radio and other technical equipment, we were now self-sufficient through the organization of the rich upland food and other resources.

Almost before anyone at Balawit noticed that I was missing, believed drunk, I was floating, refreshed, down to the rich brown earth again.

This time, dropping into an assured welcome and organized reception was plain fun. I was able to exercise my para-wit in the matter. With Eric Edmeades and Nick Combe, back at Richmond in New South Wales, we had spent a fortnight working out methods of controlling the aircraft, once the navigator brought it within the direct area; of regulating the pilot's precise movements going over the DZ, and then despatching ourselves by direct signals without the intervention of pilot, engineer or formal despatcher. This 'last word' in dropping sophistication, later officially termed Jump Master Technique, was suited to the present occasion: by now I knew this part of the uplands thoroughly. I decided, for the hell of it, to Super-Jump-Master myself so that I should land, as No 1 in the string, directly on to the Balawit

---

* I ought to make it clear that I have a deep affection for the Dutch people. Indeed, I spend quite a lot of time in Holland, when I can. My remarks on their conduct of the war in South-East Asia are not intended to be derogatory except to the senior Dutch people who were responsible for a tragically misguided policy, which involved both grossly inadequate military morale before the end of the war and unrealistic return to civilian government after it. I know that a good many of the younger Dutch, thousands of whom passed the war uselessly in Australia and elsewhere, had a much better grasp of realities as well as an aching urge to do something to win back their pre-war territories by their own efforts. I also realize that high-level politics, as between the Americans and the Dutch, made great difficulties for the Dutch Government too.

airfield; but time it so close that the other seven landed in a line, into the flooded rice fields beyond.

In my smugness, however, I forgot my invariable landing technique and gave myself a smart bruise on the coccyx from one of the bamoob internodes, intended only to interfere with the wheels of the aircraft.

* * *

We were now supplying the major intelligence information available (or required) about Japanese positions on the mainland within the possible range of Semut I. Further west, Semut II and III had begun to fill in the picture along their coastlines. The Australians intended to land first on Labuan in Brunei Bay and to extend down the coast from there (but only as far as the oilfields at Miri). It was also now our job to prepare positions behind Brunei Bay, and more widely—so that we could synchronize our first positive attacks from behind the Japanese lines, dislocate radio and other communications, and generally foul the Japanese set-up to ease the pressure and confuse the issue when the Australians landed, in mass. Related to this, we must make arrangements to ensure that the Japanese would not, in such crisis, kill prisoners and generally turn places they were about to vacate into shambles— which they had often done elsewhere, as the war spread up the Pacific.

At the same time, we had to expect that considerable Japanese forces might withdraw into the interior, possibly setting up some semi-permanent organization inside the country to trouble the allies; just as we were intending to trouble the Japanese (though they still did not know it). This involved a good deal of thinking about possible escape routes, and the disposing of our growing guerrilla forces so that Jap forces working inland could be somehow plotted as they moved, pursued, harassed and if possible stopped. This sticky business, which was presently to occupy nearly all our resources—and my nightmares —had already begun on the east side. It was a big relief to have someone of the calibre of Blondeel to take over the detail in that direction, supported by such already experienced Borneans as Jack Tredrea, Rod Cusack and Jeff Westley.

The Australian landing on Tarakan had dislodged Japanese, who gathered up others from the east coast and in May began to move inland. Naturally, I began to grow concerned for the pleasant and orderly establishment which by now was developed around HQ and air base in the rich Bawang valley at Balawit. But the nearest large forces of Japs were still a good fortnight's slogging away from that. The thing was to get at them quickly, before they got going or could do any damage to the people who had supported us and to whom we already had deep obligations.

*   *   *

To some extent, it was fortunate for us that the Japs did not yet realize we were there. They therefore had no particular inclination to come in our direction. It rapidly became evident, further, that there was some over-all retreat plan in operation. Even isolated individuals whom we picked off—but if possible first picked up and squeezed for intelligence—were heading roughly in the same direction. From Tara-kan, this was always north-west—in the general direction of the Sembakong in Dutch Borneo, through Labang or Loembis towards Pensiangan over the North Borneo border.

Though we had these movements closely plotted from the beginning —and were even able within a few days to start directing air strikes on Japanese river craft (for the Sembakong is a navigable river outside the upland formation), on to the miserable escapees—the purpose of these movements was far from clear at first. It was not until larger forces started moving over from the *west* coast, in a north-easterly direction, that we were able to calculate where the two lines of retreat might meet and see the big attraction which lay there. But this lies ahead, in an exciting enterprise which to Eric Edmeades' delight was to fall mostly within his zone of immediate command (Map C).

Eric's north-western sector was hotting up on its own account, anyway. Although we still had a clear spell before the Labuan landings, we had strict orders in no circumstances to attack the Japanese or dislocate anything until Labuan D Day, June 10th, when we should fall upon everything we could with abandon—the Japanese themselves were gatheringly restless and becoming angry. As the supply of rice, cattle, tobacco and salt, and labour from the interior began to dry up, they did, of course, notice. But the full effect was delayed for some weeks through the intervention of their Native Officer in administration, Bigar anak Debois, a wonderful citizen of the decent world.

Bigar was a Land Dayak from near Kuching, far away in the south-west corner of Sarawak. He was already an experienced junior administrative officer under the Brookes and had been posted to Lawas in the centre of Brunei Bay, opposite Labuan Island (the main Australian landing point). Lawas was and is the main outlet for all products from the interior down to this part of the coast. Trade through Lawas certainly goes back more than 1,000 years into the great Chinese commerce of the T'ang Dynasty to the far interior. The Japs were using Lawas to tap not only the rich Trusan valley behind but also the upper part of the Padas river in North Borneo (more accessible via Sarawak) and the great upland chunk of north-western Dutch Borneo, products from which could most easily come out that way. In a period when there were no political boundaries, Borneo was one indivisible territory instead of the usual four.

Bigar, an accomplished linguist, was the one man in Lawas who could speak inland languages. The Japs had come to rely upon him tremendously.

We heard well of him soon after we arrived. There were stories told of how he had protected and helped the Christian missionaries heading out up the Trusan after the Japs arrived; and of how he had effectively acted as go-between them and the Japanese, so that when they eventually gave themselves up to avoid reprisals upon the tribes, they were not in any way punished, and indeed all survived the war in internment —whereas missionaries on the Dutch side who also surrendered, were brutally murdered. Everyone said that Bigar again and again had prevailed upon the Japanese to mitigate harshnesses and repressions which, in their multiple frustrations of occupation, they periodically wished to impose upon local people; and especially upon the inland people, whom they regarded throughout, with a mixture of fear and contempt, as 'savages'.

One of the first things I had done, therefore, from way back at Bario, was send a selected special agent to contact Bigar and give him secret information of our existence. This was so successfully achieved that as soon as Eric Edmeades returned from his westward reconnaissance and another stiff trip to the south—to secure for sure our position in that at first unpromising direction—he tore off down the Trusan towards Lawas and Brunei Bay. Within only two miles of the Japs at Lawas, a quiet Murut head man, Kerus, unhesitatingly looked after this first white man. As soon as I could spare the personnel, from Westley's drop onwards, we built up on this base with excellent fellows like Lieutenant Pinkerton and Sergeant Bill Nibbs (another escapee from the regular paratroops). Edmeades was in close communication with Bigar, at first by intermediary and presently with direct meetings in the jungle dark. Invaluable information was thus obtained. For instance, Bigar had access to wireless signals coming all through this area. But best of all, we were able to keep him exactly informed of *what* we were doing, thus to co-ordinate with him the arrival of certain named upland individuals with agreed stories, and in all ways to support him from our end in his explanations of why the interior seemed to be drying up for the forces of occupation.

By the time Bigar had been through such excuses as floods, droughts, disease, death of a great chief, a plague of rice birds and rats, Japanese suspicions were well aroused. They could no longer be prevented from sending up a strong—by their then standards—force to find out what was going on and see to it that the 'dirty savages' toed the Asian co-prosperity line without further delay.

It was unfair, really; too unsporting. For, through Bigar, we had precise information about the plan, programme, personnel and equipment of this force before they had started inland. We dare not let them get *too* far up and learn our secrets. On the other hand, we dare not deal with them too soon, lest they be missed by the Japs near the coast quickly, and our whole secret too early exploded. About a hundred Trusan Muruts now had our rifles and some training in the use of them; to stop some of them getting trigger-happy was another worry. It only needed one rifle shot to give our show away.

The Muruts and Kelabits let the Japanese patrol get about seven days up the Trusan before we set an ambush where the path climbs steeply out of a creek bed above Long Semadoh. It had to be a one-sided ambush. For not one of the local guerrillas would consider being left out. And local standards of gun play were hardly refined. On a shout, this fearful blast of fire-power was discharged from behind a ridge into all the rear part of the party, which included the Japanese and their fully implicated satellites. In these early patrols they always took the precaution of sending a considerable body ahead, including conscripted locals and wretched aggregations of Javanese and Celebes Malays, carrying inferior firearms (sometimes wooden dummies) and classed as soldiers.

★　★　★

I think the Kelabits made the best soldiers on the whole in these ambush and other guerrilla affairs. But then it came easily to them, for reasons which I hope have already appeared (in Part I); and accentuated by the fact that they were almost the last people in Borneo to come under any sort of outside control towards pacification and a quiet life. Indeed, they were one of the last such people in the world. Secondly, I would put the closely related Muruts, of the Trusan river and the inter-related Potoks, Milaus and other Kelabit-Murut groups who occupy a great section of the mountainous land and upland valleys in the north-west corner of what was then Dutch Borneo. It is often said, by the unthinking, that when such people become Christians they lose a great deal. They do. But one of the things that the small proportion who by that time were already Christian definitely had not lost was the martial quality and the aggressive trait. If anything, I would say that the Christian Muruts were just an edge better than the pagan ones in fighting. They were certainly better in special jobs where they did not have to use firearms and yet had to take great risks, show energy, responsibility and daring. For instance, we used Christian Muruts, mostly from the villages on the middle Trusan, extensively as super-speed runners carrying messages between the coast and the interior; as guides moving fast and often unarmed ahead of larger parties (unarmed so that they appeared harmless if they contacted any enemy point); and as special agents and spies percolating into the coastal areas to bring back specific information.

Third, one must give credit definitely to the Kenyahs. Both the Kenyahs under Tama Weng Ajang and Tama Weng Tingang, on the Baram to the west in Sarawak and the great assemblage of Kenyahs on the Bawang-Batang-Kayan rivers to the east, who only got involved at the very end but came in boiling to fight and seething with hatred of those they regarded as their Asian oppressors. The Kenyahs had the disadvantage of being almost entirely water-borne people, much of whose life is spent either on their farms or on the river lines. Although of course they have much jungle experience, they have not the same jungle instincts and physiques as some of the hill tribes. The Ibans, or Sea Dayaks, on the other hand, are very jungley people. Where the Kenyahs have the great advantage of having powerful chiefs and clear-cut hierarchies, facilitating command and control, the Ibans are perhaps the most individualistic, classless and yet dynamic of the Borneo inland peoples. This constantly presented a problem in control. Fortunately, I only had to face it myself in one case because there were very few Ibans within the whole of the Semut I area; those there were moved in groups under distinct leaders whom I was able to attach specifically, on the north-east, to Captain Blondeel; and over in the Limbang, to Fred Sanderson.

The Japs made it easy for us, of course. It was Japanese regulations that their people should move through the jungle in boots and other standard equipment. It is impossible to do this at all quietly. But in any case, they never had enough confidence in their guides and in the general set-up, once they had moved away from the coast, to do otherwise than keep to such limited, visible paths as existed. No such inhibitions, either of footwear or freedom of lateral movement, inhibited any of our people. We did, on the other hand, suffer from an intellectual restriction which at times tended to be threateningly severe; which I had to deal with drastically from the beginning. All writers about the Dayaks and other people of Borneo have written at length about their omen birds and animals; howls, the sound of a barking deer, the call of a spider-hunter, the movement of a certain snake, can be sufficient to negate all activity, cancel a forward march, send everybody home, cause general alarm or even in some cases stop work of any kind altogether for several days at a time. Though sometimes exaggerated, these accounts have been substantially true.

Clearly, we could not operate like this. And in this one respect I did simply rough-ride over every consideration of local custom and belief. This was never ill-received, though at first received in some circles with very much misgiving. Fortunately, we had to start with the Kelabits, in many ways the most realistic, logical, and in a sense 'amoral', liberal-minded people of the interior—in ways I have tried to show in the opening part of this story. Had we been forced to start tackling this problem with the riverine Kenyahs (with their highly organized animist paganism, and aristocratic society) it might have been much more difficult to stop; and as it was, after the war was over, I was to experience difficulty on this account, with the tremendously powerful and culturally rich Kenyahs of the upper Batang Kayan round Long Nawang, with whom I was on one occasion forced to put people sitting alternately back to back in my canoe to ensure that all omens were favourable—at least to one part of my party under all conditions of movement. But such efforts by the outsider, especially the white man, are really exceedingly superficial and seldom actually called for.

To go through such motions is rather by way of paying lip service and safeguarding one's own position. It is always possible to make the others understand that necessity overrides all other considerations. This indeed is fundamental in a very large part of animism; and many observers, even highly trained anthropologists, have been more than somewhat deceived as to the extent and depth in which this type of religious or socio-theological feeling penetrates *inside* the minds and real actions of the people as compared with its superficial and of course extremely important influences in ritual, agricultural observances, long-house organization, and so on. Anyway, in effect we were able to ignore this aspect altogether during the war inside Borneo. Since then, whole tribes—including peoples not at all affected by our wartime influence—have demonstrated the point in another way; by abandoning the whole framework of old and supposedly deep-seated beliefs within a few years, to become Roman Catholics, Methodists and Seventh Day Adventists on a mass conversion scale over huge areas both of Sarawak and of what is now Indonesian territory

* * *

Anyway, our first operation went one hundred per cent. No one escaped down-hill to tell the tale. We won about twenty terrified Javanese, alive. These were so delighted to be left alive and quite kindly treated that after the long trek into the Bawang, medical treatment and bags of good rice, they settled in as the first in a long line of these conscripts who presently made us tracks and bridges, excellent vegetable gardens, male nurses and a qualified crooner. There was only one job not to give to the Javanese, as I soon discovered. They appeared to be ninety per cent kleptomaniacal, must not be left in charge of or near any kind of depot or stores. (But this was probably because of all the misery and suffering they had experienced since the Japanese had compulsorily removed them from their home island into Borneo war service.)

This so one-sided ambush greatly heightened the already high morale of our continually growing forces. With several more which soon followed, it gave reassuring indications that my subordinates could control their guerrillas; and that their guerrillas could control themselves. There was no looting, or even lopping off of heads on this occasion—or on any other occasion later, unless for some reason permission was given; or unless the forces concerned were Ibans, lowland people who had not yet got in to the Semut system of ants with firearms, but para-military, uncouth manners.

While Bigar was frantically, with our best assistance, producing runners and messages to prove that the inland Japs were held up, delayed by floods, but in no serious difficulties, the rumblings of Jap nervousness grew day by day. A new factor came in to accentuate this. Non-Japanese in their administration and military organizations, singly or sometimes in small groups, got to hear of us through their natural close identification with the local people. Jap coastal conscripts started, at first in a tiny trickle, to desert inland, to flit without explanation by night.

The first of these flitters, a Chinese, was the first of many such welcome recruits to our side. Chong Ah Onn was a long-time Medical Dresser in the Sarawak Government. He had lived, groaning, under the Japanese all these years. Directly he heard of us, he flit. By no means an athletic or youthful man, he walked dangerously unannounced into our hide-out behind Lawas. Thence he was sent up to headquarters. He had a very wide knowledge of the country and a lively sympathy for the inland people. He was simply thrilled when I put him in charge of the hospital we had just started at Bawang, arranged a special air drop to furnish it with the good old 'Z' splendour of priority drugs, and left him free to carry out medical operations on a scale he had hope-lessly dreamed of for years, the like of which still remains as a lovely sad dream in the peace-time uplands today.

Chong pined for Mrs Chong and his little Chongs, all the time. One day he came to me in tears about them. He had left them hidden, provided for and he hoped secure against Jap revenge. But he was worried. I was in a hurry; I thought so much of this gentle man that I detailed two armed men to go to Lawas at once and bring his family back. Little did I know. Several weeks later, when I had forgotten all about it, there emerged upon the plain an impressive caravan. Mrs Chong, a powerful-minded woman—but I always forgive her everything for her superb birds' nest and shark's fin soup and 'boneless wonder' chicken; and sucking pig; and roast duck; and bamboo shoots in oil—had conscripted a troop of our urgently required guerillas to transport a family of six, a baby, and more furniture than the whole of the interior had ever previously contained in one epoch.

* * *

Other recruits came up under Japanese orders as messengers and to see what was going on; then immediately came over to us. One of these was an ex-Sarawak policeman, Usop, a Dayak from Lundu, near Kuching in the south-west. He was invaluable as a fire-arms instructor and later on the leader of a guerrilla troop in his own right. Yita Singh was a handsome, six foot, jet-bearded Sikh, a cloth trader on the coast, with a passion for brandy and aggression. He, too, presently became a leader in his own right, a real killer, the one man I have known of whom I could honestly say that once aroused he neither felt nor could feel fear. Andrew Blassan, a quiet Balau Dayak, was also invaluable.

A serio-comic group who deserted from Brunei consisted of Bolang, Cusoi and Sulang. These were Christian men from the Celebes, soldiers under the Dutch, then under the Japanese; and soldiers of fortune in the fullest sense of fun. They were invaluable, because they knew a lot about weapons, simple drills and tactics. We never had to teach a Kelabit or Murut how to move or kill. But there was always an appreciable danger that in moving they might kill themselves, with things like hand-grenades; or kill each other, instead of the enemy, by a combination of over-enthusiasm and the automatic lever on a carbine or Sten gun. Cusoi and Co. knew about two inch mortars as well. We were going to want these, as special sorts of unpleasantness in night surprise or on well secured hideouts.

The chronicle of human acquisitions in these days would on its own fill a visitors' book. Two others need to be mentioned, for the record, I think. 'Tuan Aris' and 'Tuan Agong' were names often to be heard on Kelabit lips from our first landing. They stood out as shadowy figures over to the east. Who were they? *Tuan* means, in common Borneo parlance, either an important Malay religious leader or any European. Aris and Agong were said to be neither of these. What exactly they were, informants found it hard to define. They always find it hard to define what people of other races who come up among them do; impossible to define why they do it. The blanket term '*Perintah*', meaning Government, is readily extended to anyone who looks like having anything to do with any branch of administration. But although Agong was partly regarded as this, it was pointed out that the *Perintah* eastward was Dutch and he was not.

During the years of the Japanese occupation these two Tuans, Aris and Agong, had evidently grown to be important figures in the interior. As the only two outsiders, people of reportedly 'white' education and knowledge, they alone had been able to throw light on the many extraordinary events which had convulsed Borneo, expelled the white man, and replaced him with a regime of rudeness followed by hardship followed by cruelty, however remote.

Not long before we arrived—as Japanese probing of the interior had increased in the struggle for supplies and their anxieties about the American airmen at large—Aris and Agong had taken to the jungle, vanished from everyday view. Neither of them made any early approach to us, somewhat to my surprise. Probably they were too clever to believe the reports of us which had certainly been reaching them. It was not until I was established at Bawang that I one day received the momentous news that the great Tuan Aris approached.

Picking a way with some difficulty along the narrow bund between the rice fields, Aris emerged into comfortable reality as a very fat, sweaty, pale brown gentleman with a solar topee and the cleanest white clothing to be seen, at that time, this side of Sydney. His wide face and big flared nostrils, his glistening and perfect teeth, crisp waving (but not pomaded) hair and middle-age spread, belied a character sophisticated, charged with passion which he was for ever battling to control, and incorporating a cunning and a kind of cynicism which constantly and involuntarily operated, in him, against his own absolute and uppermost convictions as a fanatical Christian. For Aris, it almost instantly emerged, was a Christian convert from the Celebes who had come into the interior on behalf of an American mission before the war, and remained there after all his superiors in Christ had been imprisoned or slain (by the Japs). Aris had continued his work of proselytism throughout the occupation and with some conspicuous successes. He had not only consolidated the small beginning of the American work, but powerfully extended it. He held several thousands of the Potok, Milau and other people to the east in what was virtually a reign of terror; the terror of hell. Full of energy, devotion, eloquence, heavenly wrath, burning belief, he blasted most of the sins which these people had hitherto been cheerfully unthinking heirs to. None of his flock dare drink, dare smoke, dare move out of the long-house on Sunday, swear, (even at a dog) or raise their voices—except in the compulsory hymns before dawn, lengthy graces before and after each meal, hymns after dusk every day (trebled on Sundays).

Tuan Aris generously, even effusively, welcomed me. He put his great heart in the service of worldly Semut, *pro tem*. Lawai and Penghulu Miri and all the other pagan chiefs had seen that their super-stitions and ritual observances must be modified or suspended in this unprecedented period. Aris agreed with this in superficial principle. He agreed, for instance, that his flock might hate (the Japanese), might travel on Sunday (on duty) and on occasion allow themselves to be sworn at by runaway Sergeant Cusoi or smooth Sergeant Bolang, for the good of their skins as soldiers.

But Cusoi and Bolang and Sulang, like Yita Singh and Usop and I, introduced a terrible threat into Tuan Aris's interior kingdom of the soul's salvation. One of his most powerful arguments had been that all educated and civilized people were Christians and behaved as Christians: i.e. did not smoke, belch, swear, etc. Uncontrolled, unsupervised and necessarily unchallenged during several years, his sincere, but viciously narrow brand of Christianity, derived from American Fundamentalism and one hundred per cent belief in the Bible as irrevocably, textually, factually applicable everywhere in the world, under all conditions and at once, had led him into diverse dogmas and into unwitting emphases, occasional exaggerations, in order to impress his existing and extend his expanding flock. The presence of other outsiders over his (Dutch) side of the border was a serious disturbance of dogma. Unintentionally, we were living evidence that men could call themselves Christian and still light a cigarette without being blasted by heavenly lightning; and although myself I drank borak—yet was I not turned, into stone, like Lot's wife or the long-house which laughed at the dressed-up frog dancing.

Tuan Aris set out in all his sincerity to help. He could do little else. But he became more and more uneasy and unhappy. In the end, once he was sure the Japanese were no longer a serious threat, he became an absolute nuisance and had to be threatened. He certainly was something of a miracle, picking his way in immaculate linen with unvarying prayer book, across the tricky trails of bamboo and slippery mud between the sheets of Bawang water, waiting for another season's rice and another soul won.

Aris did us one other very good turn. He had earlier introduced ducks into the eastern interior. These ducks did exceedingly well in the uplands. He did exceedingly well selling them, from a monopoly, to all comers (Christian converts got half-price). Borneo chickens are mostly poor creatures. Aris's imported ducks were fine chaps, great layers. By some judicious requisitioning I soon had duck depots established to north and west as sidelines on all Semut's ant-heaps. These went down very well with the troops everywhere.

Tuan Agong emerged from the shadows at about the same time, but separately. The separately was an inseparable part of the life and the hate which lay between this uneven pair. Agong was also a Celebes Malay and also a Christian. He was a smaller, quieter, more thoughtful, less passionate man than Aris. He had been sent up into the interior as the only representative of Dutch government in the area after the American mission, largely through Aris, had begun to have an appreciable influence. The Dutch, unlike the Brookes on the west side of the border, had encouraged these missionaries. This was a logical part of their belief in 'development' of the country for economic purposes, to their own ultimate advantage (they thought). They wished to westernize, educate and re-orientate the inland people in a nice, vague way. They left it to the missionaries to do the spadework. They left it to Agong, as a Junior Administrator, to watch over government interests alongside Aris and over the area generally.

Agong married a nice local girl and soon made himself well-beloved. He was the equivalent, in Dutch Borneo, to Native Officer Bigar working from Lawas on the Sarawak side. Both liked and were liked by the people; were fair, kept their tempers and kept their word—three qualities which nearly all Borneans desire and expect from outsiders seeking not merely to order them but to influence them.

But Agong was quite a man of the world. He did not interpret Christianity as necessarily excluding a cigarette or a glass of rice wine. When Aris demanded that his Christians be prevented from marrying pagans, or that pagan observances be compulsorily discontinued in long-houses where there were Christians, Agong refused to intervene. Aris had little control of his temper and none of his tongue, once started. Bad blood ran high. Each disliked and distrusted the other. When they emerged and converged upon me at Bawang, I quickly found myself the thin ham in this sandwich, little Agong and Aris the huge.

Agong was also a nervous, timid man. He had learnt to be frightened of Dutch authority, more than reaffirmed by Japanese successors, for whom he was still working. He thought that, for this latter reason, we would certainly execute him in reprisal for the killing of Dutch missionaries, nuns and others which had gone (in 1941-2) on in his part of Borneo, though entirely outside his control. He had to emerge once Aris had done so. The duet was on. The two of them gave me some awful times between them. There was nothing to do, though, but plump for Agong, whose real influence was far greater.

In any case I was feeling uneasy about our intervention on Dutch territory, now verging on positive occupation. I kept on raising this point in signals and reports. HQ reassured that the Dutch were fully in the picture and fully approved. From our point of view, it was impossible to consider as binding political boundaries (unsurveyed) which at present did not exist even in administrative terms—and which never had existed in any serious sense, among the thousands inhabiting the interior of all the British and Dutch territories together. However, I felt that the least I could do, under these circumstances, was to back up Tuan Agong on the Dutch side, equally with Bigar in Sarawak.

Bigar, duly tipped off, now deserted the Japs, just before Labuan D Day, and joined us in mid-June. He could thus take charge of administrative problems which were rapidly piling on to my inexperienced head. No flicker of instruction or advice on this subject had ever been given to us before coming in. I never had the benefit of a European administrative officer with Asian experience among all the extraordinary figures that landed upon me at one time or another during the following months. It was only too obvious that if we were going to overthrow the Jap regime we must in parallel put back some other. I was worried about the effects of our dislocating the whole of the interior economy—by introducing all sorts of new services, medicines, currency and by introducing people on a large scale to new trade routes, saleable commodities and other peoples with whom they had never been in direct contact before. Psychologically I was even more worried by the possible effects of reintroducing and vigorously sanctioning the killing of human beings. How would anyone be able to stop this, click, on an external armistice? How indeed could we get modern guns away from those who had so swiftly learnt to handle them—and who fell in love with them on sight?

The first approach to an answer must be to keep close check on the normal things of life; a close record of all that we did to dislocate it; and an accurate register of the material things we distributed in the process. Here, Bigar—and presently others, such as Hugo Low and Abang Haji Adenan—played a good part in Sarawak. Tuan Agong was the only straw to clutch, with the other hand, in Dutch Borneo. I clutched him and squeezed him until his nerve ends squeaked. For months I had him sleeping within a few feet of me, referred everything that could have post-war repercussions to him. It was an impossible job. But he made the best possible go of it. I learnt to respect his integrity as I could only, among those around me then, that of Lasong Piri, the chief, and Sergeant Long at his radio day and night, placidly super-efficient.

* * *

From June 10, 1945, 23,553 men of the Australian Ninth Division (reinforced) landed in Brunei Bay, mainly on Labuan Island; plus 6,525 RAAF and 1,254 US personnel. They met at first with fierce opposition and considerable casualties. The Official War Histories must suffice to describe operations with which I was much concerned, but indirectly. I did not myself get down to Labuan until the Australians were fairly well established and had detailed a separate Auster flight for regular liaison with us up in Bawang.

At dawn on Labuan's D Day we fell as best we might upon the mainland Japanese, their co-operators, installations and communications, wherever we could get at them. In strict military terms this was not great shakes. But the wide scatter, the ferocity and the complete surprise of these attacks had a far greater effect than their simple statistical significance. Our irregular efforts gave to the unlucky enemy the impression of a general, synchronized attack. This impression was accentuated in that we were able to take over wireless and administrative posts and to kill off every Jap on routine duty along the whole of the Brunei and Sarawak installations in the huge arc of Brunei Bay and the coastal plain behind.

This was easy. For example, the Japanese in charge at Lawas—a small but then vital point in their occupation, and their control for a huge hinterland—was shot and finished off with a spear as he walked out to go to the garden lavatory, unexpectant of death, in the early morning. By mid-day, Lieutenant Pinkerton had thrown all possible signs of Japanese control out of Lawas, arrested collaborators in the district on whom we had been building up information for weeks past, and raised the Union Jack over the government offices in the fort. Further along the bay on the Limbang river—which rises in Mount Murud, flows round Batu Lawi and a fortnight's travel later flows out into Brunei

Bay in a wide delta, at one side of which is the city of Brunei—the hell-bent Sergeant Sanderson had by now built up a private army, and was creating tropical hades.

Further north-east again, just inside the territory of North Borneo, Warrant-Officer Colin MacPherson and Corporal George Griffiths were running a private war of their own around Mengalong and up towards Weston. North Borneo was indeed strictly in the zone of influence of Nick Combe's 'Agas' (Sandfly) operation, our secret sister. But in practice, Agas had had more difficulty than Semut as regards guerrilla organization. Semut's ants had therefore been given permission to spread into North Borneo until we met up with Agas sandflies from the opposite direction—which we never did. MacPherson was given this corner of North Borneo on Brunei Bay, near to Eric Edmeades now in the Padas valley above Beaufort*—Beaufort being taken by the Australian Ninth Division as the inland limit of their control on the mainland.

When I flew down to Labuan on the first convenient Auster, things were still a shambles there. The Japanese were still holed out, doing suicide attacks at night, causing a lot of dislocation. But 'Z' Special already had an advance HQ set up. Being 'Z', it had bagged the best cliff-top site, bay and bathing beach as camp. Here soon appeared Jumbo Courtney and George Crowther; and a new character, Colonel David Leach. David Leach was a New Zealander, and had served with the artillery in the Middle East and Italy, was now liaison officer between 'Z' and the Ninth Division. The need for this liaison was conspicuous. Regular Australian units landing on the mainland, naturally enough felt like conquering heroes, bringing the first news of better days and gladness to the unhappy inhabitants. So much security secrecy surrounded Semut's existence that none of them had any idea other Australians were around. It came as a nasty shock to majors and colonels, cautiously proceeding upon Limbang, Ukong, Lawas, Awat Awat, Trusan, Mengalong and elsewhere to find sergeants and even in one case a private (Driver Henry) in full occupation; and sometimes, naturally enough, behaving like rulers of separate kingdoms—for within limits, I had to encourage their egos to get the best out of them; and it was better to do this than to try to inhibit Aussie exuberance, under unusual conditions, by remote control.

---

* In the last week of June I accompanied Brigadier Porter during the battle for Beaufort, to facilitate current and subsequent liaison.

XVIIa The Ong family with 'Doctor' Ong, key-man of interior medicine in 1945. (*See p. 253*)

XVIIb Nomadic Punans who served as erratic blowpipe units in 1945. (*See p. 265*)

XVIIIa G. S. Carter, DSO, in our house at Kuching, 1958; our only surviving war souvenir, one of several hundred Japanese flags Semut captured, in background. (*See* p. 176 *on*)

XVIIIb Christian Murut soldiers from the middle Trusan river, each of whom was decorated for gallantry. (*See* p. 250)

XIXa (*above*) Nick Combe, OBE, MC, with his eldest daughter, Sheila, at Kuching recently. (*See pp.* 175, 245, 260)

XIXb (*left*) Eric Edmeades, MC, second-in-command of *Semut I.* (*See p.* 200 *on*)

XIXc Bill Sochon and family, after receiving the DSO at Buckingham Palace. (*See p.* 222 *on*)

XX Peace in a corner of the long-house. (*See Part IV*)

XXIa Kelabit mother and child (1945)

XXIb 'Tom', a Kelabit godson, born 1945, sulking in the special
Kelabit way, *kedior*, used by small boys.

XXII   A Kelabit father and son in party dress at Long Lelang, in the head-
waters of the Akar River.

XXIII Boys learning to blowpipe. (*See pp.* 65, 88, 265)

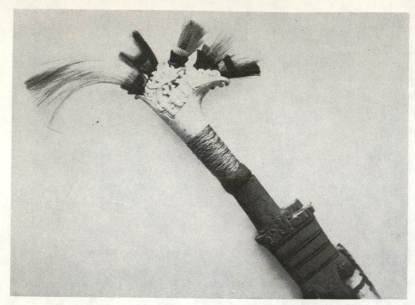

XXIVa

Three styles of inland carving—on antler handle and wood sheath of sword; on pendant of hornbill ivory; and on ear-rings of tortoise-shell.
(See pp. 11, 26, 80, 319, etc.)

XXIVb

XXIVc

It should be emphasized, here, that distances in this Borneo set-up cannot be measured on a map. Very fast jungle travel inland is ten miles a day on an established track. Except on the lower reaches of the Limbang, the whole of my area at this time involved jungle travel on foot, much of it on negligible or non-existent tracks. In the ordinary peacetime life of the interior, people had had no occasion to make some of the journeys between river systems or different racial groups, which became an essential part of our movement and organization for paramilitary purposes. And though by the middle of 1945 I had a network of radio posts and a first-class Signals Officer (Captain Richter), by now I had five seniors acting with groups of their own in the field, and all sorts of subsidiary white and Asian gangs operated semi-independently —though each within defined territorial limits—including irregulars like Sikh Yita Singh, Lundu Dayak Usop, and the three musketeers (Cusoi, Bolang and Sulang).

The possibilities for upsetting, possibly infuriating, regular forces as they spread ashore to hold a strip of coastal mainland, were therefore clearly appreciable. A peculiar additional factor was making itself felt, as well. I was concerned at the possibility that inland Tuan Aris might get out of hand and suddenly start revoking his versions of the messages the Almighty had sent him permitting Christians to take part in the war. Relations between the religious leader and the administrative leader, Tuan Agong, got more and more strained, and in general I had to take Agong's side in the arguments. I therefore thought to build up Aris by inventing a second and special role for his stricter brethren. He had several fanatical young men under him, including three imported pre-war from the Celebes as his deacons and teachers. I asked that an elite, selected by him, should not carry arms, but travel all over the interior and down to the coast, wherever there were any Christians whatsoever, inciting them to be of good heart, good informants and (when required) good fighters. The demand for ordinary soldiers in any old place had ceased. We had well over a thousand men well armed, equipped with simple denim uniforms, badges and belts. In addition we had acquired about another thousand shot-gun irregulars, armed with weapons taken largely from Jap stores.

These shot-gun irregulars were terrifying figures. They were mostly using guns that had been confiscated from the whole inland area by the Japanese, left stacked and neglected in this tropical climate for several years, then recovered and released—not always with much discrimination in the first excitement—when 'Z' people took over. On the whole, however, the discipline which these ex-head-hunters showed was remarkable. They never shot at each other on purpose. There was no case of paying off an old feud. The main difficulty was in determining what, exactly, was a Japanese legitimate target.

As I have already suggested, the Kelabits and other Borneo peoples have the woolliest ideas of group terminology and racial classification, as these things are seen through western eyes. They do not think of races and peoples as we do. They may know the names; these seldom have any substance, for them. As the wretched Javanese conscripts had been to all intents and purposes, incorporated in the Japanese forces and under Japanese orders had inflicted much beastliness on the countryside, Borneans genuinely confused the two. The more so since up to that time very few Javanese had ever been seen in this part of Borneo—the echoes of the Madjapahit Empire which ruled West Borneo from Java a thousand years ago could hardly be expected to register as race recognition in 1945.

In one case some Tagals shot a Javanese near Lawas for this reason. On paper, it looked just like murder. The man was unarmed, sitting in a hut, doing nothing but hide amidst the surrounding confusion. Probably no one except a Tagal would have shot in this instance, at this time. We already knew* that the Tagals alone had betrayed some American airmen where all other people had protected them, even with hardship and danger to themselves. It was therefore against my policy to arm Tagals at all. (I left it to the post-war governments to sort out any suitable punishment. In practice the government of North Borneo never did anything about it, so far as I know.)

These particular Tagals had acquired weapons during the taking of Lawas. Unfortunately, for them, they did their belated war work just as the first Australian platoon came that way. They were arrested for murder, under orders from an entirely ignorant officer. That is the last anyone has ever seen or heard of them to this day!

*   *   *

Another unfortunate upset occurred above Ukong on the Limbang, about the same time. Here my tough Driver Henry, with a force of about thirty Kelabits and Muruts, Tabuns and Ibans—one of several

* See pages 195 and 182.

extremely tough units recruited and trained under the authority of Penghulu Badak, after he had returned from Bario with Sergeant Sanderson—was holding a crucial position on the escape route which Japanese were now beginning to use as the Australians came on to the mainland coast. Many Japanese were stationed in the Miri and Seria oil fields west of Brunei Bay. Numbers of these started moving east along an evidently prepared line of escape—set to converge, far away to the north-east, with the similar movements already well under way from the east coast, first noticed after the Tarakan landings (see Map C).

Driver Henry set himself right across this escape line, picking off individual Japanese and small groups as they came through, with marked success. Sanderson, mostly working further up river, with a larger force, was tackling any larger numbers of Japanese, reported in advance by Henry. But the flow was still only a trickle; with strong signs—confirmed by Javanese and other conscripts taken alive—that larger and better organized groups would be coming through shortly.

The Ibans (Sea Dayaks) in the Limbang have migrated there in recent times from South West Sarawak. The Ibans are the really 'wild men of Borneo', famed head-hunters of the past. Their idea of head-hunting, killing and war was less controlled, more volatile and exhibitionist, than that of most other Borneo peoples. Moreover, the Ibans have not got a strong class system. In consequence, if in large groups together, they are not easily amenable to orders or disciplined organization in emergency—as compared with, say, the Kelabits who, though very strong individualists, basically submerge personal interests and adopt very strict discipline under their *own* leadership when necessary. For individual daring and dash the Iban is unbeatable. Where he is regimented and under rigid control from senior officers—and preferably in a minority racially within the unit—he cannot be surpassed in jungle warfare. But we could not exercise so much control in activities which, by their very nature, put a premium on individuality, irregularity and at times impulse.

Unfortunately, on this particular occasion, Henry was at his post in a depot temporarily established on the left bank of the main Limbang river. He had some very tough-looking operators scattered about, armed to the throats with some of the latest weapons, including some not issued to but immediately envied by regular soldiers, with their post-'Z' priorities!

A Kelabit is an imposing looking chap by his build, his beads, his skins and feathers and leopard's teeth ear-ornaments. The Iban has a slighter body, but is more mercurially demonstrative from moment to moment, with a delicate boned, often beautiful face, vividly dramatized by bands of blue-black tattoo stretching from the chest up the throat and right under the chin. Give this man (as Henry had done) an American carbine, a camouflaged set of jungle overalls, high canvas American marine boots, a webbed belt studded with hand grenades, a bush knife decorated with human hair, a beret with hornbill feather, and a Commando sheath dagger attached to waterproofed torch and kosh, and you have something that Auntie might well have seen in the woodshed, with permanent ill-effect.

Into this classical guerrilla set-up—with Henry lolling at ease in a pair of shorts and a bead necklace, surrounded by his devoted warriors—a platoon of Australians, probing with enterprise and due precaution, by river, unexpectedly appeared. It was difficult, after some months of such jungle experience, for the driver (=private) to treat an officer and his NCOs with a great show of respect when they started giving him orders—once they had got over the shock at his paradoxical paramilitaroid existence. Apparently the unpleasant atmosphere thus generated affected the Iban irregulars. They did not like the attitude of these white soldiers, which bordered on the contemptuous or facetious (they wrongly thought). Most of these toughs had by now taken at least one head. An Iban becomes tremendously touchy once the idea of heads swims dimly into vision.

Anyway (to cut a long saga short) while Henry was pressing some of his excellent rice wine on the Aussie other ranks round the back—the officer being on a 'tour of inspection'—several of the Ibans devoted their attentions to a prisoner taken that morning. This man, from down river, had been repeatedly reported as a Jap collaborator. Our policy (if any) in this—for in this as in most things we had no direction from above—was to treat all ordinary collaboration as explainable, excusable, and to be forgotten forthwith provided the collaborator changed his tune. There could be no question of allowing spites and hatreds against individuals to convict any man of a crime under new conditions. Only where someone had gone far beyond the needs and pressures of the Japanese occupation, had gone out of his way to exploit a position or impose cruel hardships, could he be regarded, by us, as a collaborator.

Henry's prisoner belonged to this latter category. He was waiting to be sent up to me for further examination. But while the lieutenant was having a look-see and the other ranks a quick swill, the Ibans, angered and humiliated at the way they *felt* they had been brushed aside, on ground they felt they had themselves 'liberated' from the hated Japs, now took the familiar liberty of chopping off the prisoner's head. When the officer returned to the camp clearing, he was faced with the sight of a headless trunk upon the ground. According to the Iban story —and it made a good story the way I heard it later—the officer almost fainted. And why not, indeed?

The next thing I knew about this was a top urgent message that Henry was to be put under arrest and sent down to Labuan for court martial; the charge: murder. Unlike the miserable Tagals from Mempakul, I was able to do something to protect my man in this case. Against all the efforts of a quota of legal men who decorated command positions in 9 Div. the charge was quashed from above, by Field-Marshal Blamey in person (I believe).

*　*　*

All this sort of thing made rather nervous work. I have mentioned two kinds of armament which our people carried—the regular arms supplied by parachute and the shot guns of all conditions and calibres, captured from the Japs. There was a third element which produced its due share of tertiary headache and 'Z' irregularity. The blow-pipe boys, our third arm, were something else again!

In the early days after landing, when we were not able to meet the fierce demand for fire-arms, I had sanctioned the formation of several blow-pipe groups. To the Kelabit mind, as to mine, this was much like using poison gas in Western war. It was a deadly thing to do—lest the idea of fighting with blow-pipes should be established, sanctioned by experience and subsequently continued. But after all, unpleasant though it was, the same objection applied to everything we were doing lethally, in reintroducing organized killing so soon after it had been outlawed under white influence.

As soon as firearms were dropped in numbers, I was able to replace blow-pipes with firearms, except in one broad direction. Away to the east, beyond the Kerayan, in the Toeboe and related rivers, there were numbers of nomadic people, Punans, who were most anxious to help. These people were so wild and so inexperienced in other ways, that it had not seemed wise to arm them ordinarily. Punans roam in small bands over great distances, without cultivating anything; living off wild vegetables and game.

Wizards, naturally, of quiet movement and poison-dart accuracy, we could not afford to ignore them, when and where they did come out of the shadow and seek to serve. Ordinarily, these nomads have little to do with anybody else, and practically nothing to do with administration. They had become aware of the Japs because during the occupation, the two things they really wanted from outside had ceased to be available. Living with this very simple economy, they contacted other groups to barter their beautifully patterned black-and-white mats and baskets, for tobacco and iron. Punans crave tobacco, require iron. In the dislocation of Japanese later days, the supply of both these things became so restricted that none of it got through to the last gasp, the Punan. They registered, in the simplest but strongest terms, their loathing for those responsible. They had never seen any of these monsters. They had only heard of them, from the settled people with whom they bartered, as 'Orang Gippun'. That was enough. They wanted to liquidate these Gippun and get back to tobacco.

Several remarkable operations were carried out by the eastern Punans, only nominally under the control of other personnel, operating along lines vaguely indicated by me. On one occasion, a group of them surprised a Japanese group near Malinau, behind Tarakan, as they were fording a wide river bed. They simply picked the helpless Japs off one by one, as they waded.

Death by blow-pipe is agony. I am not in a position to say whether it is worse to die from the needle stab of a dart dipped in the glucoside or in the strychnine types of poison, both of which are obtained from tree sap in the interior. The glucoside kills by shocking the heart, the strychnine by shattering the nervous system. In either case, with freshly made and applied poison liberally smeared on a barbed dart head, death or total incapacity should follow within the hour. Provided, that is, that you surprise the victim, shoot the dart into deep flesh, preferably in the back where he cannot instantly cut it out. It is best to let him have several darts in rapid succession, for safety's sake.

The dreadful advantage of blow-pipe attack is its silence. If you miss with your first, just flip in a second dart from the bamboo quiver, press lips against the pith base and with sibilant puff, barely audible, whirl the next point at a target a hundred feet, or further, away. When Punans are hunting this way, they may hold a row of darts balanced between the third and little fingers of the left hand, as these fingers can be relaxed slightly while they grip the base of the blow-pipe. The tricky bit in this: being ware that you do not prick yourself.

We had a few blow-pipes, too, at one point behind Brunei Bay for a while, with a 'Z' NCO whose name I have forgotten. This man, one day, accidentally pierced himself with a poisoned dart head. Not very deeply. Unhappily, he was on his own; and, reasonably enough, got into a flap. He was found, by his men, probably some hours later, insensible and partially paralysed. With characteristic devotion, they got him into a small boat down river and paddled him long miles across the sea to Labuan, soon after the Australian landings there. The patient could barely move and he could not speak. No one in Labuan knew what had happened. He had the hospital people properly puzzled for some days. He slowly recovered and was invalided home. But this, too, caused quite a stir among the legalists of regular militarism who (through this accident) got on to our using blow-pipe poison in our (to them) savage irregular ops.

Had they but known! Considering the human material with which we were dealing in Semut, the amount of true irregularity was negligible; the small amount of real irresponsibility extraordinary. I think it might have got worse if the war had gone on very long. But as it was, deliberate disobedience or carelessness, throughout this complicated set-up, was something like two per cent of what I had previously experienced in civil and naval intelligence studies at the beginning of the war, and then in the army at Strensall, Sandhurst, Ballymena and points east.

It was high time for liaison, however. Colonel Leach was overdue. There was risk of serious misunderstanding. I had some tormented moments when I thought that some of our irregular forces might actually come into armed conflict with the regular Australians. It makes me sweat just to remember that anxiety, sitting comfortably in a flat on top of Primrose Hill, London, thirteen years later (almost to the day).

Before I leave this somewhat painful aspect, a special accolade for irregularity must be awarded to a Potok-Kelabit boy. This young gentleman, age about fourteen, was upset at not being allowed to join the older men of his long-house and go off man hunting, eastward, with Blondeel and Sergeant Tredrea. He managed to get hold of some ·303 rifle bullets, spilled out of a storepedo. Through one of the hardwood posts supporting the long-house, he bored a neat hole, the calibre of ·303. Above this he bored a second hole, a rougher job. Into the lower hole he placed a ·303 bullet. He then waited, with Potok patience, for a buffalo to walk past, coming in for the evening salt ration. Eventually a large buffalo bull passed across his line of sight through the upper hole. As it did so, the cheerful lad delivered a smashing blow upon the base of the ·303 bullet, with a heavy stone. Result:

(i) Sad Buffalo.

(ii) Wobbly long-house.

(iii) Smashed hand—and life only saved by the skill of our good doctor, Chong.

This sort of ingenuity, most marked where fire-arms were concerned, was a great asset. On several occasions Kelabits were able to make substitutes for pieces lost out of Bren guns. Anyi of Bario, master craftsman of them all, even manufactured a substitute firing pin section for an automatic carbine. Very few fire-arm accidents occurred. Usop shot himself in the leg; a small boy was hit, but not seriously injured, at Long Semadoh; hand grenades blew two men up.

Accidents, whether involving poison paralysis, a truncated prisoner or an injured child, became dynamite once regular forces were firmly established and near to us. It was inevitable that these regular forces should at least distrust and probably dislike the 'Z' type of activity and personnel. We lived the military life that every decent soldier dreams of on active service. With 'Z', a private could have as much decision as a colonel, a major more than a regular major-general. For nearly everything that I did in wartime Borneo I answered to no one, beyond reporting by radio day-to-day positions and outlining any significant changes in plan. This is not to say that I did not obey orders. I obeyed all I could, and explained when I could not. Those under my command conducted themselves in the same way towards me. None of them took orders from anyone else except 'Z' HQ. In war this was disciplined paradise. It was also the only method of operating inside Borneo, with effect.

*   *   *

There were two ways of dealing with this explosive mixture and we tried to use both. One way was to improve relations between 'Z' and

9 Div. A lot of the trouble had arisen through excessive security and a failure to inform Divisional Headquarters, on down to company level, of our presence and movements insofar as this affected regular formations once Labuan was secured and they (the regulars) would interest themselves in the mainland. This was David Leach's new job. With his long war record as a regular soldier and his knowledge of Sarawak as a government surveyor pre-war, he was able to ease tension very considerably. But he held a very delicate position.

One sticky crisis arose, after he thought he had everything rather nice. I had come down to Labuan to consolidate better feeling. The sound of typewriters and telephones, the sight of hospital nurses and the taste of iced beer went to my head and reverted me to type. Abetted by the GSO2 in Div. HQ, an intelligent officer, I composed and impetuously submitted (without permission) through him direct a memo addressed to the Major-General, not such an intelligent man, entitled 'Borneo is Indivisible'. The diamond centrepiece of this tiara of words glittered with the truth that regular and irregular operations must be integrated; that the whole island should be thought of as one entity, if serious repercussions were not to follow, post-war. The Major-General considered this, from me, flat impertinence. An order was issued excluding 'Z' Special field commanders from having, henceforward, any direct access to Div. except when personally accompanied and bespoken by Colonel Leach. Poor David!

The second way to ease the strain and keep clear of a disastrous mix-up between Semut and Div. was simpler still. As soon as the Australians were at all established along the coast we withdrew well out of touch with them, merely vanished into the hills without further comment. This would not have been at all to the liking of our forces had it not been that in the first place the Australian regulars did not attempt or intend to move far inland; and, second, that as a result of their occupying the coastal strip in some force, more and more Japanese were pushed inland, soon more than enough to keep our hand grenades whirling and rifle sights full. By the beginning of July 1945 many Japanese were on the move deliberately towards the interior. These were naturally our concern. More than that, it would clearly be an inexplicable thing if we let these Japanese do wide-scale damage inland or destroy the lives of these, our so loyal supporters and allies.

Thus, from this time on until the end of the war, Semut ceased to be engaged in intelligence and sabotage, and decreasingly in administration. Instead, we devoted the greater part of all effort directly to killing Japanese. This battle, which was to rage and roam for hundreds of jungle and mountain miles, and continue until long after the war was over, now became my concern for all the working hours during which I was sober.

* * *

The last gasp of our *coastal* contact and conflict occurred at Sipitang at the North Borneo end of Brunei Bay. While I was on a visit to Labuan, being loved and liaisoned by Colonel Leach as usual, a dramatic landing on the 'Z' Camp beach was staged by Warrant-Officer Colin MacPherson, whom I had last seen freshly dropped up in the Bawang some months before. MacPherson, who had no idea I might be there on Labuan, and who had lost wireless contact with me inland, arrived exhausted, having paddled across the broad bay from Sipitang in the dark, seeking fresh orders and preferably aid. He reported that the considerable guerrilla forces we had raised in that area, after initial successes, were being counter-attacked and disorganized by a small, disciplined Japanese force. The situation was confused. He asked for more 'Z' men and arms. No additional men or arms were available at the moment at Labuan. Anyhow, my bosses happily said it was my business, in the first place. I was supplied with a work-boat type launch, commanded by a paratroop sergeant who had worked with Colonel Courtney on small craft operations in the Eastern Mediterranean earlier in the war.

With a bagful of pistols and grenades, MacPherson and I set out to inspect and if possible repair the damage. This looked like being a physical interlude after too much brain-work up at Bawang, which was left for Long to look after and buzz on its own a couple of days until I flew back. It was a proper Borneo night, sheet rain falling at forty-five degrees, visibility in yards, turbulent sea. The whole shoreline, alive with house lights and fishermen's torches on any ordinary night, was invisible. As we got nearer in, the towering silhouette of the Crocker Range proved that land did exist, up back.

MacPherson was confident he knew where we were. We launched off in the standard cloak-and-dagger rubber dinghy, having arranged with the sergeant skipper that two pistol shots in rapid succession meant he was to put on his searchlights, so that we could find him again where he lay at anchor off-shore. There is nothing to be said for a rubber dinghy, especially in a sea on a strong tidal shore. After a lot of thrashing about we landed all right. We landed, on extremely low tide, in a mangrove swamp. By comparison, bobbing at sea in a rubber dinghy is fun. About three hours later we emerged from the mangroves, up to the waist in mud, every exposed square millimetre of skin scratched by the tensed branches and bitten by malevolent black mangrove mosquitoes (who cares that they are not malarial?). Later, we struck sand beach. The rain had ceased. Presently the moon cleared, lucid and sweet, filtered through coconut and betel-nut palms, faintly to outline the angles of distant thatch roofs. We were on the edge of Sipitang, thank goodness.

Sipitang is a Malay village. Malays do not sleep in the dark. Each simple, square, airy, comfortable hut has a little wick set in a cup or boat or brass lamp, faintly to lighten the darkness. But this night showed no light. Painfully aware of surrounding enemy, we advanced most stealthily along the village path, employing all that remained of a military training, eroded by months of guerrilladom. Nothing stirred. There is, or was, a delightful, straggling, arched wooden bridge over the creek that runs through Sipitang. It did not seem delightful that night. It creaked abominably as we crept across, each moving separately in turn, to 'give covering fire'. On the far side of the creek, at last, a small light. We did a two-man surround of this. Peeping into the hut, nothing was to be seen. So we jumped it, as proper commandos should. In the shadow sat a man, pale-skinned and large-eyed, unaffected by our effusive entry. MacPherson recognized him as one of the local leaders. He was the only breath in the place; he had just now come back. All the rest of his people were scattered, in hiding. There had been a big Jap scare, big enough to send over the water for aid. But where were any actual Japs?

We spent a relaxed hour with this excellent man, who I thought was Chinese though he spoke fluent Malay. The discussion was fortifying. He undertook, with MacPherson, to get things back on to their feet as from early next morning. He was as good as his word. This unit did good work again directly and on until MacPherson withdrew inland, in line with our changing policy and fighting obligations, already described above.

I understood our gallant and shadowy friend to be called Miaw Sing, a good Chinese name. After the war I included him in a long list of citations which were accepted. He received the BEM. At the same time he must have received a separate citation for loyalty under his correct name, Mohamad Yassin, from the North Borneo side. He was actually a Malay, of high status and aristocratic build. I ought to have known that from his composure, squatting at ease in the shadow of an abandoned hamlet. (Anyway, he got the BEM twice, for his coolness.)

As things looked as if they were going to be all right, MacPherson saw me off in the filthy rubber dinghy, about 4 a.m. It had started raining again. I could not see much. I fired double bursts with two revolvers. Nothing happened, except that I frightened myself—just in case there were any Japs still along this part of the coast. With dawn and delight I detected the work-boat in the distance. When I climbed aboard, sergeant and crew were asleep. This is the only time in the war that the sympathy for non-officers which I had learnt the hard way as a rifleman at Strensall, let me down. The effect of such carelessness could have been serious; and I succeeded in getting the insensitive sergeant sent back to base.

*　　*　　*

While I was thrashing around in these various ways, Toby Carter in Semut II and the probes he had put out with Bill Sochon as Semut III were having their own troubles as well. They had one slight advantage over me, in that they were farther away from Labuan HQ and direct contact with regular forces. This particularly applied to Semut III, which was operating west of the farthest westerly interests engaged by 9 Div.

The distance between the south-western flank of Sochon's Semut III and the north-eastern of my Semut I was over 300 miles, with not a single rail, road or corrugated iron roof between. As the Japanese were pressed inland, and in fact handed over to Semut's tender mercy as a whole, liaison with the Australian army diminished in mass, while liaison between the three Semuts increased in significance. Especially this must be increasingly so if any part of us had Japanese movements in the direction of any other. Semut III was, in some ways, a separate affair in this respect. There was no allied pressure from the coast so that Sochon's mission had a clear run. They also had the advantage of great navigable rivers in the Rejang watershed. These equally provided good landing places for seaplanes, which could not be used anywhere in my area, alas. I flew down to Labuan in an Auster again and with Jumbo Courtney flew in a seaplane to Bill Sochon's headquarters in an imposing Iban long-house on the Rejang. Bill was having a marvellous time. In the following weeks he succeeded in pushing far down the river and capturing a series of important places, including Kapit, Song, Kanowit, and eventually the second largest town in Sarawak, Sibu. His forces were largely Iban Sea Dayaks and his main difficulty was keeping them under control. But he enjoyed another advantage. At an early stage Major John Fisher was inserted by sea-plane into Semut III. John, a lanky, hail-fellow-well-met but subtle fellow, had served as a Brooke administrative officer pre-war; he now became the first and only white one to take direct part in these operations during the war. Like Toby Carter, he did this under great personal stress. Toby's allergy had been parachutes; John's was anything to do with aeroplanes, as a result of a crash and subsequent sufferings in Timor two years before. His services in quickly re-establishing some degree of normal administration behind Sochon's advance down river saved an immense amount of trouble later on. This was particularly necessary in the Iban country, where violent passions and temper are more easily incited than among the Kenyah, Kayan, Kelabit and other less inland people to the south and east.

Semut II with Toby Carter did not rely largely on Ibans, but on the Kenyahs under the very powerful leadership of jolly, tough, steel-minded Tama Weng Ajang, paramount chief of all these people in the Baram watersheds. After visiting Sochon, we went on over and landed at Long Ikan on the Baram, Toby Carter's current headquarters. In this way, in one day, the three Semut commanders were able to tie up loose ends and concoct common plans, supervised by a decisive referee, Colonel Courtney.

The main common concern was between the north-easterly edges of Semut II in the Tutoh branch of the Baram, and the south-westerly edges of me as Semut I in the middle Limbang, where Sanderson and his roughs were at large. For as well as the Japanese flow of escapees from Brunei towards Ukong on the Limbang— which came under the savage attentions of Driver Henry's irregulars—a much larger group were now reported as escaping from farther west, down the coast. This group was said to be composed mainly of oilfield and related personnel, driven out from the Miri and Lutong field at the mouth of the

Baram, as the Australians finished their westerly mainland move and set about restoring the oil wells and refinery as a matter of utmost priority.

Toby's Semut II people had earlier taken Marudi, then been forced back again by this oilfield column, who, despite vigorous obstruction from the Kenyahs, pushed their way across into the Tutoh and headed up river. However it may have looked from the Semut II end, to me it could only appear that they were heading north-east. So they were. The numbers were variously reported as between 1,500 and 500. Whatever the total, this was a large force to have loose, heading inland. If, as it seemed, the force was well led and armed, it could throw back any opposition we could concentrate at short notice, and devastate large tracts of country inhabited by our allies—who, living in strictly centralized long-house communities, along river lines or other conspicuous features, were particularly vulnerable to any kind of large-scale attack by hungry, disciplined people. The possibilities of a 'scorched earth' policy inside Borneo are restricted, especially outside the central uplands; among the riverine and foothill peoples, food margins are usually narrow, and the business of restocking large areas at a later date looked pretty well insuperable.

The thing to do, then, was to oppose the Japs all the way, wherever they came in. To pick them off one by one, give them no rest, wear them out, lead them astray, slow them up so that they could not advance evenly on main tracks, only with much difficulty anywhere.

That was all very well, as a plan. But I began to let out some hideous squawks at the pace they were being allowed to move up the Tutoh heading straight for the Limbang. Between the Tutoh and the Limbang there is a low divide. There would be no future in continuing up the Tutoh, which then runs through tremendous gorges into a great tract of virgin jungle, inhabited solely by a handful of nomadic Punans. The divide of the Tutoh-Limbang, which is here populated, was well known to one and all. Indeed, in the turbulent days in the middle of the previous century the Kayans used to drag their canoes from the Tutoh over the watershed and down into the Limbang on head-hunting forays against Muruts and Kelabits—who were left as free game for them by the Brunei Sultanate, providing the Kayans did not turn down river to harass the coastal plain.

A specially recommended major and odd paratroops were put hastily into the Tutoh to try to slow up this Jap movement. But they were put in behind, not ahead. And their leader had exaggerated ideas (based on European experience only) of his own capacity to lead Kenyahs and Kayans. Before long—and after some very nasty radio exchanges between the Bawang and the Baram—this Japanese column therefore passed out of the area of influence of Semut II and was delivered on to my back door step, whence it was to advance and castigate me for another five months, far into peacetime.

*　　*　　*

It was a relief to get back to the beautiful highland valley of the Bawang, to the comforts of palm salad, sugar cane, mangosteen, Aris's ducks' eggs, Agong's wife's excellent rice brews, Mrs Chong's soups. Austers now came to and fro almost every day, sometimes several. The 150 mile trip over the bay from Labuan, then up the Trusan, over jungle and the magnificent mountains, building up into the enormous dramas of Murud, took an hour. Past Batu Lawi became a pleasure trip for senior officers, visiting air marshals and suchlike. Our difficulties with the regular soldiers had no effect on the regular airmen, who, anyway, had a strong fellow-feeling for parachutists. They kept us supplied with all sorts of good things. In return we sent them down loads of fresh fruit and the vegetables which our Javanese 'prisoners' were now beginning to cultivate in quantity, including potatoes, onions, brussels sprouts and radishes. The RAAF also had a craving for goat-flesh. And on one memorable occasion we sent them down an amiable Kelabit girl who—with the typical democracy of Australianism—they immediately (and seriously) entitled 'Princess'.

Pleasant, prosperous and cool the highlands were. The buzz and scramble of activity, agents, runners, visiting deputations, distributing fire-arms, registering recruits, issuing uniforms, had steadily ceased. Now it was much more a matter of constant radio messages and less hastily written reports, orders, rejoinders, revised orders and occasionally reinforcements to some trouble-spot from a reservoir of new volunteers kept in the centre. Below the top clamour, though, all this Jap movement inland was very worrying. I now felt sure that our forces could never be *beaten*. It would have taken a million Japanese to have coped with a few thousand guerillas in their own country. We could have held out indefinitely, living in and off the jungle, especially with the air support now available from Labuan. But the thought that the

Japanese could, and perhaps would, devastate this and other lovely plains, possibly settle down in the interior and have to be got out in open battle engagements, was another idea altogether, an awful one. I managed to keep it to myself, however. And with the exception of Tuan Agong, I do not believe that anyone else thought much of this danger until several months later, when it became very real.

*　　*　　*

By the middle of 1945, Semut I had some fifty white, trained military personnel, mostly officers below the rank of captain, warrant officers and senior NCOs. My command—if such it can properly be termed —extended right across Borneo from the west coast to the east, but receding a few miles at either extremity wherever regular forces landed and established themselves. This east-west movement had always been our first concern, starting with the early days of intelligence require- ments from the mainland facing the regular landings at Labuan and Tarakan islands off-shore. As the intelligence role dwindled and pres- ently vanished, we were freer to pay more attention to extensions north and south within the interior. At the same time, these became of heightening interest as Japanese pressed inland from the coast.

It is perhaps appropriate that a British officer—the only one in what had now become a largely Australian and New Zealand led unit— should make a few general observations, at about this point, about the Australian soldiers who formed the main body of Semut personnel and did much the larger part of the toughest work. I doubt if I would have been able to compete with some of the complexities of dealing with such personnel had I not had the advantage of many months working first with Jock Marshall in the New Hebrides and then years later with my own troops in training, almost all over Australia; and in the field with Australian troops in New Guinea, the Halmaheras and elsewhere. For their fundamental approach to military service was almost dia- metrically opposed to that of the ordinary English training, a general knowledge of which I had obtained. Where acceptance ruled in the west, initiative and independence played a much greater part among the Aussies. In particular, the conception of the officers as a separate class barely existed, whereas this was the fundamental assumption—allow- ing for all sorts of extraordinary situations—in Britain at least up to 1944 when I left. This relates partly to the less differentiated class structure of Australian society. But it goes deeper than that. Much of it has to do with the Australian's estimate of himself as a man. And to the outsider, this estimate sometimes seems almost as dramatized as when American children dress up as Davy Crockett and patrol the frontiers of the Yank mind. There is really a sort of exaggerated masculinity and virility among the better type of Australian men, which at times can be fairly insufferable; but which is absolutely invaluable under active service, military conditions.

This is related, in turn, of course, to the fact that a very large part of Australia is still open and relatively undeveloped; and that even the teeming towns, highly sophisticated and cultivated (e.g. Sydney or Melbourne) are surrounded by outlets for easy athletic and physico-intellectual exercises, denied to so many of the people of other continents, unless they have considerable means. But to broaden this again, all the tradition of being tough, of being masculine, is tremendously common in Australia. It is best—and to an Englishman most embarrassingly—expressed in their behaviour at parties. It is commonplace, even among well educated and well mannered Australians, for the women virtually to be left in their own corner or corners of the rooms at a Melbourne or Sydney party in a way which would be inconceivable in New York or Baltimore, irreparable in Paris or Lyons, and incredible in Southampton or Manchester.

This thing about being tough is deep inside Australian men, including those who are extremely untough. In actual fact, once they get into uniform and out in the field, it is almost impossible to separate the bank clerk from Sydney from the shearer out of the Darling Downs or the range riders from the far northern plains below Darwin. This is far from so in most countries. Thus I came to think of all my chaps, anyway, as great big rugged Queenslanders from Cape York or Cloncurry. In fact it was only after the war that I discovered, with some surprise, how remote from the truth this classification really was.

Accentuating this, again, is the tradition of actual military service among a considerable section of Australian men, which again finds no parallel in other English-speaking countries. The idea of Anzac Day always seems to me to represent this very neatly. The Australians behave on Anzac Day like the French or Americans or British behave on festivals that celebrate either peace, or some vast political, democratic, constitutional reforms. Gallipoli, too, has left its indelible mark from 1916 across generations of Australians who have no direct memory of it. (Here, I had a slight advantage too, because so many of my boy-hood evenings had been spent listening to my father and my uncle talking about that terrible campaign, in which both of them won DSOs and other distinctions.)

Thus many Australians were delighted to have the chance to be soldiers; and even delighted to have the chance to fight. Such an atti-tude was consciously rare among the British, and almost neurotic. It produced some of the best and some of the worst of our soldiers and airmen. To Australians there was nothing neurotic about it. In fact the neurotic soldier, the Strensall-equivalent, was a great rarity. So for that matter was the intellectual soldier, the sort of chap I had got to know as an officer and in cloak-and-dagger training, who had all sorts of philosophies and principles and determinations of a mental kind connected with fighting (or not fighting). Without over-generalizing, or over-simplifying, I think it would be true to say that the great majority of Australian soldiers who were any good at the job, and by definition all those who volunteered for our kind of operation, had a really good, guts-y, personal, proud, determined, individual, sensible yet passionate approach to the business of fighting Japanese. Problems of morale or anxiety just never seemed to arise at all. The only diffi-culties I had were with two officers sent me from Europe, one a senior and one a junior one, both of them with good records in cloak-and-dagger operations there; but both of them who could not keep up to the Australian pace and had, though without ignominy, to be returned to base before the conclusion of Semut's own goings-ons.

To a curious extent, the attitude of the best Australian soldiers was very similar to the attitude of the average Kelabit men, so lately forced out of head-hunting. I have tried to describe some of the basic drives in Kelabit manhood earlier in this story; I think it will be seen, by those familiar with the other continent, that there are many points in com-mon between the at least manifest, projected, wartime attitude of the tough Australian and the everyday attitude of the disciplined but individualistic, conservative yet progressive-minded, tough-for-toughness-sake Kelabit of Bario or Pa Main. In practice, certainly, an extraordinary degree of sympathy developed between Australians who had never been out of Australia before, and Kelabits who had some-times never seen a white man before; certainly never heard of Austra-lians. Although I believe I had my ear pretty closely to the ground, neither during the war nor in the thirteen years since it has been over, have I heard of any of the fifty-odd Australian personnel under my command causing any troublesome incident with a Kelabit or other Dayak person of the interior; and vice versa. And, believe me, there are plenty of stories flying about—about them, and at all times—in the middle of Borneo.

This sympathy between rugged Australian paratroopers and rugged Kelabit rice farmers, which had given me some anxiety in thought back in the Melbourne Library and on the files of 'Z' Special unit, was in a way the more remarkable since the idea of a White Australian policy was at that time much stronger in Australia than it is now—after nearly fifteen years of peace which have forced Australia to re-think its relations with the swarming millions of its coloured neighbours breathing across the Thursday Island strait, down the Gulf of Carpentaria and over Cape York. Clearly, both myself and my superiors and colleagues, such as George Crowther, had been at pains to select personnel without an extreme 'race attitude'. Even so, the thing was very deep-seated among the twenty to thirty age group in Australia at the time. Yet the strange manliness, friendliness, gayness and effectiveness of the Kelabit and other Borneo inlanders seemed to disarm such prejudice quickly, gently, invisibly, unfelt. Indeed the readiness of the Kelabits and others to learn from the Australian officers and NCOs was something to startle anyone. Their capacity for mastering the handling of a Bren gun would put almost any white soldier to shame. They were even able to carry out difficult repairs, and learned to make replacements for broken parts on Bren guns, carbines, Sten guns, entirely by observation, experiment and experience. This came both from the innate qualities of the people themselves and also from their intense interest in the operations of aggression and lethal achievement—an interest so closely parallel to that in the minds of these Aussie paratroopers themselves.

*　　*　　*

By July, the northern extremity of my control was below Tomani on the Padas river in North Borneo, just below latitude 5°north. My southern extremity was below 2° above the equator, in the upper reaches of the Batang Kayan in Indonesian Borneo.

Extensions far north had come from two directions. From behind Brunei Bay, the various sub-sections more or less under Captain Eric

Edmeades, had pushed eastward over the Crocker ranges into the Padas in North Borneo. The Crocker range here performs much the same spinal function as the ranges running in the other direction from Mount Murud, south-west, to divide Sarawak and then Dutch territory. From the Dutch side, Captain Jack Blondeel's people had also been pushing north, both in front of and in the wake of Japanese movements, away from Tarakan from the Sembakong and over into the area of Pensiangan, divided from the Padas to the west by forty miles of tormented and highly unpromising country inhabited by the least 'reliable' of the inlanders, the Tagals (the ones who had betrayed the American airmen).

Converging movements of Edmeades and Blondeel, the former north-easterly and the latter north-north-westerly, recorded the facts of Japanese intention and tactics inland to the north. Far away to the south, other Japanese were reported to be moving inland from the south-east where Australians had also landed around the Balikpapan oilfields. From Balik Papan the natural route inland was up the Mahakam and related rivers and over into the head waters of the Batang Kayan in the Long Nawang sector. Although less than 200 miles south of the Bawang valley, Long Nawang had never had any direct contact in this direction. In the land between, river and mountain systems run in wild disarray to make north and south movement, under normal conditions, impracticable if not impossible. Down there, just as farther up in Borneo, the natural movements were east and west, across the island, not along it. Along it, north and south, the spinal ranges give off a great network of ribs, veins and arteries, broadly resembling a human body, with its legs splayed out from somewhere central and south-west of Long Nawang itself.

In human terms, in those days, the distance between Long Nawang and the Bawang was virtually infinite. Yet, so great were the compulsions of the time, that some two months after we arrived at Bario, a party sent all that distance waited upon me. This party of finely built, energetic Kenyahs, provided four items of considerable importance:

(i) They confirmed that down there, also, all European and associated runaways, escaped prisoners, etc., had given themselves up or been captured in the south. More than sixty had been rounded up and murdered under atrocious conditions by a Japanese force which surprised Long Nawang directly.

(ii) No Japanese had been that way lately, but there were now repeated rumours that considerable forces were moving inland in that direction, and that their intention was to press on north through the interior.

(iii) The great Kenyah and Kayan population of the Batang Kayan had suffered deep hardship during the Japanese occupation and were now near starvation.

(iv) The great chief from Long Nawang and all the other chiefs pledged their full support to us. If we could bring them arms they would resist the Japanese advance inland, regardless of further suffering for themselves.

As pledge of this, the party was headed by the great chief's son, with Along, a brilliantly intelligent middle-class Kenyah as his interpreter and assistant; and they brought several beautiful knives, swords, shields, bark coats and other things in which these Kenyahs excel above all other Borneo people.

This news from the south—earlier quickly explored by Eric Edmeades —was now so promising, that I detailed Jeff Westley (of Lembudut memory) to go in that direction, with these Kenyahs. I gave Westley three special jobs—to spread goodwill and ensure Japanese resistance down there; to get information about practicable land routes in that direction; and particularly, to find dropping places where we could put in arms and possibly personnel should the Jap threat materialize and become a matter of serious concern. Meanwhile he carried a token message of fire-arms and reassurance.

It was now clear to me that the great grassland valley which I had originally seen, flying in the American plane on the very first sortie over Borneo back in 1944, must be in that direction. I therefore instructed the party to pay special attention to this aspect and build a large beacon, under local supervision for quick firing there, should any plane come over this, the Bahau upland.

In a suitable lull from the pressing excitements to the north-west and north-east, I took one of our Austers off, having given the ground party a fortnight's start. It was warming to find the superb valley— much the largest clear space anywhere inside Borneo—and to receive smoke signals, then go low enough to spot Westley on the ground. I dropped him messages to leave some men there, they to be permanently available to receive drops—and little knowing then that the first thing to be dropped would be me, and that I should owe my life to their strict observances of Westley's orders, despite intervening weeks of boredom and apparent uselessness, all on their own in a strange part of the country, sparsely inhabited, miserably supplied, and notably unhealthy, as the upper Bahau was to prove.

Thus screened to the south, shielded by Semut II and Semut III to the west, and well organized to the east, as far as the coast, it was possible to devote maximum attention in a northerly direction, towards Brunei Bay and North Borneo. Every day, things got hotter that way. Indeed, the messages and points to be coped with got to be almost overwhelming, especially when—owing to local difficulties of the terrain for dropping—it became necessary to send large-scale supply columns with rice and other foods through the troublesome hill country north-east of the Bawang, over to Loembis and Labang, Blondeel's bases south of Pensiangan, and just on the Dutch side of the North Borneo border.

It was impossible to continue running all the military, civilian and liaison problems through my own head. I very fortunately acquired an adjutant, at this stage, who not only coped with all the civilian and administrative side until the end of the war, but in the post-war shambles grew into a military leader on his own account. Paul Bartram was an RAF officer, one of the many mystery figures who had latterly drifted east into 'Z' Special. The mystery usually was why they had come or who had sent them. Sometimes it was nothing more than a supersecurity, double-overcheck mistake; or a case of mistaken identity, such as I had earlier suffered with the London left-winger whose name I share plus one 's'.

There was no mistake about Paul Bartram, though. Now an estate agent in Oxford, he looked just like a very tall, rather shy, thoroughly indoor Oxford don. Happily he had a tremendous streak of effectiveness (as well as efficiency) behind this facade. After a few days with him on the Bawang scene, I was freer than ever before to move about myself. The periphery of Semut command had grown so peripherily that the highly egocentric individuals dotted around it were thoroughly overdue for personal contact with their egocentric commanding officer. The beheading incident in Sanderson's sector, involving Driver Henry, was only one example of a tendency that had been growing. And the incidental experience of meeting Warrant Officer MacPherson on the rampage and sorting things out direct in the dark at Sipitang, confirmed my feeling that some of these excellent fellows needed checking pretty strongly here before we went much further. It was out of the question to tackle them all. I had to select. Otherwise it would have taken one man the best part of a year to have covered the whole area and reached every unit operating in it. Years before I had won one award from the Royal Geographical Society. This did not seem the moment to go for a second, the hard way.

⋆　⋆　⋆

The first place upon which to lavish collective attention was, clearly, to the east and north-east. We had developed slowly at first, there. But after the drops at Lembudut and the successful bosh-drop of the Westley party opening up the Bawang valley, it had been possible for the two members of our original Bario unit to move eastward, as planned. Sergeant Tredrea and Warrant-Officer Cusack had pushed right across Borneo to the east coast opposite Tarakan island; then turned, with the tide of withdrawing Japanese, north-westward along the Sembakong river and away towards the North Borneo border. Subsequently, I had been able to spare other officers and NCOs to go direct from later Bawang drops in that direction; and in particular, when I dropped back myself with Captain Blondeel, I had sent him direct towards the Sembakong, to take charge of all operations in that sector.

By that time, large Japanese forces had been building up along the Sembakong, moving slowly but steadily north-west into the headwaters of that river, around to the small but important township of Pensiangan, just across the border in North Borneo. From Pensiangan water transport becomes again impossible, as throughout the rest of this interior. But a well-developed bridle path and some ponies existed for communication another fortnight or so over the mountains into the Tenom district on the lower Padas, adjacent to the great Sapong Rubber Estate.

On this north side of Pensiangan, from the North Borneo border right up the easterly half of North Borneo, there was no effective, irregular military activity from our side. The 'Agas' sandflies had not been able to expand down that far, from their bases much further north. Across tremendously rugged terrain, even by interior standards, we had not been able to push eastwards from Eric Edmeades's people in the Padas, to intercept in that direction. The Japanese therefore had, on the map at least, a relatively steady line of retreat up there. But rapid work by Blondeel and his people soon made it, in practice, more difficult for them to get on. In the first place, irregular forces south of the border were soon well enough organized to give the Japanese a bad time as they moved by boat up the Sembakong. In this, effective air-co-operation was provided from Tarakan, destroying many small craft for the first few days and making the only possible subsequent movement by night—at the best of times unpleasant work on Bornean river. Here, some of the blow-pipe irregulars, including Punans (already mentioned as operating south of the Sesajap river), were moved up and proved effective. For the most part, however, forces in that area were relatives of the Kelabits, under various other names. These estimable hill-people do not, however, extend right away eastward as far as the Sembakong itself. There we began to get mixed up with the much less reliable Tagals, the main hill-people of southern North Borneo and the extreme north of Dutch Borneo. Also with some intermediate Mohammedan-ized groups on the rivers, notably the Tidongs, who proved unsatis-factory, from our point of view. Not because they were treacherous, but because they were both painfully mercenary and sadly timid, even in their own immediate interests.

In this somewhat insecure human context, Blondeel was fortunate in finding a large body of Iban Sea Dayaks, who for some years past had been loose in that part of Borneo, on one of the great hunting and jungle foraging expeditions which such Ibans periodically undertake. Their actual home area was hundreds of miles away to the south in the headwaters of the Balleh-Rejang river system in central Sarawak. They gladly joined up with Blondeel. And although it was against my policy to keep groups of Ibans together, for reasons already mentioned—principally the difficulty of disciplining these highly individualistic headhunters on their own—in this case it was clearly the better solution. Blondeel thus had a tough striking force around him, which also gave dominance over any less reliable elements in the local Tagal popu-lation.

These Ibans had another characteristic which—in these circumstances —was of value. The Iban idea of fighting is rather different from that of most other Borneans, such as the Kelabits. It partly derives from the nature of the over-populated, over-cultivated country in which most of them normally live. The Iban puts a premium on open displays of bravery, and, in fighting, even on frontal attack and direct assault across the open. It is this sort of fearlessness (in the western sense) which has acquired Ibans such well-earned prestige as the jungle trackers attached with regular army units in the communist war in Malaya.

Where the Iban likes assault—though not, of course, unmixed with what an Englishman would call treachery—the Kelabit prefers guile. Apart from this one unit, totalling about ninety men, around Blondeel, practically all the operations of Semut I were conducted with such guile. Guile produces economy in casualties, in this sort of country. Indeed, the only lives we lost—except for one of these Ibans—were lost through gross neglect of the rules of jungle craft, or arms' care, or in one case plain murder by the Japanese.

Perhaps to use the phrase 'rules of jungle craft' is to put it too ostentatiously. There is only one sort of rule in jungle warfare. And it is the ordinary rule of all jungle activity. The rule is, simply, *do not be smelt before you are heard; do not be heard before you are seen; and, below all, do not be seen.*

Thus, the principles involved in attacking Japanese in the jungle are precisely those involved in hunting deer or monkeys. Necessarily, through generations of group experience and years of personal experience, the male population of the interior can move in accordance with this simple law of jungle success. Almost by definition, no one from a temperate country of open places—let alone, from a land of cities and roads—can compete, in this respect, with the Kelabits. I have, in fact, actually seen a Kelabit (for a dare) *touch* a wild pig, which was in full possession of all its faculties and fit. There are plenty of records of these people getting close enough to rhinoceros to spear them, though not necessarily with lethal effect; and the rhinoceros, though regarded as one of the stupidest and most unseeing animals of the forest, has a notorious sense of scent and hearing, as well as an extreme sensitivity to vibrations and movements upon the jungle floor.

What chance had the Japanese, always moving with elaborate equipment and nearly always on the defensive, in these conditions? How could they hope to compete with the silent hunter, let alone the soundless blowpipe and poisoned dart?

There was only one way in which, inside Borneo, the Japanese could hope to cope. This was to stay as far as possible in the open, and in force. But the middle of Borneo is conspicuously lacking in open spaces—other than extremely remote ones into which we had dropped or where we had already built up our own major strength from the beginning; and these were both topographically at first and now militarily at second, critical areas for them to approach. Moreover, having no supply lines left and being surrounded by hostile people at this stage, they could hardly remain seated in one position, out in the open, forever.

Pensiangan happened to be one of the few places where they could so stay, with some kind of real line of supply and retreat not completely controlled by us. It is also deep down in awkward mountain country, particularly difficult for aircraft to get at. The Japs took Pensiangan especially seriously ; they really dug in and built themselves air-raid shelters, machine-gun posts and other fortifications. The place therefore became an important staging centre and, for a time, the only static position which the Japanese held in the face of active opposition, anywhere in the whole of Borneo—that is, after the end of June and the organized land fighting.

It was under these conditions that the Blondeel Ibans excelled themselves. They carried out splendidly courageous assaults, including on Japanese machine-gun positions. These met with mixed success. But they were arranged with such skill that we only lost one man killed and several wounded, during some weeks of irregular but harassing activity. The enemy became so harassed that they started sending out probing units and patrols to counter-attack and try to break up these angering and usually nocturnal assaults. This was precisely what our people liked best; and considerable casualties were inflicted as a result. Here, once again, jungle craft came into its own.

In one such clandestine encounter one of our more virile guerrillas was wounded slightly and temporarily knocked out; he lost touch with his troop. After a week, in accordance with local custom, his relatives celebrated his departure to the other world by slaughtering his cattle and converting his surplus rice store into alcohol. During the orgy that then ensued, he reappeared. He had fought his way back across the ranges, emerging by chance on a river which he recognized from a previous hunting trip. It is hardly necessary to point out that this man was a Tagal. If he had been a Kelabit, he would have had several years margin of safety before all the major machinery of a monstrous death feast could be put into operation to sanctify his departure.

★　　★　　★

Everywhere I found things really humming, and good. My incomparable Australians were not known to panic or even to register concern (even when seemingly lost) excepting only on one account. I am sure that had the need arisen, they would in the absence of guns, or hand grenades, have leapt from behind trees and strangled Japanese colonels with their hands. Their capacity for improvising all sorts of crude machinery and other addenda to human aggressive activity approached the stupendous. But there was one small piece of metal which, without any exception known to me, each of these excellent fellows regarded as absolutely essential. The loss of it was a threat to stability. The need to supply it was the only filip or bolster for morale which these men ever mentioned or needed. Whereas in the British army officers were constantly thinking of dealing with the men's morale; with the Australians one had the uneasy feeling that they were always thinking about the benighted CO's guts.

But the loss of one's *tin-opener* was a catastrophe to an Australian soldier anywhere. And I remember once, lethal, multi-jumping, parachute instructor Sergeant Bill Nibbs coming to me in a sort of frenzy to report such a drastic loss. The thing had got detached from his belt as he leapt off the track in face of a Japanese ambush—or rather a head-on collision owing to his own negligence; perhaps because he was thinking about tins.

For tins could move these men. Instead of decorating the walls of any hut with pin-up girls or lewd messages, nothing more delighted the Queensland or Victorian eye than a couple of well-placed tins of pork and beans or corned beef, upon a little shelf, to catch the waking wink of first daylight. Where the British, in their highly urbanized and off-the-land culture, often pray for and even make a sort of luscious phrase out of 'fresh food'—so that, to say something is 'fresh' from the sea or the strawberry patch is in a mysterious way a powerful incentive to buy—these Australians, accustomed to chew hunks of mutton *au choix*, hankered, in moments of depression or doubt, for unfresh foods, in tins. What was in the tins didn't matter so much as what was outside the inside; and awaiting a quick machine for breaking this holy grail and entering the secret heart within. It was, seriously, necessary to be sure that a small but colourful supply of basic, solid, slightly indigestible tinned foods were supplied to these fine he-men wherever they were—and some of them were in very remote, awkward-to-get-at places. If they had a couple of tins of potatoes, one of tomatoes and four of sardines or herrings in tomato oil, they could do without ammunition; they would find a way of making that stuff themselves.

One day on this trip I met Corporal Sterelny—who had already warmed my heart by volunteering to join us at short notice into Balawit without any previous training on parachutes whatsoever—and he gave me a smart (by Australian standards) salute, which included a sort of clanking sound. On inspection, I find that he had a very neat little tin opener suspended on a thong, made from jungle rotan, over the lobe of his right ear. Corporal Wheelhouse, if I remember rightly, had a tin opener brightly polished, which he had required one of his guerrillas to mount upon a sort of sword handle, with most impressive effect. Corporal Gibbs kept his in a wallet and no one else was allowed to touch it; a sacred thing.

Although capable of killing almost anything, my Australians were initially very conservative—for instance, the horror of eating goat, and the common idea that fresh fruit from the forest might somehow carry dysentery or some other disease. But the thing that shook them in the interior environment was certainly the dogs. It is difficult for outsiders to understand the Kelabit attitude to a dog. Dogs are essential in one sector of their lives, which if it may not be materially or economically very important, is psychologically of the highest significance. Dogs are the essential adjuncts to hunting, particularly hunting for pig (much the most important kind). But beyond that, few people feel about dogs. If a dog is a very good hunter, its master is liable to take particular care of it. But by and large, the dogs don't have to be particularly good or bad. They just have to scent a pig and get around it, yapping. Most any dog can do that. The hunter then comes up and does the rest. It is only a very exceptional dog which will bay other animals, such as deer. And one dog in a thousand or less will bay a Clouded Leopard and keep it treed. Such special dogs can easily be detected in the long-house. Anyi, always expert, had one several years at Bario; a fat, a sleek, cheerful dog, Anyi loved to sit (as we earlier saw) among company around the borak jar holding the creature between knees, cheeks between hands, while he dribbled boraked saliva down its receptive jaws. But such dog loving is seldom to be seen. Generally they are a pack of curs who behave inside the long-house, day or night, just about as they behave to a pig in the jungle—making an uproar and seldom bringing affairs to a personal conclusion. The idea of patting or calling a dog is, in this setting, ridiculous. Generally, you kick it, throw something at it, or take it up by the tail—too swiftly for it to snap at your hand—and swing it out of the way. This always got under the skin of the sheep shearer, the fruit farmer and the week-end sportsman from the Blue Mountains, the Grampians or rough Gippsland. No wonder. Personally, though, I think Kelabit dogs have a lot of fun. I'd rather be a bitch at Bario than a ewe on the Darling Downs, anyhow.

*　　*　　*

Having rearranged inner Borneo's tin supplies, after a quick trip to the east—or at least as quick as the tremendous climb that begins a day east of Bawang permits—I raced back to Paul Bartram at Bawang base. Things were going along reasonably there, thanks particularly to a by now very useful network of wireless stations operating throughout the interior and way down behind Brunei Bay and the Padas, under the charge of our signals officer (put in shortly after Blondeel), Captain Gordon Richter.

After a few days at base, I tore off again to revisit the Trusan and Lawas. Lawas, by now, urgently needed a second visit. I had not been there since immediately after D-Day, far back in May, when we had re-established civil administration.

There were still some odd Japanese at large in the Lawas district and we were picking them off. Generally, though, there was not enough for large numbers of already blooded guerrillas in the area to do. Speedy reorganization was due. I arrived, unexpectedly, to find the major elements concentrated around the home of an admirable Chinese, recruited much earlier by Lieutenant Pinkerton.

This fine, middle-aged, elegant looking tough was the principal trader at Merapok, up a side-branch of the Lawas river. Pre-war he had enjoyed the licence for distilling *arak* in the area. Under the enlightened auspices of 'Z' (in the form of Pinkerton and his associates) he had renewed this estimable craft.

I arrived unexpectedly in the middle of a splendid session, the principal ingredients of which were fifty semi-trained guerrillas, three big jars of pure spirit made from pineapples and two more from bananas, with a steaming still as active background. For that day, I gave this activity the fullest possible support. Next day most of these merry men reluctantly moved up to supplement the forces farther inland, who were in no danger of having little to do or anything worthwhile to drink.

The Chinese leader left with a reduced force continued to operate admirably. He was only one of the many Chinese who helped us actively. As they nearly all lived along the coast, they inevitably had less to do with Semut operations. However, one of the best of our troops was formed from about twenty Chinese, who came right up to Bawang to volunteer for service anywhere—which was gladly supplied to them. The Merapok master later came to a sad end, alas. Not long after these strange days, with warriors camped around a steaming still, he was returning from Labuan Island in a small boat, and was overtaken by a storm, close inshore. The other occupants of the boat jumped out and got ashore safely. Our friend would not abandon a large bag of coin, the result of his marginal sales at Labuan. He was last seen going down, holding the bag. This seemed a particularly inappropriate end for a Chinese who made no tiny attempt to cash in on the golden opportunities of those extravagant 'Z' days; who not only housed and fed, but also boozed, all comers for weeks, free, and warmly.

Far and away our biggest headache was building up behind Lawas, in the lower and middle reaches of the Trusan, which flows down from Murud at the extreme eastern edge of Sarawak. Here a large Japanese force had entered from behind Brunei Bay, landing in about the centre of the bay or towards the west of it, going overland across the Trusan delta, keeping well clear of the forces around Lawas, and working up the gorges into the Trusan at a group of villages in the valley of the Tengoa, a right bank tributary of the main Trusan. These Japs had come from Labuan island or from the west side of Brunei Bay. They were nothing to do, directly, with the other forces coming out into the Limbang, currently being dealt with by Sergeant Sanderson and Dr. Henry. These came from farther down the coast, south-west. Nor had either of these anything to do, directly, with the big force from Miri, still farther down the coast, which had got across the Baram and through Semut II and were now heading towards the upper reaches of the Limbang. The lower Trusan group had emerged into clear vision, as an organized force, while the others were still far back in the jungle and widely scattered. I proposed to take on what was left of all three, all of whom were heading eastward towards the Trusan, when they got to that river valley. By now we knew this valley backwards and forwards, and we had every able-bodied man in it under arms, trained, aggressive and moderately disciplined. The two forces still far away to the west, would have to make fearful marches through uninhabited country to come out here; on the way they were harmless. The Baram lot had already done their damage in the middle Limbang before we realized the full menace and while they were still being reported as coped with inside Semut II command.

Immediately, the lot already in the lower Trusan—two to three days behind Lawas—was of first concern. After assembling and reorganizing around Tengoa, they had quickly demonstrated the expected tendency to continue on east, by sending scouts up into the head waters of the Tengoa, evidently trying to seek a way across the Crocker Ranges—trackless in this part over into the Padas valley in North Borneo.

Our arrangements to deal with this lower Trusan group, still close to the coast, were three-fold: to harry them as they reformed in the Tengoa (we had already killed about fifty before they got there); to prepare harassment for them all the way along whatever line they should pursue; and intelligently to anticipate where they would emerge in the Padas in order to provide them with the warmest possible welcome at that end.

I took off on foot far into the Trusan, down it, and then over the Crockers into the Padas. I do not think I have ever walked so fast, so far, in such exhausting country. But it was marvellous to be clear of radio and paper work, to feel actually in the field and subject to the proper discomforts or hazards. My mobility helped to co-ordinate and tighten things up considerably. Also, it was exhilarating to meet Edmeades, Pinkerton, Richter, Bower and the others again, to iron out their own suspicions and complaints about treatment from headquarters, and to clarify my own ideas of what not only could but should be done in effect, on the spots.

One spot clearly deserved our utmost, although secret and squinted, attention. This spot was the Sapong Estate below Tomani, and just above Tenom, on the lower Padas.

At last, it grew clear: where all these Japs were aiming at? The Sapong Estate was at the head of North Borneo's single railway line which runs from the capital, Jesselton, down to the north corner of Brunei Bay, then turns at Beaufort (the regular Army's farthest point up river) inland up the Padas as far as Tenom. The Sapong Estate, above Tenom, was one of the biggest rubber holdings in Borneo, with many amenities unavailable elsewhere. It also had the big advantage of being a rubber estate developed well inland, blocked from the coast, inaccessible by water down river—and, in fact, hitherto thought of as being accessible only through the narrow, tremendous Padas gorge which is tunnelled by the single line railway.

The Sapong Estate had therefore been selected by the Japanese as their General Headquarters; and further as their emergency rendezvous for the whole of Borneo. This was to be the centre for their last stand, should all else collapse. The columns on the lower Trusan, trickling across the lower Limbang and heading into the Upper Limbang, as well as those from much farther east long since heading from Tarakan north-westward towards Pensiangan, all had the same intention: to concentrate at the Sapong Estate (see Map C).

Once we knew that, our own plans were much easier. In particular, at present, it was evident that the Japs in the Tengoa, estimated at approaching a thousand, would continue in that direction and almost certainly emerge over the Crockers on to the Padas after an excruciating up and down journey through very tough, entirely uninhabited, mountain country—along a general line Tengoa-Sapong, roughly north-east. This established, we arranged our available forces, nearly a thousand irregulars in all in that sector. The position at Sipitang along the coast was also now cleared, so that MacPherson could move inland towards the larger forces from that direction, scattered about around Tengoa on the Trusan and above Tomani and on the Padas. With a detailed plan for once, I hoped, not only understood but *agreed* as practicable by almost everyone concerned, I hastened back over the mountains to Bawang—making the trip from the upper Padas to Balawit in what now seems the incredible time of $2\frac{1}{4}$ days. Then I took the air down to Labuan again, to tie the ends up there. From the regulars at Labuan we needed more help in this instance. To start with, we wanted air harassment to support our ground work around Tengoa. Then we wanted to try to keep air observation on Jap inland movement. Finally, we would need to lay on something terrific upon the Sapong Estate itself—but this must only be done when we were ready to follow up and fall upon it through the cane grass and rubber trees, direct.

The RAAF were, as ever, co-operative. They provided a flight of Beaufighters detailed to this rôle. I went with the pilot in the leading Beaufighter the first time, to point targets and explain our ground control and signals, lest they shoot us up in error (which they afterwards only once did).

This first flight had one sad repercussion. The saddest thing, I think, that happened in all these operations. Other things happened more horrible bitter or flatly tragic. This one was just terribly *sad*.

* * *

The first Beaufighter strikes were aimed at surprising the Japanese who had occupied some of the tall, stilted Murut long-houses in this unusually well-cultivated (and, therefore, moderately open) valley. Our guerrilla forces were around these houses and withdrawn, for the present purpose. We knew that several hundred Japanese were clustered over there in security under and in certain houses and the farm huts dotted upon the surrounding rice fields, conspicuous from the air.

Our first attack, by a wing of Beaufighters, flipping over the ranges, swooping into the Tengoa valley within seconds, grossly surprised the Japanese. From our point of view, the main value in such attack was to force the Japanese to scatter and camp under natural cover at ground level—where they were far more vulnerable to guerrilla approach, especially at night. There was very little the Japanese could do to cope with the jungle craft of the inland peoples. And most of these people even conquered their dislike of the dark, temporarily, under the demands of this emergency time. But even in the daytime, no ordinary outsider can compete with an inlander, can hope to move so silently through the forest, can possibly expect to subconsciously side-step a thorn vine or step over a moving column of ants, two of the many things with which a Kelabit deals almost automatically—and which make the jungle seem such a difficult place to people less used to moving in it.

Apart, though, from direct approach and attack upon individuals or small posts—which we were naturally much better at than launching large-scale assaults on organized enemy positions—air attack, in scattering large groups, presented the whole enemy force with a difficult problem. Their difficulty was to keep in contact in difficult country. This difficulty was accentuated, because in no case did the escaping Japanese maintain radio communications. And in every case they had wearisome journeys, through country hitherto unknown to them. (Our influence, of course, ensured that they had no guides or porters at any stage after leaving the coast. In the very few cases when they succeeded in capturing an able-bodied local, he was ready with an ignorance of whatever language the Japs could produce; and language was not their strong suit. Anyway, it is practically impossible to force a Bornean to lead or carry for you under jungle conditions in Borneo.)

Once the Japs had got far inland, they came to depend upon keeping close and moving in column. This need was not only the result of guerrilla harassment, ambush, sneak-raid, blow-pipe. It was equally due to a sense of helplessness, bordering at times on hopelessness, as they moved through this seemingly endless succession of hills and gulleys, ridges cut by land-slides and cliffs, rivers invariably winding in deep meanders; so that to follow along one side of a river, a simple operation in theory, proves tremendously laborious in practice; and is frequently out of the question because in many rivers at each alternate bend the meander only stops as it strikes a steep hillside or rock wall which can only be crossed with difficulty, if at all, so that you must next cross the river itself to continue and follow it until the same thing happens, perhaps another half-mile farther down, on the other side. . . .

Well, while I was feeling rather powerful, directing these two-engine aeroplanes at actual and some imagined Japanese positions, one of them vanished. That is, as we reformed to fly back to Labuan, one was missing. This felt like a waste of life and plane, on an irregular, off-the-cuff operation of this sort. By now, the Australian forces were definitely showing signs of feeling that they had done their share in this war. There was a good deal of talk about risking life, mainly from the army. It was clear everywhere that the Japanese were, in fact, finished. The Borneo landings had been quite costly and complicated. There was a strong undertone of reluctance to engage personnel to their considerable danger, at this late stage. Indeed, before long, I was due to have serious trouble on this account. For the moment, it did seem awful to lose the particularly pleasant and powerful presence of Flying-Officer George, in his Beaufighter.

That afternoon and much of the following day, all available RAAF planes from Labuan—the only airfield then in West Borneo, other than ours inland—searched the Tengoa valley, which is about seven miles long; and all the land between there and the sea. There was no trace. To this day, so far as I know, no trace of the plane has been found, although the Tengoa people hunt and collect jungle produce widely all around. There is nothing surprising about that. There would not be any difficulty about losing a fleet of Comet Jets inside Borneo, without trace.

We gave up—as in war one must—thinking about Flying-Officer George after a few days. Then, after ten days, when I was back at Bawang again, I received a signal to say that he had been found but was dead. Elaborated, what happened was this. . . .

The plane had evidently crashed somewhere on the mountainside near the head of the Tengoa valley. The pilot had carried out Standing

Orders for airmen throughout this theatre. He had followed the nearest waterway downwards. A great many airmen lost their lives unnecessarily through this ill-judged order—ill-judged, that is, in a land of old rivers like Borneo, where the best thing to do if you are lost is to make for the highest ground in the district, from there look for the nearest patch of light green (cultivation) and make a direct line—regardless of obstacles—until you get there.

George was lucky, however, insofar as none of the streams in the Tengoa could possibly be more than five theoretical miles long before they reached our strongly held posts low down in the valley. Unfortunately, at the same time, the upper part of the valley was swarming with Japs. These Japs were not simply in organized groups, they were getting more and more scattered. The more scattered a Jap got the more often he got lost. If it is easy to lose an aeroplane in this jungle, without trace, how much easier to lose a man. Men without long jungle experience and innate jungle sense, can lose themselves in a few seconds and two false steps. And in the case of the Japanese, it would not help even to locate the nearest cultivation and make for it: their ambitions were in quite the contrary direction, away from the open and the locals, over the hills and far away towards the invisible, unknown Sapong Estate of *their* Standing Orders.

George had wonderfully escaped the crash-landing into the hillside. But one eye was severely injured and he had many bruises, though no actual fractures. He had his emergency kit with him, including atropine, then standard anti-malarial issue for all Australian troops. The Tengoa is very much a malarial area. Mosquitos must have made his netless nights into purgatory. He properly loaded himself with atropine, which, taken in quantity, turns the skin livid yellow. He also had his pistol; plus some food, in the form of iron rations.

Ten days after the plane was lost, this gallant man had worked his way down the mountain stream into the main Tengoa, rocky and rapid. Half a mile down the Tengoa he came upon the main camp of 'Z' guerrillas. The Japanese, having scattered, were moving irregularly higher up the valley. But stray individuals were constantly appearing from all directions, lost. Two Murut sentries on the river bank challenged George as he approached. With only one eye to see, worn out and knowing, of course, that the place was full of Japs, he evidently mistook these two tough little Asians, armed with automatics, for Japanese. Certainly, he could not understand as they shouted. He drew his pistol. His yellow skin had already made them think him Japanese: now they were sure. So they shot him before he could shoot.

We made up for this sad act as best we could. The RAAF readily understood. It was not anyone's fault. Even if we could have called the two sentries trigger-happy, they had every occasion to be: at that place and time. The Muruts themselves made a splendid grave for the dead man, in a clearing by the largest long-house of the Tengoa. Over this they erected a cairn of stone, around planted lovely flowers. This, the only direct white casualty in all Semut associations, was commemorated in solitary glory, deep in the heart of this glorious valley and generous people, several of whom had already suffered death under torture protecting American airmen, before we arrived. (Some years later, the Australian War Graves Commission removed his bones: I have not since been able to identify his grave in the long, long rows of identical crosses, drilled in their dead discipline upon the cemetery on Labuan Island.)

Within a few days of this tiny pathos, which upset many of us inside, we nearly lost Sergeant Nibbs, veteran of unnumbered parachute jumps and one of our best professional toughs. Nibbs, with a small guerrilla force, had been moving in a hurry, on a report of some Japs coming into the Tengoa from the Lawas direction. Over-confidence (the occupational disease of irregulars) caused him to lead his small column personally, to move fast without precautions and along the only main track (two feet wide). Without warning he was suddenly under fire from Japs, met nearly face to face. He and the Murut nearest to him jumped off the path, down into a narrow ravine on the left of it. The others fanned out backwards and up the hill, and started a general sniping contest with the Japs, as per schedule. The first thing I knew was Nibbs signalled as 'shot under ambush'—which certainly did not sound right to me: surely *we* were not going to start being ambushed, at this late date?

Fortunately for Bill Nibbs, he had a cocky, sparrow-sharp resolution, was as level in the head as the ground around him was not. Better still, he had with him Sabal, son of Kerus, who had first given strong aid to Edmeades and Co behind Lawas. Sabal was one of Kerus's three sons who were among the very best men we had. He and Nibbs kept together. Four days later they managed to emerge into cultivation and contact. Sabal being able to shout in dialect, they were not in danger of being shot.

Nibbs was lucky. He had the sense to be shaken by the experience. We gave him a spell away from the main trouble, while he recovered his poise.

Trouble continued to gather. Now we knew the principle underlying it, from the Japanese side, the trouble was welcome; in its way exciting.

* * *

The Sapong Estate was handsomely *out of* the way if looked at from the point of view of North Borneo being separate country; or of the coast, with Padas gorge and railway as the only visible line of approach. From our end of the island scale, however, it was attractively accessible. Various irregular units were already familiar with the country immediately to the south-west, up the Merapok and Mengalong rivers, whose head waters drain from the ranges which, on their eastern side, feed the Padas into and through Sapong. Again, separate forces engaged about the Tengoa were moving with the Japanese over into the Meligan branch of the Padas, farther south. While Eric Edmeades and his local headquarters had moved from the upper part of the main Padas valley right down river (that is northward) to near Tomani, whence there is a bicycle trail, leading swiftly into the huge rubber estate, Staff Sergeant Bower, of our original Bario drop lot, working with a lanky, tough Sergeant 'Stroke' Hayes, had established wireless and observation posts in the vicinity. Eric Edmeades, in command there, was in close contact with the local Tagal chief. We continued always to be suspicious of the Tagals, only to arm them or trust them in any way when close supervision was possible.

But these Tagals around Tomani had a special reason to hate the Japanese, with whom they were in immediate proximity. In this part of North Borneo the inland and hill peoples come down close to the area and aura of coastal influence, in keeping with the geography, the terrain itself, which makes the Padas—like the Trusan west over the Sarawak border—one of the very few big rivers in Borneo which is only lowland, level and navigable *near* the mouth.

Tagal women can be even trickier than their men. Whether or not she was glad or sorry, it did so happen that the daughter of one of the leading Tagals had been taken as a concubine by one of the senior Japanese officers, and badly treated. We also contacted a Chinese who had been employed as a stores clerk inside Jap GHQ; he was able to draw an accurate plan of the whole. We began to get, through such channels, something like the same sort of intimate inside information which Bigar had been able to provide out of Lawas earlier on. We needed every scrap of information we could get. For when I started reporting that Sapong was becoming the concentration area and final GHQ, with some 2,000 troops already there, *manifest* disbelief was expressed from Australian HQ. As far as I could learn, they were convinced that the Japanese were centred in Kuching, the Capital of Sarawak, 500 miles to the south-west, and still beyond contact with any of our forces, irregular as well as regular. (The neglect of Kuching was deliberate. It was known to be the place of internment of all surviving civilians and imprisonment for many troops; it was felt that any gesture that way might well bring savage and wholesale reprisals upon these helpless English, Australians, Dutch and French.)

Disbelief is part of the normal diet of subversion, which properly thrives upon it. (The best sort disbelieves itself, too.) Valuably, it meant in this case that the high-ups were disinterested in whatever we were supposed to be seeing and doing around Sapong. We could go and get on with it! As ever, elements in the Royal Australian Air Force could be interested separately. Indeed, it often seemed as if we needed no other credential than disapproval from the Major-General, to ensure vigorous, if informal, air co-operation from on high.

The Sapong plan, as it grew, looked like working out, again, as initial surprise from the air, followed up from the ground. Our irregular minds were directly attracted by the fact that some of the Japanese establishments there had been sited, rather ideally, in tracts of very high cane grass and rush, probably because they could easily be camouflaged and were not so readily to be expected as buildings among the thousands of acres of rubber. Our idea was that, at the critical moment, aircraft should drop incendiary bombs and set fire to this most inflammable vegetation. Simultaneously, the Tagals would perform widescale acts of murder and sabotage while our Kelabit, Murut, Chinese and other forces would cope with the wider repercussions, including the capture of selected persons and places in force.

But this entrancing plan lay some way ahead as yet. It would defeat our own objects if we showed our hand too soon. Too soon, in this, meant soon enough for the Sapong Estate to be so liquidated that inevitably escapees from it would contact Japanese columns making that way and turn them back into the fertile interior, in any and every direction.

By the same token, it was necessary to stop these columns arriving successfully at Sapong, in mass, thus rendering the place very strong. We estimated that there were under three thousand Japs, at most, already in residence, including a considerable number driven back from Beaufort, near the mouth of the Padas, when Brigadier Porter's forces had taken that place some weeks before.

To meet the first of the expected new arrivals, Eric Edmeades deployed about 200 men on the east side of the Crocker Range, around the headwaters of the Meligang, in the sector Iburu-Bole. Both these last two places fortunately had small grasslands suitable for air-dropping of supplies and if necessary reinforcements. From behind the Japs were harried all the way up the Tengoa valley. From above they were blasted wherever they made any visible concentration. When, a fortnight later, they staggered out into the welcoming, more prosperous and open country in that part of the Padas (after making a trip which in better days would merit a lecture to the Royal Geographical Society), they were given the works by our highly impatient irregulars. A succession of minor battles and many skirmishes proceeded during the following week. One day we may know, from some Japanese document, the story from their side. Until then we can only take our own observations and figures. Reliable Australian personnel accounted for one hundred dead from this lot of Japanese at the Padas, out-in-the-open, end. At least three times that number must have perished individually, shot and sometimes stabbed in the dark, lost in the jungle or by their own hand.

Suicide first appeared on this trek. Numbers of Japanese, unable to keep up with their leaders, fearful of being taken alive or simply lost, starving and desperate, took their own lives. The usual way of doing this, rather surprisingly, was by hanging. They hanged themselves by their belts from branches. This was soon to become a familiar accompaniment to the line of march of the other forces, with much further to go to reach their Sapong objective. Years later, skeletons were still being found; several times single skulls strangely dangling, ghostly jokes in a land so long scarred by head-hunting.

A horrible form of involuntary suicide also appeared in the upper Tengoa, where a few Murut rice farmers had pushed far up-river in recent years. These people had not been able to hide their harvest crops (as most of the others had), being insufficiently warned in advance of the Jap approach. Wandering Japs came upon these storage huts. There was, of course, no husked rice about. And the people in this part normally do their husking back in the long-house, so there were few ordinary pestles and mortars around the huts. Had there been plenty, it is doubtful if these Japs would have used them. They were evidently astray. They fell upon the unhusked paddy and ate it raw. Paddy taken in this way, in any quantity, speedily swells inside the stomach until that organ bursts.

Not all Jap indigestion was so extreme. They had a dreadful time of it, internally, all the same. The main Trusan-Padas force made no fires in the later part of their trek, owing to their inability to suppress the smoke as up-clue for aircraft, the flame as side-clue for crawling Kelabit and Murut. It is astonishing how conspicuous the thinnest finger of smoke is, rising out of the jungle canopy; the same with a small flame glimmering in the partial darkness of the forest floor, where few things are readily discernible for more than a few yards in the overall texture of deep green, dark brown, shadow and black.

For what it is worth, we claimed no fewer than 400 Japanese, perhaps many more, obliterated on this Tengoa exercise, from that end. Perhaps 300, maybe more, finally reached Sapong, less or more intact.

I asked Eric Edmeades to recall the first encounters as they emerged from over the Crocker Range out into the Padas, back there in July 1945; he writes:

'The fight went on all the way through Ulu Tomani, and Tomani down past Kemabong into Sapong Estate itself. Gordon Richter and I left MacPherson and Griffiths at Bole, and with Bower and a party of guerilla soldiers we carried out a follow-up operation, picking off stragglers and generally making a nuisance of ourselves wherever possible. We followed the remnants of the Japanese column into Sapong Estate where all remaining enemy forces were being regrouped at this stage. Presumably the Japanese intended their last ditch stand to be carried out here, and their strength was now variously reported at between three and four thousand.

'I next sent Sergeant "Stroke" Hayes with a wireless set to report more closely on Japanese movements and patrolling from the Sapong area. This he carried out most successfully, sitting almost on top of General Baba's HQ for nearly three weeks, with little food and often surrounded by Japanese.'

*　　*　　*

If the goings-on from the Tengoa to Sapong counted as strenuous, the Japanese column now debouching into the upper reaches of the Limbang river, fifty miles—but at least eight days walk—farther west, were warming up into something more strenuous still. In this sector, however, by June our dispositions were less favourable than on the Trusan and Padas. Sanderson's men were below and *behind* the Japs, now. This partly arose from the already described difference of opinion —to put it mildly—which had arisen between the Australian battalion, now stationed down in the mouth of the Limbang, and our irregulars farther up. The repercussions of the Ibans beheading a prisoner had prevented me from establishing a line of direct contact between our tireless and fearless forces up-river and established 'Z' HQ at Labuan Island. The practical way of supplying Sanderson was from Labuan by sea and up-river—as the Limbang, alone of all the rivers in my command area, was readily navigable for more than a hundred miles inland. It was far more difficult to work from inland, round Mount Murud.

The Jap force, variously reported between hundreds and thousands strong, which had emerged in the middle Limbang at the Madalam, having ravaged the small group of long-houses, livestock and crops in that tribuary—had first faced Sanderson and Penghulu Badak's relatively small but by now highly experienced group of irregulars, Kelabits, Tabuns, Muruts and Ibans. Many casualties were inflicted, including four on our side. There was no real hope of holding the Japs though. Fortunately, on any reckoning, they then had to travel right on up the Limbang in order to avoid the impossible mountain country lying directly ahead to the east in the ranges of Pagan Priok, little more than 6,000 feet at the highest, but enormously rugged, even for Borneo. In this section of the Limbang (above the Madalam) there was no resident population, only the hot forest and difficult river as far as the Madihit, right on the edge of the high Kelabit country, and sparsely populated by an outlying fringe of Kelabits. As we had seen to it that no craft of any kind could be available to the Japanese for this journey, they would have to walk. No one in human knowledge, or mythology, had ever done this walk. On a conservative estimate, it could hardly take less than fifteen days. That gave time to re-organize in the Madihit; and more importantly to reform our large and excellent forces in the Trusan, bringing them back up from the Tengoa lower down, and from the upper Padas eastward, to meet the Japanese after their overland crossing of the Limbang watershed south of the Pagan Priok massif. This still left them the best part of another horrible hundred miles trek from that watershed into the Sapong, every mile of the way now well understood by our people.

At this interesting moment in the Borneo war, a great misfortune fell upon us, however. Entirely without asking us and outside our conception of anything (absorbed as we were in interior enthusiasms and anxieties) two atom bombs were dropped in Japan. The war came to an end outside! Out of nowhere—for we never had time to concern ourselves with outside news—without prior warning, I was ordered to cease operations forthwith, await further orders.

MAP C.

BORNEO FROM WITHIN, 1945

This map of the northern interior of Borneo is compiled by Tom Harrisson for the Royal Geographical Society, and based on a recent air survey (incomplete), field work by D. L. Leach and T.H. (including first exploration of the Uson-Apau area) by the Oxford University Expedition 1956, and from geologists' reports. Place names underlined indicate pockets of open country used for parachute dropping or air strips (later).

Arrows show main retreat lines of Japanese forces from either side of the island towards Sapong Estate HQ in the north (1945).

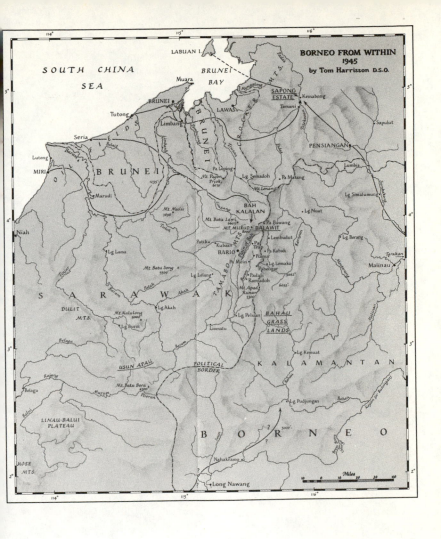

BORNEO FROM WITHIN
1945
by Tom Harrisson D.S.O.

IV

OUTCOME

'Yes', said Lord Ickenham, 'yes . . . but nothing in this world ever works out one hundred per cent satisfactorily for all parties. Thus, while A. is waving his hat and giving a series of rousing cheers, we see B. frowning dubiously. And the same is true of X. and Z.'

P. G. Wodehouse.

'The louder he talked of his honour, the sooner we counted our spoons!'

Ralph Waldo Emerson.

★　　★　　★

'The best man is the last one to pass out.'

Bawang Murut saying.
(1945)

'The best man passes out top—MAYBE!'

Sandhurst saying.
(1944)

OUTCOME

1945–6 . . . High and Low

The atomic bombs which fell, late in August 1945, on Hiroshima and Nagasaki seemed, for a day or so, to have fallen upon us also, inside Borneo. The, to us, sudden end of the war blasted plans, indeed hopes, nursed and nurtured in our particular internal abstraction. The complexity of our proliferating ant-heap had kept some sort of shape, common purpose and self-control: the intention of, and absorbed belief in, ridding the inland of every living Japanese. Beyond that, however obscurely, a feeling had been growing throughout the interior that after the war the interior might ask for something more than ever before. This feeling took the form, among an appreciable number of thoughtful inland people, of in some way associating all the different peoples realistically, as many within one 'feel'.

Until this century, more than a hundred thousand people, living roughly within the area now theoretically controlled on V-Day by Semut I, had been cut off or up into numerous small and in varying degrees isolated groups, largely in consequence of past or continuing head-hunting and related feuds and affairs. The impacts of European Government, the Dutch from the east and the British—in three different ways, through Sarawak, Brunei and North Borneo—from the west, had altered the horizons of impact. These alterations, however, were naturally conditioned to a coastal approach. Government was on and near the coast, with few and negligible exceptions. The island was divided into four territories by far inland boundaries, some of which were not even surveyed and agreed. This arrangement of Borneo into political units not only negatived the potential mobility and liberality consequent upon the gradual cessation of head-hunting, and other valuations. It actually confused and in certain respects accentuated divisions set along lines which bore no relation whatever to *any* internal reality, present or past.

I was trying to express something of this mood when I wrote the paper, in military terms, 'Borneo is Indivisible', which got me slung out of 9 Div. HQ* on Labuan.

Some of the biggest and wisest leaders inland felt that the Japanese occupation had shown up great weaknesses in the previous regime. Although the Japanese had done even worse than anyone before them, yet from the inland point of view that experience—augmented by a wide new mobility and unity since our Bario parachute drop—stimulated a fairly ill-formulated desire to try again; or at the very least, to preserve some of the advantages now enjoyed by administration from the inside, interchange of people and goods in all directions irrespective of political watersheds or past bloodsheds.

To establish this pattern with some kind of solidity, it was evidently desirable that the inland people as a whole should secure the interior as a whole; and that whatever outside administration emerged after the Japanese exit, it should have new ideas about the interior and a uniform approach thereto.

For these hopes, the war ended too soon. None of them have been realized. On the contrary, the interior of Borneo is now more divided than ever before. Discrepancies between different governments have never been more acute, and along the border hostilities have been politically aroused which had no existence or purpose before. This situation did not derive from anything then in the minds of these people; nor from the organizations and events they were currently experiencing as and after the war ended.

But V-Day blasted the hopes of a different future for the people. It came too soon for that. It also blasted the hopes of 'Z' Special enthusiasts—for instance the moment when Captain Edmeades and his lads could capture the Japanese Commander-in-Chief and present him in chains, to be flown by Auster and delivered by me (complete with a carbon copy of 'Borneo is Indivisible') to Major-General Wootten at 9 Div. HQ. Major-General Wootten seemed in need of some such medicine at this moment. His staff refused to believe in the Sapong Estate, and immediately mounted detailed plans for their big Commander to receive the surrender, adequately photographed, of the Japanese Commander-in-Chief, Baba, supposedly at Kuching. One unlucky consequence of this was that the thousands of prisoners in Kuching were held for nearly a month after the war was over. The Army would not

* See page 269.

permit anyone to relieve them until he had received the formal surrender, in due pomp and ceremony. In the event, Toby Carter, by this
time on liaison and clear of Semut II—which had no post armistice
military headaches—was the first officer most Kuching whites met, as
he managed to get in on the very first plane permitted to land on the
Sarawak river, near the town.

So far as I was concerned, the immediate effect of peace threatened
to be disastrous. I was being ordered to stop fighting, disband all irregular forces, send out immediately all my Australian personnel and as
soon as possible evacuate my own headquarters. At the same time,
some thousands of Japanese were either known or supposed to be mill-
ing about and moving inland—not only across the Limbang but latterly
towards the Long Nawang area far south, and again in the Sembakong
far on the eastern side. I was, in brief, being ordered to abandon the
whole inland and its people to the apparent mercy of by now angry and
always potentially vicious enemies.

Needless to say, I protested loud and clear. 'Z' Special, as ever, rose
to the occasion. My first orders were watered down. In conference at
Labuan, eyes winked, elbows raised, signals got blurred under orders—
orders which, had I been actually ordered to obey them, would have
left me no decent alternative but the Japanese one: suicide. After a lot
of talk and double talk, it was tacitly agreed that, orders apart, we
could not abandon our faith in this way. To do so would not only be
to expose a fine people to devastation, but also to expose the good
name of the British to undying contempt in lands which they wished,
now, at once, to reoccupy with untarnished, indeed with revarnished
honour.

This was more or less alright as far as the top brass of 'Z' was concerned. All of us in Semut were vastly assisted by our recent break-off
inland and segregation from regular forces, so that it was virtually impossible for anyone outside our unit to know what we were up to, in
detail, in the interior.

The attitude of the regular army was different. They naturally enough
insisted on reclaiming several personnel seconded to us; on prohibiting
further air sorties and use of Austers to and from the Bawang strip; and
on generally treating irregular operations as, from their point of view,
no longer properly extant. The Ruling General honoured me with an
interview, in which he told me that it was no longer possible to risk the
expenditure of a single Australian life for any such purpose. He regretted

that from now on it must be up to the inland people to fend for themselves. If my unit agreed to let me and some others stay, it could be done, he said; I was, after all, English. But I must not do anything to embarrass anyone outside the unit or endanger the lives of any Australians within it.

This estimable and very experienced officer was only saying what he had to say, under the Australian conditions. Above and behind him were Australian politicians; labour politicians who had many reservations about the war any way, all of which came welling out powerfully once the war was good and over. But regular 9 Div. HQ had further reservations about us irregulars, in addition. They didn't believe half of what we said. (For example, they still did not believe there was anything significant on the Sapong Estate.) They openly dismissed our reports of large Jap forces moving inland. They accepted that there were some Japs, but senior intelligence officers put the total in tens or at the most a couple of hundred. The rest was written off as typical irregular exaggeration, self-dramatization and the usual, altogether indiscipline. It is easy to sympathize with this view, which was maintained up to the last moment—long after the end of the war, when I was actually able to present to Labuan an imposing quantity of Japanese prisoners taken alive from about as far into Borneo as anyone could get. Meanwhile, this attitude was distressing. It put what, at first, seemed too much of a burden of responsibility back on to the shoulders of myself, Bartram (English), Blondeel (Flemish), Edmeades (New Zealand) and a few others left inland. Edmeades was by now really worn out with his constant exertions; it was a further blow to have to invalid him home at this crucial moment.

*　　*　　*

To meet this disturbing re-arrangement of tensions and prospects there was no alternative but to become *more* independent, more self-centred than ever, inside our old Semut I—and with special, revised reference to three vital matters:

    (i) Keeping our guerrillas mobilized and armed wherever and so long as there was a Japanese threat.

   (ii) Keeping confidence and existing goodwill going throughout the area.

  (iii) Planning for the possibility that a few of us might be left a long time on our own with local people in the interior—faced with Jap refusal to surrender or belief in surrender, but instead Jap determination to stay, survive and resist inland.

I therefore set about, as rapidly as possible, covering all traces and clues which might lead outside to the coast; and sending out any personnel liable then or later to become disgruntled. Fortunately, the nucleus of the most experienced were absolutely loyal to the people of the inland in general. This did not prevent me, all the same, from later receiving a curious letter from a senior Australian NCO. This gentleman claimed that he had in his possession papers, signed by me, which proved that I ignored and even cancelled High Command orders to cease operations and altered these—as he saw it, over-ruled these—to cause all forces engaged with, close to or faced in the near future with Japanese, to carry on under arms, contrary to the Armistice. He proposed to publish this material in Australia unless . . .

During these tricky negotiations and chicaneries—which parent SOE in Europe and offspring 'Z' in Australia had ably prepared me for over and above any innate aptitude—it was imperative that the Kelabits and others should not suspect the tremendous danger under which they lay: the danger that total demobilization would be enforced. Safeguard for this was simply achieved. We collected up the arms from the several hundred people in 'safe' sectors, as, for example, the Bawang and Bario, where there was no apparent danger and a mood of better-than-peace-time security. I signalled that these troops had been demobilized and the men taken off strength. I was duly ordered to write the arms off as impossible to return to a regular unit for check or destruction under present conditions. I then reissued the arms to the same people, as demobilized reservists who must be available on call at runner notice. This gave a comfortable sense of something up the sleeve; a sense that was fortified whenever I carried out the weekly inspection of rifle and carbine ammunition, hand grenades and mortar shells, which had been built up over several months in our base depots. It was a formidable armament.

The only trouble about Balawit and the Bawang valley generally, lay in its geography. What before had been of great advantage, became much less satisfactory with no further air links, dropped supplies or elaborate personnel.

* * *

We had, back in March, practically vacated the Plain of Bah in the Sarawak Kelabit uplands, in favour of the better centralization and mobility available from the east side of Mount Murud, once Semut II and III had secured all the land west of Bario and the Tamabo ranges, as far as the coastal plain behind the South China Sea. Under war conditions, all this territory was Japanese-held. Now, over V-night, the Dutch once more proclaimed Dutch Borneo. We were actually occupying it, though.

A large part of Semut I organization and activities was all of a sudden recognized to be in Dutch territory. And having tacitly permitted us to exercise a very wide and—as far back as Melbourne—widely known control over all the northern part of Dutch Borneo, the Dutch Government, within a week, declared amazement at our existence. They began to demand, from this freshly unexpected and politically powerful side, our immediate withdrawal. Oh dear!

I do not know enough about the inner politics of what went on between the British, the Australians and Dutch back at GHQ level in Australia and around MacArthur. I never got near to a Dutchman (except my Captain Jack Blondeel, who was part Belgian Flemish) during the war and none of them appeared in our part of Borneo until long after it was over. But I did know that the highest Dutch either were amazed or feigned amazement when a full report of the existence of our Dutch Borneo operations was described in a summary report that I had to submit, immediately after the close of final hostilities.

This thing quickly grew serious.

Back in our main 'Z' Headquarters at Morotai in the Halmaheras, they sent for me urgently. Next thing I knew, briefed by our new CO, Brigadier Jock Campbell (he had succeeded John Chapman-Walker), I was on my way in a comfortable aircraft back to Australia. I was accompanied by a senior officer in a unit that I now heard about for the first time, the Dutch equivalent of 'Z'. It was rather like being under open arrest, he seemed to think. But it was the most comfortable travel I did any time, anywhere, in the war. I was, so to speak, the guest of the Dutch military and government even unto their wonderful camp outside Brisbane in Queensland. The object of this sudden operation was: to clear up the position as between Semut I and the Dutch. The Dutch idea (as far as I could understand or was given to understand) was that once I had solved the problems of the Limbang forces at large on the Sarawak side, I should join the Dutch service and clear up the north part of Dutch Borneo as a Colonel in the Dutch army and military administration, on their behalf. This idea seemed so absurd, that it inevitably intrigued. It was logical 'Z'. It would also give me a reasonable chance to continue influencing that part of the interior, possibly to its advantage.

Jock Campbell had given me certain limits beyond which I must not go. His general brief was that I had nothing to apologize for: that the Dutch had been kept fully informed of what we were up to; but that in the general interests of 'Z'—Dutch goodwill, peace and the Borneo people involved—I should consent to co-operate to any degree consistent with 'Z's' own principles (*sic*), British dignity and my existing status as a British officer attached to the Australian Army—who could, however, easily be seconded to the Dutch for a period. With this characteristically cloak-and-dagger intellectual background, I came to Brisbane in a mood of hopefulness, but without too much over-confidence. I was rudely disillusioned as to Dutch intentions. First I was kept waiting for three days before anyone above the rank of a major could spare time to speak to me. Eventually, I was summoned to an hotel interview—shades of Northumberland Avenue, but without any shabbiness, underhand or off-handedness—with General Spoor, then head of the Dutch 'Z' equivalent and other bodies, subsequently in supreme command over Indonesia (where he died before the final Dutch downfall in Asia).

Spoor adopted a direct, one could almost say crude, approach. He did not approve of the extent to which we had established ourselves in Dutch Borneo. He knew we were there, but had been misled as to the extent and depth of our doings. He would, under the circumstances, accept me as a temporary take-over to get things back nearer normal, disarm all guerrillas, hand over as soon as possible to his nominee. I tried to argue that this process was impracticable. I implied that it was practically criminal, in that it would expose Dutch subjects to great risks as well as the Dutch to humiliation. He was too intelligent a man to disbelieve my analysis of possible peace-time Japanese movement and even possible settlement inland. But he was too much of the Dutch army and administrative mind (of that time) to be able to accept any offer or interpretation which could in any sense be taken to reflect on the sovereignty and on the capacity of the Dutch themselves, in their colonies. After a dreadful half-hour I put it to him something like this:

Myself: 'Sir, if you do not employ me, my commanding officer instructs me to withdraw without further delay, from Dutch Borneo on to the British side of the border. This will mean abandoning the largest part of those who supported us in the war and some of the most courageous and likeable people I have ever met. To do so would be an insult to them, to me and in the long run, Sir, to you, the Dutch—unless you are prepared, at once, to take alternative measures, provide personnel to whom I can hand over our whole set-up forthwith. As I understand it, my headquarters are prepared to accept such an arrangement, if you so wish.'

Spoor: 'Nothing of this kind is possible. Either you will continue in Dutch Borneo as an officer subject to Dutch orders and regulations; or you will unconditionally withdraw in the shortest possible time, to be agreed without any further observations from you or your unit.'

Myself: 'Sir, I only care about this thing from one point of view. I hope I am not being too sentimental or absurdly romantic when I say that I feel very deeply indeed about these people. I cannot feel any differently about them or any less devotion to them, whether they are now to be classed again as the subjects of the Dutch, the British or anyone else. I must implore you to consider what will happen to them if you only think of this matter in terms of military or immediate political precedent or prestige.'

At this, Spoor, a fine man of his kind, with good mind and high character, commenced to explode upon me. I countered this attack, taking both of us wholly by surprise (both of us) by bursting into tears. I did feel that bad about the dilemma then. Spoor had the goodness to stop talking, offer me a cigarette—which he deliberately had not done before—and bring our painful interview to an end.

I remember nothing else of two wild days and nights on the town in Brisbane—the only city in the Commonwealth which has official (and graded) brothels. One angle is, however, recalled for me by a long letter I lately received from Miss Lenore Morris; it starts:

'When I read yesterday's *Evening Standard*, I decided it would be too much of a coincidence—Christian name Tom, Harrisson spelt with a double "s", and *Borneo*—for you not to be the Major Tom Harrisson who played an important part in the Borneo operations of Services Reconnaissance Department ("Z" Special Unit, AMF) prior to and during the Allied invasions there towards the end of the War. So, I thought I'd send a written "hello", although you won't have the least idea of my identity.

'I was a cipher operator in the Australian Women's Army Service, attached to "Z" Special Unit—SRD—and in the later stages of SRD's existence, when its headquarters moved to Morotai, etc., I transferred from Melbourne to Brisbane. It was there, 2nd Floor, Bank of NSW Building I think it was, that I met you, back from Borneo for a few days, when you dictated to me a detailed Top Secret report on the Borneo operations, which I typed back in draft form. I don't even remember now to whom you were sending it, possibly SOE in London; seeing the paragraph about you in the paper has brought back memories of SRD and "Z" I had forgotten until now. I've been wondering what has happened . . . .'

I flew back to Morotai next morning. Jock Campbell was furious at my account of what happened. And it so happened that a need to express our British reaction turned up, just at this moment, in the usual 'Z'-ish way.

*　　*　　*

It was now well into September 1945. So far as the interior of Borneo was concerned, what we had earlier reported as a large Japanese force was now in the Upper Limbang, not at present being attended to by anyone, since dynamite Sanderson and wild-boy Henry had been withdrawn by sea. But it did not seem possible that these Japanese could emerge from the tangled hinterland of the upper Limbang for a long time to come. The official, high-up, regular view was that if they existed at all (except in 'Z' reports) they could in any case never emerge as a threat anywhere else. They would surely perish in this uninhabited country. Long since, they must have run out of their own supplies and —according to our own reports—could not obtain any more if and as they advanced through unmapped and unknown country, full of physical hazards and obstacles, precipitous mountains, gorges, rock beds, river rapids, interspersed with wide tracts of characterless jungle providing no clues: and nothing promising ahead.

There was a good deal in this view, clearly enough. But we already had direct experience of the toughness and unflinching will of Japanese leadership under these circumstances, from the extraordinary way they had got themselves up the Tengoa, out of it and—at least as a relic—at last into the Sapong Estate, that way. It did seem reasonable, however, to hope that only a few of the Limbang lot would emerge; that these would take a long time; and that the considerable forces now secretly disposed to meet them as they came into the Trusan valley would be able to cope on their own. We anticipated, moreover, that those who did emerge would make either down the Trusan and over via the Tengoa, or get right across the Trusan into the Padas, making, of course, for the Sapong again. In either direction, they had to pass through days of organized hostility and areas which were sufficiently sparsely populated yet highly organized to prevent their doing serious damage to local property and to prevent them obtaining appreciable food supplies.

Thus suitably and maybe wishfully reassured, I was offered a new attraction. Reports were being received, not only through our own 'Z' sources, but also from the regular Australian formations at Balikpapan (off the south-east corner of East Borneo) to the effect that large forces of Japanese had moved inland from the south-east and were heading generally inland and northward, via the Batang Kayan and Long Nawang. This possibility had already been anticipated. As it was now emerging into probability, and as the position around the densely populated Batang Kayan and south of our guerrilla area was still completely obscure, unknown from first-hand report, it was agreed (by whom?) that I should myself now abandon the Bawang valley—a fact that could at once be reported to the Dutch without their having to realize that Paul Bartram and others were still up there—and be dropped away to the south, to sort things out there, well within Dutch territory but far out of conceivable Dutch knowledge.

*　　*　　*

I celebrated my thirty-fourth birthday that night, in the by now relative luxury of Morotai, a Halmahera war hell only a year before—when we had Navy Search flown thence for the first time over Borneo and the Bahau. Jack Finlay gave me a tremendous party, assisted by various amiable English ladies who had now appeared on the scene in the uniform of the classy FANYS. We took off before dawn next morning, in a Liberator once more.

We, for this trip consisted of air crew, plus me and two others. One of these two was a highly competent signals sergeant, whom I did not know before, never saw again, and cannot remember his name. The other was a brigadier who, they whispered, was a Fellow of the Royal Society, a master-mind on radio, radar and the like. I was given three, and three only, instructions, before I passed out again in the bomb bay:

(i) to find out about the supposed Jap movement up from the south-east and do whatever was necessary to cope;

(ii) to come back myself as soon as I could;

(iii) (and this was the one most emphasized) to get our radio immediately set up and a message (in clear) back to Moratai *before* the brigadier had touched ground on his return flight, so that my message could be received by him as he landed—and prove the miraculous efficiency of 'Z' signals!

I do not know what all this showing off was about, or if he really was a scientist; but 'Z' clearly acted thus to impress. I was far too full of drink and short of sleep to take it all in. But freshly thirty-four, polished in the art of 'Z'-manship, I had carefully failed to mention to anyone that Jeff Westley had already taken a radio down that way, and set it up with initial contact and careful subsequent storing on the great grassland which I had seen on my first reconnaissance flight, and where I now intended to drop. I also took the precaution of writing a message for the signals sergeant to send, immediately he could get to the set. Our own set he could ignore, of course, in the storpedo containing the equipment being dropped with us.

* * *

The navigator shook me back into consciousness in due course, six hours later. I looked out to see, for the third time, this magnificent open valley (first seen from Navy Search a year before). It looked like Central New Guinea, not jungular Borneo. Not a tree to be seen anywhere on it, just miles and miles of rolling grass. The pilot on the intercom, pointed out that the wind was blowing too fast for dropping and the cloud too much for him to be able to come down safely in such a rugged place. Harrisson, true to his faith, plus hangover, said never to worry, he would jump-master himself and his sergeant into this enormous DZ, which no one could anyway miss, blast it all.

As an added refinement, I elected to jump-master the sergeant out in front of me. As I shot out of the camera hatch into the usual enchantment, after him, I gave the brigadier a snappy salute, slipping on my parachute pack, feet dangling. I hope the brigadier was impressed by this. He surely *must* have been impressed by receiving, as he landed at Moratai, the good sergeant's signal that we had both landed safely, recovered the radio and were getting on with things all right. The sergeant indeed had done perfectly, fallen right on to Westley's old marker, being led straight to the radio by the reception committee, who had been waiting through so many weeks. He'd at once got on to the air and done his stuff. But while the brigadier was reading the message and no doubt being suitably impressed, I was dangling from the top of a 200 foot tree, slowly but surely dying.

The delay in my reflexes had been sufficient to let me go out over past the sergeant, in space time. My physical condition—once surprisingly emerged into full, cold air at the unusual dropping altitude of 10,000 feet (the mountains around went up to 7,000, and the cloud to 9,000)—was such that I could not even contemplate competing with a strong cross-wind, blowing me further off centre. After some emasculated efforts to manipulate my suspension cords and sail the chute into the wind, I flopped and descended, crabwise. A superb panorama stretched out below. From this height the great grassland valley showed pale as silver in an endless surround of dark virgin forest and towering peak. The setting was wilder even than Bario behind Batu Lawi and Murud. This is, I think, the wildest, and in its particular way, the grandest, piece of all Borneo.

The wind and my ineptitude carried me, slung away, from this height. I realized that I was going to achieve the astonishing feat of missing what must be about the largest DZ south of Siam. There was not anything I could do about it. I came right across the valley and over a ridge, where up-eddies and air currents played with me as if I was some sort of tubular glider out of control. They presently deposited me, with a smash, sideways on to the forest canopy at about 4,000 feet, upon a very steep hillside.

Fate poised me for a few seconds, a crucified gibbon, spread over the superb top-knot of a huge gum. Then I began to slide. Looking down, it was difficult to doubt that I was about to break my neck on the face of the ravine, 200 feet below. But when I got about a quarter of the way down (entangled head first in my harness, my feet wrapped up in the lines) I came to a shuddering stop. After a few reverberating bounces up and down in the air, I settled, set for eternity. A single broken branch in the tree top had pierced the parachute silk and held it. I owed that to Bill Sochon, testing his hundred-time job at Bario months before.* My 'chute was, therefore, brand new, and held.

* See page 224.

Sober at last, but greatly staggered, I presently managed to get my feet below my head and look something more like an old Harrovian and a gentleman should when in trouble. But I was so suspended that I could not do anything more. I was too far from my own tree or the next to swing in either direction without starting something serious up on my single securing point overhead. I had not the strength to climb up the lines, even if I could have cleared the harness without falling out.

I therefore remained as I was. I had jumped wearing a fur-lined coat, bartered long before with an American. The sun pierced the canopy as it rose towards noon, fried me as I hung. Before long I must have passed out again.

I woke to find myself swaying alarmingly. The sun was well past noon and I past hope. I could no longer feel my body below the waist, where the harness and the pressure of suspension held me as in a vice of pure misery. The wind had got up. I must soon be unhooked from above, to crash down below.

I managed to assemble enough strength to look up and watch dissolution. Instead, the extraordinary sight of a small, yellow man, wearing only a loincloth and a cap with a hornbill feather, perched in my tree top on the theory—as I subsequently learnt—that if he unhooked the 'chute it would open again before it hit the ground. He was trying to free me and it. I summoned all the invective in all the Borneo dialects I had ever heard swear in. This caused him to reconsider: his position and mine.

By and by, one way and another, he got other people (I am not sure how) to build an enormous ladder and improvised pulley, between my tree and the next. Down this device, some twenty little agile, excited, laughing Borneans lowered me, with great gentleness to the ground. They carried me over the ridge, into and across the blissful grass, by now supervised by my steady, calm sergeant, his radio chore performed.

Lucky for me, Westley's reception committee had been alerted directly they heard a plane approaching. They had watched it circling and then us drop. They had seen me go wildly astray and set out to search the hillsides. The Kenyah who found me—for these were not Kelabits or other hill groups, but Kenyahs and Sabans at the north edge of their, and south of our, inland range—had, he said, heard me groaning before he saw me dangling.

I lay on a beautifully made bamboo bed and soothed my soul. Soon, reaction set in. Blame someone else—a 'Z' speciality. Well, if we were so marvellous pleasing the brigadier with that radio, our own could now have something extra for itself. I sent a snorter complaining of the pilot's ineptitude and whatever else I could scrape up. I received this treasured reply:

'Never in the history of royalty, has so high a rajah been delivered upon so high a tree so high as thee.'

Next morning I was *literally* black from waist to my knees, presumably the effect on my circulation of hanging suspended for hours. I suffered no other ill effects. Three days later, having passed a few formal signals, reported nothing serious in the immediate vicinity of what I now realised to be the Bahau river valley (flowing into the Batang Kayan farther down), and having got the all-clear to proceed south and investigate, I told the sergeant to throw all wireless sets in the river, gave him our last bag of gold and some good men to see him out to the coast in his own good time, and pushed off south myself, freer than I had ever felt in the previous five years.

*   *   *

Ever since I first came to Borneo I had been hearing about Long Nawang in the upper Batang Kayan river. Now I had the chance to go there. I was out to take it. I would move as fast as I possibly could; but I was not going to miss seeing what all native tradition and legend claimed as the great culture centre of the Kenyah-Kayan and other river people living between the coastal Malays and Dayaks on the outside and the upland Kelabits, Muruts and others of the highlands.

Carrying reserves of arms, accompanied by the Kenyah reception committee and many others recruited upon the way, I set out down the Bahau and then overland on a long march to join the Batang Kayan higher up. Another four days further paddling upriver in a long canoe, we were there.

Long Nawang is, perhaps, the most impressive community in Borneo and among all the inland people famous far beyond experience, as are only, in another way, the mountains of Kinabalu and Batu Lawi hundreds of miles to the north. Thousands of people live in a series of longhouses at Long Nawang, jumbled up together with a teeming profusion of life, in quantity as well as quality not to be equalled among the hill peoples. In Borneo, it is only when you live on a river that it is possible to concentrate large numbers of people in one place, whence they can go about practically all their kinds of business on the water, by canoe.

As well as that, the people of Long Nawang belong, broadly, to the senior clan of the Kenyahs, who differ from nearly all other Borneo people by being divided into cryptototemic groupings which have largely faded in recent times and remain most strongly represented by the universal respect and seniority given to Long Nawang itself. Among the Kenyahs, then, the class structure is far more pronounced than among Kelabits and other people farther north. High aristocrats do relatively little work and the demand which can be made upon the population by a man like the paramount chief of Long Nawang are very considerable. A glowing example of the result was the towering house, made of the usual jungle materials, but on a monumental scale, in which this chief, aged and slowly dying, received me. The centre wall had been raised to fifty feet in height. The whole of this was decorated with a marvellous tree of life which he told me had taken the best artists of the whole Batang Kayan months to achieve. The tree was crowned, as ever, with splendid Rhinoceros Hornbill, rampant.

Here, and everywhere else I went on the Batang Kayan, I was presented with beautifully carved swords and knives—the metal of the blade carved and embossed equally with the horn handle, and horn sheets sewn on to the sheaths. I asked the old man what, in all the world, *he* wanted most. He said, my combined ·22 rifle and 410 shotgun. I gave him this and he proceeded to whang high velocity American cartridges into the tree of life, glowing in the half-dark from where we sat, on a raised platform held by four magnificently carved monsters.

There is no place, in this book, to go into the character, culture and activity of the Kenyahs. It need only be said, here, that they are in many ways a more placid, slower-to-fire, sweeter people than the Kelabits of the uplands. They look quite different, largely because the upper part of the body is greatly developed by constant canoeing, in contrast to the lower half of a Kelabit who is for ever walking. There are many other differences, which do not obscure basic similarities in outlook on most of the fundamental issues of life, as they apply within Borneo.

The issue with which I was currently concerned was, of course, our friends—the war was over—the Japanese.

The expected forces of Japs had not and never did arrive in Long Nawang, as it so happened. Apparently they turned back much farther south. Some of them holed up in caves and were not discovered until two years after the war was over, a great sensation. Only two got to Long Nawang in their innocence.

One of the characteristic differences between Kenyah and Kelabit was demonstrated on this sinister occasion. Under the directions of the great chief, the two men were brought before him, but kept down below the house, on the ground. Their wrists and ankles were then carefully broken. They were left to crawl about through the village among the pigs, goats, dogs, hens (none of Tuan Aris's ducks here, alas) until they perished. No human touched them until it was time to throw the corpses into the river, in final contempt.

One particular reason for the Kenyah hatred of the Japanese derived from an incident early in the war, at Long Nawang. In peace time this had also been an important Dutch post, the only major administrative post situated anywhere far inland in Borneo. When the Japanese arrived on the coast at the end of 1941, many Europeans moved inland. Long Nawang was the natural southern focus, offering the armed security of a regular Dutch camp. There was a great deal of confusion at this time, particularly in Sarawak, where some felt it was their duty to stay at their posts, some that they must escape to fight another day. From the Sarawak coast in the west, the trek to Long Nawang involves weeks of slogging up the Rejang river beyond the navigable head waters and over into the Batang Kayan by an easy pass. Some fifty Europeans set out upon this journey. But about half turned back, gave themselves up to the Japanese and mostly survived the war in intern-ment at Kuching. The remainder, under one of the Brooke Residents, a strong leader of most uneven temperament, finished up at Long Nawang.

Eventually, there were quite a lot of English and Dutch subjects, plus some American missionaries and others at Long Nawang. Evi-dently they felt very safe here. Like Major-General Wootten and 9 Div. HQ, they underestimated Japanese capacity for vigorous travel and jungle sense. The Japanese sent up a warning that if they did not sur-render voluntarily and come down, as by now all other Europeans except one had done, the Japs would take action. Some months later some Kenyahs from the Mahakam side came dashing in to say that the Japanese were only a couple of days away, in strength. The Dutch officer in command of the post militarily, did not believe this. The Kenyahs were put into the beastly little lock-up (four cells) which the

Dutch kept for their interior purposes. Three days later, these cells were occupied by the wretched wives of such Europeans and Americans as had gathered here *en pair*. The men were all dead. The Dutch commander, the Brooke Resident and some others are said to have been killed, as they were playing cards, by the first Japanese mortar shell from across the river, into their verandah. The rest were rounded up, lined up, a little back in the scrub, shot down and buried in a communal grave. No-one escaped. The Kenyahs escaped reprisals, because it could fairly be held that the Dutch were occupying an established situation by force. No doubt, too, at this stage the Japanese did not wish to alienate the most powerful single chief and community in all Borneo.

*　　*　　*

Before dumping the radio in the Bahau, I had advised Labuan of my intention to proceed to Long Nawang. After four happy days there (very reminiscent of time spent among a junior branch of the same people around Mount Dulit, with the Oxford Expedition of 1932), a two-engined Mitchell reconnaissance plane came over, clearly searching for me around the only permanent buildings in all this part of the island. I signalled, was dropped some comforts and trade goods, accompanied by an urgent order—of the 'or else' type—to return immediately to the coast, as new troubles were brewing up north and west, over in Sarawak.

Immediately had to be a comparative term. With regret on both sides, the next day I set off in a fine, long canoe, accompanied by the chief's deputy and his grandson—who, I hear, is now the chief. We had twenty paddlers, picked men who could paddle hour after hour. It took, if I remember rightly, eight days steady going to get down the Batang Kayan, this lovely river torn with exciting rapids in the upper reaches, and every few miles studded with groups of long-houses or single long-houses, one of which, at Long Po, was more than half-a-mile long when I was there. In most of these communities, and notably at Nakramo, there are craftsmen, carvers and smiths, who specialize in making beautiful objects—a specialization which is possible when a Borneo community is sufficiently large and communications comparatively easy. On my way down I gathered, as gifts from chiefs and head men, greatly delighted at the first white in years and at news of

Japanese defeat, a collection of Kenyah art which still decorates my life, as I write; and which can never be made again, by anyone, alas: for these things die with the second half of the twentieth century.

We had to change boats, but not crews, half way. The Batang Kayan is broken, half of the way down, by miles of impassable rapids, the Brem Brem. Boats are deposited at either end, used interchangeably by people going up and down river. We took a new boat from below, and spent the last few days of our paddling in a swiftly widening river of powerful tides, which sometimes held us for hours.

Nothing could have been a nicer change from the previous months, of walking and climbing, dropping, reporting, arguing and intriguing. The two Kenyah leaders and I quietly sat in a comfortable, covered section and were paddled through glorious gorges, innumerable variations on the same theme of scenery and natural history; wherever there were humans, we were received as princes, until, at reluctant last, we reached Tanjong Selor, in the mouth of the mighty river.

There I was brought up against the outside with the proper bang. The decrepit Sultan, surrounded by so-called advisers, most of whom were wall-eyed (perhaps from looking into his pockets sideways) was amiable but frightened. He entertained me to a formal Malay luncheon and explained that I alone knew about the inland people, but must not despise him in that he knew nothing, since he—although ruler of the whole of the territory as far as the British Border—was prohibited from ever moving inland, owing to a traditional curse upon any member of his family who ever did so. With due Mohammedan courtesies he presented me with a fine *keris* dagger. Not to be outdone, I presented him with my favourite parachute, intact except for the small hole which had secured my blackening hulk from the Bahau forest canopy. Before I left, he had rigged this sheet as a canopy for his seedy gilt throne. I went across the river to the empty Dutch government house. Here I found cause for his unease and my discomfort. The first Dutchman had arrived from Tarakan a few days before. He was not aware of my impending presence; but he was, of course, well aware that 'Z' people had been operating from further north in this direction, and that Blondeel with a large force had come down the coast from the Sembakong as far as the mouth of the Batang Kayan some months earlier. He had therefore, I now learnt, issued frightful threats about what would happen to anyone co-operating with the British. These threats were effective in preventing the Malay caretaker from permitting me, voluntarily, from using the place at all. With marked reluctance, I therefore performed perhaps the last act of force ever to be perpetrated by a British officer in Dutch territory overseas.

Next day I said sad farewell to my Kenyah friends, who now had to face at least treble the journey against the stream, back to Long Nawang. I persuaded the two-hearted Sultan to lend me the only motor boat then in the area to take me over to Tarakan, where there were still Australian forces in occupation alongside the returning Dutch. The inboard engine broke down on the short sea journey, so I ended up paddling, anyhow. From Tarakan, a sea-plane took me over Borneo once more to Labuan, in the middle of October.

★　　★　　★

'Z' HQ at Labuan was humming with signals from my adjutant left in charge in the Bawang. Paul Bartram was reporting that the Japanese who had passed through the Baram into the middle Limbang, had not dwindled away, as anticipated, but were believed to be now clear of the Limbang watershed and on their way down a tributary called Adang, into the main Trusan valley. This, as he correctly saw, was serious. In my absence, all white personnel had been withdrawn from the Limbang, the Trusan and the Padas, as well as the whole of Dutch Borneo, apart from Bawang and the vicinity. Our only remaining signal station was the old base one beside the Bawang airfield, with Sergeant Long. There were no more RAAF Austers; the airfield was already going back into scrub. The atom bombs had exploded nearly two months ago.

It had been the official intention, directly on my return, to close down in the Bawang and everywhere else inland, also. But if Bartram's reports were correct, this was only to be done over my dead body. The familiar arguments of authenticity began once more. Poor 9 Div. could not accept our reports at face value. They held the view that the Jap force was exaggerated. They were able to quote my own evidence, to show that similar reports from the south-east had been disproved by my recent, first-hand contacts on the Batang Kayan. It was difficult, sitting on Labuan Island in Brunei Bay, to demonstrate the difference between the validity of native observations and statements in sectors where we had been established for months, as compared with those in which we had never been properly established at all. Many of the older Australians could only think of native Borneans by their more familiar scale of Australian aborigines. All, on this view, were primitive, childish, and utterly unreliable blacks.

The third standard argument also reappeared with the odd forces of practical good sense as well as politics. From my side to re-establish the situation and get what I believed to be considerable Jap forces under control before they did disastrous damage inward, required assistance —for the first time—from 9 Div. HQ. This assistance was at this stage essential, because the Semut full set-up had been almost disbanded; and because, regardless of actual operations involved, if I took any appreciable number of Jap prisoners, I could hardly be expected to treat them as simply a Semut affair, in this peace-time?

This last argument did attract the legalists in 9 Div. I only had to roll it on my tongue a little, to imply some sort of ghastly atrocity; the slaughter of prisoners-of-peace. And, although they said they did not believe that there were many Japs, they also knew that it could be true. Where would the area commander and his staff stand if they had made no provision for this? As they (wrongly) supposed that all 'Z' personnel were automatically head-hunters, poison darters and general gangsters, their unease was both enjoyable and readily exploitable.

Brigadier-General Windeyer had taken over from Major-General Wootten not long after the termination of hostilities. Wootten soon achieved his ambition and received an important politico-military appointment in Australia. Windeyer was a lawyer of distinction in civil life; as soon as the war was officially over he started behaving very much like one in the military life of Borneo. The pros (which alone win wars) became as weighty as the cons, the fros as numerous as the tos, the sides of the argument always at least bi-lateral—conditions of thought which affected several levels of decision in ways not necessarily suitable to the continuation, in reality, of military conditions over a large part of the mainland. But by now, political pressure in Australia was becoming so strong, that the Generals who wished to come out of the war with continuing merit hardly *dared* to enter into any obligations which continued to be of strictly military and lethal character. No one could have been better suited to carry out this ambivalent—and indeed contradictory, and sometimes no doubt painful—rôle than Windeyer. In my case, he had to both admit and deny that the war was *in fact* not over inside Borneo, alas . . .

It was on this basis, alone, that it was finally agreed I might be landed back at Lawas and return up the Trusan, aided by air liaison and if necessary supply (only) drops from Labuan. There was no question of my receiving any fire support from the air. Nor was I to take any arms with me, except on my own person. Further, as a special concession, I was allowed to ask for two volunteers from 'Z' personnel already withdrawn from the field, who would be allowed to return to the mainland with me if they so wished. All my own proved personnel had already been flown back to Australia. But I had the great good fortune to meet up, for the first time, with Major Rex Blow, tall, assured, blond, perpetually chuckling; disarmingly pally, hail-fellow, athletic; invisibly but very clever; and fast off his feet.

I had no military or other practical need for Blow or any other volunteer once I was launched up the Trusan. I relied on rallying our trained guerrillas, using the arms we had quietly cached or redistributed immediately after the armistice and orders to demobilize. But I did decidedly feel that in view of the long awkward background of tricky relations between regular and irregular forces, I wanted someone Australian with me, so that there should be another confirmation on whatever I said I did. More so, also, to deal with whatever *others* said I did, now or later. As permission to use an Australian regular officer of seniority was refused, I took volunteer Major Blow as the next best thing, an irregular but an Australian already with a fabulous war record, DSO and bar, American Silver Star, etc. Lest Rex—who is now a senior administrative officer in North Borneo—get vexed with me (and it makes me shudder to think of it) let it be hastily said that he was perfect for the purpose. Rex was one of the very few Australians, out of thousands, who survived the prison camp at Sandakan in North Borneo. Nearly all his comrades died in appalling circumstances, in the great Japanese death march from Sandakan to Ranau in the foot-hills of Mount Kinabalu—the Borneo parallel of the Burma 'railway of death', but much more frightful. Rex had escaped to the Philippines and become a famous guerrilla leader there. After many adventures, he had got out to Australia, joined Gort Chester and Nick Combe in the 'Agas' operations in North Borneo, and there distinguished himself with numerous acts of anti-Japanese fury and ecstasy. Rex, survivor of Sandakan camp in North Borneo and the worst of Philippine guerrilladom, has gone through the sonic barrier of fear. He had about reached that dangerous edge where there is sense of invulnerability; the nearly trance which the Malays can sometimes attain out of a seemingly infinitely peaceable ease, suddenly. One of my worst concerns, indeed, was the restraint of Rex, in his over-total disregard for risk. To have him with me was an invaluable buttress in Austropolitics; his corpse, however, would be the worst burden I could carry, court martial stuff ('not another Australian life', etc., were the words of Generals Wootten and Windeyer which echoed in my Angli-ears).

Duly, Rex and I set off up the wide Trusan valley, assisted by a pleasant young signals officer whose job it was to keep 9 Div. in the picture for everything we did. He soon fell into the spirit of this peculiar enterprise. As we moved up, everywhere we were greeted with warmest enthusiasm. Many of these good people felt, as I had done earlier, that the war ended too soon, so far as the inside of Borneo was concerned. As well as our tried Murut-Kelabit guerrillas, we quickly re-acquired the lion-heart Sikh, Yita Singh; the mercurial Dyak leader, Usop; and a gang of other, still hovering, soldiers of fortune or fighters for fun. It was really quite like going back to the beginning, the early days of enthusiasms and wholesale recruiting back at Bario, before we had even seen the Bawang or the colour of Jap eyes.

Four days hard going brought us to Long Semadoh, well up the Trusan. It was a difficult trip, as the heavy October rains flooded every river; and on this track it is necessary to cross rocky rivers and muddy streams repeatedly. In this country, a river a few inches deep in dry times can swell to a raging height of ten feet in as many hours. We suffered a bit from this. The Japanese, now not far away, had been suffering from this sort of thing and much else, ever since they set out into the green and shadow, back five months and three river systems ago. For there was no longer any doubt about the Japanese. Indeed, we were *just* in time. As we sweated, waded the nominal fords and wallowed in the universal mud which all tracks had temporarily become, our forward contacts reported a large body of men encamped about a day's walk farther up river from Long Semadoh.

This was something of a surprise to start with. I had expected that when they debouched into the main Trusan valley they would turn down, making for the good old Sapong Estate. Strange as it may seem, these Japanese did not believe the war was over. Like most Japanese then, they had no other idea than that Japan would fight to the last drop, without surrender.

We had the strongest possible evidence of this attitude, in drops of our own blood. Immediately after the armistice, while Sanderson was still in touch with this force before it turned high up the Limbang, he had sent four of his Kelabit and Iban volunteers over to the Jap forces, unarmed, to tell them that the war was over and that if they now laid down their arms, all would be well. The reply of the Japanese commander was to execute all four men forthwith.

We had with us, as we approached them again, an educated English-speaking Japanese officer with orders signed by the Japanese Commander-in-Chief (General Baba)—whom 9 Div. had at last unearthed on the Sapong Estate?—telling them they must surrender, to me, at once. Our business now was to get this officer, with this order, to them. But how?

As we came to the long-house above Long Semadoh, we collected one clue to the reason they had turned south inland and up-river, instead of north-east. As we learnt later, they had established nocturnal contact with two Muruts at this point. These two Muruts, one of them subsequently the leading Christian convert of the area (Rajah Bigshot), had pinned a note, offering peaceful surrender and supplies and information, to the side of the long-house, in the night. This note we presently acquired. The following night they had crept up and had a conversation with a Japanese, speaking Malay, which the leading local could talk too. The Japanese, highly suspicious from past experience of guerrilla ambush and surprise, explained that their greatest need was for salt. Also that they sought to contact another Japanese force which had set out before them from farther along the coast—and which was, of course, the Tengoa force with whom we had already done our bit of battle.

The Muruts were able to tell them that this force had suffered many casualties forty miles down river. And that there was salt only twenty miles up river, welling out of the ground in rich springs. These two pieces of information apparently decided the Japanese to turn up river, away from expected further attack; they had no expectation of any armed enemy lying farther inland at all. Their need for salt was drastic. Not wise to the ways of the jungle, they did not know how to extract it from wild palm; or to substitute for it by consuming every fragment of every animal, from Sambhur deer to stream shrimp. In the deep jungle heat, on the tormenting marches, through country along routes which no Bornean would dream of taking (knowing better if longer ways), constant perspiration and effort had sapped the vitality of a people who always like plenty of salt and spices. Salt had become a kind of mirage, a craving, an obsessional ache. Soldiers were hanging themselves, along the way—or at night from the house beams—thinking of home and feeling no salt in the bone. Some of them left pathetic notes with their bones, so quickly stripped by the blood (and salt) hungry mammals and insects of Borneo—which has no vultures.

Unhappily for the Japs, before they had acquired more accurate information, something aroused their suspicion. Maybe it was some incidental noise of the night, one of a thousand natural disturbances which can jar on the taut nerves of tropical darkness. Whatever it was, without warning, several hidden gunmen within the house, opened fire on the Murut envoys who—to put it politely—broke off contact, without further comment.

* * *

The radio operator was having trouble in keeping contact with 9 Div. on Labuan and again contact with Paul Bartram, through Long, in the Bawang. We now urgently needed the latter contact. On their wave, 9 Div. urgently bombarded me with cautions and extra instructions. When we could not get through, owing to our rapid movement and the impossibility of getting a good aerial up clear of the forest, they sent an old one-engined 'Wirraway' over, dropping notes wherever they could see people; luckily for the pilot he did not go far enough up to see Japs and be shot.

As I was supposed to have no arms—let alone a private army with me—and as we were clearly heading up for a private war in peace, I was excessively bothered by trying to keep the peace with 9 Div. and avoid their reaching a state of nerves where they would actually call the whole thing off. I now sat, suffering, by the set, to try to get across a complete picture, my version. Rex went on ahead with the forces we had accumulated, to get right on the path of the Japs.

The operator and I also bashed away at the set to get through to the Bawang. Happily, we succeeded. It was good to find Paul Bartram already fully alert.

As the Japanese pushed on up the Trusan (taking a main tributary called the Kalalan) they came out into the wide, fertile, irrigated plain which, in the very head of the Trusan valley, at the foot of Mount Murud, corresponds exactly with the other and greater plains over the watershed in the Bawang, and further east, south as well as west, to the Plain of Bah and Bario.

It must have been a wonderful feeling after all these months in the jungle, for them to come out on to the plain, to be able to see for miles —and to see at this season, the brilliant green of young rice as well as the muddied hides of highly edible buffaloes. The people of the Kalalan plain, being adequately warned, had removed themselves and all the cattle they could. But many of the domestic animals are not domestic in the western sense, and strongly resent being driven or led. The first thing the Japs did was to set about shooting all the meat in sight. In the process, they came about a mile out into the open—and went within forty yards of the salt springs which they were seeking, but which lie off the track, and inconspicuous, softly bubbling mud holes surrounded by scrub.

When they were nicely out in the open, several hundred of the Bawang troops carefully deployed under Bartram, Cusoi, Bolang and Sulang (our three musketeers from the Celebes) and Bolang's younger brother, Alexander (who had emerged from being a clerk to the Japanese at Tarakan) pelted them with small arms and machine gun fire. Taken more by surprise than ever before, many Japs fell in these few minutes, with the smell of a new comfort as they fell.

No one can properly reconstruct what happened in the following two days. Japanese and Borneans were mixed up all over the plain and beyond its edges. Only one Bornean was lost. The Japanese re-formed and concentrated around a long-house on a knoll, at about the middle of the open plain, still in fair shape.

Rex, Yita Singh and the rest were now pressing behind them, from the down-river side, and exchanging sporadic bursts of fire, over the open rice fields, which were just high enough to give cover, but well overlooked against close approach by Japanese outpost positions. The Japanese, almost out of ammunition, were holding their fire. From the inland side, where Bartram had an abundance of ammunition stored, anyone could hurl, approach, aim or throw individually or collectively, though with negligible effect.

I came chugging up with the radio to find Yita Singh walking about in the open, men dotted about in the ditches, and Japanese visible less than half a mile away at their camp on the Knoll.

There had already been a good deal of waving of white flags from our side, to suggest, somewhat feebly, that we wanted peace. At last, a clear way could now be seen to launch our Japanese colleague upon his confreres directly.

Equipped with a white flag about ten times the size of the one which had first met me at Bario, our envoy sloshed across the fields in full view of both sides. A handsome black and white harrier swept ahead of him for a hundred yards, quartering the rice fields for mice and pipits. The first shrikes had arrived and were sitting, pale bellies barred, on odd posts. As he went he started up the first of the phalaropes moving south from the Arctic. Else than that, nought seemed to breathe.

In about an hour, the white flag reappeared, followed by several bodies. In a highly inconsequential 'ceremony', the Japanese commander handed me his sword, as we stood beside a rice hut, which I remember was almost falling down as a relic of the previous harvest season. This was on the last day of October 1945.*

I said that I would come up to the camp after a meal and a rest. Late that afternoon, with Rex, Yita Singh and one or two more, I did so. It was an impressive spectacle.

Five hundred and sixty Japanese, mostly soldiers, still in fairly full uniform, were paraded on the cleared ground beside the house. They were arranged in ranks and seniorities. The firearms and swords of all were stacked in an orderly manner. Before each man was a neat pile of his remaining equipment and reserve clothing. Shattered and worn by months of a journey which by any other account earned the highest geographical awards, it was slightly shaming to be faced with the proud relic of a force still disciplined, nine-tenths of it looking much more soldierly and effective than any of us, except Yita Singh.

The Japanese commander could not speak any English; but his second-in-command could. They were extremely courteous. They accepted surrender unconditionally. They were entirely at my disposal. They included, after a few initial suicides, 500+ bodies, including two bodies of hospital nurses in excellent shape in both cases (one pregnant).

To replace the headache of coping with 9 Div., who did not now

* In the Official War History volume *Military Administration in the Far East*, by F. S. V. Dennison (HM Stationery Office, 1956) it is stated (p. 184) that Japanese forces in the Upper Trusan surrendered on November 8, 1945. The British Borneo Civil Affairs Unit (BBCAU) then established 'a simple form of administration even in this remote area'. This simple form can only have been me? Later I am referred to by name (p. 192) as taking a prominent part inland, in civil affairs, along with Lt-Col G. P. Hill. Between us, 'a more ambitious administration was established than the area had known before the war'. I cannot conceive, though, who Col Hill was. Surely I cannot have become so Irreparably 'Z' as to develop dual personality and draw double pay?

matter any more and soon expressed themselves quite satisfied for once, came the problem of disposal of this force, much of it unfit for further travel for some time ahead.

Additional supplies, drugs and surgical kit, vitamins and bulk foods not immediately available on the spot—owing to the denial precautions taken locally—were dropped from the air, by my suddenly benevolent masters, who, at this stage, incited a press despatch widely quoted through the world, describing purely 9 Div. (regular) operations successfully to complete the rounding up of Japanese in the Borneo interior!

But there were difficulties in keeping so many people on the Kalalan plain. With a twinkle in eyes which had long brushed aside the tears shed over General Spoor, I decided to move everything over the border, into the Bawang valley at Balawit, where we had our own remaining organization, communications and far larger food and supplies easily available. With the consent of Penghulu Lasong Piri and Tuan Ajong, two adjacent long-houses were vacated and turned into prisoner-of-war camps. I left it to Rex to organize this whatever way he liked. The signals officer went back to the coast, and Sergeant Long soon after, alas. It would need several weeks to get our prisoners into shape to be marched out the quickest way, back down the Trusan to Lawas.

I had to revert to other immediate concerns. The first of these was to wind up our old headquarters, a couple of miles away from the prisoners' camp. There were great quantities of stores which came in very handy to reward the many hundreds of excellent people, who had rallied to the bullet for the second time. I must have repeated, in reverse, all the contacts, shaking hands and bottoms-up in farewell, with which the beginning of these proceedings had been initiated. With Tuan Agong, now presumably back as a Dutch civil servant—though he had had no word from anywhere—the goodbyes were protracted, lasted for nights. But sense came out in the end, things were reasonably tied up, Paul Bartram vanished alas towards Oxford, and I aimed my heart back at Bario, where it most belonged.

Jubilant, I shot hot-foot, over the spinal range and across the western plain to the old, sentimentally moving knoll on which perched Lawai Bisarai, Anyi, Tayun, and all the other friends who made Bario—and had made it all for me. Great things had happened there. I had forgotten how many Javanese prisoners we had sent over, once rehabilitated from their Japanese experiences. These industrious fellows had made acres of vegetable gardens on the rich ground, near the long-house. With the Kelabits, they had also built me a special house, separately. For Lawai was sure, in his mind, that I would keep my promise and come back to live there after the war was over.

*　　*　　*

I now had every reason to think highly of the Javanese as gardeners as well as thieves. But I was staggered to emerge on to the plain and see the glittering spectacle of terrace upon terrace of bright green vegetables all the way round the long knoll running out from the range beyond the long-house—hitherto coarse grass, buffalo and cattle grazing ground only. Here, aided subsequently by seeds thoughtfully sent to me by Sergeant Fred Sanderson, on his return to civilian life (fruit farming in New South Wales), in the following months I grew what must easily stand as the best garden yet in Borneo; and what might indicate, very faintly, the future potential of this kind of interior country. For once, in the tropics, I was able to satiate my lust for vegetables with:

Lettuce, cabbage, kale, cauliflowers (these only moderate); parsnips, small beetroots, white beet, magnificent carrots; peas, runner beans, french beans, long beans, peanuts; exquisite new potatoes and luscious raspberries; cucumber, ladies' fingers, egg fruit, tiny and tremendous radishes; melons (but not water melons, too wet), pumpkins, gourds, sweetcorn, Job's tears; things whose names I never discovered or cannot now recall.

*　　*　　*

To Bario, reports from across the Tamabos showed that there were still spatterings of Japanese who had split off or got lost from the Limbang force we had captured. Some had wandered into side valleys. Several of them had reached a Kelabit long-house beyond Kubaan, unarmed and dying, there been taken in by the Kelabits—according to my post-armistice orders—and were now settled down happily in hospitable company. I had long since sent to round up these men, with instructions that they should remain at Bario and be usefully employed, not brought across to the (Dutch) Bawang until further instructions.

All the Javanese who were well and strong, I now took back with me as Dutch citizens, returning eastward to the Bawang; after reassuring dear Bario that I would soon be back and stay—this time, a long time.

The Javanese I handed over to the administrator, Tuan Agong, who was presently able to send them down to Tarakan and have them repatriated. In a fortnight or so, proceeding back up the valley, into the upper Trusan again, I sent word ahead to Rex Blow that I was coming to inspect his prisoner-of-war camp and make final arrangements for their return, with him, to the coast from Bah Kalalan.

I expected to find a scene of desolation and distress, the ravages of Rex's revenge upon the Japanese whom I had left entirely at his mercy, without instructions which it would have been impertinent (as well as useless) to give to him. This did not worry me, particularly. Certainly I did not expect to be met, along the track, by Rex heading a male voice choir of combined Japanese and Kelabits, singing what sounded something like the Eton Boating Song—perhaps an Australian's idea of bliss for an Old Harrovian? Rex then gaily led on to his own quarters, a pleasant wooden house on the hillside overlooking the unfenced camp. Here the best in food and drink was served, with giggles, by the two Japanese hospital nurses and Lasong Piri's new little wife. For the evening, Rex had laid on a large-scale entertainment, including more singing, dancing, wrestling matches, Japanese and Kelabit games and an inter-racial tug-of-war.

In this, all the races we ever had to do with got into the act. Rex moved everywhere, benign father of a fantastically varied flock, which included Chinese and Japanese, Indian, Javanese, Malay, Murut and Kelabit, some Kenyahs, odd Tagals, Dusun, Potok and Milau, stray Punans. Nowhere lay any trace of hatred. It was peace at the highest level! And it augured well for any residual fears I might still have held about our ill effects on the latent head-hunting and feuding, classic in all the interior's past.

Bemused, entranced and reassured, I climbed the small hill and went to bed with Rex—and the nurses.

The war was properly over, it seemed.

Bound Stone Tool, Kelabit

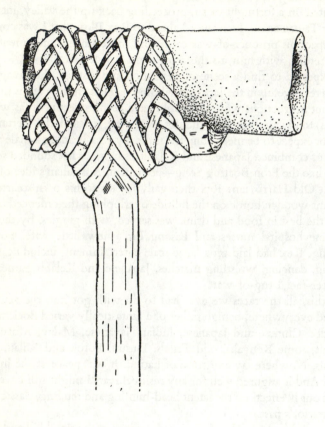

V

NOW

'And now the fancy passes by,
  And nothing will remain,
And miles around they'll say that I
  Am quite myself again.'
                    A. E. Housman (*A Shropshire Lad*)

'For with the troubles of memory are closely linked the heart's intermissions. It is, no doubt, the existence of our body, which we may compare to a jar containing our spiritual nature, that leads us to suppose that all our inward wealth, our past joys, all our sorrows, are perpetually in our possession. Perhaps it is equally inexact to suppose that they escape or return. In any case, if they remain within us, it is, for most of the time, in an unknown region where they are of no service to us . . .'
                    Marcel Proust (*Cities of the Plain*)

PRIMROSE HILL

1958 . . . NW1

Cleaning up the detritus of those exacting months of fighting, sniping, blow-piping and spying, making sure we left no permanent trouble or lasting urges to kill on, and trying to control drastic change within reason, kept me very busy for months. Not until late in 1946 could I come down to the coast with a free conscience accompanied (to the alarm of all there) by my valet and handyman, the last stray Japanese picked up after the rest had left (with Rex Blow) for the coast.

Sitting snugly by the fireside in a pleasant flat (£14 a week) on Primrose Hill, overlooking Regents Park Zoo and much else in smoky autumn London, only the nice things easily come to mind when one tries to feel floating down from the camera hatch on the Plain of Bah long ago. Goodness me, it is thirteen years now since I woke in the cool Bawang morning to the high song of the bulbuls, the dawn shriek of kingfishers along the edges of the ricefields, and coolly jingling water in the bamboo pipes from the hillside, with the gentle breath of a pretty little Japanese face still asleep on the plain wooden pillow.

There have been many faces and places since then. But substantially I have lived and still do live there or thereabouts. Nowadays, I occupy, albeit somewhat fidgetily, that Curatorial chair from which Mr E. Banks, over a quarter of a century ago,* blasted the uncouth and unsuitable explorers from the universities, foremost among them I. The sting of those sparse words then was one thing making me not only eager to go back to Borneo in war but ready to stay on in peace. I cannot possibly pretend that I have satisfied myself—let alone anyone else—that Mr Banks was fundamentally incorrect in his estimate. Nowadays, however, it is left to me, similarly, to criticize others in this field. It has thus become easier to see his point of view.

* See page 153.

But Sarawak is no longer the sort of country which Mr Banks could really like anyway. The days of his White Rajah Brookes are over; and their rule simply remains, as the basis of some of the best of feeling and foundation in a country undergoing enormous changes and immense accelerations and revaluations (largely economic), sometimes without very well-defined directions. In staying, because one likes—or rather has grown to love—the people and places, it is possible to help, in a small way, in these quite painful transitions out of the age of Balang Lipang saga, rice-gold, head-hunting, omen birds and the calendar of yellow wagtails, into phases of literacy, declined tradition, rejected craftsmanships, new ideologies.

Immediately, in the post-war years, it was possible to arrange civil air-drops for the people in the Upper Limbang and Tutoh, to repair the damages of the Japanese columns coming through there before. It was possible to establish the first schools in the interior, liberally assisted by the residual funds of cloak and daggerism. It was possible, for the first time, to climb splendid Mt Batu Lawi, which we had earlier called Mt 200; and to place under the shining 'female' peak's summit a Kelabit carved plaque to Graham Pockley and his crew who had not returned from dropping us early ants on to the Plain of Bah far below. Many other things could be done which had to be done. For the Kelabits and other interior people were not deeply scarred by the war as such, and most certainly did not, in any sense, revert to the more unpleasant parts—from the outside point of view—of their culture. On the contrary these extraordinary (in their experience) incidents led to a great hunger for new ways of life and thought. Where, then, when we dropped we were unable to find anyone who could speak Malay for two days, now every man, woman and child can speak Malay. Several can speak adequate English. A young Kelabit from Batu Patong, Jala Lai, recently represented Sarawak at a Colombo Plan show. Within a day's walk of Bario now there are six Government Civil Servants!

Close on the heels of a new regime, missionaries waded in (free of Brooke and other controls) as spiritual paratroops, to perform impressive mass-conversions. Today, you should not smell the pungency of *borak* readily on the plain of Bah. Salt is no longer currency—only cash. Kelabits may not smoke any more; and they are not permitted (by their faith) to grow tobacco even for export. The songs to be sung in the long-houses are sung before dawn and after dark—hymns translated by the Australian fundamentalist pastors, accomplished linguists. On Sundays no one should go out of the long-house except for some urgent purpose. Even drawing of water or gathering firewood is against this Christian ethic. From the poorer classes (the 'bad' people of the old idea) have grown up a race of Christian canons, teachers, deacons, vergers, urgers and gurus, who dominate the conduct of the interior, and in many respects are more powerful than the Government or traditional leaders and chiefs.

No one will ever make a megalithic monument again? Tattooing, long hair, flashy beads, leopards' teeth, bored ears, exposed breasts, loin cloths, slit skirts, bone hairpins, leg bangles: all these and much else are OUT. The cycle of *irau* funerary and exchange festivities is now centralized on Easter and Christmas, as Christian observances. The churches seek a tithe of all produce. But they prefer money or marketable goods to rice; which has meant that the intricate procedures of upland irrigation have sharply declined since—with the absence of the feasts and drinking and without any alternative incentive—there is no purpose in making larger farms than are absolutely necessary, and nothing left to be proud of in excess harvesting.

Unhappy Kelabits are now going down to the coast and working for wages, some of them abandoning the interior for harvests at a time. Whole villages (like Kubaan lately) have suffered seriously in consequence.

Some things have kept going though, almost underground. Thus, within the public area of Kelabit sexual privacy, the cult of the pierced penis by palang has continued to spread, thighly. Also, under the surface, the next generation (growing up) is beginning to wonder at some of the things their seniors so rapidly acquired. Particularly so, as it is now possible to see several Christian sects operating side by side—even (if you can be at the right place at the right time) three different sects carrying on competitive religious services at the same time in the same Baram long-house.

And even the pip-squeakest new deacon is still internally afraid of an old lion like Penghulu Lawai, who has duly beaten everyone out and got old Balan's old jar* until himself, all right. Anyi, alas, is untimely dead. But Tayun, though he has a perfect set of gold teeth and children now, is just the same sort of person he always was: intelligent, charming, gay, purposive, full of initiatives and curiosities. He often comes and

* See page 35.

stays with us down at Pig Lane in Kuching. For I am afraid I am getting rather lazy; and, as the incentives for visiting the uplands grow less, there is less and less that is strange in them still to visit.

There is no defeatism in that, though. Far from it. For example, Toby Carter and I kept our eye in, recently, by climbing Mt Kinabalu (the mighty 'Black Widow' of American Air Force uplift). We stayed for days in the tiny Pakka Cave, at 10,000 ft. under the summit, looking out over the vast expanses of inside Borneo, once our peculiar empires.

No: there is no cause for despair. And to long for a Bario past is simply, ineffectively romantic. The transitions of this time are just some in a long-long sequence, among people essentially mobile, liberal, experimental and enterprising. Things may be very different even in another ten years; and perhaps I may be even still around to see them. It is now about to become easy to get back to Bario again; by the end of this year the airstrip I built there originally is going to be re-opened as part of the Government sponsored 'feeder service' of aircraft through the interior.

How far away it does seem, though, on this smoky autumn European day. All the same; and if you just stand still by the map of London spread out under the frame on top of Primrose Hill, in a few moments comes recapture: in pieces, the falling notes as Penghulu Lawai ends his long chanting of Balang Lipang Surang, singing harsh, yet moving (and borak-swayed) at the end of the old, the seemingly eternal, *irau* party around the glistening dragon jar centuries ago out of China, in megalithic mood and the spirit life:

> Then Udan Panit and Junkeloko said to Balang Lipang, 'We have been here a long time; the drink is finished and we should go home. For a long time we have not been in our own long-houses.'
>
> Then Balang Lipang replied: 'All right, go home, Junkelokong, Junkeloko, Udan Panit, for my drink is finished —go today! I have nothing more to give you, my drink is finished.'
>
> All the visitors then got up and put on their clothes, their hats, their other things, ready to go home.
>
> They went along the long-house and out onto the end platform, down the ladder and into the jungle and so on.
>
> After they had all gone, Balang Lipang said to his father Burong Siwang (after talking of many things), 'How

about rice, father Burong Siwang? If there is little (left)
we had better make a rice-clearing, or how shall we fare
for food later—perhaps the people will starve, and what
good is there in hunger?'

And Burong Siwang said to Balang Lipang, 'You speak
wisely, child. You shall lead our people to make rice-
clearings, for if not they may starve later on, and that
would not be pleasant.'

On this thoroughly practical Kelabit note, the singing ends. Or,
rather, gives way to other music. And anything, really, may be sung;
maybe in relays—non-stop for a week, if you like. But not in Hamp-
stead; and not for the time being in the new Christian Utopia of the
uplands, where the ultimate sanction for such pagan exercise can only
(at present) be the everlasting bonfire. But fires and hells—like feuds
and wars and cultures—constantly perish around the equator. Before I
get involved in that whole new story of the last thirteen years (or
13,000)—and the next several—I better stop: and stop thinking. Instead,
I think, I will just stroll down the hill to the Zoo, refresh my mind by
chatting with that big orang-utang, from Borneo. Avoiding, of course,
the 'Teddy Boys' at the corner of Prince Albert Road—more petri-
fying, they, than any head-hunter or drunken far Kelabit dream.

T. H.

London,
October, 1958.

END NOTE

It would not be right if the reader got, from what has gone before, the idea that the para-military operations described (in Part III) were of special importance, within the 'Z' (SRD) context. To correct any such impression I can quote from a booklet produced by the unit on the occasion of unveiling its special War Memorial on Garden Island, Western Australia; this states:

'By the end of the war, SRD (Z Special) had grown to a force of 1,500 officers and OR's (mainly Australian but including many British, New Zealand, Canadian and South African operatives) and had raised and equipped some 6,000 native guerrillas.

'The Unit had inflicted some 1,700 casualties on the Japs at the cost of some 112 white lives.

'*Eighty-one operations* had been carried out behind the enemy lines in practically every area from New Guinea to Borneo and the China and Malayan coasts. Resistance groups had been trained for the Philippines, and the interior of British North Borneo and Sarawak virtually reoccupied. It became quite apparent that the Japanese High Command had *no* answer to these activities.

'The extent of the successes achieved during such a short period of clandestine and unorthodox warfare are in themselves a tribute to the courage, determination, resource and endurance of the Australian and other Commonwealth personnel who took part in them. Indeed the courage displayed is to some extent reflected by the large number of decorations awarded to so small a Unit.'

What distinguished *Semut*, Operation Ant, as such, was the scale of country we were able to cover owing to the remarkable response of the native peoples of Sarawak and all within Borneo. Thus the same booklet officially credits my Semut I with 'over 1,000 Japanese killed', out of the 'Z' total of 1,700. On the other hand, of the 112 white lives, *none* were lost in Semut I (or II, or III) operations, which also cost (to the best of records) only 11 Asians, including two blown up by their own hand-grenades and four murdered by the Japs when acting as peace envoys (on the Limbang).

Nearly all those mentioned (and many not) in the latter part of my story were decorated for their war services. Toby Carter and Bill Sochon with the DSO, Sgt Sanderson with the Distinguished Conduct Medal. Eric Edmeades, Jack Blondeel and Pinkerton received the Military Cross. Other officers such as Jeff Westley and Gordon Richter the MBE; Sgts Long, Tredrea, Barry, Macpherson and others the MM; many more the BEM. On the civilian side, N. O. Bigar, Chong Ah Onn, Penghulus Lawai and Miri, Badak, Kerus, Sabal and many more received honorary military decorations (MBE, BEM, King's Medal for Courage, etc.). In all, more than 150 awards. It is a matter of deep regret to me that we were not allowed to put in Dutch citizens for recognition; and that their own governments did nothing subsequently to acknowledge the courage of men like Tuan Agong and Penghulu Lasong Piri and Senghir. The answer, though, lies in their hearts—and I hope, in some small degree, in the tribute I have tried to pay in these incomplete pages.

Perhaps my (successful) citation to the British Empire Order for Lawai of Bario may then make a proper end note for all these gay and gallant people; it read:

'BARIO was the starting place of all SEMUT. Semut party dropped there "blind". LAWAI was the first chief to greet us. From our landing he put the whole of his energy and loyalty into furthering our cause. He organized the whole area to collect our stores, prepare our jungle camp, feed us, guard us, and act as our intelligence agents. By putting his people wholly at our disposal he was, in those days, running a big risk, for the Japs were still dominant in BORNEO, and we were negligibly weak.

'LAWAI, though a hill man in an area rarely visited by whites or touched by Government, readily took this risk. He was absolutely invaluable in arranging, consolidating and maintaining our base area. Through his support, it was possible successfully to bring in SEMUT II at BARIO and move them south to further extensions. It is no exaggeration to say that more than any other one native in BORNEO, LAWAI has promoted the success of SRD ("Z") activities.

'When we moved from BARIO to BAWANG, LAWAI continued his aid by guarding our stores cache, by defending the track from the TUTOH and by collecting and sending to BAWANG regular intelligence from the UPPER TUTOH. Frequently he came over to BAWANG, two days' walk, to bring presents of food, salt, tobacco and buffalo. In August he built a fine house for us on the hill above BARIO, for use as an HQ in cleaning up the Interior and for later Civil purposes.

'At no time did he seek profit or ask for himself. Never did he refuse a request, time and time again he anticipated our needs.

'LAWAI is a great gentleman, a natural leader, a wonderfully loyal subject of the Crown, a credit to his splendid race.

T. H. Harrisson,
OC SEMUT I.'

Lastly I put in American Dan Illerich (p. 242) for a Military Medal; but this was disallowed by U.S.

T. H.

INDEX

Abang Haji Adenan, 258
Abyssinia, 155
Adang, 323
Agan, 30, 33, 41, 45, 55, 56
Agan Plandok (Mouse-deer), 48–51
Agas, 175–7, 188, 260, 325
Akar, 113, 204, 221
Alaska, 69
Aldershot, 168
Along, 281
Amat, 195
American, Americans, 139, 141, 144, 146, 239–42
Anyi, 44, 47, 56, 72–3, 86, 89, 113, 131, 268, 288, 331, 339
Apo Rewat, 181
Aran Tuan, 207
Arctic Phalaropes ('Baby Boat'), 69
Argus Pheasants, 18
Ashley, Lady Sylvia, 157
Astor, 166
Auster, 242, 260, 273, 275, 281, 306–7
Australia, Australians, 138–9, 141, 144, 146, 177, 211, 212, 232, 276–7, 286–9, 294, 298, 307–9, 314, 324
Awat Awat, 260

Baba, General, 300, 306, 327
Bahau, 18, 19, 39, 85, 109, 151, 281–2, 318
Bah, Plain of, 4, 5, 6, 32, 67, 71, 82, 91, 93, 108, 112, 137, 139, 151, 199, 211, 222, 310, 338 (see also under Bario)
Bah Kalalan, 238, 328, 331, 333
Baker, Dr John R., 155, 157
Balan, 32, 34–44, 122, 339
Balan Ding, 91
Balang Lipang, 7, 8, 10, 53, 80–1, 93, 340
Balawit, 234, 237–8, 240, 242, 245–7, 292, 308, 331
Balikpapan, 188, 280, 314
Balio, 114
Balleh-Rejang, 284 (see also Rejang)
Banks, E., 152–3, 181, 183–4, 194, 197, 202, 223, 337–8
Baram, 5, 6, 15, 18–20, 37, 45, 56, 102, 109, 116, 151, 154, 176–7, 179, 181–2, 196, 203–4, 210–11, 221, 230, 273, 275
Bario, 5–6, 9–10, 15, 18, 21–33, 36–7, 55–6, 61–2, 64, 67–78, 82, 84–6, 90, 93, 95–6, 99–103, 107–10, 112, 117–22, 124–6, 128–31, 133, 183, 186, 191, 195, 197, 203, 205–6, 211, 213–14, 216, 221, 225, 233, 237–8, 240, 248, 280, 288, 308
Barry, Sergeant, 139, 193, 195–7, 200, 202, 204, 207–8, 210, 221, 228–9, 343
Bartram, Paul, 282, 289, 308, 314, 323, 328–9, 331
Batang Kayan, 18, 22, 26–7, 85, 109, 111, 151, 238, 251, 279–81, 318, 320–2
Batu Apoi (see under Mount Batu Apoi)
Batu Lawi, 20, 56, 79, 83, 149, 151–2, 192, 196, 211, 213, 217, 241, 275, 338 (see also Mount 200)
Batu Patong, 15, 18, 70, 102
Batu Song, 152
Bawang, 17, 23, 37, 83, 91, 109, 111, 123, 126–7, 185, 213, 216, 219–20, 230, 234–5, 238–40, 242, 245, 247, 252–3, 275, 280, 289, 292, 307–8, 314, 323, 328, 333
Beaufighters, 292–3
Beaufort, 260, 291, 299
Beaulieu, 173, 235
Beaurepaire, Ernest, 174, 177
Beaurepaire, Sir Frank, 174
Belalang, 35, 96, 98, 123
Benoeang, 238
Bevin, Ernest, 164
Bigar anak Debois, 247–9, 253, 257, 343
Bird, Terence, 157
Bisaya(s), 71, 217
Blackheath, 161
Black Widow (Mount Kinabalu), 148–9 (and see under Kinabalu)
Blamey, Field-Marshal, 141, 144, 265
Blassan, Andrew, 254
Blondeel, Captain Jack, 244, 246, 251, 280, 283–5, 308, 322, 342
Blow, Major Rex, 176, 325, 328–31, 333, 337
Bolang, 254, 256, 261, 329
Bolton, 24, 159, 180
Bower, Staff Sergeant, 139, 193, 195, 197, 201, 204, 207, 211, 220, 237, 291, 297, 300
Bray, Reginald, 155, 158
Brem Brem, 322
Brisbane, 311–12
Britain, British, 158, 140–1, 144, 175
Brooke, Humphrey, 167, 170–1

344

Brooke (White Rajah Brookes – references to their regime and personnel), 71, 90, 141–2, 152, 179, 180, 182–3, 197, 205, 206, 208, 210, 213, 218–19, 223, 234, 248, 257, 273, 338
Brown Shrike (*Neropa*), 68
Brunei, 188, 216–17, 219, 260, 273–4, 279, 305
Brunei Bay, 5, 13, 17, 21, 25, 93, 149, 188, 204–6, 212, 214–15, 229–30, 235, 237, 241, 246, 248, 259, 282
Bulan, 10, 11, 14
Burma, 140
Burong Siwang, 7–8, 80–81, 94, 340

Campbell, Jock (Colonel, subsequently Brigadier), 244, 310–12
Cambridge, 152, 155
Carter, Major G. C. (Toby), 176, 178, 179, 185, 203–4, 210, 221–2, 226–9, 231, 235, 272–4, 307, 340, 342
Catalina, 174, 177
Celebes, 247, 254–5, 261
Ceylon, 174
Chapman, Freddie Spencer, 140
Chapman-Walker, Colonel John, 143–4, 216, 310
Cheshire, 171
Chester, Colonel Gort, 176, 325
Chesterton, G. K., 136
Cheyney, Lt, 242
Chief Anyi, 72
Chinese, 6, 14, 31, 209, 248, 253, 289–90, 297–8, 333
Chong Ah Onn, 253, 268, 343
Christian(s), 9, 236, 250, 255–7, 339, 341
Christie, Agatha, 2
Clark, General Mark, 176
Clarke, Louis, 155
Clouded Leopard, 36, 288
Colonial Development Corporation, 173
Combe, Major N. G. P. (Nick), 175, 178, 245, 260, 325
Communist Chinese, 173
Cook, Squadron Leader (RAAF), 147, 151
Courtney, Colonel (Jumbo), 176, 184, 244, 260, 273
Crocker Ranges, 237, 241, 270, 280, 291, 299
Crowther, George, 178, 260
Cusack, Warrant Officer (Rod), 201–2, 204, 206–7, 211, 220, 246, 283
Cusoi, 254, 256, 261

Daily Mirror, 160
Dakotas, 174
Darling Downs, 186
Darwin, Australia, 139, 203, 207, 211
Dayak(s), 10, 247, 250–1, 254, 318

Dayang, 11
Dayang Agong, 132–3
Douglas, 191
Douglas, R. O., 181–3, 184, 195, 197
Dryden, 190
Dusun, 333
Dutch, 140, 144, 245, 310, 320, 322
Dutch Borneo, 37, 150, 184–6, 188, 218–20, 231, 247, 250, 258, 310–11, 323

Edmeades, Captain Eric, 200, 203, 204, 207, 210, 221, 231, 235, 244–5, 247–9, 260, 279–81, 291, 297–8, 300, 306, 308, 342
Egerton-Mott, Colonel, 173, 180, 223
Ellis, Everard, 188
Elton, Charles, 156
Emerson, Ralph Waldo, 304
English, Colonel I. M., 184

Fairbanks, Douglas, 157
FANYS, 314
Finlay, Colonel Jack, 176, 184, 216, 244, 314
Fisher, Major John, 273
Fitzgerald, Scott, 2
Flight 200, 185–6
Force 136, 140
Formosa, 69

Galle, Ceylon, 174, 176
Gascoyne, David, 161
George, Flying-Officer, 294–5
German air-raids, 163
Gibbs, Corporal, 288
Giraud, General, 176
Glen, A. R., 155
Gollancz, Victor, 160
Great Sandy Island, 175
Green Howards, 172, 143
Griffiths, Private Bob, 240
Griffiths, Corporal George, 260, 300

Hallam, Sergeant, 201, 211, 220, 228
Halmaheras, 139, 146, 147, 151
Harrow, 155
Hayes, Sergeant 'Stroke', 297, 300
Helmeted Hornbill, 36
Henry, Driver, 260, 262–4, 273, 290, 313
Hill, Lt-Col G. P., 330
Hiroshima, 140
Hitler, 161
Hollandia, 146, 185
Horsnell, WO, 224, 227
Hose, 152, 182
Housman, A. E., 336
Hutchinson, George, 163

Ibans, 182, 250–2, 262, 263–4, 273, 284–6
Iburu-Bole, 299

Illerich, Dan, 242, 343
Indian, 333
Indonesian Borneo, 5, 230, 252, 279
Institute of Sociology, 161

Jala Lai, 338
Jap, Japan, Japanese, 3, 137–8, 139, 140, 145, 174, 176–7, 179, 196–7, 199–203, 205, 207, 209–10, 212–15, 217, 219–21, 230, 234, 241–2, 244, 246–9, 251, 253, 259–61, 263, 266, 269–70, 273–5, 280–1, 283, 285, 290–5, 299–300, 306–8, 313, 319–21, 323, 325–30, 332, 333
Japanese Sparrow Hawk, *Kornio Piting*, 68
Javanese, 252, 262–3, 275, 331–3
Jennings, Humphrey, 161
Jesselton, 149, 291

Kampong Rajah, 30, 72–4
Kanowit, 273
Kapit, 273
Kassim, Sgt Abu, 224, 227
Kayan(s), 10–11, 18, 20, 25, 67, 71, 91, 97, 113, 126, 179, 182, 204, 210, 217, 221, 273–5, 281, 318
Kalabit, 152, 181–2 (and see Kelabit)
Kelabit(s), 3–133, 138, 145, 150, 173, 179, 180, 182–3, 194–6, 199, 205, 207–14, 216–17, 220, 227, 232, 249–51, 254, 262–3, 265, 273–5, 278–9, 285, 293, 298, 301, 309, 318, 320, 332, 333, 338 (and see Kalabit)
Kemabong, 300
Kemaloh, 242
Kenyah(s), 10–11, 18–19, 24, 61, 67, 71, 85, 91, 102–3, 113, 123, 126, 129, 179, 182, 204, 210, 221, 251–2, 273–5, 280–1, 317–19, 320–3, 333
Kerayan, 83, 97, 109, 111, 238, 265
Kerus, 248, 343
Kijang, *barking deer*, 50
Kinabalu, 67, 69, 79, 148–9, 175, 224, 340
King Cobra, 193
Knox, Brigadier-General, 184
KRRs, 166, 194
Kubaan, 19, 32, 33, 35, 38, 43, 56, 74, 111, 122–3, 204, 210, 214, 216, 227
Kuching, 153, 184, 203, 247, 298, 306–7, 339
Kudat, 149

Labang, 247, 282
Labuan, 147, 149, 188, 212, 230, 242, 244, 246, 247–8, 259–60, 267, 269, 270, 275, 292, 301, 306–8, 321, 323–325
Lake Bunut, 177
Lambah, 183, 195 (and see Bario)
Lasong Piri, Penghulu, 216–19, 240, 242, 259, 331, 343

Lawai Bisarai, 7, 10, 23, 25, 28, 29, 33, 35, 37, 39, 41–2, 47, 56, 71, 73–4, 76, 86, 89–92, 107, 113, 121, 128, 132, 183, 194, 196–7, 206–7, 214, 221, 256, 331, 339, 343
Lawas, 235, 248, 253, 259, 289–90, 331
Leach, Colonel David, 260, 269–70, 302
Legge, Stuart, 161
Lembudut, 233, 238–9, 283
Lian, 54–6
Libbun, 113, 116, 133, 238
Liberators, 3, 137, 147, 149, 185–6, 191–2, 199, 222, 245, 314
Limbang, 109, 214, 216, 217, 220, 230, 238–9, 251, 259–60, 263, 273–4, 290, 292, 301, 307, 313, 323, 338
Loembis, 247, 282
Long Akah, 225
Long Bawang, 218
Long Ikan, 273
Long Lelang, 20, 225
Long Marong Akan Dalan, 8, 80, 94
Long Nawang, 251, 280–1, 307, 318–20, 321–3
Long Po, 321
Long Semadoh, 249, 268, 326
Long, Sgt, 224, 228, 237, 240, 242, 259, 270, 323, 328, 331, 343
Low, Hugo, 180, 258
Lun Aran, 132–3
Lundu, 254
Lutong, 273
Lu'un Ribu, 48, 50–1, 94, 130 (see Tuan Ribu)

Ma'at, 122
MacArthur, General, 139, 140–1, 144, 146
MacPherson, Warrant-Officer Colin, 260, 270–1, 282, 292, 300, 343
Madalam, 301
Madge, Charles, 160–1
Madihit, 301
Madjapahit Empire, 262
Magpie-Robin, 64
Mahakam, 280, 320
Malay(a)(s), 140, 177, 179, 236, 249, 271, 318, 323, 333
Malekula, 155, 157, 159, 166, 179–80
Malinau, 266
Malinowski, Professor, 161
Manchuria, 69
Manila, 137, 140, 146
Manning, Tom, 155, 158
Marseilles, 158
Marshall, A. J. (Jock), 157, 276
Marudi, 84, 90, 209, 274
Mass Observation, 137, 161–4, 167, 187
Melanesia, 155

Melbourne, 137–8, 143, 151, 174–5, 180–1, 184, 213, 234
Melbourne Argus, 184
Meligang, 299
Mempakul, 265
Mengalong, 260, 297
Merapok, 289, 297
Miaw Sing, 271
Milau(s), 97, 99, 250, 255, 333
Mindanao, 146, 186
Mindoro, 146
Ming, 10
Miri, 205, 246, 263, 273, 290
MI5, 173
Mohamad Yassin, 272
Mohammedan, 21
Morotai, 146, 147, 149, 151, 185, 244–5, 310, 313–14
Morris, Miss Lenore, 312
Morshead, Lt-General Sir Leslie, 243
Mountbatten, Admiral Lord, 140
Mount Batu Apoi, 149, 213
Mount Dulit, 151–2, 154–5, 167, 180
Mount Everest, 148
Mount Kalulong, 151–2
Mount Murud (see under Murud)
Mount 200, 149, 151, 192 (and see Batu Lawi)
Mouse-deer, 48, 94
Mulu, 152–3
Murud, 4, 5, 7, 9, 11, 15–17, 20, 39, 56, 67, 70, 73, 79, 83, 91, 108, 133, 137, 139, 181, 185, 214, 216, 234, 239, 275, 280, 310, 328
Murut(s), 11, 67, 70–1, 216, 235, 241, 248–50, 254, 262, 274, 295–6, 298, 301, 318, 326–8, 333

Nakramo, 321
New Guinea, 139, 146, 151, 185
New Hebrides, 155–7
Newport, Isle of Wight, 164
Ngelawan Rajah, 35
Ngewelan Ribu, 129
Ngomong Sakai, 207
Niah Caves, 6
Nibbs, Sergeant Bill, 248, 287, 296
North Borneo, 175, 177, 186, 188, 219, 224, 241, 248, 260, 262, 282–3, 297, 305, 325
Northern Ireland, 172
Northumberland Avenue, 172–3

Official War History, 330
Orang Gippun, 266
Owen, Frank, 172
Oxford, 155
Oxford University Expedition 1932, 152, 155, 173, 179, 202, 223, 321

Oxford University Expedition 1956, 302–3

Pa, 15
Pa Bawang, 59, 185
Pa Bengar, 15, 72–4, 83, 89, 131
Pacific, 138, 147, 246
Pa Dali, 15, 18, 107, 116, 130, 205–6, 220
Padas, 241, 248, 279–80, 291–2, 297, 299, 323
Pagan Priok, 301
Pa Kabak, 231–33
Pa Koerid, 238
Palaeolithic Stone Age, 6
Pa Labid, 182
Pallid Thrush, *Padawang,* 68–9
Palog I-it, 51–3
Palog Raja, 51–3
Pamabo, 181, 182 (and see Tamabo)
Pa Mada, 15, 25, 27, 68, 129–30
Pa Main, 15, 22, 62, 96, 99, 107, 113, 127, 130, 207, 230–1, 237
Papeete, 180
Pa Potok, 234
Papuans, 146
Pa Tik, 111, 123, 210
Pa Trap (Palungan), 15, 23, 25, 27, 33, 56, 207
Pease, Humphrey, 163
Penghulu Badak, 216–17, 218–19, 220, 239, 263, 301, 343
Penghulu Miri, 131, 205–6, 208, 210, 220, 228, 236, 256, 343
Penghulu Puding, 54
Pensiangan, 247, 280, 282–3, 286, 292
Percy Sladen Trust, 157
Perintah, 254
Perth, 174
Philippines, 139, 187, 325
Pied Harrier, 133
Pinkerton, Lieutenant, 248, 259, 289, 291
Plain of Bah (see Bah)
Pockley, Squadron Leader Graham, 186–7, 338
Porter, Brigadier, 260, 299
Potok(s), 250, 255, 267, 333
Prentice, Dave, 244
Primrose Hill, 337
Prisoners of War, 198, 204 (and see Americans, 239–242)
Proust, Marcel, 336
P'Umur, 15, 110, 113, 132, 207
Punan(s), 5, 71, 133, 265–6, 274, 284, 333
Pungga Pawan, 124, 183
Pun Maran, 26, 29, 40, 42, 47, 68, 71, 76, 79–80, 90, 104, 113, 119

Qantas, 176
Queensland, 151, 185, 193

RAAF, 149
Rajah Bigshot, 327
Rajah Omong, 107, 131, 205, 208 (and see Penghulu Miri)
Rajah (Tom Harrisson), 208, 213, 215, 221, 228
Ra Mudoh, 15, 220
Ranau, 325
Recce Corps, 172
Reed Warblers, 195
Rejang, 229, 272, 284, 320
Rhinoceros, 8
Rhinoceros Hornbill, 319
Richmond, New South Wales, 178, 245
Richter, Captain Gordon, 261, 289, 291, 300, 343
Ringway, Manchester, 178, 180, 235
Robertson-Glasgow, R. C., 190
Royal Geographical Society, 152, 157, 238, 302/3 map

Sabal (Penghulu), 296, 343
Saban(s), 18, 39, 85, 102, 123
Sambhur deer, 12, 44, 77, 215, 327
Sandakan, 325
Sanderson, Staff Sergeant Fred, 139, 193, 196-8, 202-3, 205, 208, 211, 214, 216, 220, 239, 251, 260, 263, 273, 282, 290, 301, 313, 326, 332, 342
Sandhurst, 166, 171-2, 267, 304
Sapong, 291-2, 297-9, 300, 302, 306, 313, 326-7
Sarawak, 5, 90, 91, 141-2, 144, 150, 152-4, 175, 177, 183, 186, 188, 203, 206, 209-10, 218-19, 247, 252-3, 258, 305, 320
Sarawak Museum, 153, 181-2, 195, 223
Sargasso Sea, 19
Sawankalok, 25
Schneeberger, Dr W. F., 184-6, 199, 209, 220, 234
Scrub Typhus, 193
Sedge Warblers, 195
Sembakong, 247, 280, 283-4, 322
Semut, Operation, 175-6, 188, 197-8, 201, 220, 223, 228, 235, 260, 269, 276, 324, 342
Semut I, 197, 233-5, 246, 272, 285, 305
Semut II, 210, 215, 221-2, 229, 246, 274-5, 307, 310
Semut III, 229, 246, 272, 310
Senghir, 343
Seria, 263
Sesayap, 109, 185
Shackleton, Lord (Eddy), 153, 154
Shakespeare, 2, 136
Shangri-La, 9, 10
Shell Company, 184-5
Siam, Siamese, 28, 120
Siberia, 69, 70

Sibu, 273
Sina Manalad, 49
Sina Nurun, 48-9
Sipitang, 270-1, 292
Sochon, Bill, 179, 203, 210, 222-4, 228-9, 272-3, 316
SOE (Special Operations Executive), 173
Solomon Islands, 146
Song, 273
South China Sea, 19, 147, 149, 310
South-east Asia, 71
Spitzbergen, 155
Spoor, General, 311-12, 331
SRD, 143, 175, 178
Stein, Gertrude, 190
Sterelny, Corporal, 288
St John, Spencer, 180
Strenshall, 166-71, 180, 194, 267, 272
Sulang, 254, 329
Sulu Archipelago, 148
Sung, 28
Swan Lake, W. Australia, 174
Swatow, 34
Sydney, 143

Tabun(s), 216-17, 262, 301
Tagal(s), 71, 241, 262, 265, 280, 284, 286, 297-8, 333
Tahiti, Tahitians, 157-8, 179
Tama Abo, 183 (see Tamabo)
Tama Balan, 91
Tamabo, 5, 7, 11, 19, 20, 32, 38, 56, 67, 72, 74, 79, 109, 125, 131, 133, 137, 181, 185, 192, 204, 210-11, 216, 227-8, 229
Tama Bulan, 132, 207
Tama Labang, 68, 111
Tama Manalad, 49
Tama Nurun, 48-9
Tama Uding, 91
Tama Weng Ajang, 221, 250, 273
Tama Weng Tingang, 250
T'ang, 6, 28, 248
Tanjong Selor, 322
Tarakan, 5, 17, 151, 188, 204, 212, 229-30, 235, 239, 242-4, 246, 263, 280, 284, 292, 323
Tayun, 10-15, 41, 42, 47, 56-7, 83, 86, 113, 130, 199, 331, 339
Telang Usan, 20
Tengoa, 290, 292, 294-5, 299, 327
Tenom, 283
The Observer, 166
Thesiger, Wilfred, 155
Tidongs, 284
Timor, 213
Tinjar, 151-2, 154, 176, 179
Todd, Ruthven, 161
Toeboe, 265
Tokid Rini, 20

Tokud Udan Panit Tutub Long Midang, 7, 81–2, 93
Tomani, 279, 291–2, 297
Tredrea, Staff Sergeant Jack, 201, 204, 206, 211, 220, 231, 233, 239, 246, 343
Trevelyan, Julian, 162
Trobriands, The, 156, 161
Trusan, 67, 109, 219, 220, 230, 235, 241, 249, 260, 275, 289–90, 292, 297, 314, 323, 325–6
Tuan Agong, 254–5, 257–8, 261, 276, 331, 333
Tuan Aris, 254–8, 261
Tuan Ribu, 47
Tuan Sandinglut, 183
Tutoh, 183, 273–4, 338

Udan Panit, 340
Ukong, 260, 262, 273
Ulu Tomani, 300
Unilever, 159
Uson-Apau, 302/3 map
Usop, 254, 256, 261, 268, 326

Wagtails, 68–9
Wallace, Alfred Russell, 180
West Borneo, 176, 178

West Houghton, 160
Westley, Lt Geoffrey (Jeff), 234, 238, 246, 281, 315–16, 343
Weston, 260
Wheelhouse, Corporal, 288
Whitehouse, Brigadier D. (Torpy), 243
White-winged Black Tern, *Ut Bario*, 69
Whitley, 191
Wild Ox, 8
Windeyer, Brigadier-General, 324, 326
Wirraway, 328
Wodehouse, P. G., 136, 304
Wootten, Major-General, 306, 320, 324, 326
Worktown, 160, 162–3
Wyatt, Woodrow, 162
Wyck Rissington, 156

Yellow-Crowned Bulbul, 64
Yellow Wagtail, *Sensulit*, 68
Yita Singh, Sikh, 254, 256, 261, 326, 329–30

'Z' Special, 137, 175, 179, 185–6, 188, 193, 209, 210, 213, 215, 222–3, 232–3, 244, 260, 269, 306–7

CAMBODIA

GEORGE COEDES
Angkor

MALCOLM MacDONALD
Angkor and the Khmers*

CENTRAL ASIA

PETER FLEMING
Bayonets to Lhasa

ANDRE GUIBAUT
Tibetan Venture

LADY MACARTNEY
An English Lady in Chinese
Turkestan

DIANA SHIPTON
The Antique Land

C. P. SKRINE AND
PAMELA NIGHTINGALE
Macartney at Kashgar*

ERIC TEICHMAN
Journey to Turkistan

ALBERT VON LE COQ
Buried Treasures of Chinese
Turkestan

AITCHEN K. WU
Turkistan Tumult

CHINA

All About Shanghai: A Standard
Guide

HAROLD ACTON
Peonies and Ponies

VICKI BAUM
Shanghai '37

ERNEST BRAMAH
Kai Lung's Golden Hours*

ERNEST BRAMAH
The Wallet of Kai Lung*

ANN BRIDGE
The Ginger Griffin

CHANG HSIN-HAI
The Fabulous Concubine*

CARL CROW
Handbook for China

PETER FLEMING
The Siege at Peking

MARY HOOKER
Behind the Scenes in Peking

NEALE HUNTER
Shanghai Journal*

REGINALD F. JOHNSTON
Twilight in the Forbidden City

GEORGE N. KATES
The Years that Were Fat

CORRINNE LAMB
The Chinese Festive Board

W. SOMERSET
MAUGHAM
On a Chinese Screen*

G. E. MORRISON
An Australian in China

DESMOND NEILL
Elegant Flower

PETER QUENNELL
Superficial Journey through
Tokyo and Peking

OSBERT SITWELL
Escape with Me! An Oriental
Sketch-book

J. A. TURNER
Kwang Tung or Five Years in
South China

HONG KONG AND MACAU

AUSTIN COATES
City of Broken Promises

AUSTIN COATES
A Macao Narrative

AUSTIN COATES
Macao and the British, 1637–1842

AUSTIN COATES
Myself a Mandarin

AUSTIN COATES
The Road

The Hong Kong Guide 1893

INDONESIA

DAVID ATTENBOROUGH
Zoo Quest for a Dragon*

VICKI BAUM
A Tale from Bali*

'BENGAL CIVILIAN'
Rambles in Java and the Straits
in 1852

MIGUEL COVARRUBIAS
Island of Bali*

AUGUSTA DE WIT
Java: Facts and Fancies

JACQUES DUMARÇAY
Borobudur

JACQUES DUMARÇAY
The Temples of Java

ANNA FORBES
Unbeaten Tracks in Islands of the
Far East

GEOFFREY GORER
Bali and Angkor

JENNIFER LINDSAY
Javanese Gamelan

EDWIN M. LOEB
Sumatra: Its History and People

MOCHTAR LUBIS
The Outlaw and Other Stories

MOCHTAR LUBIS
Twilight in Djakarta

MADELON H. LULOFS
Coolie*

MADELON H. LULOFS
Rubber

COLIN McPHEE
A House in Bali*

ERIC MJÖBERG
Forest Life and Adventures in the
Malay Archipelago

H. W. PONDER
Java Pageant

HICKMAN POWELL
The Last Paradise

F. M. SCHNITGER
Forgotten Kingdoms in Sumatra

E. R. SCIDMORE
Java, The Garden of the East

MICHAEL SMITHIES
Yogyakarta: Cultural Heart of
Indonesia

LADISLAO SZÉKELY
Tropic Fever: The Adventures of
a Planter in Sumatra

EDWARD C. VAN NESS
AND SHITA
PRAWIROHARDJO
Javanese Wayang Kulit

HARRY WILCOX
Six Moons in Sulawesi

MALAYSIA

ODOARDO BECCARI
Wanderings in the Great
Forests of Borneo

ISABELLA L. BIRD
The Golden Chersonese: Travels
in Malaya in 1879

MARGARET BROOKE
THE RANEE OF
SARAWAK
My Life in Sarawak

SIR HUGH CLIFFORD
Saleh: A Prince of Malaya

HENRI FAUCONNIER
The Soul of Malaya

W. R. GEDDES
Nine Dayak Nights

C. W. HARRISON
Illustrated Guide to the Federated
Malay States (1923)

BARBARA HARRISSON
Orang-Utan

TOM HARRISSON
Borneo Jungle

TOM HARRISSON
World Within: A Borneo Story

CHARLES HOSE
The Field-Book of a Jungle-Wallah

CHARLES HOSE
Natural Man

W. SOMERSET
MAUGHAM
Ah King and Other Stories*

W. SOMERSET
MAUGHAM
The Casuarina Tree*

MARY McMINNIES
The Flying Fox*

ROBERT PAYNE
The White Rajahs of Sarawak

CARVETH WELLS
Six Years in the Malay Jungle

SINGAPORE

RUSSELL GRENFELL
Main Fleet to Singapore

R. W. E. HARPER AND
HARRY MILLER
Singapore Mutiny

MASANOBU TSUJI
Singapore 1941–1942

G. M. REITH
Handbook to Singapore (1907)

C. E. WURTZBURG
Raffles of the Eastern Isles

THAILAND

CARL BOCK
Temples and Elephants

REGINALD CAMPBELL
Teak-Wallah

ANNA LEONOWENS
The English Governess at the
Siamese Court

MALCOLM SMITH
A Physician at the Court of Siam

ERNEST YOUNG
The Kingdom of the Yellow Robe

Titles marked with an asterisk have restricted rights.

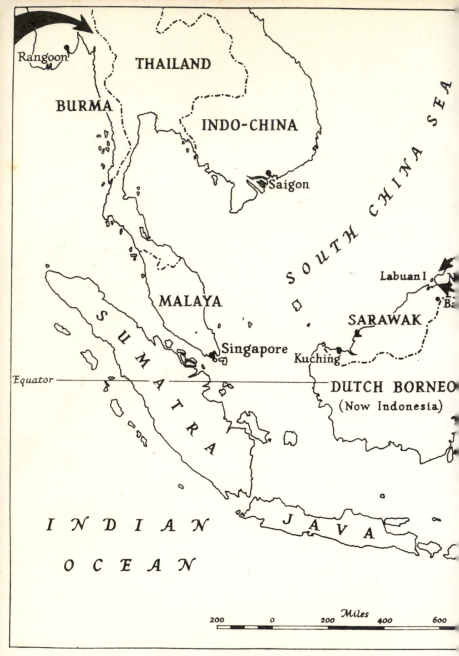

Map A

BORNEO IN SOUTH-EAST ASIA, 1944-5.

The great drives of war in the Far East swept northwards from New Guinea, with the American forces under General MacArthur, and from India east into Burma under Admiral Mountbatten. They left a great intervening area of exposed flank; and for a long time, relatively